FIGHTING FIRSTS

FIGHTING FIRSTS

FIGHTER AIRCRAFT COMBAT
DEBUTS FROM 1914-1944

JON GUTTMAN

CASSELL&CO

Cassell & Co
Wellington House, 125 Strand, London WC2R 0BB

First published 2000

British Library Cataloguing-in-Publication data:
A catalogue record for this book is available from the British
Library

ISBN 1 85409 443 2

Distributed in the USA by
Sterling Publishing Co. Inc.,
387 Park Avenue South, New York, NY 10016-8810

Edited, designed and typeset by Roger Chesneau

Printed and bound in Great Britain

CONTENTS

PREFACE

Of all military aircraft, fighters hold the most exclusive mystique—perhaps because, of all military aircraft, fighters are the type that can afford the least compromise. There have been numerous occasions when desperate combatants managed to achieve a surprising degree of success by improvising the most unlikely available aircraft into bombers, attack planes and reconnaissance aircraft. There is far less room for ingenuity in the realm of fighter aircraft, however. When the goal is to seize and maintain control of the air, the confrontation is direct, with the prospect of one of only two possible outcomes. If a pilot and his aeroplane are better, he and his side win; if his enemy is superior, he loses—and often dies.

Although aircraft—in the form of balloons—have appeared in battle since 1794, the concept of air superiority dates to 1914, during World War I. Since then, the development of fighter aircraft has been an ongoing see-saw battle, with each new design leading to another. Like sports and racing cars, fighter planes became sleeker and their performance greater as the competition intensified—but, in contrast to peacetime competition, they also became deadlier. And with each new development the pilots had to adjust to higher speeds and higher gs—something they did not always do ungrudgingly. The alternative, however, was to suffer the fate of those 'seat-of-the-pants' Italian fighter pilots who were loath to give up open cockpits, or of the Japanese who regarded dogfighting ability as the primary determinant of a fighter's worth—to be literally left behind by newer, faster opponents.

Aside from the adrenalin rush of aerial combat itself, a great cause of excitement among fighter pilots is the arrival of a new aeroplane. As they admire its lines, the questions fill their minds. Will it be all that the manufacturer claims it will be? Will I be able to adjust to its idiosyncrasies? Above all else, will it give me the edge I need to win?

This book explores the first combats for a variety of famous fighters of World War I, the conflicts of the so-called 'interwar years' and World War II—a 30-year period that saw the birth of the fighter concept and its maturity on the threshold of the Jet Age. Most of the aircraft described are fairly well known

7

to aviation historians, and a few names, such as Fokker Dr.I, Messerschmitt Me 109, Mitsubishi Zero, North American Mustang and Supermarine Spitfire, are familiar even to the most non-aviation-minded layman. Not so well known are the circumstances of their combat debuts, where some, such as the Zero, made their mark almost from the outset but in which others, like the Bristol F.2A, showed rather less promise than they would ultimately realize. Still others, like the Fiat C.R.32 and the Nakajima Ki-43 *Hayabusa*, enjoyed deceptively greater initial success than their outdated designs deserved.

While a certain amount of space must be devoted to the technical development of these famous fighters, these studies of first combats serve as a reminder that it is the human factor, with all its special quirks, that inevitably came into play when these deadly flying machines first fired their guns in anger. It is the pilots who determined how a new aeroplane performed, and the results were not always in direct relation to the aeroplane's capabilities. To cite a particularly striking example, the Brewster Buffalo, long vilified for its wretched performance against the Japanese Zero and *Hayabusa* fighters in the Pacific, actually saw combat for the first time over Finland nearly six months earlier—and, thanks to the skill of the Finnish pilots, enjoyed a generous measure of success over its Soviet opponents that its American and British users would have found unbelievable.

Some of the pilots became as famous as the aircraft they flew, and some of the first men to fly the fighters recounted in this volume are exactly those whom the lay reader would expect. For example, the first aerial victory scored in a Fokker Triplane was achieved by the man most popularly associated with it— Manfred von Richthofen, the Red Baron. Likewise, although Georges Guynemer may not have gained the first aerial victory credited to a Spad 7.C1, he did score the first for two other Spads in the development of which he played a prominent role—the cannon-armed Spad 12.Ca1 and the twin-gun Spad 13.C1. Other fighters had combat debuts that were more obscure and sometimes, as in the case of the Supermarine Spitfire and the Vought F4U-1 Corsair, less than auspicious. Several famous types did not even enter combat with the countries that designed them, although an American did score the first aerial victory for the North American P-51 Mustang—albeit while serving in the Royal Canadian Air Force!

Some beginnings are more famous than others, and what began for this writer, in all honesty, as a casual literary lark, soon took on the trappings of an often frustrating scavenger hunt—one, it must be added, that he could not have completed alone. Among the friends and colleagues who lent a hand to the project, I particularly wish to gratefully acknowledge the assistance of Frank W. Bailey, Jerzy B. Cynk, Norman L. R. Franks, Predrag Jelic, Lt-Gen Heikki

Nikunen (Finnish Air Force, ret.), Henry Sakaida, Stanislaw Skalski and Greg van Wyngarden, as well as the late Svein Heglund, Robert S. Johnson and Eino Ilmari Juutilainen.

The comparison of the strengths and weaknesses of fighters will go on as long as there are men who fly them. This study, however, will compare them from a somewhat narrower perspective: how did they do at the very beginning?

Jon Guttman
Leesburg, VA

Chapter 1

FIRST BLOOD

The Earliest Fighters, 1914–1916

When Austria-Hungary declared war on Serbia on 28 July 1914, she began a chain reaction that rapidly plunged the world into a struggle that would be carried out not only on land and sea but in the air. Aircraft were then nothing new to warfare. The French had introduced observation balloons to the battlefield in 1794, and that means of intelligence-gathering was subsequently employed in numerous other conflicts, such as the American Civil War, the Franco-Prussian War and the Spanish-American War. The Italians introduced aeroplanes during their 1911 campaign in Libya, not only for reconnaissance but also for bombing. Aeroplanes were also much in evidence during the Balkan Wars of 1912 and 1913. It was during World War I, however, that airmen began to take air power seriously enough to try to take control of the sky by eliminating the other side's aircraft.

Britain's Royal Flying Corps (RFC) has often taken credit for the first air-to-air victory, although that claim is not without its qualifications. The main protagonist was Lieutenant Hubert D. Harvey-Kelly, who at 8.20 a.m. on 13 August had had the distinction of landing the first RFC aeroplane on French soil since the war began—Royal Aircraft Factory B.E.2a No 347. Harvey-Kelly's unit, No 2 Squadron, soon commenced reconnaissance operations and it was during one such patrol on 25 August that three of its B.E.s encountered a German Rumpler Taube. Harvey-Kelly and his observer, Lieutenant W .H. C. Mansfield, immediately attacked the enemy plane with whatever small arms they carried, to which the German pilot responded by bringing his plane down to earth near Le Cateau. Harvey-Kelly landed nearby and saw the enemy pilot and observer running into some woods. He gave chase, but was unable to overtake them. He then returned to the Taube and, after taking some trophies from it, burned it and took off again.

On the following day a Russian pilot actually destroyed an enemy plane in the air, albeit by means that few of his colleagues would want to emulate. The drama began on 25 August when an Austro-Hungarian Albatros two-seater dropped a bomb on the airfield of the 11th Detachment of the 3rd Aviation

11

Company, Imperial Russian Air Service. The Austrian observer, *Oberleutnant* Friedrich *Freiherr* Rosenthal, owned several large estates in territory that by then had been occupied by the Russians, so his action may have been inspired by a degree of personal rancour. His attack, however, was taken equally personally by one of the Russian pilots, *Stabs-Kapitän* Piotr Nikolaevich Nesterov.

Born in Nizhny Novgorod (now Gorky) on 27 February 1887, Nesterov had graduated from the aviation school in March 1913. Flying over Syretsk military aerodrome on 8 September of that year, he put his Nieuport IV through a complete loop in the vertical plane—the first airman to complete what was then known as a 'death loop'. For that achievement, Nestorov was put under 10 days' arrest for 'undue risk with a machine, the property of his government'. However, he was later pardoned, promoted to *Stabs-Kapitän* and, on 23 November, awarded the Russian Aero Club Gold Medal.

Appointed commander of the 11th Detachment in February 1914, Nesterov tried to develop a training regimen for his pilots that he described in prophetic terms:

> I am perfectly convinced that it is the duty of every military aviator to be able to execute looping flights and gliding flights. These exercises must certainly be included in the training programme, as they will play a great part in the aero-combat. Such a combat will resemble a fight between a hawk and a crow. The aviator who is able to give his craft the mobility and flexibility of motion of the hawk will be in a better position to seriously damage his opponent.

When Rosenthal's Albatros appeared over the town of Zholkov on 26 August, Nesterov set out to put his theories into practice. Flying a Morane-Saulnier G two-seat monoplane, Nesterov attacked the Austro-Hungarian machine with a pistol on two separate occasions, but accomplished nothing. When Rosenthal made a third appearance that day, Nesterov jumped into the cockpit of Morane-Saulnier G No 281 without bothering to fasten his seat belt, and when one of his lieutenants came up to offer his Browning pistol Nesterov replied, 'That's all right; I shall manage without it.' Taking off and gaining altitude, Nesterov then dived on the Albatros and rammed it. Wing fabric wrapped around the Morane-Saulnier's propeller shaft and the two aeroplanes were momentarily locked together, then the Albatros spun into the ground, killing Rosenthal and his pilot, *Feldwebel* Franz Malina. Any hope that Nesterov may have had of regaining control of his machine was lost when he was thrown from the careening plane; his body was found 30 or 40 feet from the wreckage.

For his sacrificial victory, Nesterov was buried in Askold's Grave, a resting place for heroes in Kiev, and he was posthumously awarded the Order of St George, 4th Class, on 22 July 1915. His status as a pioneer of military aviation was also honoured later by the Soviet Union, which on 3 December 1951 renamed the town of Zholiva in Lvov province Nesterov, and renamed the Zholkovsky region as the Nesterov region.

The first confirmed aerial shoot-down occurred on 5 October 1914 when a French Voisin 3LA two-seat pusher of *Escadrille V.24* flown by *Sergent* Joseph Frantz, with his observer, *Sapeur* Louis Quénault, using a rifle, downed an Aviatik two-seater over Jonchery-sur-Vesle, near Reims, killing Sergeant Wilhelm Schlichting and *Oberleutnant* Fritz von Zangen of *Flieger Abteilung 18*. After that, the airmen of both sides began experimenting in earnest with means of more effectively clearing the skies of their counterparts.

The most useful weapon for accomplishing the task was the machine gun, but the most efficient way of using it was at first determined by how to fire it without shooting one's propeller off. In the circumstances, there were initially two schools of thought regarding fighting aircraft: one advocated large flying fortresses with anything from one to three gunner's positions, and the other single-seat scouts in which the pilot aimed his gun by aiming the plane itself at the target. Ultimately, the latter came to be recognized as the best fighters, but the problem of clearing the propeller arc remained to be solved.

The first successful single-seat fighter was a crude improvisation based on a Morane-Saulnier L two-seat parasol reconnaissance plane. The idea was to mount steel wedges on the propeller, so that any bullets that struck it would most likely be deflected aside. One of the early advocates of the system, *Sergent* Eugène Gilbert of *Escadrille MS.23*, abandoned it when two of his friends were killed by ricocheting bullets during ground testing. Another prewar pilot in neighbouring *MS.26*, Roland Garros, also discussed the idea with Raymond Saulnier, who devised steel deflectors that could be bolted on to the propeller blades. Garros and his mechanic, Jules Hue, improved on Saulnier's design by narrowing the width of the propeller blades at the point where the deflectors were attached. Garros then installed the modified airscrew on a Morane-Saulnier L armed with a forward-firing Hotchkiss machine gun and, attaching himself to *MS.23* at St Pol aerodrome, went up looking for trouble.

Garros was on a bombing mission to Ostend in the morning of 1 April 1915 when he encountered a lone Albatros two-seater and immediately attacked. *Gefreiter* August Spacholz and *Leutnant* Walter Grosskopf of *Fl. Abt. 40* thus had the dubious distinction of being the first aircrew to be shot down by a single-seat fighter. Over the next two weeks, Garros was the terror of the Western Front, attacking any German aircraft he could find. He brought down an Aviatik on 15 April and another Albatros three days later, but shortly after scoring his third victory his luck ran out and he was forced down behind enemy lines—either due to engine trouble or to a single rifle bullet through his fuel line by a German soldier, depending upon whose story one believed.

The Germans were delighted to have captured France's hero of the hour and even more pleased to have got their hands on the secret of his success. The Germans soon discovered flaws in the system, however. While French copper-jacketed ammunition bounced off the deflectors, German steel-jacketed bullets tended to shatter the wedges.

One of the aircraft designers whom the German High Command had asked to adapt or even improve upon Garros's deflectors, Anthony Fokker, had a better idea. Since 1913 Franz Schneider of the Luft Verkehrs Gesellschaft (LVG) had held a patent for using a series of cams and rods attached to the trigger bar to interrupt the machine gun's fire whenever the propeller was in its way. Schneider's idea had been strictly theoretical up to that time, but Fokker put it into practice, adapting it to the 7.92 mm Parabellum 08/14 machine gun and his M.5K single-seat scout. Similar in appearance to the Morane-Saulnier H shoulder-wing monoplane, the Fokker M.5K differed in having an airframe of steel tubing, rather than wood, and was powered by an 80 hp Oberursel rotary engine.

The German High Command ordered 30 of Fokker's *Eindecker* (monoplane) scouts armed with the synchronized machine gun armament, which were initially designated M.5L/MG but subsequently standardized as E.I. Several were assigned to Döberitz for pilot training, while the rest were farmed out to front-line units, to be used by their most experienced pilots.

Among the fighter's early recipients was *Leutnant* Kurt Wintgens, a bespectacled, 20-year-old army officer's son from Neustadt. After some time as an observer, Wintgens began training as a pilot and demonstrated such innate skill that he was assigned to fly a Fokker with *Feldflieger Abteilung 67*, then *Fl. Abt. 6.* It was with the latter unit that he claimed a Morane-Saulnier Parasol east of Lunéville at 6 p.m. on 1 July 1915—a success which, had it been confirmed, would have been the first German fighter victory, for it probably resulted in the wounding of *Capitaine* Paul du Peuty and *Lieutenant* Louis de Boutiny of *MS.48* that day. Wintgens claimed another Morane-Saulnier Parasol on 4 July, again without confirmation. He then transferred to *Fl. Abt. 48* on 5 July, although he stated in a letter to a friend that he had been granted what amounted to a roving commission. Finally, on 15 July Wintgens downed a Voisin over Schucht, and went on to score two more victories by early 1916, when he came down with influenza. Returning to action that spring, he resumed his scoring with a Nieuport 12—probably flown by *Maréchal-des-Logis* Léon Beauchamps and *Sous-Lieutenant* Debacker of *Escadrille N.68*—on 20 May, and by 30 June he had brought his total up to eight, for which he became the fourth German fighter pilot to be awarded the *Ordre Pour le Mérite* on 1 July. Wintgens' official score reached nineteen when he was shot down in flames over Villers Carbonnel by *Lieutenant* Alfred Heurteaux of *Escadrille N.3* on 25 September 1916.

Another early recipient of Fokker *Eindecker*s was *Fl. Abt. 62*, the ranks of which included a 24-year-old *Leutnant* from Dresden named Max Immelmann. Immelmann had been flying LVG two-seaters with the unit since March 1915, and was overjoyed when his flying section was assigned two E.Is for escort and hunting duties. Another pilot who got to fly the new type was *Leutnant* Oswald Boelcke, who had already proved his mettle on 4 July when he and his observer, *Oberleutnant* Heinz von Wühlisch, flying LVG C.I 162/15, destroyed a Morane-Saulnier Parasol over Valenciennes, killing *Lieutenants* Maurice Tetu and de la Rochefoucault of *MS.15*.

Although the two budding fighter pilots were close friends, the only thing they held in common was an aggressive spirit and a shared belief that the Fokker E.I represented the future of aerial warfare. Immelmann was self-centred, arrogant and unpopular; one of his instructors accused him of having 'a truly childish temperament'. Boelcke, though almost a year younger than Immelmann, was more mature in attitude and was the more experienced pilot. Although Boelcke preferred to think of himself as being as much of a 'loner' as Immelmann, he proved to be a natural leader and the mentor for a future generation of German aces. Boelcke himself once wrote, 'You can win the men's confidence if you associate with them naturally and do not try to play the high and mighty superior.' While Boelcke thought nothing of taking German nurses up on 'joy rides' (for which he was censured by his superiors) and courted a young French girl who lived near his base, Immelmann seemed to have only one woman in his life—his mother.

As the 'old hand' in the flying section, Boelcke got the first chance to fly the *Eindecker*, and attacked a French two-seater in June 1915. He was still unfamiliar with the E.I's characteristics, however, and when he dived and loosed a long burst at the French machine, his gun jammed. A nearby German two-seater crew swore they saw the French plane go down, but nobody saw it crash and it went unconfirmed.

On 1 August, flying crews of *Fl. Abt. 62* were sleeping off the previous evening's drinking binge when they were shaken awake by bombs falling on their aerodrome. B.E.2cs of No 2 Squadron RFC were staging a surprise raid on Douai. Immelmann scrambled into whatever flying garb was available and took off in Fokker E.I 3/15, followed soon afterwards by Boelcke in E.I 1/15. The B.E.s, too stable for their own good, made easy targets for the Fokkers, and Immelmann quickly brought one down, landed next to it and took its pilot, Lieutenant William Reid, prisoner. Boelcke also lined up a target, only to suffer another gun jam. After pounding on the mechanism of his LMG 08/14, he gave up and returned to Douai. For his feat, Immelmann was awarded the Iron Cross 1st Class.

Boelcke finally got his chance in the evening of 19 August, when he downed a Morane-Saulnier biplane. Soon the formidable pair would wreak such havoc on Allied reconnaissance planes as to achieve a measure of local air superiority. 'They treat my single-seater with a holy respect,' Boelcke wrote. 'They bolt as quick as they can.'

Disobeying orders to stay within his own lines, Boelcke began to hunt in Allied territory. When he was almost shot down by an Allied plane while attacking another, however, he realized the flaw in lone-wolf tactics. He formulated the idea of two Fokkers working as a team, with a wingman flying slightly above and to the side, to guard the leader's tail. He and Immelmann soon put that idea into practice. In spite of a friendly rivalry that developed between them, they worked quite effectively as a team, with encouraging results. Their scores were tied at six on 12 January 1916 when both were awarded the *Ordre Pour le Mérite*. On 18 June, however, Immelmann—then with fifteen victories to his credit—was killed when his Fokker E.III, 246/16, suffered structural failure while attacking a Royal Aircraft Factory F.E.2b pusher of No 25 Squadron crewed by Captain J. R. McCubbin and Corporal J. H. Waller. The British credited him to McCubbin and Waller, but the Germans attributed his loss to a malfunction of the machine gun's synchronization system, resulting in his shooting his own propeller off. Immelmann's name lives on in a manoeuvre he developed to regain altitude, involving a half loop with a half roll at the top.

On the same day that Garros fell into German hands, 18 April 1915, *Sergent* Eugène Gilbert was being transferred to a newly formed *escadrille, MS.49*. Upon learning of his friend's capture, Gilbert embarked on a personal campaign that he best summed up with the words he emblazoned on the side of his aeroplane: *'Le Vengeur'*. Gilbert's machine was a Morane-Saulnier N, a racing and aerobatic single-seat monoplane that Garros and he had flown before the war. The Model N featured extra stringers that gave the fabric-covered fuselage a rounded, streamlined shape, and a large cone-like propeller spinner. The deflectors that Garros had employed on his modified Morane-Saulnier L were ultimately meant for the smaller, nimbler single-seater, and Gilbert set out to continue what his friend had started.

Gilbert's quest for revenge began with an indecisive combat on 6 June, although he may have killed the enemy plane's observer, since the Germans recorded the death of *Leutnant* Fritz Rössler of *Fl. Abt. 34* that day On the following day he was credited with driving an enemy plane down behind German lines near St Amarin, which was added to three previous victories he had scored in two-seaters. Gilbert claimed a two-seater in flames on 11 June, and although it was never confirmed, he may again have killed the observer, *Leutnant* Joachim von Maltzahn of *Fl. Abt. 48*, and wounded his pilot, *Vizefeldwebel* Rudolf Weingarten. Gilbert achieved ace status on 17 June when he shot down another Aviatik two-seater of *Fl.Abt. 48* north-east of St Amarin, killing the pilot, *Vize-*

feldwebel Hugo Grabitz and wounding his observer, *Leutnant* Karl Schwartzkopff, but Gilbert's own plane was badly shot up in the fight. Gilbert's fighting career as *'Le Vengeur'* ended on 27 June when his aeroplane suffered engine trouble during a bombing raid and he was compelled to force-land in Rheinfelden, Switzerland. After two attempts, he finally escaped from Swiss internment, but he was killed in an accident at Villacoublay on 17 May 1918.

A somewhat modified version of Gilbert's Morane-Saulnier, the Model Nm (the last letter signifying *militaire*) was put into production by the French and saw some use in the summer of 1915, but the deflectors were never a satisfactory solution to the problem of firing a machine gun through the propeller arc. The fighters were never allotted to squadrons in more than twos or threes, and some early aces, such as Jean Navarre, Georges Pelletier d'Oisy and Jean Chaput, scored a few victories in them before moving on to the more practical Nieuport scouts.

Although the Morane-Saulnier N did not last long in French service, it did see more extensive use in the RFC, equipping No 60 Squadron in the summer of 1916. By that time, the deflector system and the plane on which it was mounted were completely outdated, and the unit suffered heavy casualties. Four examples of the Morane-Saulnier I, with a 110 hp Le Rhône rotary in place of the original 80 hp rotary and an Alkan synchronization mechanism in place of the deflectors, were delivered to No 60 Squadron, while others served in the Imperial Russian Air Service. The installation of a heavier and more powerful engine only made a tricky aeroplane even harder to control, however, and one of No 60 Squadron's pilots, Lieutenant William M. Fry, tellingly described it as the only plane he ever flew that gave the constant impression that it was doing its sincere best to kill him. Enlarging the wings on the Morane-Saulnier V did little to alleviate the problem. The last of the Morane-Saulniers were withdrawn in October, No 60 Squadron re-equipping with other scouts of French design, Nieuport 16s and 17s. By then, the Morane-Saulniers had been in service much too long, but they left behind a stigma in the minds of the RFC's senior officers that would also persist far longer than it should have—an almost pathological distrust of, and prejudice against, monoplanes.

While Morane-Saulnier sought to fire a machine-gun through a spinning propeller, Nieuport literally found a way around the problem. The progenitor of a line of Nieuport fighters, the XB—the 'B' signifying that it was a biplane version of the Type X monoplane—was developed by Gustave Delage in 1915. Unlike most biplanes, the single-spar lower wing was of much narrower chord than the upper, to which it was braced by V-shaped interplane struts, giving the pilot and the observer, who sat in front of him, a greatly improved downward view. Introduced into military service as the Nieuport 10 and powered by an 80

17

hp Clerget or Le Rhône 9B rotary engine, the two-seater was soon being flown by French, British, Belgian and, later, Italian aircrews.

When the matter of armament began to be addressed, Nieuport put a central aperture in the upper wing centre section, allowing the observer to stand up and fire a rifle or carbine over the top of the propeller arc. Inevitably, Allied pilots improvised means of mounting a lightweight Lewis machine gun above the upper wing, and then the observer's cockpit was faired over, turning the plane into a single-seat fighter. Nieuport eventually developed a standard mount that allowed the Lewis gun to be pulled down by the pilot so that he could reload it.

Contemporary with the Nieuport X was the much smaller Nieuport XI, a monoplane that was likewise given the sesquiplane, or 1½-wing, arrangement of the XB. Originally designated the BB-XI, and later given the military designation 11.C1 (the suffix signifying *chasse*, or fighter, single-seat), this proportionately smaller and aesthetically pleasing relative of the Nieuport 10 came to be known popularly as the *Bébé* (Baby) Nieuport.

The prototype Nieuport XI flew in the summer of 1915 and production commenced that autumn. Among the earliest recipients of the *Bébé* was the Royal Naval Air Service (RNAS), which had already placed substantial orders for Nieuport 10s and which seems to have received its first Nieuport 11 in November 1915.

By the end of 1915 fifteen French *escadrilles* were equipped with Nieuports, and they unleashed them to take the sky back from the Fokkers. One of the earliest to re-equip with the Nieuport 10 was *MS.3*, a reconnaissance unit that had shown considerable aggressiveness even while flying Morane-Saulnier L parasols. The unit's first air-to-air victory had been scored on 3 July 1915 when its commander, *Capitaine* Antonin Brocard, attacked an Albatros two-seater of *Flieger Abteiling 2* over Dreslincourt and, though armed only with a carbine, brought it down, killing the observer. Then, on 19 July, *Caporal* Georges Marie Ludovic Jules Guynemer went up in a Morane-Saulnier L with an improvised machine gun mount in the rear cockpit, manned by his mechanic, *Soldat* Jean Guerder, and the pair shot down an Aviatik between the lines, killing *Unteroffizier* August Ströbel and *Leutnant* Werner Johannes of *Fl. Abt. 26*. Both Guynemer and Guerder were awarded the *Médaille Militaire* for their feat. *Escadrille MS.3* began receiving Nieuports in July, and it moved from Vauciennes to Breuil-le-Sec on 16 August. Brocard shot down an enemy plane north of Senlis on 28 August.

The French were not alone in making aggressive use of their Nieuports. At 10.11 in the morning of 12 September a Nieuport 10 of the *2ème Escadrille Belge* attacked an Aviatik two-seater and sent it down to crash at Oudstuivekenskerke. The Nieuport's pilot was *Sous-Lieutenant* Jan Olieslagers, a prewar champion motorcycle racer and aviator, known as 'The Antwerp Devil'. His success was confirmed as the first Belgian aerial victory to be scored in a single-seater, as well as the first of an eventual wartime total of six for Olieslagers.

Escadrille MS.3 was fully re-equipped with the sesquiplanes and officially redesignated *N.3* on 20 September. Its next success occurred on 5 December 1915 when *Sergent* Guynemer took off in a modified single-seat Nieuport 10 with an infantry Lewis gun, complete with stock, mounted above the wing and brought down an Aviatik over Bois de Carré. Guynemer struck again on 8 December, shooting down an LVG between Roye and Nesle and killing *Vizefeldwebel* Kurt Diesendahl and *Leutnant* Hans Reitter of *Fl. Abt. 27*. On 14 December Guynemer teamed up with a two-seat Nieuport 10, crewed by *Adjudant* André Bucquet and *Lieutenant* Pandevant, in shooting down a Fokker *Eindecker* over Hervilly.

Early in 1916 single-seat *Bébés* began to replace the Nieuport 10s. Guynemer received Nieuport 11 N836, on the fuselage of which he applied the legend '*Le Vieux Charles*', a reference to *Sergent* Charles Bonnard, a well-liked member of the old *MS.3* who had transferred to the Macedonian Front. He was flying that plane on 3 February 1916 when he encountered and attacked an LVG near Roye He later wrote:

> I did not open fire until I was at 20 metres. Almost at once my adversary tumbled into a tail spin. I dived after him, continuing to fire my weapon. I plainly saw him fall in his own lines. That was all right. No doubt about him. I had my fifth. I was really in luck, for less than ten minutes later another plane, sharing the same lot, spun downward with the same grace, taking fire as it fell through the clouds.

German records only mention one fatality from the combat—*Leutnant* Heinrich Zwenger, an observer of *Fl. Abt. 27*, killed between Roye and Chaulnes. Both LVGs were confirmed, however, to which double victory Guynemer added a seventh success on 5 February with an LVG downed at Herbecourt, again killing the observer, *Leutnant* Rudolf Lumblatt of *Fl. Abt. 9*.

Another early Nieuport fighter unit was *C.65*, which was originally formed at Lyon-Bron on 2 August 1915 as an *escadrille provisoire de chasse*, with two Nieuport 11s, three Nieuport 12 two-seaters and three Caudron G.4s. The unit's first success, an enemy plane forced to land on 16 October, involved a two-seater crew, and not until 21 February was it redesignated a full-fledged fighter squadron as *N.65*. Long before that, however, *N.65*'s first success in the *Bébé* Nieuport was achieved by a hero about as far removed from Guynemer in temperament as could be imagined—Charles Nungesser.

While Georges Guynemer was a sickly 20-year-old boy driven by a single-minded devotion to his country, Charles Eugène Jules Marie Nungesser was an athletic man of the world who had raced cars, boxed and learned to fly while in Argentina before the war. During the early days of World War I Nungesser had served with distinction with the *2ème Régiment des Hussards*, earning the *Médaille Militaire* before transferring into aviation in November 1914 and earning his military pilot's brevet on 17 March 1915. Assigned to *VB.106*, he flew 53 bombing missions in a Voisin 3, the front nacelle of which he personalized with a black skull and crossbones. In the early morning hours of 31 July *Adjudant* Nungesser and his mechanic went up in a new Voisin armed with a Hotchkiss machine gun—an unauthorized flight, since Nungesser was supposed to be on standby duty that night. However, as fortune would have it, five Albatros two-seaters staged a raid on Nancy that night and the Voisin crew were able to catch one and send it down to crash. For deserting his post Nungesser was confined to his quarters for eight days; for downing the German aeroplane he received the *Croix de Guerre*. His commander subsequently sent him for training in Nieuports, in which he could put his hell-raising attitude to more productive use.

Such was Nungesser's background when he joined *N.65* in November 1915 and received Nieuport 11 N880. Delighted with the new fighter, he soon decorated its fuselage sides with a more elaborate version of the macabre personal marking that had adorned his Voisin—a black heart, bordered in white, with a white skull and crossbones, over which was a coffin flanked by two candles. While flying it to *N.65*'s aerodrome at Malzéville on 26 November, he celebrated his return to the Front by buzzing Nancy, flying around the church steeples, looping over the town square and zooming down the main street as low as 30 feet. When he landed, he found that a telephone call from the town elders had preceded him, and he was greeted with a dressing down from his commander, *Capitaine* Louis Gonnet-Thomas, who caustically remarked that he should be scaring the *Boche*, not his fellow Frenchmen.

Nungesser obeyed in his own way: he refuelled his Nieuport, flew over the lines and gave an even wilder aerobatic display at a German aerodrome. The Germans were too astonished to fire at him, and upon his return Nungesser reported to Gonnet-Thomas: 'It is done, *mon capitaine!*'

Nungesser was rewarded with another eight days of house arrest, but on 28 November he was permitted to take his plane up to practice gunnery on ground targets. He had barely taken off, however, when he spotted two Albatros two-seaters crossing the lines near Nomeny. Climbing to 8,000 feet and placing the sun at his back, Nungesser attacked. One of the Germans fled, but the other fought—and fought well. Nungesser made four passes at the plane, each time closing to 100 feet and using up a drum of ammunition without effect. Then, after placing his last drum on his Lewis gun, he went directly at his opponent, ignoring the gunner's return fire as he closed to 30 feet before emptying the magazine into the Albatros. The pilot was hit and the Albatros went into a dive, but Nungesser reported a scene that took much of the triumph out of his second victory:

The observer, still alive, clung desperately to the mounting ring to which his machine gun was attached. Suddenly the mounting ripped loose from the fuselage and was flung into space, taking with it the helpless crewman. He clawed frantically at the air, his body working convulsively like a man on a trapeze. I had a quick glimpse of his face before he tumbled away through the clouds . . . it was a mask of horror.

The observer whose fall Nungesser witnessed was *Leutnant* Wilhelm von Kalkreuth of *Brief A.M.*, whose body was found at Nomeny. His pilot, *Vizefeldwebel* August Blank, crashed to his death at Mailly. Nungesser had trouble eating and sleeping for some time after that, but he eventually got over it. Gonnet-Thomas helped—he commuted the remaining six days of his arrest and recommended that he be made a *Chevalier de la Légion d'Honneur*, an honour that Nungesser received on 4 December. In spite of numerous crashes, Nungesser survived the war as France's third-ranking ace with 43 victories to his credit—only to vanish during an attempt to fly non-stop across the Atlantic Ocean in May 1927.

Early in 1916 ambitious pilots in some *esadrilles*, such as *N.38*, began installing 110 hp Le Rhône 9J engines in place of the original 80 hp rotaries. By mid-1916 the more powerful version of the aircraft was in production as the Nieuport 16. The slight increase in speed, however, was offset by sluggish handling and dangerous nose-heaviness.

Nieuport realized that, in order to develop, its 'baby' would have to grow. Therefore, it increased the overall wing area from 13.30 to 14.75 square metres and redesigned the fuselage with more streamlined cowl panels as well as accommodation for a synchronized Vickers machine gun. The Nieuport 17, also known as the '15-metre Nieuport', provided an ideal combination of higher performance and outstanding flight characteristics that soon led the Germans to copy its sesquiplane layout.

The first Nieuport 17s are alleged to have been sent to *Escadrille N.57* in May 1916, although it is not certain when they flew their first mission alongside the Nieuport 11s and 16s with which that squadron was already equipped, and in one of which *Sous-Lieutenant* Jean Firmin Louis Robert had downed a Fokker *Eindecker* for the unit's first victory on 25 April. *Sergent* Louis Coudouret started the month's scoring on 4 May when he sent an LVG two-seater crashing near Hermeville, for his first of an eventual six victories. The squadron acquired an experienced member on 7 May when *Sous-Lieutenant* Jean Chaput transferred over, after having already been credited with three victories with *Escadrilles C.28* and *N.31*. Nine days later Chaput showed his mettle by attacking an Aviatik over Esparges and severely damaging it. *Lieutenant* André Bastien forced an enemy plane down behind its own lines the next day. *Adjudant* Léon François Acher did the same on 19 May, although he was badly wounded in the course of the fight. *Lieutenant* Charles Dumas sent an Aviatik down to crash near Eparges on

21 May, and on the following day *Lieutenant* André Charles Dubois de Gennes and Chaput each flamed German balloons, the latter's victory bringing his total to five and conferring acedom. The Nieuport 17's first month ended on a blue note, however, when the recently promoted *Lieutenant* Robert failed to return from a mission on the 24th.

While the French and Germans were addressing the matter of developing an effective single-seat fighter, the British were doing so in their own way, with one airman in particular playing an instrumental role. In October 1914, the same month that Frantz and Quénault scored their aerial victory, No 6 Squadron RFC arrived in France, its flying personnel including a 23-year-old officer from a distinguished military family named Lanoe George Hawker.

When his unit traded in its ungainly Henry Farman pushers for somewhat faster B.E.2cs, Hawker began complementing his reconnaissance patrols with more aggressive activities, such as a bombing attack on Zeppelin sheds, for which he received the Distinguished Service Order.

In 1915 No 6 Squadron began to receive F.E.2 (Fighter Experimental, Type 2) pushers, armed with a 0.303-inch Lewis machine gun in a gunner's pit in front of the pilot, to escort the B.E.s. The squadron also acquired a single-seat Bristol Scout C, serial number 1609, for short-range, front-line reconnaissance flights. Designed by Frank Sowter Barnwell for the British & Colonial Aeroplane Co. Ltd, the Bristol Scout was originally powered by an 80 hp Gnome Lambda 9-cylinder rotary engine, and it flew for the first time in February 1914. Its wing, which had a span of only 22 feet, employed ailerons rather than the older but still prevalent wing-warping for lateral control. Compact and clean for its time, the Scout embodied the biplane fighter configuration that would remain essentially standard for more than twenty years to follow.

Captain Hawker had the privilege of ferrying the single-seater in from St Omer on 3 June. On 7 June he wrote: 'I have a beautiful new toy, a new Bristol Scout that goes at 80 and climbs 5 or 600 feet a minute! I'm having a machine gun fitted to see how they like it.'

The gun to which Hawker referred was a lightweight 0.303-inch Lewis, but he faced a problem that the F.E. pusher crews did not have to deal with—finding a way to fix such a weapon to a single-seat tractor aeroplane so that he could fire it without shooting his own propeller off. Hawker devised a solution, which Air Mechanic E. J. Elton duly fabricated, mounting the gun so that it could fire forward, downwards and outwards at an angle. The arrangement avoided the propeller arc but posed a challenge as far as aiming was concerned.

Nevertheless, Hawker sallied forth on 21 June 1915 and attacked a DFW two-seater over Poelcapelle. It was officially credited to him as 'brought down out of control', although there is no evidence of any aircraft or crew losses in German records. On the following day Hawker overturned his 'beautiful new toy' during a forced landing and it had to be taken to No 1 Aircraft Park for repairs. It was replaced by another Bristol C, No 1611, on which Hawker promptly installed his Lewis gun mounting and resumed his hunting.

In the course of three sorties on 25 June Hawker attacked three German aircraft. During his second combat he forced an Albatros two-seater of *Flieger Abteilung 3* to land near Passchendaele at about 6.45 p.m., then succeeded in shooting down another in flames south-east of Zillebeke fifteen minutes later, killing *Oberleutnant* Alfred Uberlacker and *Hauptmann* Hans Roser, also of *Fl.Abt. 3*. Hawker was credited with a double victory and subsequently awarded the Victoria Cross—the first man to receive Britain's highest decoration for air-to-air combat. Hardly one to rest on his laurels, he flew more patrols in the Bristol until No 1611 was withdrawn to the air park on 22 October. After that he continued to seek combat in the F.E.2s, supplementing the gunner's firepower with his own Lee-Enfield rifle.

Flying F.E.2 4227 with Lieutenant A. Payze as his observer on 2 August, Hawker attacked a German two-seater and forced it to land at Wulverghem. Hawker was credited with a second 'double' on 11 August when he and his gunner, Lieutenant N. Clifton, destroyed an Aviatik two-seater at Houthem at 3.45 p.m. and downed an attacking Fokker *Eindecker* in the area of Lille-Roubaix at 7.15 that evening. Returning to Bristol Scout 1611 on 7 September, Hawker shot down an enemy biplane over Bixschoote for his seventh victory. Hawker was now not only Britain's pioneer single-seat scout pilot, but her first ace.

Posted back to England late in 1915, Captain Hawker was sent to Hounslow on 28 September to take command of the RFC's the first single-seat fighter unit, No 24 Squadron. The squadron's equipment, the de Havilland D.H.2, represented yet another early method for a machine gun-armed single-seater to circumvent the propeller. After leaving the Royal Aircraft Factory to join Aircraft Manufacturing Co. Ltd in June 1914, Geoffrey de Havilland had designed a two-seat pusher fighter of similar configuration to the RAF's F.E.2, the Airco D.H.1. In the early summer of 1915, however, he introduced a more compact single-seat version, the D.H.2, which was sent to France for operational evaluation on 26 July.

The new scout's front-line debut could scarcely have been less promising. Its 100 hp Gnome Monosoupape rotary engine had to be replaced immediately upon its arrival in France. The aircraft was attached to No 5 Squadron but disappeared over the lines on 9 August. The Germans subsequently dropped a message stating that the plane's pilot, Captain R. Maxwell-Pike, had died of his wounds, but otherwise they did not indicate whether the plane had been shot down or had crashed after another engine failure. A German photograph showed that the plane had flipped over on its back upon landing, but was otherwise quite intact. In spite of their being presented with an almost-perfect advance look at Britain's latest fighter, however, for more than a year thereafter the Germans tended to misidentify D.H.2s as 'Vickers scouts' in their combat reports with curious regularity.

In spite of the disastrous loss of the prototype, Airco put the D.H.2 into production and the first example was delivered to No 18 Squadron on 9 January 1916, while another went to No 11 Squadron two days later. Back in Britain, No 24 Squadron got its first D.H.2 on 10 January, and by the time the newly promoted Major Hawker took his unit to Bertangles, France, on 10 February, its strength was up to twelve D.H.2s.

In its original form, the D.H.2 carried a Lewis gun with a 47-round magazine within a fairing on the port side of the pilot's nacelle. The production version placed the gun centrally within the front of the nacelle on a vertical shaft that gave it a considerable range of movement. In practice, Hawker judged what he called the 'wobbly mounting'—which required the pilot to fly the plane with one hand and aim his weapon with the other—to be utterly useless and devised a clamp to fix the gun in a forward-firing position. Higher authorities prohibited such practice, but Hawker ultimately came up with a compromise—a spring clip that would theoretically allow the pilot to release the gun for flexible use at will. In practice, Hawker's men almost never unclipped their guns when they went into battle.

Another problem encountered in the D.H.2 was its tendency to fall into spins, which caused a number of training accidents. At that time little was known about how one could recover from a spin, but Hawker understood the concept of centralizing the controls and repeatedly put his plane into a spin and pulled out of it to show his pilots that it could be done. He also dealt with the numbing cold that had to be endured in an open nacelle, with no engine to shield and warm the pilot, by designing fur-lined flying clothes, including the hip-high 'fug boots' that would become a popular item among British airmen throughout the war.

Once its personnel had gained sufficient experience and confidence in the D.H.2, No 24 had its first engagement with the Germans on 19 March. On 2 April Second Lieutenant D. M. Tidmarsh officially opened the squadron's account when he shot down an enemy plane over Bapaume. On 25 April, three of No 24's D.H.2s were escorting a B.E.2c of No 15 Squadron when they were attacked by a flight of Fokker *Eindeckers*. The D.H.2s turned on the enemy, drove down one of the monoplanes and chased off the rest. That action sealed No 24 Squadron's confidence in the D.H.2, and from then on its pilots attacked all German aircraft they encountered without hesitation.

The Fokker bogey had been laid and the Allies had retaken the sky. But they would not hold it for long.

Chapter 2

Biplanes,
Boelcke and the Baron

Halberstadt and Albatros Scouts, 1916–1917

By the time the Battle of the Somme commenced on 1 July 1916, Allied fighters had virtually retaken command of the sky. *Major* Wilhelm Siegert, commander of the *Idflieg* (*Inspektion der Fliegertruppen*, or Inspectorate of Aviation Troops) wrote in outspoken retrospect:

> The start of the Somme battle unfortunately coincided with the low point in the technical development of our aircraft. The unquestioned supremacy we had enjoyed in early 1916 by virtue of our Fokker monoplane fighters shifted over to the enemy's Nieuport, Vickers and Sopwith aircraft in March and April. Our monthly aircraft output did not even allow a squadron to be equipped with a common type. For example, *Flieger Abteilung 23* had a complement of five different aircraft types.

By October 1916 the aerial balance of power began to shift again. In large degree Siegert attributed the German resurgence to the 'enterprise of Boelcke and his "school" in conjunction with the new Halberstadt D.III fighter'.

Originally formed on 9 April 1912 as the Deutsche Bristol Werke Flugzeug GmbH to build Bristol aircraft under licence, the Halberstädter Flugzeugwerke GmbH produced an original design, the B.I biplane, in 1914. A product of technical director Karl Thies and Swiss-born Hans Burkhard before the latter left the firm to join Gotha, the B.I was powered by an 80 hp Oberursel rotary engine, but its successor, the B.II, used a 100 hp Mercedes inline engine. Both types were used as trainers, although their controls were noted to be more sensitive than most such aircraft. Those flying characteristics were no doubt on Thies's mind in early 1916 when letters from Boelcke, Immelmann, Wintgens, Otto Parshau and other aces expressed an urgent need for a successor to the Fokker *Eindecker*s. Anthony Fokker responded in May 1916 with the D.I, a biplane powered by a Mercedes engine that was otherwise similar in structure to the E.III and which proved to be only a marginal improvement. Thies designed a more compact, sturdier, single-seat version of the B.II, with a forward stagger to the double-bay wings and a 100 hp Mercedes D.I engine. On 26 Febru-

25

ary 1916 static testing of the Halberstadt D.I, as the fighter version was called, produced a safety factor of 5.78, which contrasted markedly with the fragility shown by the Fokker D.I, D.II and D.III. An initial production contract for twelve aircraft was placed in March and the new fighter was officially flight-tested and accepted in May.

It is generally believed that the first Halberstadt D.I was intended for Max Immelmann, but he was killed four days before it arrived at Douai on 22 June 1916. Boelcke visited the aerodrome later that month and wrote:

> One evening I flew the new Halberstadt biplane—that was the first appearance of this machine at the Front. Because it had a slight resemblance to the British B.E., I was able to completely surprise an Englander. Undetected I got within 50 metres and 'shot his jacket full'. But since I was too fast and did not have the machine in hand like my Fokker, I had to dive under the Englander. He turned around at once and began to descend. I went after him; the belt jammed and I had to turn away. By the time I had located the problem, the enemy was gone.

A few days after that promising first flight, Boelcke was ordered to take leave to Turkey, so he did not have time to become better acquainted with the Halberstadt. By 29 June, however, there were eight Halberstadt D.Is, now powered by 120 hp Mercedes engines, at the Front. Two were delivered to *Fl.Abt. 32* by *Leutnante* Gustav Leffers and Franz Diemer, who flew them with the unit's fighter detachment, called *Abwehr Kommando Nord*. Leffers was probably flying the Halberstadt when he shot down an F.E.2b of No 11 Squadron RFC over Miraumont on 9 July, although Allied witnesses misidentified it as a Fokker.

Halberstadt D.Is and D.IIs proliferated in the months to follow, and became an important transitionary fighter for the Germans—not only as a technological advancement in itself but as equipment for new, specialized fighter squadrons, or *Jagdstaffeln*, that began to form in August 1916. *Abwehr Kommando Nord* became the nucleus for *Jagdstaffel* or *Jasta 1*, under the command of *Hauptmann* Martin Zander, on 22 August, although its initial standardized aircraft complement was composed of less desirable Fokker D.Is and D.IIs. Boelcke, recalled from Turkey on 11 August, formed *Jasta 2* on 27 August, its initial equipment including two Fokker biplanes and the first front-line example of another new fighter type, the Albatros D.I.

Built in the summer of 1916, the Albatros D.I was based on a racing plane with a plywood fuselage developed just before the war began by Robert Thelen, supervisor of the Albatros design committee. Although the single-bay, twin-spar wing structure was standard for the time, the D.I featured a streamlined plywood fuselage with a neatly cowled 160 hp Mercedes D.III engine and a spinner over the propeller. Taking advantage of the more powerful engine, Thelen built the new fighter to carry not one but two synchronized 7.92mm Parabellum 08/14 machine guns, an arrangement that more than doubled the rate of fire. Although it was not as manoeuvrable as most of its Allied opponents, German airmen soon decided that they could live with the superior speed and firepower of the Albatros. Early D.I fliers, however, complained of the way the upper wing and the trestle-type centre-section struts blocked their upward vision. Thelen responded by lowering the upper wing and supporting it with N-shaped cabane struts splayed outward, designating the modified result the D.II. He also later replaced the drag-producing 'ear' type radiators on the fuselage sides of the D.I and early D.IIs with a Teeves und Braun radiator installed flush within the centre section of the upper wing.

Nimble and viceless though the Halberstadt D.II had been, the Albatros D.I made an even more dramatic impression on its pilots. One of the earliest members of *Jasta 2*, *Leutnant* Erwin Böhme, wrote of the Albatros fighters: 'Their climb rate and manoeuvrability are astonishing; it is as if they were living, feeling beings that understand what their master wishes. With them, one can dare and achieve anything.'

Boelcke scored *Jasta 2*'s first victory while flying a Fokker D.III, bringing down a D.H.2 of No 32 Squadron north of Thiepval on 2 September and cordially showing its uninjured pilot, Captain R. E. Wilson, around his aerodrome at Bertincourt before sending him off to the prisoner-of-war camp. Boelcke continued to fly Fokker and Halberstadt scouts over the next two weeks, adding six more Allied aircraft to his score, until 16 September, when five Albatros D.Is and one D.II arrived. Later that same afternoon, *Leutnant* Otto Walter Höhne flew a patrol in one of the new D.Is and brought down an F.E.2b of No 11 Squadron at Manacourt at 6 p.m. The crew, Second Lieutenant A. L. Pinkerton and Lieutenant J. W. Sanders, were taken prisoner.

On the following day Boelcke inaugurated an innovation more significant than the Albatros—a team effort at gaining local air superiority. At 11 a.m. he led five of his men towards British lines and spotted fourteen British aircraft heading for Marcoing railway station. Boelcke led his formation to intercept them, but the British reached their target first and were bombing the station when Boelcke's flight arrived. While Boelcke held back in order to be ready to help any inexperienced pilot who got into trouble, five Albatros scouts dived on the bombers and their escorts, broke up the formations and then proceeded to go after lone targets.

One of Boelcke's young disciples, *Leutnant* Manfred *Freiherr* von Richthofen, pursued an F.E.2b which took evasive action and led him on a merry chase until he was able to get a good shot into the engine compartment. The F.E. finally came down at the German aerodrome at Flesquières, and Richthofen landed nearby to inspect the first of the 80 aircraft that he was destined to bring down.

The observer, 21-year-old Second Lieutenant Thomas Rees of No 11 Squadron, was dead; the pilot, 19-year-old Second Lieutenant Lionel B. F. Morris, died shortly after being taken to the hospital at Cambrai.

Another F.E.2b team from No 11 Squadron, Second Lieutenant T. P. L. Molloy and Sergeant G. J. Morton, were somewhat more fortunate than Rees and Morris, being brought down alive south of Thescault by *Leutnant der Reserve* Hans Reimann for his second victory. Boelcke himself downed another of No 11 Squadron's F.E.s over Equancourt, Captain D. Gray and Lieutenant L. B. Helder also becoming POWs. Finally, *Leutnant* Böhme, who felt that one could do anything in an Albatros, opened his account by bringing down a Sopwith 1½-Strutter of No 70 Squadron, its pilot, Second Lieutenant Oswald Nixon, being killed and the wounded observer, Lieutenant R. Wood, being taken prisoner.

That night a German Army tradition was broken and a new air force tradition established when enlisted men were permitted to join the officers in the squadron *Kasino* to celebrate. Amid the festivities, Boelcke pinned the Iron Cross First Class on Böhme. Richthofen, who had already received that decoration, wrote a letter that evening to a jeweller in Berlin, ordering a plain silver cup, two inches high and one inch wide, on which was to be inscribed: '1. Vickers 2. 17.9.16.'

The Albatros D.II, combined with the adoption of the 'Boelcke Dicta', resulted in another reversal of fortune over the Western Front in the autumn of 1916. *Jasta 2* would be the vanguard of a general resurgence of German air power, during which Boelcke would bring his personal score up to 40 before being killed in a mid-air collision with Böhme on 28 October 1916. Böhme managed to bring his stricken plane down, but blamed himself for the death of his beloved mentor and Richthofen only narrowly dissuaded him from committing suicide. Death caught up with Böhme of its own accord on 29 November 1917 when he fell victim to an Armstrong Whitworth F.K.8 crew of No 10 Squadron, but not before he had accounted for a total of 24 Allied aircraft and received the *Ordre Pour le Mérite*.

The New Year brought a new fighter to the growing number of *Jagdstaffeln* as the first Albatros D.IIIs arrived. Inspired by the manoeuvrability and improved downward vision of the Nieuport 17.C1, the Albatros design team tried to achieve the best of both worlds by applying a sesquiplane wing arrangement to the D.II. The result, which featured two wings with a long curving rake at the tips, the lower of which was of considerably reduced chord, certainly looked more graceful than the squared-off wings of the D.II. However much they may have enhanced the appearance, manoeuvrability and climb rate of the D.III though, the lower wing in the sesquiplane arrangement displayed a disturbing tendency to twist about on its axis during a prolonged dive.

Manfred von Richthofen had sixteen victories to his credit when the first D.IIIs reached *Jasta 2* on 7 January 1917. Before he could try the new plane out, however, he was reassigned to *Jasta 11*, a fighter squadron attached to the *6. Armee* which had accomplished nothing since it became operational at La Brayelle, north-west of Douai, on 11 October 1916. Richthofen was to take over command from *Oberleutnant* Rudolf Emil Lang, who in turn would take command of a new unit, Royal Württemberg *Jasta 28*.

Richthofen received the *Ordre Pour le Mérite* on 12 January, and eight days later he arrived at *Jasta 11*'s aerodrome at La Brayelle. At that point Richthofen, deciding that camouflage did nothing to hide his plane, went the opposite route and had it completely overpainted in red. When his men protested that he would be too vulnerable to being singled out by the enemy, Richthofen suggested that all of them adopt some red as a unit marking, and add an additional colour for personal identification.

Richthofen inaugurated his new all-red Albatros D.III to combat on 23 January, shooting down an F.E.8 single-seat pusher fighter of No 40 Squadron over Lens and killing its Australian pilot, Second Lieutenant John Hay, for *Jasta 11*'s first and his seventeenth victory. On the following day he brought down an F.E.2b west of Vimy, the wounded crew of which, Captain Oscar Greig and Lieutenant John E. Maclennan of No 25 Squadron, were taken prisoner. Richthofen again landed nearby his victims, but it was not solely for the purpose of having a chat: in the course of the combat, his wing had cracked during a dive. Richthofen's confidence in the new D.III was seriously shaken and he reverted to the Halberstadt D.II for much of his flying until the end of March 1917, scoring as many as eleven victories in the older but more reliable fighter. Eventually, Albatros was able to strengthen and brace the wing cellule enough to make the D.III satisfactory, and, in the hands of Richthofen and the aggressive pilots he inspired, *Jasta 11* made it the terror of the Western Front in April 1917.

By the spring of 1917, the fundamentals of air-to-air combat were in place, but few of its pioneers were around to see the fruition of their efforts. Garros was a prisoner of war, while Immelmann, Boelcke and Wintgens were dead. Nor did Major Lanoe Hawker live to see the arrival of newer, more efficient fighters at No 24 Squadron. He was leading his men as usual on 23 November 1916 when he engaged in an epic, ten-minute duel with an Albatros D.II of *Jasta 2*. At last, running low on fuel, Hawker tried to make a break for home, but he was shot down and killed, as victory number eleven for Manfred von Richthofen.

Hubert Harvey-Kelly, victor of the RFC's first aerial combat, had a somewhat longer career than Hawker's, eventually rising to the rank of Major and commanding No 19 Squadron before he too became a victim of the new form of warfare he had helped to pioneer. He was flying a Spad 7.C1 as he took off from Vert Galant aerodrome at 10.00 in the morning of 29 April 1917, accompanied by Second Lieutenants Richard Applin and W. M. Hamilton, to patrol the area around Douai. There they encountered eight Albatros D.IIIs, five of which were described as silvery-gray and three of which were red. The bright-coloured Germans were from *Jasta 11*, led by Hawker's killer, *Hauptmann* von Richthofen, who by then was gaining notoriety as 'The Red Baron'.

Six Sopwith Triplanes of No 1 Squadron, Royal Naval Air Service, were also in the area, so Harvey-Kelly confidently attacked the Germans. The Triplanes indeed joined in and claimed three Albatros scouts as 'out of control' in the course of the twenty-minute mêlée. Things turned out disastrously different for the Spads, however, as Applin was sent crashing to his death in a swamp near Lecluse by Manfred von Richthofen, who claimed him as his 49th kill—and the first of four that he would gain before the day was over. Hamilton was more fortunate, being brought down and taken prisoner, the thirteenth victory for the Baron's younger brother, *Leutnant* Lothar von Richthofen. Harvey-Kelly crashed after a duel with another of *Jasta 11*'s Albatros pilots, dying of head wounds in a German hospital three days later. He was the tenth victim of *Leutnant* Kurt Wolff.

Chapter 3

A DEADLIER BREED

Fighter Development, 1916–1917

By the end of 1916, the essential fighter configuration had been defined: a single-seater with a forward-firing machine gun, usually synchronized to fire through the propeller. For the rest of World War I, aircraft manufacturers of the warring powers were engaged in a constant struggle to improve the breed, seeking to gain that edge in speed, climb or manoeuvrability that would bring them control of the sky. Neither the Allies nor the Central Powers were able to attain that goal for long, before the other side came up with a new type that would equal or surpass the performance of the current world-beater.

An aeroplane's worth often depends on its powerplant, and the water-cooled, 8-cylinder marvel that Swiss engineer Marc Birkigt created in 1915, the 150 hp Hispano-Suiza 8A, was to inspire several great Allied fighters. The first had its origins in the dissolution of the French *Société provisoire des Aéroplanes Deperdussin* and its resurrection in August 1914 as the *Société anonyme pour l'Aviation et ses Dérivés*, still retaining the company acronym of Spad. In its new incarnation, Spad also retained Deperdussin's talented designer, Louis Béchereau.

Among Béchereau's first wartime designs was the Spad A2, which sought to solve the problem of firing a machine gun past the propeller arc by placing a gunner in a pulpit held by means of struts in front of the propeller and its 80 hp Le Rhône rotary engine. Although placed into limited production, the Spad A2 and its 110 hp successor, the A4, were too terrifying—the front gunner having little chance of survival in the event of a nose-over upon landing—to last long. The basic airframe, however, was sturdy and sound. On 4 June 1915 Béchereau applied for a patent for the plane's single-bay wing cellule, which featured intermediate struts of narrow chord, to which the bracing wires were attached at the mid point. That arrangement added strength and, by reducing vibration in the wires, reduced drag as well.

Béchereau's next fighter, the Spad G, used the same airframe and rotary engine as the A2 but dispensed with the gunner, instead mounting a remotely controlled machine gun in a sizeable housing in front of the propeller. That,

31

too, was a failure, but then Béchereau adapted the airframe to two new developments—the 150 hp Hispano-Suiza 8A engine and a synchronized 0.303-inch Vickers machine gun. At first called the Spad HS, the prototype had a large conical spinner in front of a circular radiator. The spinner was soon abandoned but the radiator was retained, although it would undergo several changes in configuration to address an early spate of cooling problems.

First flown in April 1916, the Spad HS was an instant success and the French air service placed its first order for 268 of the new Spad 7.C1, as it was officially designated, on 10 May 1916. The Royal Flying Corps and the Royal Naval Air Service were also quick to order the new fighter.

An early recipient of the Spad 7 was *Sous-Lieutenant* Georges Guynemer, the leading ace of *Escadrille N.3 'Les Cigognes'*, who scored his fifteenth victory in Spad 7 S113 over Hyencourt on 4 September 1916, his victims being the Aviatik C.II crew of *Leutnante* Hans Steiner and Otto Fresnius.

Production of the Spad 7 got off to a slow start, but eventually some 3,500 were built, serving in numerous air arms around the world. Aces from France, Britain, Russia, Belgium, Italy and the United States all scored victories in Spad 7s at one time or another in their careers, as did André Bosson and Jacques Roques, two Swiss volunteers who became aces in French service. Problems with the later twin-gunned Spad 13's geared Hispano-Suiza engine made it necessary to retain the Spad 7 in front-line service until the end of the war, and French fighter pilots were still training in Spad 7s as late as 1928.

By the time the RFC received its first Spad 7 for evaluation on 9 September 1916 the Royal Aircraft Factory at Farnborough was engaged in designing its own Hispano-Suiza-powered fighter. In fact, RAF engineer Frank W. Goodden had had two ideas in the works as early as June. One, designated the F.E.10 (Fighter Experimental No 10), was a rather impractical-looking contraption with the pilot and his machine gun perched in front of the propeller in a nacelle braced to the undercarriage and upper wing in a manner similar to that used by the gunner of the unsuccessful Spad A2. The other, designated S.E.5 (Scouting Experimental No 5), was similar in overall layout, but with the engine in front and the pilot seated aft of the wings—essentially a smaller, more compactly proportioned single-seat version of the B.E.2c. Not surprisingly, the conventional design was selected for further development, but the F.E.10's vertical tail surfaces were retained in lieu of the smaller fin and rudder originally proposed for the S.E.5.

When the first 21 French-made Hispano-Suiza 8A engines were delivered to the RFC on 20 September, most were earmarked for installation in British-built Spad 7s, but two were used to power the first and second S.E.5 prototypes, A4561 and A4562. On 28 November the Royal Aircraft Factory received its first example of the new geared 200 hp Hispano-Suiza 8B, which it subsequently installed in the third prototype, A4563—thereby creating the first S.E.5a.

S.E.5 A4562 broke up during a test flight on 28 January 1917, killing Major Goodden. Simple modifications corrected the plane's structural problems, however, and the first production S.E.5, A4845, cleared its final inspection on 2 March 1917. The first production batch of S.E.5s did not make a promising impression on their pilots, who complained of poor lateral control—a shortcoming that was alleviated somewhat, but never entirely, by shortening the wingspan and reducing the rake of the wing tips. Early production S.E.5s also featured an overhead gravity tank, a large half-canopy that pilots came to call 'the greenhouse' and a mechanism that could raise or lower the pilot's seat. The mixed armament consisted of one 0.303-inch Vickers machine gun in the fuselage, synchronized by means of a new Constantinesco CC Fire Control Timing Gear which frequently failed, and a 0.303-inch Lewis gun mounted above the upper wing.

The first S.E.5s were assigned to No 56 Squadron under Major Richard Graham Blomfield, a new unit that nevertheless had the benefit of a hand-picked cadre of experienced pilots. The most famous of the 'old hands' was the 20-year-old leader of 'A' Flight, Captain Albert Ball, an eccentric but brilliantly aggressive 'loner' whose exploits as a Nieuport pilot in No 60 Squadron were already legendary in the RFC. Ball, whose score then stood at 32 victories, had high expectations for the S.E.5, but, after giving the first prototype a ten-minute test flight on 23 November 1916 he remarked with bitter regret that the new scout had 'turned out a dud'.

On 7 April thirteen S.E.5s of No 56 Squadron landed at Vert Galant aerodrome, joining the Spad 7s of No 19 Squadron and the Sopwith Pups of No 66 Squadron. The unit and its new fighters reached the Front at the start of the Battle of Arras, a British offensive that was meant merely as a diversion for the larger French push that would be launched along the Aisne river on 16 April.

Ball had made no secret of his dislike for the S.E., and when Major-General Hugh Montague Trenchard visited the sector, Ball flew to Le Hameau and entreated him to replace the new fighters with Nieuports. Trenchard lent him a sympathetic ear and Ball was convinced that the S.E.s would be replaced, but he had already taken the liberty of modifying his personal S.E.5, A4850, while at London Colney. He replaced the 'greenhouse' with a small Avro windscreen, which reduced drag and gave the pilot better access to the upper Lewis gun. He also removed the adjustable armoured seat and replaced it with a board until a simpler seat could be installed. The Lewis machine gun mounting was altered, with the slide lengthened by two inches to make it easier for the pilot to replace the ammunition drums. Ball discarded his synchronized Vickers gun and replaced it with an obliquely mounted, downward-firing Lewis. He also removed the petrol and water gravity tanks from the upper wing and installed long Spad-type exhaust pipes. Ball noted that his alterations resulted in a considerable improvement in performance, but he still regarded the S.E. to be 'a rotten machine'.

Not all of Ball's modifications met with approval in the RFC—the obliquely mounted, downward-firing Lewis gun was not a good idea—but many of them were adopted for production aircraft, and the S.E.5 was the better for it. The undercarriage wheels were also moved further forward and the external over-wing tank was replaced by internally fitted fuel and water gravity tanks behind the leading edge of the upper wing centre section, which was also strengthened and covered with plywood to withstand the recoil of the Lewis gun.

Snow and bad weather delayed test-flying in the modified aircraft until 13 April. Ball was told that afternoon that Trenchard had authorized him a Nieuport for his personal use, although he still had to fly S.E.5 A4850 on squadron patrols. Ball was delighted, and that evening Captain Henry Meintjes flew Nieuport Scout No B.1522 in from Candas, while Ball brought in his modified S.E.5.

The first operational S.E.5 patrol was dispatched at 10.18 a.m. on 22 April, the pilots' enthusiasm being somewhat tempered by orders that they were on no account to cross the front lines. Ball led 'A' Flight in A4850, but one of his five planes dropped out when Gerald Maxwell developed engine trouble due to a failure of the oil to circulate properly. At an altitude of 11,000 feet Ball spotted an Albatros two-seater over Adinfer and attacked. Although he fired three drums of ammunition into the enemy plane at a range as close as 150 feet, the German managed to escape in a steep dive over the lines, at which point Ball had to break off the chase. Another enemy plane was seen at noon, but it was too far away to engage. Meintjes led 'C' Flight on another patrol that afternoon, but it was equally unproductive.

Cyril Crowe led the squadron's first offensive patrol the next morning, but again the British encountered no enemy activity. Ball, however, had taken off on his own at 6 a.m., flying his Nieuport between Douai and Cambrai with the expectation of encountering a German en route to or from one of those aerodromes. Indeed, two Albatros two-seaters appeared 8,000 feet over Cambrai, and Ball carried out his usual tactic—a dive, then a pull-out underneath his quarry, at which point he pulled up his wing-mounted Lewis gun and fired at the underside. The first German eluded him, but Ball slipped under the second, fired half a drum of Lewis into it and then pursued his diving prey until it crashed into the side of the road between Tilloy and Abancourt. Thus No 56 Squadron's first official victory was not scored in the unit's assigned aircraft.

Ball found and attacked another Albatros a few minutes later, but its pilot was an experienced hand and throttled back when Ball dived to the attack, causing him to overshoot. With the tables turned, the German put fifteen bullets in the spars of the Nieuport's bottom wing. Ball dived away and landed safely at 8.45, but his Nieuport was out of action until a new lower wing could be installed. Ball therefore flew his second patrol of the day in his unloved S.E.5.

Taking off at 10.45 and climbing to 12,000 feet, Ball spotted an Albatros C.III over Adinfer, dived, pulled up and opened fire—only to suffer a gun jam. Apparently forgetting that he had another Lewis gun in his plane, Ball landed at Le Hameau aerodrome, rectified his jam and took off again. At 11.45 he sighted five Albatros scouts over Sevigny and again dived to the attack, firing 150 rounds into one opponent, which fell out of control and burst into flames before reaching the ground. The other four Germans put some rounds into Ball's plane, but he used the S.E.'s superior diving speed to escape. Three-quarters of an hour later Ball encountered yet another Albatros C.III north of Cambrai, dived underneath and fired half a drum of Lewis into it. The German pilot, *Vizefeldwebel* Egert of *Flieger Abteilung 7*, retired in a steep dive, made a good landing and then helped his observer, *Leutnant* Berger, who had suffered a severe neck wound in Ball's attack.

Meintjes led a five-plane patrol up at 1.15 that afternoon, but half an hour later Lieutenant William B. Melville turned back with engine trouble and his S.E.5, A4852, overturned while landing and was wrecked. The rest of the flight chased a German two-seater south of Lens but failed to bring it down. In the final sortie of the day Ball led Lieutenants Clarence R. W. Knight and John Owen Leach in search of enemy balloons, but they returned empty-handed at 5.35.

So ended the S.E.5's first day. Only the redoubtable Ball had shot anything down, but squadron morale was high. Disappointing though they had been at the onset, the modified S.E.5s had not performed badly. Even Ball came to appreciate the aircraft, and used it to add eleven victories to his final total of 44, before being killed in it shortly after a costly run-in with the Red Baron's Circus on 7 May 1917. The replacement of the S.E.5's 150 hp Hispano-Suiza with a more powerful 200 hp model, along with further refinements, produced the S.E.5a, the first of which began arriving at No 56 Squadron in June. Fast, rugged and almost viceless, the S.E.5a became a mainstay of the RFC and later of the RAF over the Western Front right up to the end of the war. The first unit to employ it, 'Fighting Fifty-Six', was also the most successful, being credited with 401 victories by the end of the war and producing numerous famous aces, two of whom—Ball and James Thomas Byford McCudden—were awarded the Victoria Cross.

In the same month that the S.E.5 saw combat for the first time another British fighter was having a far less auspicious debut. Although it, like the S.E.5, would evolve into one of the great fighters of the war, the first Bristol F.2As to cross the lines added to the notoriety of 'Bloody April'—and to that of the Flying Circus.

In 1916 the RFC began seeking a replacement for the intolerably vulnerable B.E.2c. The Royal Aircraft Factory responded with the R.E.8, while Frank Barnwell at Bristols designed the R.2A, a two-seater which had the fuselage raised above the lower wing by struts in order to improve the pilot's view over the upper wing. A revised version of the Bristol design with unequal-span wings and a 150 hp Hispano-Suiza engine was designated the R.2B, but it was quickly superseded by another variant, with equal-span wings and a new Rolls-Royce Falcon I engine. At that point the Bristol design was being regarded as a reconnaissance fighter, and by the time the first prototype, A3303, flew on 9 September 1916 it had been redesignated the F.2A. With its side-mounted 'ear' radiators replaced by a circular radiator within a deeper nose cowling, A3303 underwent its official tests between 16 and 18 October, using both a two- and a four-blade propeller. The RFC was already impressed with the new plane's potential, and testing only confirmed its decision to order 50 production examples. The first operational F.2As were delivered to No 48 Squadron in December, armed with a synchronized 0.303-inch Vickers gun and a 0.303-inch Lewis gun on a Scarff ring in the observer's cockpit. After training at Rendcombe, No 48 Squadron was deployed to Bellevue, France, in March 1917, its aircraft being held until the start of the Battle of Arras in the hope of their achieving a degree of surprise over the enemy.

As with the S.E.5s of No 56 Squadron, the Bristol crews of No 48 Squadron were led by a cadre of veteran flight and deputy flight leaders. Captain A. T. Cull had seen considerable action, and Captain Alan M. Wilkinson was already credited with ten victories flying D.H.2s with No 24 Squadron. Captain William Leefe Robinson, who had been awarded the Victoria Cross for destroying Schütte-Lanz airship *SL11* over north London on the night of 2/3 September 1916, was the most famous of No 48 Squadron's flight commanders, but he also had the least experience in the more intense fighting environment that had developed over the Western Front.

Largely ignoring the higher speed and greater manoeuvrability that the Bristol offered over two-seat reconnaissance aircraft, Robinson adopted the tactic of closing up the flight when attacked so that the rear gunners could concentrate their fire. He then took up six F.2As at 10.00 in the morning of 5 April, to conduct an offensive patrol to Douai. By the time the Bristols neared Arras at 11.00, German ground observers had reported their presence to the fighter unit at Brayelle, and soon five Albatros D.IIIs of *Jasta 11* were taking off to intercept them, led by *Leutnant* Manfred von Richthofen.

As the Germans closed in, the Bristols closed up, their gunners waiting for the enemy to come within range. Then the Albatros scouts bore in fast, twin machine guns blazing, and almost immediately a Bristol fell out of formation and was forced down near Lewarde by Richthofen himself. Its wounded crew, Second Lieutenants A. N. Leckler and H. D. K. George, were taken prisoner, but George died of his wounds shortly afterwards.

While Richthofen hastened to re-join the chase, *Vizefeldwebel* Sebastian Festner drove down Robinson and his observer, Second Lieutenant E. D. Warburton, both of whom became prisoners of war. Catching up with another Bristol near Cuincy, Richthofen downed Lieutenants A. T. Adams and D. J. Stewart, who were also wounded and taken prisoner, their only consolation lying in both having survived their run-in with the Baron. A fourth Bristol was brought down by *Leutnant* Georg Simon, resulting in another wounded air crew, Lieutenant H. A. Cooper and Second Lieutenant A. Boldison, falling into German captivity. The remaining two F.2As limped home full of holes, their crews claiming to have shot down two of their attackers. In fact, Richthofen lost none of his 'gentlemen' or their planes that day.

Two more patrols were flown by No 48 Squadron on 5 April, each returning unscathed and each claiming to have downed an enemy plane; one, an Albatros D.III 'out of control', was credited to Wilkinson and his observer, Lieutenant L. W. Allen, as Wilkinson's eleventh victory. Nevertheless, to say that the Bristol fighter's first day of combat had fallen short of expectations would be an understatement. For four somewhat dubious claims, the squadron had lost four aircraft and eight men—one of whom, a publicly adored VC recipient, was as much of a moral blow to Britain as he was a feather in the cap for the Red Baron's Circus.

In spite of that disastrous initial showing, another 200 Bristol fighters were ordered for the RFC, modified with longer-span tailplanes and a slope to the upper fuselage longerons. The first 150 F.2Bs, as the altered Bristols were called, used Hispano-Suiza engines, but the next 50 were powered by the 220 hp Rolls-Royce Falcon II, with radiator shutters to help control the engine's temperature. Even while Bristol Fighters were being delivered to Nos 11, 20, 22, 48, 62 and 88 Squadrons, pilots were realizing that the new plane's speed and manoeuvrability would be more effectively brought into play if it were flown aggressively like a scout with a sting in the tail rather than as a typical two-seater. They changed their tactics accordingly, and the Bristol F.2B went on to acquire an outstanding fighting record.

Having provided the British forces with the excellent Pup and Triplane scouts in 1916, Sopwith did not produce a new single-seat design until December

1916—six months after the Triplane—and, structurally at least, it differed little from its predecessors. The F.1 biplane had a shorter, deeper fuselage than the Pup, with the rotary engine, cockpit and guns concentrated closer up front. To facilitate production, Sopwith eliminated dihedral on the one-piece upper wing and compensated by doubling the dihedral of the lower one. The most significant improvement offered in the F.1 was the replacement of the single 0.303-inch Vickers machine gun of the Pup and Triplane with a twin-gun installation partially covered by fairings that looked somewhat like a hump from the side, leading to the plane being christened 'Camel'.

The first F.1 was powered by a 110 hp Clerget 9Z rotary engine when Harry Hawker got in its cockpit and, as he put it, 'bounced into the air' from Brooklands aerodrome on 16 December 1916. Subsequent prototypes were powered by several other engine types. The first production batch from Sopwith used either the 130 hp Clerget 9B or the 150 hp Bentley B.R.1.

Similar though it may have been in construction, the Camel's altered configuration gave it flying characteristics that differed radically from those of the docile Pup and the manageable Triplane. The torque of the rotary engine, combined with the concentration of weight up front, endowed it with breathtaking manoeuvrability but also made it murderously unforgiving of pilot error. Few if any German aircraft could match a Camel in a right-hand turn, but failure to compensate for the torque during take-off or landing could send a careless pilot careening into the ground. Pilots who mastered the Camel's idiosyncrasies swore by it; those who did not swore at it—provided they survived to do so.

The first unit to use the Camel in combat was No 4 Squadron RNAS, which began replacing its Pups with the new type in the first week of June 1917. On 4 June Flight Commander Alexander M. Shook, patrolling in N6347, attacked an enemy plane fifteen miles off Nieuport. The German dived steeply and escaped into a dense sea haze. Shook was up again the next day when he sighted fifteen German aircraft between Nieuport and Ostend and immediately attacked. He was more successful this time, sending an enemy scout down to crash on the beach and shooting a second down out of control. The first combat loss occurred on 13 June when Flight Sub-Lieutenant Langley F. W. Smith, an American volunteer from Chicago, Illinois, who had already been credited with eight victories flying Pups, was killed in N6362: according to some witnesses, his Camel broke up while he was stunting above the German aerodrome at Neumünster. On 25 June Shook and Flight Sub-Lieutenant Arnold J. Chadwick attacked a German two-seater and its escort of scouts. In the course of the mêlée Chadwick managed to shoot down the two-seater in flames.

A harbinger of somewhat different things to come came in the early morning of 4 July when five of Naval 4's Camels encountered sixteen Gotha bombers flying at an altitude of between 12,000 and 15,000 feet, 30 miles north-west of Ostend. Shook attacked one of the Gothas and last saw it diving and trailing black smoke. He then attacked a second bomber until his guns jammed. Shook was subsequently awarded the Distinguished Service Cross for his part in the action, but his fellow pilots were equally keen to come to grips with the twin-engine giants. Flight Sub-Lieutenant Sydney E. Ellis dived into the centre of the bomber formation and fired 300 rounds into one of the Gothas, which stalled and fell away erratically, with brown smoke spewing from the rear gunner's cockpit. Flight Sub-Lieutenant Albert J. Enstone claimed to have damaged one Gotha in the fight and forced a second down low over the Netherlands.

The Camels of Naval 4, joined by those of Naval 3, accounted for several more German aircraft over the next few days. On 10 July, however, Flight Sub-Lieutenant E. W. Busby was killed in action, and two days later Naval 4 was reminded of the Camel's unforgiving nature when Ellis spun into the ground and was killed instantly. Nevertheless, overall it had been a satisfactory first month for the touchy but nimble debutante that would eventually fly with the RNAS, the RFC and the Royal Air Force over every battle front, would be credited with more aerial victories than any single fighter type of World War I and would endure as one of the most famous aircraft of the war—and of all time.

Two other British fighters of less conventional configuration than that of the S.E.5, Bristol and Camel were doomed to less successful careers. Late in 1916 Geoffrey de Havilland built a tractor-engine successor to his D.H.2, powered by a 110 hp Le Rhône 9J radial and armed with a synchronized Vickers gun that could be elevated as high as 60 degrees in order to attack opponents from below. The most unusual feature of the D.H.5, however, was the placement of the pilot forward of a back-staggered upper wing, which was intended to give him as good a forward view as a D.H.2 pilot had had. Although its 100 mph speed at 10,000 feet was a distinct improvement over the D.H.2's 77 mph, the D.H.5 was slower and climbed less rapidly than the Sopwith Pup, and its service ceiling of 14,300 feet was less than the Pup's 17,500 feet. In spite of that, 400 D.H.5s were ordered on 15 January 1917.

The first D.H.5s reached No 24 Squadron on 1 May, although the unit still had a few of its old and hopelessly obsolescent D.H.2s on strength when the Battle of Messines began on 7 June. The D.H.5's first success came on 25 May when Second Lieutenant Stanley Cockerell, a D.H.2 veteran, shot down an Albatros D.III over Ligny for his sixth victory. Only nineteen other claims were to be made by the squadron, however, before it was re-equipped with S.E.5as, and in only two cases were the enemy aircraft seen to crash.

D.H.5s also equipped Nos 32, 41, 64 and 68 (Australian) Squadrons, but successes were few and more frequently the D.H.5 pilots experienced the frustration of enemy aircraft escaping by outrunning or outclimbing them. The ruggedly built D.H.5s performed yeoman service as ground strafers during the Battle of Cambrai in November 1917, but attrition to ground fire and enemy fighters was inevitably high. Even while No 64 Squadron was bringing its new D.H.5s to the Front in October 1917, No 41 Squadron was beginning to replace its D.H.5s with S.E.5as. Later No 24 Squadron's historian wrote: 'On December 25th the Squadron received the best of all Xmas presents—a new machine— and both pilots and mechanics heaved a sigh of thankfulness to heaven. The new machine was the S.E.5 with 200 h.p. Hispano Suiza engine.' By January 1918 the last D.H.5s had been withdrawn from the Front.

Among the most advanced single-seat designs to enter British service during World War I was also the most underutilized. Designed by Frank Barnwell— creator of the redoubtable F.2B—the Bristol M.1A was a monoplane fighter that first flew on 14 July 1916. Its appearance could not have been more untimely, for at that time the Morane-Saulnier Nm monoplane was taking part in the Battle of the Somme with No 60 Squadron, making a wretched name for itself and for monoplanes in general. By mid-October the RFC's commander, Major-General Hugh Trenchard, was cancelling all further purchase orders for Morane-Saulnier scouts and was left with a near-pathological antipathy for all things with single wings.

That was unfortunate, because the Bristol had none of the Morane-Saulnier's faults. Although its thin wings were wire-braced to the fuselage under-side and a rounded pylon above the cockpit, they proved to be sturdy enough to withstand the stresses of combat and had ailerons rather than wing-warping like the earlier French monoplane. The Bristol's tail surfaces had horizontal and vertical stabilizers, making it far less tricky to fly than the Morane-Saulnier, and the synchronization mechanism for its single Vickers machine gun was more reliable than that of the Morane-Saulnier I and V—to say nothing of the terrifying propeller-mounted metal deflectors on the Morane-Saulnier Nm. The most remarkable feature of the Bristol monoplane was the performance it achieved with the mere 110 hp of its Clerget 9Z rotary engine—130 mph and the ability to climb to 10,000 feet in 8½ seconds, as compared to the 109.4 mph top speed of a Morane-Saulnier I, which took twice as long to reach 10,000 feet. Later, test pilot Oliver Stewart rated the Bristol M.1's manoeuvrability as superior to that of the S.E.5a and the Sopwith Snipe, the latter of which was a 1918 design.

Bristol took steps to remedy the prototype's principal shortcoming—a com-plete lack of downward visibility—by removing a section of fabric from the right wing root of the revised M.1B, which also featured a pyramidal bracing pylon above the cockpit. The first M.1B, A5139, went to France and on the 23rd it was flown by three veteran pilots, including Lieutenant D'Urban V. Armstrong and Captain Roderic Hill, both of whom had flown Morane-Saulnier monoplanes in No 60 Squadron. Hill and the third pilot, Captain A. M. Lowery of No 70 Squadron, wrote favourable reports about the Bristol, but Trenchard had made up his mind about the new monoplane before he even read them, citing its limited downward view as the official excuse to reject it out of hand. Front-line fighter pilots who had heard about the Bristol and who hoped to see it issued to their squadrons were flabbergasted. 'It is true that the downward and forward view was slightly restricted,' Oliver Stewart wrote, 'but there was not a fighting pilot of experience who would not have exchanged that view for the speed and climb of the Bristol Monoplane with alacrity and enthusiasm.'

Although no Bristol monoplane ever fought over the Western Front, in June 1917 three M.1Bs, A5140, A5141 and A5142, were shipped to Palestine in response to desperate pleas from Brigadier-General W. G. H. Salmond for modern fighters to support large-scale operations that were about to commence there. They arrived in August and were assigned to the newly forming fighter unit, No 111 Squadron at Deir el Belah, where they flew alongside Vickers F.B.19 Bullets, Bristol F.2Bs, D.H.2s and a Bristol Scout D. Soon after joining the squadron, A5142 was modified, with both wing root panels uncovered and the machine gun repositioned from the left to a central position. Later it was apparently transferred to Heliopolis, Egypt, to serve as a trainer with a camera gun and with its spinner removed to improve engine cooling.

Lieutenant W. S. Lighthall of No 111 Squadron recorded his impressions of the M.1B in desert service:

> These were far ahead of their time aerodynamically, but were fragile and difficult to get in and out of due to a low triangle of struts over the pilot's cockpit and the close proximity of the Vickers gun which had a tendency to break the pilot's nose in a bad landing.

The first success for No. 111 Squadron was achieved on 8 October by a Bristol Fighter team, Second Lieutenant R. C. Steele and Lieutenant John J. Lloyd Williams, who brought down an Albatros D.III. The German plane was subsequently repaired and given several evaluation flights by Captain A. H. Peck. Steele and Lloyd Williams downed a second Albatros D.III on 15 October, and the team of Peck and Lloyd Williams had accounted for three other enemy planes by 8 November. With regard to the Bristol monoplanes, the Squadron History noted that they 'had some usefulness in that they made it a little more difficult for the enemy airmen to reconnoitre, except from great heights, but their very limited endurance prevented them from being used to escort the long distance strategicial reconnaissance aeroplanes'. Major-General W. Sefton Brancker, who took command of the Middle East Brigade in October 1917, wrote: 'The Bristol Monoplanes and Vickers Bullets are not very much good except to frighten the Hun; they always seem to lose the enemy as soon as he starts manoeuvring.'

M.1B A5141, in fact, became No 111 Squadron's first operational loss, although its pilot, Second Lieutenant Edgar Percival, returned on 16 November. His squadron colleague, Lighthall, wrote of the incident:

> Edgar Percival, later a well-known aircraft designer and owner of the Percival Aircraft Company, had a forced landing in a Bristol Monoplane far behind the Turk lines in the Judean hills. He only saved his nose by ducking very low and took the bump on the top of his head. He crawled out of the mess of the struts and wires, cowed some hostile Arabs with his Very pistol, and made them guide him through the Turkish lines and home to our squadron at Megdil.

However good the aircraft might have been had it fought over the Western Front, the Bristol M.1B's debut over Palestine was distinguished primarily by Percival's desert adventure. By March 1918 more fighters with greater range and a better adaptability to a desert environment, in particular the S.E.5a, were available to No 111 Squadron and the last of its monoplanes were withdrawn. On 3 August 1917 the War Office ordered 125 Bristol M.1Cs, which had panels cut out of both wing roots and were powered by the 110 hp Le Rhône engine, but they, too, were destined to see action only in sideshows. On 2 March 1918 No 72 Squadron arrived at Basra, equipped with D.H.4s, S.E.5as, Spads, Martinsydes and eight M.1Cs. The Bristol monoplanes got off to a unique start in Mesopotamia when two of them gave an aerobatic display before some Kurds, resulting in the entire tribe switching its allegiance from the Turks to the British. Other than that, No 72 Squadron's M.1Cs gave good service in the ground attack role.

A handful of M.1Cs were also shipped to Nos 17 and 47 Squadrons in Macedonia in early January 1918. On 1 April 1918, while the Royal Flying Corps and Royal Naval Air Service were being amalgamated into the Royal Air Force, 'A' Flight of No 17 Squadron and 'B' Flight of No 47 Squadron were being amalgamated into a new unit, No 150 Squadron. Although No 150 was specifically a fighter squadron, its equipment was far from homogeneous, consisting of S.E.5as, Bristol M.1Cs and Nieuports, to which would later be added some Camels. It was with No 150 Squadron that the Bristol M.1C finally got the opportunity to show its worth in air-to-air combat on 25 April 1918, when Lieutenant Arthur E. de Montainge Jarvis—then still officially on No 17 Squadron's roster—fired 150 rounds at a DFW C.V over Yenimah and last saw it descending in a steep dive toward Rupel Pass. Later that same morning, Jarvis in M.1C C4913 and Lieutenant Acheson G. Goulding in an S.E.5a attacked another DFW near Nihor, and in spite of an attempt by two Albatros D.IIIs to intervene they sent it down vertically over Angista, apparently on fire. On the next day Jarvis in his M.1C and Lieutenant J. J. Boyd Harvey in a Nieuport attacked a DFW over Prosenik and sent it crashing into Hristos Gully. The M.1Cs were quite successful over Macedonia, and one of their pilots, Captain Frederick D. Travers, even managed to claim five victories while flying one, his wartime total being nine. Nevertheless, it is doubtful whether more than 35 M.1Bs and M.1Cs saw any combat use, the rest being employed as trainers. The Bristol, however, would not be the only promising monoplane fighter design destined for a disappointing career before the war was over.

While the Camel was able to coexist with the S.E.5 and Bristol F.2B in the RFC, France's general satisfaction with the Spad 7 undermined the prospects of numerous other creditable fighter designs finding acceptance. Nieuport produced some refined variants on the Nieuport 17—the 17*bis*, 23, 24, 25 and 27—but they served primarily as supplements until enough Spad 7s or 13s were available to replace them. By late 1917 the sesquiplane, with its structural limitations, clearly had no future and Nieuport's engineers devoted themselves to a biplane, the 28.

Another promising Spad competitor had its origins in 1916 when Emile Eugène Dupont left Ponnier to become chief designer for René Hanriot's firm, which at that time was licence-producing Sopwith 1½-Strutters for the *Aviation Française*. In the summer of 1916 Dupont created a compact single-seat fighter powered by a 110 hp Le Rhône 9J engine, the HD.1. Structurally conventional, of the usual wood and canvas aside from aluminium cowl panels, the HD.1 was notable primarily for its W-shaped cabane strut arrangement, similar to that of the Sopwith 1½-Strutter, and for the greater size and dihedral of its upper wing in relation to the lower wing. In spite of its angular fuselage and wings, the HD.1 was unusually well proportioned and stands alongside the Sopwith Pup as one of the most aesthetically pleasing aircraft designs of the war.

First subjected to proof-loading tests in January 1917, the Hanriot HD.1 was test-flown soon afterwards, but its performance, while creditable, was not judged sufficiently improved over the Nieuport 17's or the Spad 7's to justify its acceptance for French service. Unlike many of its contemporaries, however, the HD.1 got a second chance when it attracted the attention of the Italian Military Mission in Paris. Italy had been at war with Austria-Hungary since May 1915, and, although Italian designers produced some good bombers and reconnaissance planes, they had yet to produce a successful indigenous fighter. Hanriot were therefore contracted to send some of their HD.1s to Italy, while the Societá Nieuport Macchi at Varese obtained a licence to build 1,700 HD.1s of its own, allegedly gearing up for production as early as November 1916. Macchi built 125 HD.1s in 1917 and 706 in 1918. The first HD.1s began arriving at the *76a*

Squadriglia at Borgnano in the summer of 1917, flying alongside and eventually replacing entirely the unit's mixed complement of Nieuports and Spads.

Among the earliest HD.1 recipients was *Tenente* Flavio Torello Baracchini, who had just transferred to the *76a* from the *81a Squadriglia*, in which unit he had already scored eight victories in Nieuports. Assigned a Hanriot-built HD.1, Baracchini decorated it with his personal motif of four aces—spades, hearts, clubs and diamonds. He wasted little time in putting the new machine through its paces, shooting down an Austro-Hungarian plane over Lom on 17 July 1917, just three days after his arrival at the squadron. He downed another enemy plane over Tolmino on 29 July, and teamed up with *Capitano* Francesco Baracca of the *91a Squadriglia* to down a Brandenburg C.I of *Fliegerkompanie 10* behind enemy lines near Val di Sava on 3 August. Baracchini's next claim was over a balloon on 7 August, but for some reason it was not confirmed. He was credited with an Oeffag-Albatros scout the next day, but during the combat he was wounded in the left jaw and he had to be hospitalized at Udine. Baracchini would return to the Front in March 1918 and served with his old outfit, the *81a Squadriglia*, until he was wounded again on 25 June. He would not fight again, but by then his score—officially downgraded from 30 to 21 after the war—was enough to make him Italy's third-ranking ace.

By mid-1918 the Hanriot HD.1 was the principal Italian fighter, with Spads and Nieuports playing a supplementary role in the squadrons. Among its many successful exponents was Italy's second-ranking ace, Silvio Scaroni, who scored at least nineteen of his 26 victories in HD.1s.

In June 1917 the exiled *Aviation Militaire Belge* also ordered 125 HD.1s from the Hanriot company, the first of which arrived on 22 August and was assigned to the *1e Escadrille* at Le Moëres. That unit's pilots had been so content with their Nieuport 17s that they had already declined an offer to replace them with Spad 7s. They likewise rejected the first HD.1 out of hand, starting with the squadron's leading ace, André de Meulemeester, and followed by Jan Olieslagers and so on down the line to the most junior member, Willy Coppens. Coppens was still flying the squadron's last Nieuport 16, the poorly balanced and treacherous flight characteristics of which he hated with a passion, so he was more than game to give the HD.1 a try. His serendipity upon discovering how well the Hanriot handled soon converted Coppens's squadron colleagues, and, once they had overcome some early problems with gun jams and inaccurate sights, the pilots of the *1e Escadrille* did quite well with the fighter that France rejected. Coppens eventually became the H.D.1's greatest exponent—and Belgium's leading ace—with a total of 37 aerial victories, 26 of which were balloons.

In addition to the improved performance it gave to the S.E.5a, the geared 200 hp Hispano-Suiza 8B engine led to the development of another famous

French fighter, the Spad 13.C1, and to one of the war's most heavily armed single-seat fighters, the Spad 12.Ca1. The conception of both fighters was also heavily influenced by the Spad 7.C1's most enthusiastic exponent and France's leading ace at the time, Georges Guynemer. In December 1916, Lieutenant Guynemer wrote a letter to Spad's chief designer, Louis Béchereau:

> The 150 hp Spad is not a match for the Halberstadt. Although the Halberstadt is probably no faster it climbs better, consequently it has the overall advantage. More speed is needed; possibly the airscrew could be improved.

Hispano-Suiza came up with one answer to that problem by increasing the compression ratio of its original engine to produce the 180 hp 8Ab. On 11 June 1916 the company successfully bench-tested a new, geared V-8 engine, the 8B, which could produce 208 hp at 2,000 rpm at ground level. Béchereau tested the new engine in the Spad 7 but soon concluded that a somewhat larger, more robust airframe would be necessary to accommodate it. In addition to its size, the Spad 13.C1, which was ordered into production in February 1917, had rounded wing tips, forward-staggered cabane struts with a frontal bracing wire and twin 0.30-calibre Vickers machine guns. *Sous-Lieutenant* René Dorme, one of the many aces in Guynemer's *Escadrille Spa.3*, flight-tested one of the new Spad 13s at Buc on 4 April 1917, and at least one was undergoing evaluation in a front-line *escadrille* on 26 April. In spite of the aeroplane's maximum speed of 124 mph and climb rate of 13,000 feet in eleven minutes, problems with the Hispano-Suiza 8B's spur reduction gear was to delay the Spad 13's introduction at the Front and would handicap it for months thereafter. In November 1917, for example, units were reporting that their Spad 13s were grounded two days out of three because of engine malfunctions.

Another suggestion that Guynemer had made to Béchereau at the end of 1916 had been for a fighter capable of mounting a cannon. Since the geared Hispano-Suiza engine raised the propeller above the cylinder heads, Birkigt was indeed able to arrange a 37mm Puteaux cannon with a shortened barrel to fire through a hollow propeller shaft. Taking matters from there, Béchereau designed an enlarged version of the Spad 7, which was designated the 12.Ca1 (for Type 12, cannon-armed single-seater).

In spite of its unusual armament, the Spad 12 did not look like a freak—in fact, with its lack of bulged fairings on the cockpit and slightly forward-staggered wings, it was one of the most elegant-looking Spads ever built. Inside the cockpit, however, the cannon breech protruded between the pilot's legs, necessitating Deperdussin-type elevator and aileron controls on either side of the pilot instead of a central control column. When *Capitaine* Guynemer flew the Spad 12 in the spring of 1917 he recorded a maximum speed of 137 mph at ground level and a maximum ceiling of 23,000 feet. The main shortcoming that Guynemer saw in what he called his '*avion magique*' was the fact that the 37mm cannon was a single-shot weapon that had to be reloaded by hand. However, the Spad 12 also had a single synchronized 0.30-calibre Vickers machine gun, which could be used to help sight the cannon on a target before it was fired or to help the pilot fight his way out of trouble after the cannon had been fired.

The first operational Spad 12, S382, was delivered to Guynemer at *Spa.3* in July 1917. During the new fighter's first front-line sortie on 5 July Guynemer attacked a DFW C.V two-seater, but the enemy gunner managed to inflict such damage that Guynemer was compelled to disengage and send away his Spad 12 for nearly three weeks of repairs. It returned to the squadron on 20 July, and on the 27th Guynemer used it to shoot down an Albatros fighter between Langemarck and Roulers with eight machine-gun rounds and one cannon shell, killing *Leutnant der Reserve* Fritz Vossen of *Jasta 33*. He downed a DFW C.V over Westroosebeke the next day using two shells and 30 bullets, but again his victim's return fire caused enough damage to send S382 back to the repair shop, this time until 15 August.

Guynemer scored a double victory on 17 August—one German two-seater with machine-gun fire alone and a second with the cannon—but an inconclusive fight with an aggressive two-seater crew the next day put the cannon Spad temporarily out of action once more. In spite of the cannon fighter's mixed fortunes, Guynemer's performance resulted in Spad getting a contract for 300 aircraft. It is doubtful that anywhere near that number were built, however, for the few cannon-armed Spad 12s that saw service in 1917 and 1918 proved to be a handful for any but the most skilled pilots, such as Guynemer and the consummate hunter who would eventually surpass him as France's ace of aces, René Fonck.

While Guynemer waited for his cannon fighter to be repaired, he received the first Spad 13, S504, armed with twin Vickers machine guns with 380 rounds each. He wasted no time in blooding that new machine on 20 August, when he used it to shoot down a DFW C.V over Poperinghe. That first Spad 13 victory was also Guynemer's 54th—and last.

On 24 August, Guynemer visited the Spad factory at Buc to inspect the repairs to his Spad 12 and recommend new improvements. Typically for Guynemer, who seldom rested, he was in a dangerously nervous state and on the 28th he commented to a friend, 'I shall not survive.' After returning to *Spa.3* he took off with *Sous-Lieutenant* Benjamin Bozon-Verduraz on 8 September, but bad weather forced them to abort their patrol. With the weather still unsuitable for flying on the 9th, Guynemer attended Sunday mass at St Pol-sur-Mer. He took off in S504 on 10 September, but had to land at a Belgian airfield when the plane's water pump control became stuck. After returning to *Spa.3*, Guynemer borrowed *Lieutenant* Albert Deullin's Spad for another patrol and attacked a large number of German aircraft, but took four bullets in his plane and was forced to land with a disabled air pump. Returning by automobile, he took off in another borrowed Spad, but this time the fuel overflowed due to a loosened carburettor cover and Guynemer was again compelled to land when the engine caught fire.

Visibly annoyed by the day's bad luck, Guynemer ordered his mechanics to have S504 working and ready to fly at 8.00 the next morning, but fog delayed take-off until 8.25 a.m. on 11 September. He was to have been accompanied by Bozon-Verduraz and *Sergent* Louis Risacher, but the latter's engine was having trouble starting and Guynemer impatiently took off with Bozon-Verduraz only.

The haze disappeared at 5,000 feet altitude, and at 12,000 feet the Frenchmen spotted a DFW C.V north-east of Ypres. After making a desultory wave to Bozon-Verduraz, Guynemer dived on the German from above and behind. Bozon-Verduraz followed him, fired, missed and then pulled up when he noticed eight German aircraft approaching. The enemy formation turned away, behaving as if its pilots had not noticed either Spad, so Bozon-Verduraz went back to find Guynemer, only to see no trace of him or the DFW. Following another indecisive combat over Poperinghe, Bozon-Verduraz returned to St Pol-sur-Mer at 10.20, his first words being 'Has he landed yet?'

Guynemer never returned, and it would be another month before anything was learned of his fate. The Germans announced that *Leutnant* Kurt Wissemann of *Jasta 3* had killed the great ace for his fifth victory, but by then Wissemann himself was not available for comment, having been killed on 28 September by two S.E.5as of No 56 Squadron flown by two of Albert Ball's disciples—Captain Geoffrey Hilton Bowman and Lieutenant Reginald T. C. Hoidge. A sergeant of the German 413th Regiment certified that he had witnessed the Spad's crash and identified Guynemer's body, noting that the ace had died of a head wound, although one of his fingers had also been shot off and a leg was broken. An Allied artillery barrage drove the Germans back before they could recover or properly bury the body, which thus vanished amid the chaos that was the Western Front.

Whatever the tragic circumstances of his death, Georges Guynemer went into French legend as the country's second ranking ace who, popular myth insisted, had flown so high he could never come down. The Spad 13 went on to greater things, although attempts to improve its lateral flying characteristics by squaring off the wing tips with added pocket extensions proved to be another of Spad's more frightful ideas. The final production version, built with squared wing tips from the outset, became one of the most famous, if not one of the best, fighters of World War I.

As Allied fighters improved and proliferated, their adversaries began to feel their control of the air, even on their side of the lines, slip away. In June 1917 the Germans introduced a more refined version of the Albatros D.III, the D.V, but its sesquiplane wing layout proved to be even more vulnerable to stress and failure than that of its predecessor. A strengthened version, the D.Va, was heavier, but that handicap on its performance was offset somewhat by the development of a higher-compression Mercedes engine, the D.IIIa. In spite of Albatros's continued commitment to quantity production, however, the *Luftstreitskräfte* needed a new design, or its fighter units would lose their tenuous hold on the sky.

One potential solution appeared in the late spring of 1917 when the prototype Pfalz D.III made its first flight. Designed by the engineering team for the Bavarian Pfalz Flugzeugwerke GmbH headed by Rudolph Gehringer, the D.III had been built in response to the same general appeal from the *Inspektion der Fliegertruppen (Idflieg)* for a fighter to match the Nieuport 11 and 17 that had led to the development of the Albatros D.III and D.V. Unlike the Albatros scouts and the many Nieuport copies produced by other German firms, the Pfalz was not really a sesquiplane but a biplane with a smaller lower wing, braced with U-shaped cabane and interplane struts. The fuselage, constructed in two halves from three-ply veneer strips, incorporated a compound wing root, along with integral fin and tailplane surfaces, based on Pfalz's previous experience building the unsuccessful Roland D.II under licence.

Accepted and put into production in mid-1917, the shark-like Pfalz D.III was one of the most rakishly handsome aircraft of its time. When the first three arrived at the Front at the end of August, however, the reaction was less than enthusiastic. *Leutnant* Werner Voss, commander of *Jasta 10*, received one of the first machines and flew it on at least a few operational missions, but he is said to have preferred the superior rate of climb and manoeuvrability of his Albatros D.V to the newer plane's stronger wing structure and better diving characteristics. Similar complaints of relatively sluggish handling characteristics and performance indicative of an unfavourable power-to-weight ratio undermined the Pfalz's popularity as it arrived in quantity at *Jastas 4* and *10*, as well as Bavarian *Jastas 16, 32, 34* and *35*, during the autumn of 1917. Another unappreciated feature was the enclosing of the D.III's twin machine guns within its fuselage—a drag-reducing measure that nevertheless made it impossible for the pilot to reach them if they jammed in combat.

At about the same time he received the disappointing Pfalz, Voss got something more to his dogfighting taste in the form of the nimble Fokker F.I triplane.

Another early Pfalz recipient, *Leutnant* Oskar *Freiherr* von Boenigk, a member of *Jasta 4* who was flying D.III 1396/17 in September, may have been among the first to demonstrate that, in the right hands, the Bavarian shark had teeth. On 3 September he downed a Camel over Houthem and also claimed a Pup that could not be confirmed. He was credited with another Sopwith over Poelcapelle on 9 September, bringing his personal score to five before being posted to take command of *Jasta 21* on 21 October. Other German aces would have their share of success in the Pfalz, which later that year would get an altered lower wing with rounder tips, enlarged horizontal tail surfaces, guns raised above the fuselage where the pilot could clear jams and the high-compression Mercedes D.IIIa engine, resulting in the Pfalz D.IIIa. Produced in greater numbers than the D.III, the improved D.IIIa became one of the principal German fighters in the spring of 1918, but its performance was at best barely the equal of its Allied opposition and its pilots desperately yearned for something significantly better.

Germans were not the only airmen in the Central Powers who longed for a fighter to match those of the Allies in 1917. Like Italy, Austria-Hungary was unsuccessful in developing an effective indigenous scout design in the early war years, its pilots using German designs such as the Fokker E.III and Brandenburg D.I, the latter of which had been created by a design bureau headed by Ernst Heinkel. A biplane braced by a unique junction of eight interplane struts into a star-like arrangement and featuring a deep fuselage whose rear upper decking tapered aft into a vertical stabilizer, the Brandenburg D.I or KD (*Kampf-Doppeldecker*) entered production for the *Kaiserliche und Königliche Luftfahrtruppen* (LFT) in May 1916. *Oberst* Emil Uzelac, commander of the LFT, personally test-flew the new fighter on 7 November 1916—and promptly crashed, suffering concussion. Nevertheless, the Brandenburg D.I (series 65), fitted with a Type II VK canister holding an MG 08/15 machine gun and ammunition above the upper wing, was committed to the Front and on 3 December *Oberleutnant* Godwin Brumowski of *Flik (Fliegerkompanie) 12*, flying D.I 65.53, teamed up with *Linienschiffsleutnant* Gottfried *Freiherr* von Banfield of the Trieste Naval Air Station and *Zugsführer* Karl Cislaghi of *Flik 28* to bring down a Caproni Ca.1 bomber over Mavinje.

Only two other victories would be scored by Brandenburg-built D.Is. One of its pilots, *Zugsführer* Julius Arigi of *Fluggeschwader 1*, added a vertical stabilizer and an enlarged rudder which improved the KD's flight characteristics somewhat, and which were incorporated in the 72 D.Is (Series 28) built by the Phönix firm. Phönix-built D.Is took a reasonable toll on Italian aircraft, virtually in spite of themselves, thanks to the skill of their pilots. Still, by June 1917 *Flik 41J*, a crack fighter squadron organized along the lines of Richthofen's *Jasta 11* by its commander, *Hauptmann* Brumowski, was reporting that 'the KD is absolutely useless . . . the best pilots (and only they can fly the type) are shackled, ruin their nerves and perish in crashes over the airfield, without their expert skill achieving anything'.

At about that time Austrian versions of the Albatros D.II and D.III, licence-built by the Oesterreichisches Flugzeugwerke A.G. (Oeffag) and powered by 185 hp Austro-Daimler engines, were entering service. Later versions of the D.III, constructed with greater care and better a grade of wood than the German Albatros scouts, and powered by 200 hp and finally 225 hp Austro-Daimler engines, would be the most successful fighters to serve in the LFT—and the best of the Albatros sesquiplane series. Nevertheless, neither the Phönix-built Brandenburg D.I nor the Oeffag-Albatros D.III were indigenous fighters, but refinements of foreign designs.

The first true Austrian-designed fighter was almost rejected out of hand before it reached the drawing board. On 8 June 1916 Julius von Berg of the Oesterreichisch-Ungarische Flugzeugfabrik 'Aviatik' GmbH proposed a fighter to use a 160 hp Daimler engine and a similar single-seat reconnaissance design to be powered by a 120 hp Daimler. Both were rejected by the LFT's *Fliegerarsenal* (*Flars*) because it wanted Aviatik to concentrate on manufacturing Knoller C.II two-seaters rather than pursue their own projects. When *Oberst* Uzelac heard of Berg's intentions in August, however, he intervened and Berg was allowed to proceed.

Just two months later, on 16 October, Aviatik fighter prototype serial 30.14 was ready for its test flight at Aspern. Combining a flat-sided wooden fuselage with Knoller-style wings featuring a reflex curvature, the 30.14 underwent a somewhat wobbly first flight, and when its test pilot, *Feldwebel* Ferdinand Könschel, throttled down for a landing it suddenly plunged into the ground, killing him. In spite of that discouraging start, Aviatik engineer Julius Kolin was convinced that the centre of pressure shift had been responsible for the crash and set about redesigning the wing. Several follow-up prototypes were built and tested, until success was finally achieved with 30.19, which first flew on 24 January 1917. Test-flying the machine on 31 March, *Flars* pilot *Oberleutnant* Oskar Fekete praised its 'fabulous climb and enormous manoeuvrability'. The new fighter was subsequently ordered into production as the Aviatik D.I.

On 15 May 1917 aircraft 30.19, retrofitted with an improved one-piece upper wing, was sent along with the first production Aviatik D.I, 38.01, to *Fluggeschwader 1* on the Izonso Front for combat evaluation. *Hauptmann* Karl Sabeditch took 30.19 up for its first front-line mission on 18 May, with an unsynchronized machine gun mounted on the upper wing. On the 23rd he managed to shoot down a Caproni Ca.1. In July Aviatik 30.19 was so badly damaged that it had to be written off, but it had demonstrated the D.I's worth.

The Aviatik D.I, also called the Berg D.I, was produced by a number of sub-contractors and appeared in equally numerous forms, using a succession of increasingly powerful engines, a variety of radiator configurations and different forms of armament ranging from single guns firing over the upper wing to synchronized twin weapons buried in the cowling and finally the twin guns in front of the cockpit that pilots favoured. Although extraordinarily nimble for an aeroplane powered by an inline engine, the Aviatik D.I occasionally suffered wing failures as a result of shoddy construction, depending on the manufacturer, and, in spite of the ubiquity it achieved by the end of 1917, Austria's first fighter never achieved a significant level of ascendancy over any of its Allied counterparts.

Having already improved the Brandenburg D.I, Phönix set about creating a replacement for it and unveiled two prototypes in June 1917. One, bearing the serial 20.14, introduced a wire-less variation on the Nieuport sesquiplane wing cellule, designed by Leo Kirste, which combined a 'V' interplane strut with a third strut that braced the lower wing to the middle of a somewhat elongated Brandenburg D.I fuselage. The 20.15, designed by Edmund Sparmann, utilized a more conventional, wire-braced wing cellule based on his observations of German aircraft—and the pros and cons of the Nieuport-style sesquiplane layout as employed on the Albatros D.III and D.V. Test flights showed the 20.15's wing to be more robust than that of the 20.14, in addition to which it provided a better climb rate and flight characteristics that were vastly superior to those of the Brandenburg D.I. The 20.15's speed was not significantly higher than that of the Brandenburg, but that could be remedied by installing a more powerful engine than the 185 hp Daimler—which it got in the form of a 200 hp Hiero. Production of the Phönix D.I began in August 1917, its armament consisting of two synchronized machine guns mounted on either side of the engine.

Austria-Hungary had a more poorly developed industrial capacity than Italy, and the arrival of Phönix fighters to the Front was considerably delayed. In November 1917 *Oberst* Uzelac learned that 50 D.Is were in storage, still awaiting the installation of machine guns and the new Zaparka synchronization system. Again taking matters into his own hands, he arranged to have the aircraft delivered to front-line units, where their armourers would install the armament as it arrived. By December Phönix D.Is were entering the inventories of *Fliegerkompanien 4D, 15D, 17D, 48D, 54D* and *66D*, where they were to serve as escorts to those units' reconnaissance aircraft, and at fighter *Fliks 14J, 30J, 60J, 61J* and *63J*.

Activated in November 1917 and dispatched to Italy the following month, *Flik 60J* was based at Grigno in the mountainous Val Sugana, about 60 miles north-north-west of Venice—a most unforgiving environment for taking off and landing. Fully equipped with Phönix D.Is of series 128, 228 and 328, the unit's initial flying personnel consisted of the commander, *Oberleutnant* Frank Linke-Crawford, and six enlisted pilots. Linke had already been credited with thirteen victories while flying Brandenburg D.Is and Oeffag-Albatros D.IIIs in *Flik 41J* under the tutelage of the formidable Brumowski, and it may have been he who blooded the Phönix in fine style. On 10 January 1918 he took off in D.I 228.16, accompanied by *Stabsfeldwebel* Kurt Gruber, another veteran with five victories to his credit, in D.I 228.24. Over Val Stagna they encountered what Linke described as a 'Sopwith two-seater' accompanied by escort fighters and attacked. In short order they sent the two-seater—which was most probably a SAML of the *115a Squadriglia*, crewed by *Sergente* U. Lenzi and *Sottotenente* S. Achenza—down just within the Italian side of the lines, followed shortly afterwards by one of its Nieuport escorts. It is possible that the Nieuport was from the *79a Squadriglia*, another of whose members, *Sergente* Antonio Reali, claimed an unidentified enemy fighter over Primolano, although it was not confirmed; Reali would eventually be credited with eleven out of the 29 victories he claimed in the course of the war. Since Austria-Hungary credited shared victories in the French manner, two were added to both Linke-Crawford's and Gruber's personal accounts. Both men would add an individually scored victory to their tallies before the month was over.

Opinions varied regarding the Phönix D.I's merits. During a flight comparison in September 1917 it was judged to be superior in speed and climb rate to the Oeffag-Albatros D.III and to have better flight characteristics than the Aviatik D.I. A German report in October stated that the Phönix 'possesses totally amazing qualities, especially the quickness of manoeuvre and stability when throttled down. The pilot can stall the aircraft virtually on the spot and drop several hundred metres without losing control.' In February 1918, however, *Flik 60J* reported that the 'D.I is not favoured by pilots because the speed and climb are inferior to the Nieuport, Spad and Sopwith fighters'. *Flik 30J* complained that it was too slow and 'almost too stable for quick combat manoeuvres'. Whatever its faults, the Phönix D.I, like the S.E.5a, the Spad 13 and the Pfalz D.IIIa, acquired a reputation for sturdiness and for the ability to escape trouble in a high-speed dive without fear of its wings coming off, as was the case with the Nieuport 17, Albatros D.V and Aviatik D.I. The Phönix D.I and its successors, the D.II, D.IIa and D.III, also did much to provide Austria-Hungary's small but spirited LFT with a competitive fighter of its own design.

Chapter 4

THE TRIPLANE CRAZE

Sopwith Triplane and Fokker Dr.1

World War I aviation was dominated by the biplane. Monoplanes were potentially faster, but they could not be practical until engineers could design a reliable means of bracing their wings. With a biplane, on the other hand, the two wings provided a matrix for the wooden spars and struts and the bracing wires that held the whole arrangement together.

The potential of the internal cantilever wing structure was first proved when Professor Hugo Junkers's all-metal J.1 monoplane first took to the air in December 1915, but that and other cantilever airframes would not work on fighter planes until they could be made light enough to be propelled by engines producing only 80 to 160 hp. Eventually a fighter with wings of wooden cantilever structure did take to the air, and it proved itself a match for any biplane in the sky. Ironically, however, the Fokker Dr.I was not a monoplane, but a step in the opposite direction—a triplane!

The process that led to what amounted to a brief 'triplane craze,' from which the Fokker triplane emerged, began with a series of aircraft from the British firm of Thomas O. M. Sopwith and his chief designer Herbert Smith. The first was a handsome single-bay, two-seat biplane with a 110 hp Clerget 9Z rotary engine, which was passed by the Sopwith experimental department on 12 December 1915—the same day that the Junkers J.1 first flew. This was somewhat ironic, since the Sopwith was of conventional wood and wire construction but its layout was advanced for its time, with a synchronized Vickers machine gun for the pilot and a flexibly mounted Lewis machine gun for the rear gunner. It also had an adjustable tailplane, the incidence of which could be modified by means of a handwheel in the pilot's cockpit. The 1½-Strutter, as it was dubbed because of its W-shaped cabane struts, was the first true two-seat fighter when it entered production in February 1916.

Although the 1½-Strutter had originally been ordered by the Admiralty, the need for air superiority for the coming British Somme offensive resulted in 27 production aircraft being transferred from the Royal Naval Air Service to the Royal Flying Corps in the summer of 1916. Formed to use the new type on

13 April, No 70 Squadron flew its first combat mission on the opening day of the Somme offensive when four 1½-Strutters took off at 6 a.m. on 1 July 1916. They met no aerial opposition and returned with useful information on German troop movements and rail activity around Cambrai. On the following day the same four Sopwiths, accompanied by Martinsyde G.100 Elephants of No 27 Squadron, were reconnoitring Cambrai and Douai when they were attacked by six German aircraft. One Sopwith that was lagging behind the group, piloted by Second Lieutenant J. Manly, was picked out for special enemy attention, but he and his observer, Second Lieutenant R. C. Oakes, managed to fend off their attackers and all the aircraft returned safely to Fienvillers aerodrome.

The first casualty occurred five days later when Captain G. L. Cruikshank, with his 19-year-old cousin, Second Lieutenant A. J. T. Cruikshank, acting as his observer, led three Sopwiths an another reconnaissance to Cambrai and became separated from the two accompanying aircraft. Cruikshank's plane was attacked by three Fokker *Eindecker*s and had to fight a 22-minute running battle, during which he made it to Allied lines but with his plane damaged and his observer seriously wounded. Captain Cruikshank landed at St Omer in the hope of finding better medical facilities for his cousin, but Second Lieutenant Cruikshank died of his wounds later the same day.

Two more Sopwiths were lost to anti-aircraft fire on 7 July and another was lost with its crew on 19 July. Five of the 1½-Strutters attacked a Roland C.II on 20 July, but the only result was that Manly was wounded in the face and shoulder and had to be hospitalized. The squadron finally scored its first victory as four Sopwiths were escorting No 27 Squadron's Martinsides on a bombing mission to Hervilly on 29 July, when its aircraft were credited with driving an enemy plane down out of control.

Good though it was, the Sopwith 1½-Strutter did not remain an effective fighter for long. By the time a second unit, No 45 Squadron, arrived in France on 15 October German biplane scouts such as the Halberstadt D.II and Albatros D.II were outperforming it in both speed and manoeuvrability. From then on its versatile airframe was employed in other tasks—as a reconnaissance plane and as a bomber.

Sopwith's next fighter design originated with a small, lightweight, single-seat, single-bay biplane, powered by a 50 hp Gnome rotary engine, which had been designed in the autumn of 1915 by test pilot Harry Hawker and was generally referred to as 'Hawker's Runabout'. The frail machine produced such remarkable performance, including a maximum speed of 84.6 mph, that the Sopwith staff began working on a smaller, more compact and robust version, to be powered by an 80 hp Le Rhône rotary engine for military purposes. The prototype that emerged from their efforts was cleared on 9 February 1916, and subsequent testing by the Admiralty resulted in a glowing report. The plane had a maximum speed of 110 mph at 6,500 feet and climbed to 10,000 feet in 12 minutes 29 seconds, but what really distinguished it was its ease of handling combined with outstanding manoeuvrability, as well as the excellent visibility from the cockpit—all wrapped up in one of the most nicely balanced and aesthetically pleasing aircraft of the war. The RNAS put in its first order for the little fighter in April 1916, and when Major-General Hugh Trenchard read a copy of the Admiralty's report on it he promptly pencilled in a concise comment of his own: 'Let us get a squadron of these.'

Armed with a single Vickers machine gun using the Sopwith-Kauper synchronizing mechanism, the plane was officially designated the Sopwith Scout but was more popularly known by another name. Allegedly, it was then-Colonel Sefton Brancker of the RFC who, upon seeing the new fighter alongside its larger two-seater forebear, exclaimed, 'Good God! Your 1½-Strutter had had a pup.' Whatever its origin, the sobriquet 'Pup' rapidly proliferated in spite of all official efforts to discourage its use.

The first Pups arrived at No 1 Wing RNAS, based at Dunkerque, in July 1916. The single-seater's first success may have occurred at 3.30 p.m. on 24 September when Flight Sub-Lieutenant Stanley James Goble sent an LVG two-seater down out of control near Ghistelles. This was the third victory for the Australian-born Goble, who had claimed two earlier ones while flying Nieuports and would survive the war with a total of ten. By the end of 1916 Pups were also being operated with considerable success by No 8 Squadron RNAS. Also used by RFC squadrons in 1917, the Pup earned the affection of all who flew it, its performance in dogfights being particularly distinguished by its ability to maintain altitude in a turn. Its only serious weaknesses were its single gun and the slow rate of fire of its synchronizing mechanism.

By the spring of 1917 German fighters, using more powerful engines and armed with twin machine guns, were rendering the Pup obsolete. By then, however, another fighter had emerged from the Sopwith stable, which was similar to, and at the same time strikingly different from, the Pup. Back in the spring of 1916 Herbert Smith had set to work designing a successor to the Pup that could climb faster, fly higher, manoeuvre as well if not better and, if possible, afford better visibility for the pilot. The result of his efforts, which emerged from the Sopwith hangar on 30 May 1916, was not a biplane but a triplane. Even more surprising than the fighter's configuration was the fact that the added wing did not adversely affect its performance.

Since the overall wing area was being distributed among three wings instead of two, Smith felt that he could make all of them of relatively narrow chord, which provided a correspondingly small change in the centre of pressure at various angles of attack. The fuselage and tail, which balanced the plane, could be also shorter than they needed to be on an aeroplane with a wider-chord wing. The narrow wings, moreover, interfered less with the pilot's view, and the middle set was mounted in line with the pilot's eyes. In addition to that, the wings' narrow chord gave them a high aspect ratio, with an efficient ratio of lift to drag. They were constructed with a shorter span and with ailerons on all three wings, both of which factors endowed the plane with an increased roll rate. The triplane's manoeuvrability was further enhanced by Smith's use of a 130 hp Clerget rotary engine and his placement of the heaviest weights—engine, pilot, fuel and armament—near the centre of gravity.

Although the Sopwith Triplane prototype was built in only three months, test pilot Harry Hawker was so pleased with it that he looped it just three minutes after take-off. Two weeks later the prototype, N500, was dispatched to 'A' Squadron of No 1 Naval Wing at Furnes, near Dunkerque, for front-line evaluation and flew its first combat mission just fifteen minutes after its arrival.

After some flights over the lines, the prototype Triplane got into its first serious fight on 1 July. Its pilot at the time, Lieutenant Roderic Stanley Dallas, a 24-year-old Australian from Mount Stanley, Queenland, attacked a German two-seater six kilometres off La Panne and sent it down out of control for his fourth victory. On 30 September Dallas took up N500 again and was credited with a German fighter out of control south-west of St Marie Capelle. Dallas would later score thirteen more victories in Triplanes with No 1 Squadron RNAS, as 'A' Squadron was redesignated after being fully equipped with the new fighter in December 1916.

In the early months of 1917 Sopwith Triplanes dazzled their opponents with their performance, and even during the general slaughter of British aircraft known as 'Bloody April' they took a disturbing toll of the German *Jagdstaffeln*. As had been the case with the Nieuport sesquiplane fighters in 1916, the *Inspektion der Fliegertruppen* reacted by requiring German aircraft manufacturers to produce a triplane fighter to counter the Sopwith. The response was perhaps greater than the triplane, with intrinsic limits on its development potential, warranted, but by the end of 1917 virtually all German firms had come up with at least one triplane design. Only two, the Fokker Dr.I and the Pfalz Dr.I, would enter production, and only ten of the latter were ever built.

Ironically, the most famous triplane in history was created by the man who was the least enthusiastic about building one. In 1917 Anthony Fokker had been applying the concepts of Hugo Junkers and Claude Dornier on metal internal cantilever wing structures to a wooden box structure. He envisaged a monoplane or a sesquiplane fighter as the ultimate airframe on which to realize the potential of that structure, but in April 1917 he was ordered by *Idflieg*—rather to his chagrin—to design a triplane fighter like the Sopwith.

As with the Sopwith Triplane, the fuselage of which was little changed from that of the Pup, Anthony Fokker's triplane was based on an experimental (*Versuchs*) biplane that he had been building for Austria-Hungary, the V4. A simple steel tube structure covered in fabric, the V4's fuselage offered better stability than the more streamlined fuselages of Fokker's experimental V1, V2 and V3. To that Fokker added three wings of torsion box structure, but in the interests of hastening production and saving weight he covered them with fabric rather than plywood. Further lift was provided by the undercarriage axle, which was also of aerofoil section. Powered by a 110 hp Le Rhône rotary engine, the altered Fokker V4 displayed such outstanding performance—especially with regard to climb and manoeuvrability—that Fokker was authorized to proceed with two pre-production aircraft for front-line evaluation, work on which began on 11 July. Among the principal modifications on the F.Is (as the pre-production V4s were designated) were increased wing area, more effective, balanced ailerons and the addition of interplane struts. The F.Is were delivered to *Jagdgeschwader I* on 28 August 1917 and allocated to Germany's two most illustrious aces at the time—*JG I*'s *Geschwaderführer*, *Rittmeister* Manfred *Freiherr* von Richthofen, and *Leutnant* Werner Voss, commander of *Jasta 10*.

Richthofen was not in the best of health or spirits at that time. He had been wounded in the head on 7 July and he was still feeling the effects. He was also depressed because the Albatros D.V, with its unreliable wing structure, remained the only type available to his Wing, while Allied fighters were improving in quality and increasing in quantity. Flying D.V 2059/17 on 26 August, he had managed to shoot down a Spad 7 of No 19 Squadron for his 59th victory, but in a letter to home two days later he admitted:

> I have made only two combat flights [since returning to the Front] and both were successful, but after each flight I was completely exhausted. During the first one I almost got sick in the stomach. My wound is healing frightfully slowly; it is still as big as a five-Mark piece. Yesterday they removed another splinter of bone; I believe it will be the last.

The arrival of Fokker F.I 102/17 did much to raise the baron's spirits. He and his 'gentlemen' of *Jasta 11* had already been flying Fokker D.Vs to accustom themselves to the idiosyncrasies of the rotary-engine fighters before they arrived in quantity. Voss wasted no time in taking up his Fokker, F.I 103/17, and flying it around the vicinity of Marcke to demonstrate its capabilities to all four *Staffeln* of *JG I*.

British bombers raided German aerodromes west of Courtrai on the night of 31 August, but on the following day Richthofen led his pilots into battle in F.I 102/17. He described what followed:

> Flying the triplane for the first time [in combat], I and four gentlemen of *Staffel 11* attacked a very courageously flown British artillery-spotting aircraft. I approached [until] it was a mere 50 metres below me and fired twenty shots, whereupon the adversary went down out of control and crashed on this side [of the lines] near Zonnebeke.
>
> Apparently the adversary had taken me for a British triplane, as the observer stood up in his machine without making a move to attack me with his machine gun.

Richthofen's 60th victory had been over R.E.8 B782 of No 6 Squadron RFC. Its pilot and observer, Second Lieutenants J. B. C. Madge and Walter Kember, were both killed.

Voss and Richthofen both took up their triplanes on the morning of 3 September, when a *JG I* patrol pounced on a flight of Sopwith Pups from No 46 Squadron RFC. One of its members, Lieutenant Arthur Stanley Gould Lee, described the action in a letter home:

> The news is not good. The squadron has taken a hammering . . . The first patrol ran quickly into trouble, five of 'A' Flight . . . met Richthofen's Circus and had a hectic scrap. The Pups were completely outclassed by the D.Vs and most of their share of the fighting consisted of trying to avoid being riddled. Mac [K. W. McDonald] and Bird were seen going down over Hunland. [Richard] Asher might have reached the lines. Two chaps who got away, badly shot about, said that one of the Huns was flying a triplane, coloured red. It must be a captured naval Tripe, I suppose.

McDonald was brought down by *Leutnant* Eberhardt Mohnicke for his sixth victory, while Richthofen got into a long-unning battle with Pup B1795(Z), finally bringing it down south of Bousbacque. Richthofen reported:

> I was absolutely convinced that in front of me I had a very skilful pilot, who even at 50 metres did not give up [but] continued to fire and, even when flattening out [before landing] fired at an infantry column, then deliberately steered his machine into a tree. The Fokker F.I 102/17 is absolutely superior to the British Sopwith.

The uninjured pilot, Second Lieutenant Algernon F. Bird, was taken prisoner. Richthofen, elated at the rare prospect of meeting a live victim, hastened to the scene, as did Anthony Fokker, eager to record the event on his cine camera. The old Baron was evidently back, smiling confidently. Bird, too, had reason to present the camera with a nervous but self-satisfied smile. Although a vanquished prisoner of war, he had done his duty to the last, including the destruction of his machine so that the enemy would not get it intact—and, on top of it all, he could legitimately tell his grandchildren that he had survived a run-in-with the 'bloody Red Baron'.

Voss also had a successful morning, bringing down a Sopwith Camel of No 45 Squadron, flown by Lieutenant A. T. Heywood, north of Houtem at 9.25 a.m., for his 39th victory. In the afternoon of 5 September Voss, with *Leutnant* Erich Löwenhardt as his wingman, attacked a patrol of Pups from No 46 Squadron and, though unable to shoot any down, he outmanoeuvred them and put bullets into practically every one before breaking away. Later, at 3.50 p.m., he shot down another of No 46 Squadron's Pups over St Julien, although its pilot, Second Lieutenant Charles W. Odell, survived. Fifty minutes after that Voss downed a Caudron over Bixshoote as well.

On 6 September Voss shot down an F.E.2d, flown by Lieutenant J. O. Pilkinton and Air Mechanic Second Class H. F. Matthews of No 20 Squadron, over St Julien. On that same day Richthofen went on a four-week leave, designating *Oberleutnant* Kurt von Döring commander of *JG I* in his absence. Voss, now the second-ranking German ace after Richthofen, was in an ideal position to catch up with his friendly rival, and he made the most of it on 10 September by downing two Camels, flown by Second Lieutenants A. J. S. Sisley and O. C. Pearson of No 70 Squadron, followed by a third British plane for which he was credited but for which no corresponding loss has been determined. At 10.30 a.m. on 11 September Voss and *Oberleutnant* Ernst Weigand—who generally dealt with adminstrative matters for *Jasta 10* on Voss's behalf—each claimed a 'new type Spad' over Langemarck, and Voss downed a Camel over St Julien at 4.25 that afternoon, killing Lieutenant Oscar L. McMaking of No 45 Squadron.

While Richthofen was away on leave, Fokker F.I 102/17 went to one of his most trusted lieutenants, Kurt Wolff, who at the age of 22 was victor over 33 Allied aircraft and commander of Richthofen's old red-nosed squadron, *Jasta 11*. Wolff had been wounded in the left hand during a fight with the Sopwith Triplanes of No 10 Squadron RNAS on 11 July. He returned to *Jasta 11* exactly two months later, on 11 September. On the following day Wolff learned that *Kaiser* Wilhelm II had promoted him to *Oberleutnant*, but he wrote his fiancée:

> I am depressed only because I receive this honour without having shot down one [since 7 July]. For until now I have already had the bad luck of scuffling with about twenty Englishmen and have not brought down one of them . . .

On the afternoon of 15 September Wolff led a patrol in the new triplane when they encountered a flight of eight British biplane scouts. Unknown to Wolff, his opponents were once again from Naval 10, which, significantly, had replaced its Triplanes with new Sopwith Camels. At 3.15 p.m. Flight Lieutenant D. F. Fitzgibbon had taken the flight up, rendezvoused with five de Havilland D.H.4 bombers at 4.10 and escorted them over the lines to Bryke Wood. At 4.30 the British spotted four German fighters and went down to investigate, only to see them dive off. At that point the Camel pilots found themselves under attack by what they described as five Albatros D.Vs and four triplanes (despite the fact that Wolff's was the only German triplane in the area at that time).

A general mêlée ensued, during which Flight Lieutenant Norman M. McGregor closed to 25 yards of an enemy triplane and sent tracers into it before turning away to avoid colliding with his quarry. When last seen by the British, McGregor's victim was going down in a nose dive. His fifth credited victory was indeed Kurt Wolff, whose body was found in the wreck of F.I 102/17 near the village of Nachtigal, north of Wervicq. Following a funeral service befitting a knight of the *Ordre Pour le Mérite* at St Joseph's Church in Courtrai, Wolff's remains were sent to his parents' home in Memel (now Klaipada, Lithuania).

In the meantime Voss had done nothing to close the gap on Richthofen's score since 11 September. He was still keen to do so, but one of his *Jasta 10* pilots, *Leutnant* Aloys Heldmann, noticed that the past few weeks' activity was taking its toll: 'He was on edge; he had the nervous instability of a cat. I think it would be fair to say that he was flying on his nerves. And such a situation could have but one end . . .'

On Sunday 23 September Voss took off early and at 9.30 he destroyed a D.H.4, crewed by Second Lieutenants L. J. Bramley and J. M. de Lacey of No 57 Squadron, south of Roulers for his 48th victory. Upon returning, he joined his brothers Otto and Max for lunch, where they discussed plans for his upcoming leave. At 6.00 that afternoon Voss led the last patrol of the day, accompanied by *Leutnant* Gustav Bellen and *Vizefeldwebel* Rudenberg, while *Oberleutnant* Wiegand followed, leading *Leutnante* Julius Bender and Max Kühn in a second flight. There were cloud layers all over the Front as the *Jasta 10* formation headed towards Zillebeke, but there were plenty of British aircraft in the area, offering Voss the enticing prospect of ending the day with a nice round score of 50.

On the other side of the lines eleven S.E.5as, comprising 'B' and 'C' Flights of No 56 Squadron RFC, had left their aerodrome at Estrée Blanche at 5 p.m. Leading 'B' Flight towards Houthulst Forst, Captain James T. B. McCudden spotted a DFW C.V, led his flight to attack it and sent it diving vertically into the ground north-east of Houthem. The flight was about to attack six Albatros scouts when McCudden noticed an S.E.5a over Poelcapelle with an enemy triplane on its tail. 'The SE certainly looked unhappy,' McCudden remarked, 'so we changed our minds about attacking the "V" strutters and went to the rescue of the unfortunate SE.'

The 'unhappy' S.E. pilot was Captain Harold Alan Hamersley of No 60 Squadron, two flights of which were returning from a patrol at 6.25 p.m. when

Hamersley, flying behind Captain Robert L. Chidlaw-Roberts, noticed what he thought was a Nieuport being dived on by an Albatros. Hamersley reported afterwards:

> I swung across to attack the D.V and what I had thought was the Nieuport turned towards me and I realized that it was a 'Tripe' as we spoke of them. It was a little below me and I put my nose down and opened fire. The 'Tripe' passed under me and as I zoomed and turned the Hun was above me and heading straight at me, firing from about 30 degrees off the bow. There was a puff of smoke from my engine and holes appeared along the engine cowling in front of me and in the wings. Realizing I could do nothing further in the matter, I threw my machine into a spin. The Hun followed me down, dicing at me while I was spinning and I had to do an inverted dive to get away.

Chidlaw-Roberts tried to intervene but only fired a few rounds before the German triplane whipped around behind him and shot up his rudder bar. Thereupon Chidlaw-Roberts said, 'I retired from the fray and that is all I saw of it.'

At about that point McCudden's flight intervened, he diving on the triplane from the right and Second Lieutenant Arthur P. F. Rhys Davids from the left. Voss saw them and reacted with what McCudden described as

> . . . not a climbing or an Immelmann turn, but a sort of flat half-spin. By now the German triplane was in the middle of our formation and its handling was wonderful to behold. Its pilot seemed to be firing at all of us simultaneously, and although I got behind him a second time I could hardly stay there for a second.

Captain Keith L. Caldwell, No 60 Squadron's New Zealand-born commander, had led the rest of his patrol to Hamersley's aid, but at that point he noticed that

> . . . a Flight of 56 Squadron's SEs (and a very good one too) had taken Voss off its tail and were busy with him in their midst. It was then really 56's affair and six to one was pretty good odds we felt. We were more or less spectators and in my opinion there was little room to join in.'

Nearby, 'C' Flight of 'Fighting 56', led by Captain Geoffrey Hilton Bowman, had had several fights of its own when its pilots noticed that McCudden's 'B' Flight was having a surprisingly difficult time with two German fighters—a triplane and an Albatros D.V that had also entered the fray, and which co-operated rather well with Voss for a time. Firing at targets of opportunity, Voss got on Second Lieutenant Victor P. Cronyn's tail, and although the Canadian managed to dive away his wings were so badly damaged that he spent the night uncontrollably perspiring and unable to sleep. Lieutenant Keith K. Muspratt was also driven out of the fight and compelled to land at No 1 Squadron's aerodrome with a bullet in his radiator. That still left Voss having to deal with such paladins as McCudden, Rhys Davids, Bowman, Reginald T. C. Hoidge and Richard A. Maybery. At one point McCudden saw the triplane 'in the apex of a cone of tracer bullets from at least five machines simultaneously', yet, as Maybery expressed it, 'he seemed invincible'.

The Albatros had left the mêlée by then, although none of No 56 Squadron's pilots claimed to have shot it down. Voss, however, was still full of fight and put his plane through a manoeuvre that several of his opponents remarked about. Bowman, for example, said:

> I, myself, had only one crack at him: he was about to pass broadside on across my bows and slightly lower. I put my nose down to give him a burst and opened fire, perhaps too soon; to my amazement he kicked on full rudder, without bank, pulled his nose up slightly, gave me a burst while he was skidding sideways, and then kicked on opposite rudder before the results of this amazing stunt appeared to have any effect on the controllability of his machine. Rhys Davids was then on his tail.

Rhys Davids, who had already replaced two drums of Lewis ammunition in the course of the fight, fired another drum and an equal quantity of Vickers bullets into the triplane, at such close range that the two aircraft almost collided:

> I saw him next, with his engine apparently off, gliding west [Rhys Davids reported]. I dived again and got one shot out of my Vickers; however, I reloaded and kept in the dive, I got another good burst and the triplane did a slight right-hand turn still going down. I now overshot him (this was at 1,000 feet) zoomed, and never saw him again.

At that juncture Rhys Davids encountered a red-nosed Albatros to the south-east and attacked it as well, forcing it to crash-land. Its pilot was probably *Leutnant* Karl Menckhoff of *Jasta 3*, who survived. Voss was less fortunate. After ha had dazzled his opponents for some ten minutes, it is possible that fuel exhaustion, after an hour and a half of combat flying (about the limit of a Fokker triplane's endurance), had been the ultimate cause of his death before Rhys Davids' guns. Voss's F.I came down at Plum Farm, about 700 metres north of Frezenberg, and, because fighting was still going on in the area, his body was hastily buried near the crash site. The wreckage was allocated the captured number G.72 and provided British intelligence with its first, albeit incomplete, look at the new aircraft type, although only a few instruments could be salvaged.

Although neither of the Fokker F.Is had had long careers, they left an impression on both sides of the lines that has since been seared into aviation annals. Voss' spectacular last dogfight made him and his triplane the talk of Nos 56 and 60 Squadrons, and arguably even more legendary among his enemies than among his own countrymen. Richthofen's first successes in the type gave the Fokker triplane a virtual seal of approval for full-scale production and an association with the Red Baron that persists to this day—at the expense of the

Halberstadt and Albatros scouts in which he gained the lion's share of his 80 victories.

Fokker Dr.Is made their way into *JG I* and other units in October, during which time Richthofen had his pilots train in Fokker D.Vs as a transitionary measure to accustom themselves to compensating for the torque of the rotary engine aircraft. Patrols were being flown over the lines by the end of the month, but on 29 October *Jasta 11* lost *Vizefeldwebel* Josef Lautenschlager, who was shot down and killed by a German fighter. After personally investigating the matter, Richthofen ascertained that the *Kogenluft-Nachrichtenwesen* (Air Intelligence and Communications Service) had failed to inform squadrons in the *IV Armee* area about the new Fokker and that the German pilot had mistaken Lautenschlager's Dr.I for a Sopwith Triplane. Consequently Richthofen not only saved the pilot from a court-martial but arranged to have him transferred to *JG I*, where he went on to a creditable career—although his name has never been disclosed.

On the following morning, 30 October, Richthofen was leading a patrol when his brother Lothar was seen to glide down with his engine off, to make a successful forced landing near Zilverberg. Minutes later, as Manfred tried to land, his triplane broke up and he crashed. Richthofen emerged from the wreckage unharmed and subsequently learned just how lucky he had been. On that same day *Leutnant* Heinrich Gontermann, 39-victory ace and an *Ordre Pour le Mérite* recipient, was test-flying his new Dr.I 115/17 over *Jasta 15*'s aerodrome at La Neuville when the ribs broke away from the upper wing spar and he crashed, dying of his injuries that evening.

On 31 October 19-year-old *Leutnant der Reserve* Günther Pastor of *Jasta 11* crashed to his death near Moorsele after the upper wing of his triplane, Dr.I 121/17, suffered structural collapse. On 2 November an alarmed *Idflieg* grounded all Fokker Dr.Is pending an investigation by a *Sturzkommission* (crash commission). The conclusion reached by the investigation was that the triplane was intrinsically sound but that condensation collecting inside the wing had eroded the integrity of the glue, which played as important a role as the nails in holding it together. Among other things, Fokker were ordered to strengthen the attachment of the ribs to the box spar, to put greater reliance on transverse nailing rather than glue, to ensure the integrity of the joints, to varnish the inside of the wing to protect it from water damage and to redesign the ailerons. Such measures solved the worst of the Dr.I's problems and by December deliveries had resumed, not only to *JG I* but to other *Jagdstaffeln*.

Although too slow fully to realize its role as an offensive weapon, the Fokker Dr.I became the principal instrument for achieving local air superiority during the German offensive of March 1918. It never completely eclipsed the Albatros or Pfalz scouts that supplemented its meagre numbers (a peak of 171 at the

Front in April 1918) but in the right hands it could be a deadly weapon. A few German pilots, most notably Josef Jacobs, were still flying Dr.Is in preference to faster but less nimble types right up to the final months of the war. Ultimately the triplane fighter in general proved to be a developmental dead end, but the exploits of the Sopwith and Fokker pilots gave them a notoriety in their own time and a fame in postwar years all out of proportion to their numbers and actual importance.

Among the Dr.I's many victims was the first pilot to achieve success in a triplane fighter. Following the incorporation of the RNAS into the Royal Air Force in April 1918, Major Roderic S. Dallas flew S.E.5as as the commander of No 40 Squadron. In that capacity he brought his final tally up to 32 before being killed in action by three Fokker Dr.Is on 1 June. Dallas was the sixth of an eventual seven victories credited to *Leutnant* Johannes Werner of *Jasta 14*—and the last before Werner got the chance to trade his triplane in for a newly delivered Fokker D.VII biplane on 9 June.

Chapter 5

PASSING GLIMPSES
OF THINGS TO COME

Fighters of 1918

The year 1918 began with months of precarious promise for the Central Powers. Russia, torn asunder by the Bolshevik Revolution in November 1917, had sued for peace. The Italian Army, disastrously routed at Caporetto on 26 October, had retreated to the Piave river and seemed on the verge of ultimate collapse. The United States had declared war on Germany on 6 April 1917, but only the first inexperienced contingents of its small but rapidly expanding army had arrived at the Front at the beginning of 1918. 'The columns of the enemy press were crammed with fantasy-like statements [about how] thousands of American aircraft would flow over Germany and force it to seek peace,' recalled the *Luftstreitskräfte*'s commander, *Generalleutnant* Ernst von Hoeppner, after the war. As 1918 dawned, however, such propaganda had little foundation in reality and the Germans saw an opportunity—perhaps their last—to mobilize their troops on the Western Front for a final all-out push to eliminate the British Army, take Paris and compel both Britain and France to sue for peace before the Americans could bring their resources fully into play.

When Operation 'Michael' was launched on 21 March 1918 German ground forces in the West were the most powerful and murderously efficient that they had ever been since the war began. For the air arm that was expected to clear the skies for the offensive it was a different matter. Although there were now three crack *Jagdgeschwader* organized to achieve local air superiority and the number of *Jagdstaffeln* had doubled through the so-called *Amerika-Programm*, their personnel and equipment betrayed the realities behind the rapid expansion. Most of the *Amerika-Programm Jasta*s formed after June 1917 consisted of a veteran commander and perhaps a small cadre of experienced men, surrounded by hastily trained pilots who would soon have to learn their trade the hard way. The best fighter on hand was the Fokker Dr.I, back in *Jasta* strength since Anthony Fokker had rectified the shoddy production techniques that had lain behind the wing failures they had suffered in October 1917. The Dr.Is, however, soon proved to be less than the world-beaters that were needed to maintain air superiority on the offensive, being slower than all Allied fighters except the Sopwith Camel—and the Camel could match the Fokker in a dogfight. Complementing this dubious vanguard were Albatros D.Vas and Pfalz D.IIIas, which at best were no more than an even match for their Allied counterparts.

Ironically, on the other side three new fighters were already making their way to Allied front-line units. Two of them fell disappointingly short of expectations, however, and the third was never given the full utilization it deserved.

Developed in the summer of 1917, the Morane-Saulnier AI was another in a long line of rotary-engine monoplanes built by that company. Generally conventional in construction, the AI was powered by a 150 hp Gnome Monosoupape 9N engine, with a series of stringers fairing the fuselage smoothly past the rounded metal cowling to a point at the tail. The slightly swept-back upper wing was mounted above the fuselage in a parasol arrangement by means of a trusslike strut system. Static testing of the structure yielded a safety factor of 8.5, and during flight tests at Villacoublay in August 1917 the prototype climbed to 3,000 metres (9,840 feet) in 7 minutes 45 seconds and reached a speed at that altitude of 134.5 mph. That performance was considered phenomenal for a rotary-engine fighter, and since the Spad 13 was experiencing trouble with its geared Hispano-Suiza engine the French ordered the Morane-Saulnier AI into production, any number from 1,100 and 1,300 being built. The earliest AI variant, armed with a single 0.303-inch synchronized Vickers machine gun, was designated the MoS.27.C1 while a later twin-gun version was called the MoS.29.C1.

The Morane-Saulnier's reputation preceded it when *Escadrille N.156* learned that it would be the first to receive the new fighter on 4 February 1918. Among the first pilots sent to ferry the aircraft in was *Caporal* David Endicott Putnam, a Lafayette Flying Corps pilot who was serving in the unit along with fellow-American volunteers *Caporaux* Walter John Shaffer and Wallace C. Winter. When Shaffer went to Plessis-Belleville to pick up his plane on 8 February he met Putnam and later wrote that 'He was greatly elated over the speed and climbing ability of the Morane and told me how nicely it worked in the air.' Shaffer's impression was that 'it was tiny, but it is so beautifully proportioned and the lines so racy-looking that a more beautiful "zang" was never built'.

By 9 February *N.156* had been fully re-equipped and was redesignated *MS.156*. Two other *escadrilles*, *MS.158* and *MS.161*, were fully equipped with MoS.27s by 4 March and 21 February, respectively. One of *MS.158*'s Americans, *Caporal* Rufus R. Rand Jr, was equally impressed after a few front-line flights, stating that with a few alterations it could be one of the best fighters on the Western Front.

Jubilation gave way to trepidation on 26 February, however, when *Lieutenant* Jean Toutary, *MS.156*'s executive officer, lost his wings while performing aerobatics over the squadron aerodrome near Châlons-sur-Marne. Then, on 8 March, five of *MS.156*'s planes encountered two German two-seaters over the lines and two of them dived to attack. One of the Morane-Saulnier pilots discovered that his gun was jammed and pulled up to clear it. The other pilot, *Caporal* Winter, continued his dive until suddenly his wings folded up and he plunged like a stone to the ground.

Wally Winter's death saddened the *escadrille* and raised a lot of uneasy questions regarding the MoS.27's capabilities. Postwar German records reveal a curious anomaly—a Morane-Saulnier credited to *Leutnant* Julius Keller of Royal Saxon *Jasta 21*. Had he come to the rescue of the two-seaters and fired on Winter from above and behind, unnoticed by Winter's French squadron colleague? Whatever the actual cause, the high initial expectations for the Morane-Saulnier AI plummeted as fast as Winter's broken plane.

Most of *MS.156*'s pilots resumed flying missions in Nieuport 27s, but at least one of them was not so readily intimidated by the MoS.27. On 14 March Dave Putnam, who had just been promoted to *sergent*, attacked and claimed an Albatros near Nauroy, although it was only counted as a 'probable'. On the following day he downed a Rumpler over Beine, which was credited as his third victory.

As combat around Reims intensified, Putnam grew more aggressive, but his tendency to fight deep in enemy territory prevented most of his claims from being homologated. On 12 April he attacked a flight of German fighters over St Hilaire-le-Petit and claimed two of them, but neither was confirmed. He claimed a triple victory on 23 April but again it went unconfirmed. On 15 May he teamed up with *Caporal* David Guy to shoot down a German aeroplane over Somme-Py, after which Guy claimed another over Nogent-l'Abbesse. Again, both victories were only recorded as 'probables'. On that same day *Caporal* Émile Boucheron of *MS.158* crashed while trying to land his Morane-Saulnier at Maissonneuve.

The first twin-gun MoS.29s arrived at *MS.156* on 18 May, but by then their cause was lost. Two days later Shaffer wrote:

> And now we have changed airplanes again, getting Spads this time . . . The Moranes, I am sorry to say, have been given up, owing to their weak construction, which could not stand the strain 'chasse' work entails. I say sorry, because not only was it fast, but so small that as one pilot said, it would be maneuvered around a clothes pin . . .

Escadrilles 158 and *161* had already given up the last of their MoS.27s on the previous day, 19 May, and were redesignated *Spa.158* and *Spa.161*. Subsequent production Morane-Saulnier AIs had their wing structures bolstered with extra wires or struts, but for the rest of the war they were relegated to the advanced training role.

Another elegant French newcomer, the Nieuport 28 represented a break at last from the manufacturer's series of nimble but fragile sesquiplane fighters, which by mid-1917 were reaching the end of their development potential. At that time Nieuport had tried a two-spar lower wing on its Nieuport 24 in an attempt to make it rugged enough to accommodate a 160 hp Gnome rotary engine. More fundamental changes were deemed necessary, however, and on 14 June 1917 a new Nieuport took to the air—this time a true biplane, with a stringered fuselage similar to that of the 24 and 27 but longer and slimmer, although the tail surfaces were virtually identical to those of the 24 and 27. The leading edges of the wings were covered with three-ply laminated wood sheet and the ribs were capped with tapering ply strips, and the smaller lower wings held the ailerons.

Test-flown in November 1917, the final version of the Nieuport 28.C1 was one of the best-looking aircraft of World War I, but in spite of a creditable performance, including a maximum speed of 128 mph, the *Aviation Française* did not regard it as sufficiently improved over the Spad 13 to warrant production. That should have been the end of the story, but, like the Hanriot HD.1, which became the principal fighter of the Italian and Belgian air arms, the Nieuport 28 got a reprieve from obscurity by another country that was desperate for a fighter. At that time the United States still had yet to develop a fighter capable of matching its German counterparts over the Western Front, and French Spad production was still insufficient to equip US Army Air Service (USAS) squadrons. Therefore Nieuport received an order for a total of 297 fighters for the USAS. The 95th Aero Squadron, based at Villeneuve, received the first complement of the new fighters at the end of February 1918 and the 94th Aero Squadron was fully equipped with them by mid-March. No machine guns had accompanied the aeroplanes to the squadrons, but for a time the Americans flew unarmed patrols in them for the sake of familiarization and pilot morale. It was soon determined, however, that the 95th's pilots had inadequate gunnery training and the unit was withdrawn until 2 May. Meanwhile the first machine guns reached the 94th—albeit only enough to mount one, rather than the specified two, on each plane—and the unit flew its first armed patrol on 28 March.

On 9 April the 94th was transferred from Villeneuve to Gengoult aerodrome near Toul. Senior officers of the American Expeditionary Force were sceptical about the Nieuport's capabilities and viewed them as a temporary measure until enough Spad 13s were available to replace them. Meanwhile, by letting them operate over the relatively quiet Toul sector, they expected the American fighter pilots to gain experience and confidence against second-line opposition, before eventually re-equipping with Spads and being turned loose against Germany's best.

Besides such forgiving conditions in which to test their mettle, the 94th's pilots had the benefit of an extraordinary cadre of 'old hands'. The commander, Major John Huffer, was a Lafayette Flying Corps volunteer with three aerial victories to his credit. His operations officer, Major G. Raoul Lufbery, was the leading American ace with sixteen victories, all scored while serving in the famed *Escadrille Spa.124 'Lafayette'*. Two of the flight leaders, Captains James Norman Hall and David McKelvie Peterson, were also veterans of the Lafayette Escadrille.

The Nieuport 28's first day of combat was to be a memorable one. It began in the early morning hours of 14 April, when Captain Dave Peterson led First Lieutenants Edward V. Rickenbacker and Reed Chambers over the lines. Thick fog persuaded Peterson to abort the mission, but Rickenbacker and Chambers mistook his reason for turning back as being engine trouble and continued with the patrol. The duo were subjected to anti-aircraft fire and, as they turned back toward Gengoult, two fighters were dispatched from Royal Württemberg *Jasta 64*'s aerodrome at Mars-la-Tour to intercept them.

Evidence has since surfaced to suggest that one of the German pilots, *Vizefeldwebel* Antoni Wroniecki, had a hidden agenda when he led *Unteroffizier* Heinrich Simon against the intruders. Of Polish extraction, Wroniecki nursed a secret hatred of the Germans and hoped that an Allied victory might result in the resurrection of his partitioned homeland from the ruins of the German and Austro-Hungarian empires. Wroniecki later told his captors that he had planned to 'lose' Simon in the fog, land at the Allied aerodrome and then join the French air service. Both *Jasta 64* pilots were still lost themselves, however, when they emerged from the clouds over Gengoult.

Upon seeing an Albatros D.Va and a Pfalz D.IIIa appear over their field, the Americans dispatched two more Nieuports, this time flown by First Lieutenant Douglas Campbell and Second Lieutenant Alan F. Winslow, to engage the Germans. In five minutes it was all over, with both enemy planes brought down—though not without some contradictory details. Winslow was officially credited with bringing down the Albatros intact, with Simon only suffering a few bruises. Campbell was credited with Wroniecki and later stated: 'He shot at me before I saw him, and had the advantage of higher altitude than I did during most of our combat.' Campbell was nevertheless able to turn the tables on his opponent and shot the Pfalz D.IIIa down in flames, the pilot being badly burned and, according to some accounts, dying of his injuries shortly afterwards.

A convincing argument can be made that the Americans, upon learning that Wroniecki wanted to go over to their side, deliberately exchanged the pilots' names and aircraft to give the impression that Wroniecki was dead, in case he were to fall into German hands later. Adopting the pseudonym Wrobelewski, Wroniecki joined General Jozef Haller de Hallenburg's 'Blue Army', a force of Polish volunteers being organized to serve under the French, and subsequently transferred to an *Escadrille Polonaise* that was being organized at Sillé-le-Guillaume. The war ended before the unit could get into action, and Wroniecki went on to establish an unsuccessful airline in Poland (its failure partly due to his preference for Farman airliners over more efficient Junkers types because of his continuing animosity towards all things German). After that Wroniecki enjoyed somewhat more success in Germany during the late 1930s—as a Polish spy.

Doug Campbell's victory that morning of 14 April 1918 was the first scored by an American-trained USAS fighter pilot (Winslow was a Lafayette Flying Corps man with previous experience in French *Esdadrille N.152*). The Nieuport 28's place in history was assured, and it would later make more of an impression as Campbell, Rickenbacker and several other pilots went on to become aces in it. The Nieuport 28 would also figure in the dramatic death of Raoul Lufbery while trying to bring down a German two-seater on 19 May, and it would also give two prominent American aces some hair-raising experiences when the wing fabric tore away on the aircraft flown by First Lieutenant James A. Meissner on 2 May and on Rickenbacker's on 17 May. A poor grade of glue was found to be the cause of the fabric failure, but a more serious problem was discovered with the single-valve Gnome Monosoupape engine, which required a 'blip switch' to slow it down by cutting the ignition to some of the cylinders. While the ignition was off, fuel was pouring from the valves and accumulating under the cowling, often resulting in a fire when ignition was restored to all cylinders. Less well-known was a tendency of the engine's rigid and improperly annealed copper-tube fuel lines to crack due to vibration—a problem acute enough for Brigadier-General Benjamin Foulois to ground all Nieuport 28s until more flexible fuel lines could be installed.

In spite of those faults, the Nieuport 28s favourably impressed their pilots with their manoeuvrability and excellent handling characteristics. The 94th and later 95th Aero Squadrons established a good record over the Toul sector, and two more squadrons, the 27th and 148th, had been equipped with the type when all four were finally transferred on 28 June to Touqin aerodrome, twenty miles south of Château Thierry, in anticipation of a new German offensive along the Marne. There harsh reality set in as the four squadrons, newly organized into the 1st Pursuit Group, suffered heavy losses at the hands of the *Jagdgeschwader* and first-string *Jastas*, equipped with Fokker D.VIIs. By the end of July sufficient Spad 13s were available to re-equip the American units, and by 1 August the Nieuport 28 had disappeared from the USAS front-line roster.

While the Morane-Saulnier AI and Nieuport 28 fell below the high expectations that attended their arrival at the Front to various degrees, a British fighter was proving rather better than expected. First flown at Martlesham Heath in June 1917, the Sopwith 5F.1 was an attempt to give the pilot as good an all-round view as possible in a biplane that would employ the 200 hp Hispano-Suiza. Structurally conventional like virtually all Sopwith fighters, the 5F.1 was a back-staggered biplane with a relatively deep fuselage and the centre section placed directly over the pilot's head. Performance was comparable to that of the S.E.5a, and Sopwith got an initial order for 500 of the Dolphin, as the 5.F1 was christened.

In order to improve forward visibility further, the frontal radiator of the prototype was replaced with a tapered cowling and radiators in the wing roots, though they were later moved to the fuselage sides. Tail surfaces were modified and the original armament of two synchronized Vickers guns was doubled by mounting two Lewis guns on the forward spar of the centre section. After testing with both four-and two-blade airscrews in September 1917, the latter was standardized for the Dolphin.

By 31 December 1917, 121 Dolphins had been accepted by the Royal Flying Corps, and the first examples were delivered to No 19 Squadron in January 1918. In spite of the promise the new fighter had shown during trials, many British pilots looked askance at its appearance. The negative wing stagger reminded them of the D.H.5, which had proved to be a poor performer in air-to-air combat. The fact that the pilot's head protruded above the upper wing did not sit well with them, either: if the plane turned over on landing—which, given the waywardness of its Hispano engine, was a distinct possibility—the pilot was exposed to the danger of a fractured skull or a broken neck. Sopwith addressed the latter problem by adding a protective steel framework over the centre section and break-out panels on the fuselage side as an emergency exit in the event of the plane turning over on its back.

Things got off to a poor start at No 19 Squadron when Second Lieutenant A. A. Veale was killed in an accident in Dolphin C3826. Nevertheless, the squadron's pilots practised away at their new machines and soon took a liking to their manoeuvrability and general flight characteristics, which proved to be superior to those of their old Spads. They also found the Dolphin's cockpit more warm and comfortable than that of the average open-cockpit scout.

The Dolphin's baptism of fire came over Comines at 10.05 a.m. on 25 February when one of No 19 Squadron's patrols, comprising both Dolphins and Spads, engaged an equally mixed German flight that included a Fokker Dr.I and three Pfalz D.IIIs. During the fight the triplane got on the tail of Lieutenant J. L. McLintock's Spad and was about to fire a lethal burst when Canadian

Lieutenant John D. de Pencier, in Dolphin C3841, got on the German's tail and with a quick burst sent it down out of control. The triplane had already done its damage, however: McLintock was last seen descending in a shallow glide and it was later learned that he had been taken prisoner.

The Dolphins' next fight occurred over Gheluwe on 8 March when a flight came under attack by five red Albatros scouts. Captain Patrick Huskinson turned the tables on one of his adversaries and shot it down. Another Albatros got on to Captain G. N. Taylor's tail and was about to shoot him down when Captain Oliver C. Bryson got behind it and with a 12–15 round burst hit its structure, causing its wings to break and fold up. The German spun down and was credited as Bryson's twelfth and final victory of the war. In contrast to the earlier combat, Bryson was in time to save Taylor, who returned unhurt. The squadron's only casualty was Second Lieutenant F. J. McConnell, who was wounded but made it back to the aerodrome.

By the middle of March the pilots of No 19 Squadron were 'sold' on the Dolphin. In addition to being more nimble than the Spad, it proved to be capable of sustaining an even greater amount of punishment and still return home. A second Dolphin unit, No 79 Squadron, arrived with its full complement in February, while in April No 23 Squadron exchanged its Spads for Dolphins and No 87 Squadron brought its Dolphins to the Front. All four units gave outstanding accounts of themselves throughout the war, yet no further Dolphin squadrons were destined to see service over the Front and the type disappeared from first-line service soon after the Armistice. In spite of its unusual appearance, no satisfactory reason has been ascertained for such scant utilization of what may well be the most seriously underrated fighter on the Western Front.

So it was that German fighter pilots could hope for no more than quantitative parity with the Allies when 21 March rolled around. There was talk of superior new fighters being developed at home, but none had reached the Front when Operation 'Michael' commenced. Over the next month the *Jagdflieger* did their best with what they had and spent at least some of their time between missions wondering when those new fighters would finally arrive.

Idflieg had in fact been seeking the answer to their prayers with a fighter competition held at Berlin's Adlershof airfield in January 1918. The 31 aircraft entered ranged from improved versions of current mainstays, such as the Albatros D.Va and Pfalz D.IIIa, to original, innovative and often imaginative designs. Although the majority of the fighters were to have utilized the 160 hp Mercedes D.III powerplant or its higher-compression relative, the D.IIIa, a few entries used rotaries, including the Siemens-Schuckert Werke's SSW D.III.

The Siemens-Schuckert electrical corporation had been involved in aviation since 1907, but its first production aeroplane, built in mid-1916, was essentially a copy of the Nieuport 11. Only 65 SSW D.Is were built before the original 150-plane order was discontinued in June 1917, but a modified variant, the D.Ib, achieved an eye-opening climb rate of 5,000 metres (16,400 feet) in 20.5 minutes by the use of an over-compressed, 140 hp version of the 9-cylinder Siemens-Halske Sh.I engine. This and other Siemens-Halske engines were counter-rotaries, in which the propeller and cylinders rotated in an opposite direction to the crankshaft. This resulted in greater propeller and cooling efficiency, better fuel economy, reduced drag, lower weight and a greatly reduced gyroscopic effect. With SSW working on a 160 hp 11-cylinder counter-rotary engine, the Sh.III, *Idflieg* ordered a fighter based on the new powerplant as early as November 1916. The engine was not ready for flight-testing until June 1917, but on 5 August twelve-victory ace and SSW test pilot *Leutnant* Hans Müller flew the D.IIb prototype to an altitude of 7,000 metres in a record-setting 35.5 minutes. Further experiments with various wing configurations and propeller types ultimately led to the D.III, which featured wings of unequal chord and a four-blade propeller to allow for a shorter undercarriage.

On 26 December 1917 *Idflieg* ordered twenty pre-production SSW D.IIIs, of which four were entered in the First Fighter Competition in January 1918. Again Müller put his plane through some impressive paces, displaying exhilarating manoeuvrability and climbing 6,000 metres in 21.5 minutes on 21 January. Pilots who were unused to the SSW fighter's high rpm and unusual handling characteristics were less favourable in their appraisals, however, finding the D.III a hot handful, especially when it came to landing. SSW modified the D.III further to address their complaints, and, in response to Manfred von Richthofen's general lament that 'all aircraft at the Competition were too slow', new wings of shorter span and equal chord (based on the D.III's lower set) were installed on a new version, the D.IV, which sacrificed climb rate for greater level speed. Encouraged by the SSW fighter's overall performance, *Idflieg* ordered 30 D.IIIs on 1 March, followed by an order for 50 more on 23 March and 50 of the new D.IVs on 8 April.

The first six SSW D.IIIs were delivered to *Jagdgeschwader III* on 16 March, but the principal recipient, *Jagdgeschwader II*, got its first nine machines on 6 April and its overall complement was up to 35 by 18 May. *Jasta*s 12 and 19 of *JG II* were then equipped with Fokker Dr.Is, and consequently their pilots' experience with rotary engines would help in making the transition to their assigned SSW D.IIIs. *Jasta 19*'s commander, *Leutnant der Reserve* Walter Göttsch, received D.III 8346/17 on 6 April and had its fuselage painted white, but he never got to fly it in combat. On 10 April he was killed in his Fokker Dr.I while pursuing an R.E.8 over British lines and was subsequently credited to Lieutenants H. L. Taylor and W. I. E. Lane of No 52 Squadron, although he may just as likely have been a victim of ground fire. Göttsch was posthumously credited with the R.E.8 for his twentieth victory, but, while Lane was wounded in the leg, Taylor had in fact made a hasty landing behind Allied lines that German observers mistook for his being shot down.

As the German offensive proceeded, the SSWs were kept discreetly on their own side of the lines while the pilots familiarized themselves with them in between offensive patrols in Dr.Is or, in the case of *Jastas 13* and *15*, Albatros D.Vas and Pfalz D.IIIas. Two successes were attributed to the SSWs, however, and they were probably achieved on 20 April, when *Leutnant der Reserve* Hans Pippart, Göttsch's successor in command of *Jasta 19*, intercepted and destroyed a Bréguet 14B.2 of *Escadrille Br.127* on the German side of the lines west of Chauny, and on the following morning, when *Leutnant der Reserve* Ulrich Neckel of *Jasta 12* bagged another Br.127 Bréguet that had penetrated the lines en route to St Quentin. During a visit by SSW engineer Bruno Steffen to *JG II* on 22 April, the *Geschwaderkommandeur*, *Hauptmann* Rudolf Berthold, praised the D.III for its 'brilliant' rate of climb, the 'faultless' combination of airframe and Sh.III engine and how the fighter had gained the trust of its pilots.

Berthold's praise proved to be somewhat premature. After seven to ten flying hours the engines began suffering from such ills as overheating, spark plug ejection, faulty magnetos, bearing failure, faulty throttles, piston heads disintegrating and complete engine seizure. By 23 May *JG II*'s D.IIIs had been withdrawn pending the rectification of their engines' faults. Berthold, however, remained a believer in the type and urged that 'the Siemens fighter be made available as quickly as possible, for, after elimination of the present faults, it is likely to become our most useful fighter aircraft'.

SSW D.IIIs and D.IVs began returning to front-line service on 22 July, their engines replaced by Sh.III(Rh) powerplants built under licence by the Rhenania Motorenfabrik A.G. (Rhemag)—which curiously suffered from none of the problems that had plagued the SSW-built originals—and portions of their cowlings cut away to allow better cooling. Generally, D.IIIs were assigned to *Kampfeinsitzer Staffeln* for home defence because of their superior climb rate, while the faster and more manoeuvrable D.IVs went to *Jastas* on the Western Front. Once pilots had mastered the SSW's 'hot' handling characteristics they were almost unanimous in their praise for it as the best fighter at 4,000 metres or higher. Unfortunately for the *Luftstreitskräfte*, only 136 SSWs had reached operational units by 11 November 1918.

While the SSW D.III attracted an unusual share of attention at the Fighter Competition, the overall star was unquestionably Anthony Fokker's V11 biplane. Hastily built for the competition, the V11 was based on the fuselage and tail of the Dr.I but employed a biplane version of the wooden box spar construction employed on the triplane. The lower wing was smaller than the upper to improve downward visibility and was built in one piece, with a cut-out arranged in the steel tube fuselage frame to accommodate it. The ailerons, installed only on the upper wing, were also made of steel tube and were fabric-covered. Streamlined steel tubing also served as interplane and cabane struts, with no bracing wires. The V11 featured a radiator mounted in the nose, rather than on the fuselage sides or the upper wing.

Even after its fuselage was lengthened to compensate for the Mercedes inline engine, Manfred von Richthofen found the V11 to be overly sensitive and unstable in a dive. Fokker immediately responded by lengthening the fuselage further and adding a vertical stabilizer. Both the V11 and the improved V18 were tested at the Fighter Competition, and Richthofen and numerous other German fighter pilots were unanimous in their praise for the Fokker biplane's overall performance, including its ability to retain its manoeuvrability at high altitude and to 'hang on its prop'. Fokker was immediately given a 25,000-mark contract to build 400 of the new biplane, which was given the military designation D.VII. Of additional personal satisfaction to Fokker was an order for both the Johannisthal and Schneidemühl factories of his rival, Albatros, to manufacture the D.VII under licence, with a five per cent royalty going to Fokker.

Fokker D.VIIs began to reach the Front in April 1918, the first examples, not surprisingly, going to Richthofen's *Jagdgeschwader I*. *Leutnant* Aloys Heldmann of *Jasta 10* claimed to have used one in combat in the middle of the month, but there is no evidence that the new biplanes scored any official aerial victories until the end of May. Certainly they inspired enthusiasm in every pilot that flew them, yet the Red Baron himself was still flying a Dr.I when he scored his 79th and 80th victories on 20 April, and when he was killed—either by Australian ground fire or by Captain Arthur R. Brown of No 209 Squadron—while pursuing his 81st the following day.

A possible reason for the slow transition was that *JG I* was heavily involved in the German offensive, continually moving from aerodrome to aerodrome. On 21 May the *Geschwader* moved from Cappy to Guise and was given a week's rest before the offensive was renewed, this time against the French along the Marne river around Château Thierry. The pilots of *Jastas 4, 6, 10* and *11* made use of the welcome 'down time' to familiarize themselves with the D.VIIs, under orders to limit their orientation flights to rear areas only. As a result, the late Red Baron's 'Circus' felt ready when the offensive was launched and the Fokker D.VIIs were unleashed in full force on 27 May.

Curiously, *JG I* recorded only one modest aerial success amid the first day's hectic activities. At 6.15 in the evening *Jasta 4* attacked a formation of Bréguet

14B.2 bombers over Pont-Arcy and two were claimed by *Leutnant* Viktor von Pressentin *genannt* von Rautter, of which one was confirmed as his fourteenth victory. *Escadrille Br.126* lost a plane that day, along with its crew of *Sergents* des Salles and Lingueglia.

Amid the confusion of this third phase of the German offensive, a curious double mystery arose. On one hand, the British reportedly acquired a Fokker D.VII, serial number 2184/18, found near Achiet-le-Grand on 27 May and given the captured aircraft registration number G/5/12. The only German loss that even begins to match such an acquisition is that of *Leutnant der Reserve* Rudolf Windisch, commander of *Jasta 66*, who was brought down while attacking a French aerodrome, probably by *Sous-Lieutenant* Souleau and *Maréchal-des-Logis* Cavieux of *Spa.76*. Typifying officers placed in command of *Amerika-Programm* units, Windisch was a 22-victory ace. He was also photographed in the cockpit of a Fokker D.VII, the aircraft bearing a personal marking of a leaping stag on the fuselage side, suggesting that as a seasoned *Kanone* he may have had the rare privilege for that time of receiving one of the new fighters. Perhaps it was his plane, or the remains thereof, that were recovered by the British in the sector. Adding to the day's anomalies were conflicting reports that Windisch had been taken prisoner and that he had been killed—shot while trying to escape, perhaps? In any case, the general configuration of the Fokker D.VII did not remain a German-kept secret for long.

That was a moot point, however, because, after more than a month in which the aircraft was cautiously introduced to the Front, the last few days of May saw the Fokker D.VII burst into almost instant prominence. At 5.30 in the afternoon of 28 May *Leutnant* Fritz Friedrichs of *Jasta 10* was credited with destroying a balloon south of Chevigny for his sixth victory, although Allied records identified no corresponding loss. *Jasta 10* lost one of its pilots on 29 May when *Leutnant der Reserve* Rademacher came down behind Allied lines and was taken prisoner; his plane, however, was one of the *Staffel's* few remaining Albatros D.Vas. On the following day *Leutnant der Reserve* Johann Janzen of *Jasta 6* downed a Spad over Beauvardes for his ninth victory.

The afternoon of 31 May saw another engagement with the Bréguets southwest of Soissons, *Leutnant* Rautter downing another of the bombers at 12.55 p.m., killing *Sous-Lieutenant* Maurice Béranger and his gunner *Sergent* Wolf of *Br.29*. Moments after scoring his fifteenth victory, however, Rautter himself was shot down and killed, either by return fire from the Bréguets or by a Spad flown by *Adjudant* Gustave Daladier of *Spa.93*, who claimed a Fokker Dr.I but may have confused its silhouette with that of the new, unfamiliar D.VII. *Jasta 4's* commander, *Leutnant der Reserve* Ernst Udet, downed another Bréguet 14 five minutes later for his 24th victory, his victims being *Sergent* Martin and *Soldat*

Galbrun of *Br.29*. At 2.35 p.m. it was *Jasta 6*'s turn as *Leutnant der Reserve* Hans Kirschstein claimed a Bréguet over Grand-Rozoy, his victims possibly being *Caporal* Lecomte and *Maréchal-des-Logis* Garcette of *Br.129*. At 7.40 that evening *Leutnant* Martin Skowronski of *Jasta 6* scored his first success over a Bréguet near Marizy-St-Mard, and *Hauptmann* Wilhelm Reinhard, Richthofen's chosen successor as *Geschwaderkommandeur*, scored his fourteenth victory over a Spad near Bonneuil five minutes later. *Oberleutnant* Erich-Rüdiger von Wedel of *Jasta 11* completed the day's activities by downing another Spad for his third victory over the Bois de Bourbillon at 8.40 p.m.

June saw a proliferation of Fokker D.VIIs, accompanied by glowing reports from their pilots and awed reactions from their Allied opponents. There seemed to be only three things wrong with the D.VII. The first was a tendency for its incendiary ammunition to overheat and explode, which was alleviated by cutting ventilating holes in the cowling and ultimately remedied with improved ammunition. Many pilots also thought that the Fokker would benefit from a more powerful engine, and later that summer it got one—the 185 hp BMW, which gave the aircraft markedly better performance, especially at altitudes of 18,000 feet or higher, and made it truly the terror of the Western Front.

The third great fault of the Fokker D.VIIs was that there were not enough of them to satisfy the demand, and the fighters produced to supplement them almost invariably suffered in comparison when appraised by the pilots who had to fly them. In mid-May the Roland D.VI, a product of the Luftfahrzeug Gesellschaft mbH featuring a fuselage built up of wooden clinkers like a boat, was assigned to *Jastas 23b, 32b, 33* and *35b*. Its performance was not better than that of the Albatros D.Va, and in late May *Jasta 23b*'s commander, *Leutnant der Reserve* Otto Kissenberth, flew a captured Sopwith Camel in preference to his unit's Rolands. August saw the appearance of the Pfalz D.XII at the Front, although its frontal radiator and 'N' shaped interplane struts caused Allied pilots frequently to mistake it for the Fokker D.VII. The Pfalz, however, featured the same semi-monocoque plywood fuselage as the earlier D.III, and wings with a drag-reducing, thin aerofoil section inspired by the Spad, conventionally wire-braced with two bays of interplane struts. In his postwar memoirs, *Jagdstaffel Unsere Heimat*, *Leutnant* Rudolf Stark mentioned that his command, *Jasta 35b*, accepted Pfalz D.XIIs on 1 September 'only after much discussion and long telephone conversations', and that every pilot 'climbed into the new machine with preconceived notions and immediately voiced all manner of complaints'. His mechanics were already so 'spoiled' by the Fokker D.VII's cantilever wings that they complained of the renewed labour required to keep the Pfalz's guy wires adjusted between missions. Later, Stark admitted, the Pfalz D.XII turned out to be a fairly good plane that 'climbed well and could fly along with the

Fokker D.VII in all respects, and in a dive it was a bit faster. But in turns and combat it was slow and could not compare with the Fokkers.'

Two noteworthy exceptions among the Fokker D.VII's maligned stablemates were the SSW D.III and the D.IV, once their engine problems had been rectified. Another was also a Fokker product—a monoplane which, like the Morane-Saulnier AI, elicited great expectations, only to fall disappointingly short of them.

When *Idflieg* held a second Fighter Competition at Adlershof between 27 May and 21 June 1918, Anthony Fokker and his staff entered the V28, a parasol monoplane powered by a 110 hp Oberursel Ur.II rotary engine. Fokker's experiments with cantilevered wing structures bore fruit with a lightweight plywood-covered wing that gave the plane outstanding climb and manoeuvrability, while its placement at eye level by means of streamlined steel-tube struts gave the pilot a remarkably good view in all directions. Judged the best rotary-engine fighter of the competition, the V28 was accepted for production as the E.V on 3 July, but Fokker had already taken the liberty of starting production two weeks prior to receiving the official order. Fokker's chief engineer, Reinhold Platz, later claimed that the E.V may have cost 'less man-hours than any other World War I aircraft'; in any case, on 5 August the first E.Vs, powered by 110 hp Oberursel engines, arrived at *JG I*. *Leutnant* Richard Wenzl, commander of Jasta 6, recalled:

> In terms of aviation technology, the machine was outstanding, despite the fact that it had been designed for the more powerful 140 hp rotary engine. In about a minute and a half it climbed to 1,000 metres and in eight minutes to 3,000 metres, but then, [as a consequence of] a characteristic of engine torque, the performance fell off. Nevertheless, in terms of climbing ability and technical performance, this machine was superior to all previous [fighters], even the much slower [Fokker] triplane.

By this time the last German offensive had been stopped and it was the Allies who were on the advance. *JG I* fell back to the aerodrome at Berne on 11 August. Once the unit had settled in there, *Jasta 6* chalked up its first success in the new monoplane on 16 August when *Leutnant der Reserve* Emil Rolff shot down a Camel for his third victory, its pilot, Sergeant P. M. Fletcher of No 203 Squadron, being taken prisoner. Later that same day, however, another E.V crashed during a test flight and its pilot, *Vizefeldwebel* Lechner, was injured.

On 18 August the RAF's intelligence staff began alerting front-line units that 'Fokker monoplanes have been issued to at least two pursuit flights now working in the Somme area'. Then, suddenly, things went frightfully wrong for the E.V. On 19 August Rolff was putting one of the new fighters through its paces over Berne when his wing suddenly broke up at an altitude of 300 metres and he crashed to his death. Sensing a reprise of the misfortunes that had befallen the Dr.I, *Idflieg* immediately grounded all E.Vs. A special crash commission concluded that condensation that had entered through wing breathing holes had begun to rot the flying surfaces from within. Improper spar dimensions and faulty construction at Fokker's Perzina factory were also blamed for the flaws in an intrinsically sound design.

On 24 August E.V production was suspended until the shoddy production techniques were rectified. Fokker responded by building a new wing with strengthened spars, more careful assembly and a varnish-coated interior. It was successfully load-tested on 7 September, and *Idflieg* permitted production of the monoplane, now redesignated D.VIII, to resume on 24 September. The first D.VIII was accepted on 8 October and additional wings were built to be retro-fitted to the 139 grounded E.Vs. Too much time had been lost, however, and Rolff's fleeting success remains the only positively recorded aerial victory attributed to the much-touted cantilever Fokker monoplane before Germany surrendered on 11 November 1918. Likewise, there is no evidence that an even more advanced design, the Junkers D.I all-metal low-wing monoplane, ever saw combat before the Germans agreed to the Armistice.

While the Germans—in a curious prelude to the closing months of a later war—experimented with innovative fighter designs that came too little and too late, Britain was introducing one more new type that could not have been less radical in concept—the Sopwith Snipe. Begun in mid-1917 as a Camel successor, the Sopwith 7F.1 featured wings of equal dihedral, with the upper wing centre section lowered to the pilot's eye level in order to improve his forward and upward vision, which had been a shortcoming of the Camel. The plane's prototypes evolved over the months that followed, adapting the 230 hp Bentley B.R.2 rotary engine, increasing the wing span with a two-bay rather than the original single-bay interplane strut layout and adopting altered tail surfaces. After being tested at Martlesham in February 1918 and undergoing operational front-line evaluation at St Omer in March, the 7.F1 Snipe was ordered into production, seven companies being contracted to build 1,700 of the new fighter. Although its fundamental structural make-up was little changed from that of the Pup of 1916, the Snipe chanced upon a historic distinction after the RFC merged with the RNAS on 1 April 1918, becoming the first new fighter to enter service with the Royal Air Force.

The first unit to employ the new Sopwith in battle, No 43 Squadron, received its first Snipe on 12 August and reached its full strength of 24 in mid-September. For several weeks the squadron's pilots alternated between orientation flights behind the lines in the new planes and combat patrols in their old Camels until the latter were fully phased out. Pilots found the B.R.2 engine to be commendably reliable and the Snipe, with a maximum speed of 121 mph at 10,000 feet, a better overall performer, though little more docile than the Camel. Full activity was resumed with a front-line patrol on 23 September. On the morning of the 27th No 43 Squadron's Snipes and the S.E.5as of No 1 Squadron were escorting No 107 Squadron on a bombing raid against the railway station at Bohain when the bombers were attacked by Fokker D.VIIs at 9.15. No 1 Squadron intervened first, Lieutenant B. H. Mooney claiming a D.VII in flames over Bertry and Lieutenant C. W. Anning sending one down out of control near Bevillers. Ten minutes later it was No 43 Squadron's turn as Captain Cecil Frederick King and Lieutenant Charles C. Banks drove a Fokker D.VII down out of control near Cambrai. Five minutes later another Snipe pilot, Lieutenant R. S. Johnston, sent a second D.VII down out of control south-east of Cambrai. Two days later Captain Augustus Henry Orlebar sent another D.VII down out of control over Renaucourt, bringing his wartime total to seven. In all, No 43 Squadron claimed ten enemy planes in the last six days of the month, without loss.

No 4 Squadron Australian Flying Corps got into action with its Snipes in October and No 208 Squadron RAF was just commencing operations when the Armistice was signed on 11 November 1918. The most famous Snipe of all, however, was E8102, a personal machine assigned to Major William George Barker while attached to the Camel-equipped No 201 Squadron, The Canadian ace fought an epic duel with at least fifteen Fokker D.VIIs on 27 October and survived to receive the Victoria Cross.

An alternative Snipe variant, completed in April 1918, was powered by the 320 hp ABC Dragonfly radial engine, which gave it a startling maximum speed of 147.8 mph at 10,000 feet. This type, too, was ordered into production, eventually being renamed the Sopwith Dragon. Unfortunately for the British, the Dragonfly engine proved to be as unreliable as it was powerful, handicapping the careers of the Dragon and several other promising fighters that had been designed around it. The Dragon never achieved squadron service, whereas the Snipe would remain a postwar RAF mainstay until 1927.

When World War I began, the fighter plane did not exist. The war's last year showed how far aviation in general had come, and the sleek, swift fighting machines of 1918 had showcased many of its most noteworthy structural refinements. Nevertheless, a good many of the innovations managed to be too far ahead of their time. While the immediate future was claimed by conventional wood-and-wire biplanes like the Bristol F.2B and the Sopwith Snipe, aeroplanes featuring such refinements as radial engines, monoplane wings, cantilever wing structures and all-metal construction generally proved to be less practicable as fighting machines than as passing glimpses of things yet to come. It would not be long, however, before the state of the art caught up with the concepts they had pioneered.

Chapter 6

A NEW GENERATION

Fighters of the Spanish Civil War, 1936–1939

The aeroplane had proved itself to be a useful addition to armies' arsenals from the earliest months of World War I, and had developed rapidly in the crucible of that conflict by the time the fighting officially ended on 11 November 1918. Less than eighteen years later, the aeroplane would play an essential role in starting another war.

When conservative political, religious and military factions, led by General Francisco Franco y Bahamonde, rebelled against Spain's five-year-old Republican government on 18 July 1936, it was the prompt dispatch of German transport planes to Franco's aid that made it possible for him to airlift 8,000 of his troops from Morocco between 20 July and the end of August, thereby establishing a viable base for his Nationalist forces in southern Spain. The conflict that ensued saw the testing of aircraft designs and tactics regarding their use that would be instrumental in the second world war, which would begin just months after the Spanish war ended.

Three fighters of the Spanish Civil War stand out as classic embodiments of the changing state of the art during the 1930s. The Fiat C.R.32 was typical of its time, yet essentially no more than a sleeker, higher-powered, structurally more advanced variation on the standard World War I formula—a biplane with fixed landing gear and an open cockpit. Nevertheless, it performed its duties very well—perhaps too well, in retrospect, for the good of the Italians who built it. In comparison, the Soviet Polikarpov I-16 represented a radical advance, being the first low-wing monoplane fighter with retractable landing gear and an enclosed canopy to enter production. The Messerschmitt Bf 109, though essentially no more than a structural and aerodynamic refinement of I-16's basic formula, was nevertheless sufficiently advanced to be prototypical of most of the aircraft that duelled for the sky in World War II—and improved versions of the Messerschmitt fighter itself would be up there with them, right to the end.

Although the League of Nations introduced an embargo against the shipment of arms to the warring Republican and Nationalist forces in Spain, great quantities of French, Czechoslovakian, American and British weaponry, including aircraft, found their way to the two sides by various subterfuges. Three dictatorial powers that perceived an ideological stake in the conflict were more open in their support. With a strong Communist constituency ensconced in the elected Spanish government, Soviet leader Josef Stalin shipped tanks, aircraft and airmen to aid the Republican cause. His arch enemies, Adolf Hitler of Nazi Germany and Benito Mussolini of Fascist Italy, saw a kindred spirit in Spain's Falangist General Franco and began sending thousands of fighting men, as well as equipment, to bolster the Nationalist Army.

Among Italy's contributions to the Nationalist war effort was the Fiat C.R.32. The C.R.32's pedigree dated to 1923, with the C.R. (Caccia Rosatelli), the first of a line of fighters designed by Celestino Rosatelli, featuring two wings of unequal span, braced by a girder-like set of Warren truss struts. The C.R.20 of 1926 introduced an all-metal airframe and the C.R.30, which appeared in 1932, featured a 600 hp Fiat A.30 liquid-cooled engine, streamlined spats for the main and tail wheels and an armament of either two 7.7mm or two 12.7mm Breda-SAFAT machine guns synchronized to fire above the engine. The C.R.32, which first flew on 28 April 1933, was basically a scaled-down, more compact and more refined C.R.30. The 592 hp Fiat A.30 RA engine gave it a maximum speed of 237 mph at 10,000 feet. Ailerons, balanced by 'park bench' tabs, were installed in the upper wing only and the rudder and ailerons were statically and dynamically balanced. Stable and yet extremely manoeuvrable and sensitive on the controls, the Fiat also had an exceptional diving speed, while its robust wing structure lent confidence to the pilot.

The Fiat C.R.32 was numerically the most important fighter in the *Regia Aeronautica* by the summer of 1936, when hostilities broke out in Spain. Wasting little time in providing support to Franco's cause, Mussolini dispatched twelve Savoia-Marchetti S.81s to Spanish Morocco on 31 July—three of which were lost en route—followed by twelve C.R.32s, which arrived at Melilla aboard the freighter *Nereid* during the night of 12 August. Secretly flown to Tablada, near Seville, the Fiats formed the *1a Esuadrilla de Caza de la Aviación de El Tercio* (1st Fighter Squadron of Army Aviation) under *Capitano* Vincenzo Dequal on 21 August.

Initially flown by Italians only, the Fiats—nicknamed '*Chirris*' by the Spaniards after the Italian pronunciation of the letters 'C.R.'—were soon asserting themselves over the mixed bag of aircraft then available to the *Fuerza Aéreas Republicanas*. Their first victim was a Hispano-built Nieuport-Delage NiD 52, downed near Cordobá on 21 August, but the victorious Italian pilot, *Sottotenente* Ceccarelli, allegedly collided with a CASA Bréguet 19 that he was attacking shortly afterwards. *Sergente* Magistrini scored the next victory for the Fiats on 27 August when he encountered and shot down a newly delivered, unarmed

Dewoitine D.372 parasol monoplane fighter over Guadix aerodrome, killing its Spanish pilot, *Capitán* de Haro. The Italians' first setback occurred on 31 August when three C.R.32s encountered two D.372s and a Hawker Fury flown by *Comandant* Andrés García Lacalle near Talavera de la Reina, resulting in two Fiats being shot down by the Dewoitines and the third returning damaged. One Italian pilot, *Sergente* Castellanini, bailed out and managed to make his way back to Nationalist territory. *Tenente* Monico was less fortunate, being captured by Republican militia, shot out of hand and dragged along the ground by an uncontrolled mob.

Meanwhile more C.R.32s were arriving in Spain, and by mid-September a second squadron had been formed, under the command of *Capitano* Dante Olivera. By then the pilots of the *1a Escuadrilla* were starting to refer to their unit as '*La Cucaracha*' (The Cockroach) after a popular song of the time. Three Spanish pilots had joined the unit at that time—*Capitán* Joaquin García Morato, *Capitán* Ángel Salas Larrazábal and *Teniente* Julio Salvador Díaz-Benjumea. By the end of the war Salas would have sixteen enemy aircraft to his credit, Salvador's score would stand at 24 and García Morato would be the war's leading ace with 40.

September 11 saw the Fiats in full stride, claiming two Bréguet 19s and five fighters. Two of the Republican aircraft were credited to Magistrini and a NiD 52 was credited to García Morato, who had previously scored his first victory flying a Republican NiD 52 and his second in a German Heinkel He 51B. By the end of the month García Morato's score stood at eight, making him the war's leading ace—a status that he never relinquished. The Nationalists, with the generous assistance of the German and Italian allies, had achieved air superiority, but that situation was about to undergo an unexpected change.

The two fighters that the Soviet Union sent to Spain in October 1936 represented a transition in aircraft configuration. One, the radial-engine *Istrebitel* (fighter) I-15, developed by Nikolai N. Polikarpov in 1933, had brought indigenous Soviet fighter design to a par with that of Western nations for the first time, but it was nevertheless a biplane with fixed landing gear and an open cockpit, its principal departure from convention being the cranked upper wing that earned it the Russian nickname of *Chaika* (Gull). In dramatic contrast, the other type, the I-16, was the world's first low-wing monoplane fighter with an enclosed cockpit and retractable landing gear.

Development of the I-16 began as a result of conceptual studies undertaken in 1932 by Professor Andrei N. Tupolev, head of the TsKB (*Tsentralny Konstruktorskoye Byuro*), leading to the development of the ANT-31, or I-14, in May 1933. Polikarpov, who had assisted in the I-14's development, was subsequently transferred to the TsKB at Factory 36 to develop the I-15 biplane. Polikarpov, however, was convinced that he could create a fighter incorporating all of the I-14's innovations in the lighter airframe. Joined by A. G. Trostyanski, he set about developing a prototype, the TsKB-12, which was first flown by test pilot Valery F. Tchkalov on 30 December 1933. Powered by a 480 hp Shvetsov M-22 9-cylinder radial engine (a licence-built Gnome-Rhône 9AsB Jupiter, which was itself a French version of the Bristol Jupiter), the TsKb-12 reached a maximum speed of 190 mph. A second prototype, designated the TsKB-12*bis*, used a more powerful 710 hp M-25 (licence-built Wright Cyclone SGR-1820-F3), which yielded an impressive performance when it was test-flown by Tchkalov in January 1934, including a speed of 218 mph. When difficulties were encountered in the I-14, the Soviet government authorized production of the TsKB-12 under the military designation I-16.

The first 30 I-16 Type 4s, powered by M-22 engines, were primarily meant as trainers to help biplane pilots make the transition to the new monoplane. The first major production model, the Type 5, used the M-25 engine and began to reach Soviet squadrons in the summer of 1935. The enormity of the Polikarpov design team's achievement can be appreciated when it is remembered that the first Messerschmitt Bf 109 did not take to the air until September 1935, the first Hawker Hurricane did not fly until November and the first Supermarine Spitfire not until March 1936.

Advanced though the aircraft was in overall configuration, the structure of the I-16 Type 5 was not quite state-of-the art. At a time when all-metal, flush-riveted, stressed-skin construction was becoming common in Western Europe and the United States, its monocoque fuselage comprised four longerons and eleven half-frames of pine, over which were glued strips of birch to form a varnished surface called *shpon*. Its wings were of chrome-molybdenum steel alloy, with duralumin wings and control surfaces. Although the centre section and leading edges of the wings were aluminium-skinned, the rest of the wings, ailerons and control surfaces were fabric-covered.

The landing gear was hand-cranked up or down by means of cables. The forward-sliding canopy was extremely narrow and confining for the pilot, and exposure to propeller-driven sand and dust tended to give it all the clarity of bottle glass. Pilots had such difficulty gaining confidence in the enclosed canopy that it was eventually dispensed with on later I-16 production models. The Type 5 was armed with two wing-mounted 7.62mm ShKAS machine guns.

Nationalist pilots who first encountered the I-16 over Spain quickly dubbed it the 'Boeing', implying that it was a copy of the American Boeing P-26. The sobriquet was as inaccurate as it was disparaging, because, for all its novelty in its brief time (1933–35), the P-26 had nothing in common with the I-16 other than being a radial-engine, low-wing monoplane. For one thing, the I-16 Type

5's speed of 283 mph was almost 50 mph faster than the P-26A's maximum of 234 mph. In spite of its superior speed and climb compared to those of its biplane contemporaries, the I-16 was surprisingly nimble as well, with feather-light ailerons and an outstanding roll rate. Unlike the I-15 and other biplanes, however, it was extremely difficult to fly, being unforgivingly sensitive on the controls and easy to stall if not given constant attention by its pilot from take-off to landing.

The Russians made no secret of their new fighter, unveiling it in the May Day flypast of 1935 and at the *Salone Internationale Aeronautica* in Milan, Italy, in October. Western observers, however, dismissed the short, stubby little fighter as a hollow piece of Soviet propaganda. When the Spanish Civil War broke out, the I-16's creators found an opportunity to put their design to a real test—and a venue where it would have to be taken seriously.

The Soviet government established diplomatic relations with Spain in August 1936 and voted to send military aid to the Republic later that month. Stalin neither expected nor wished to make significant Communist inroads in Madrid, but in the wake of Hitler's Anti-Comintern Pact with Mussolini he had no desire to see Franco's forces, aided and influenced by the Germans and Italians, come to power. Stalin's other motive was based more on capitalistic than social-ist principles: he drove a hard bargain for his military aid package, for which the Republic paid in Spanish gold, for example, the equivalent of $35,000 US for each I-15. The first 25 I-15s and 31 I-16 Type 5s were shipped to Spain in mid-October 1936, along with 141 pilots and almost 2,000 technicians and mechan-ics, who would operate the aircraft in combat even while they were training Spanish Republican pilots in their use. In February 1937 the Republic obtained a licence to build its own I-15s. Spain also began producing its own I-16 Type 10s, with 730 hp M-25A engines and the armament doubled by the addition of two synchronized 7.62mm machine guns, in the summer of 1938.

Officially dubbed the '*Yastrebok*' (Falcon), the I-16 was more popularly, if unofficially, known as the '*Mushka*' (Fly) among its Russian pilots, and the Repub-licans promptly referred to it as '*Mosca*' as well, while the I-15 was referred to as the '*Chato*' (Snub-Nose). After initially calling it the 'Boeing,' the Nationalists came to refer to the I-16 as the '*Rata*' (Rat), a term that became universal among the Germans, Italians and their allies in the years to come.

Once the aircraft were assembled, the first contingent of Soviet fighters was deployed in twelve-plane squadrons around Madrid, which was about to face a major Nationalist offensive. The I-15-equipped *1a Escuadrilla de Chatos*, under Major Pavel Rychagov (under the thin Spanish alias of 'Pablo Palancar') was set up at Campo XX at the El Soto estate near Algete, sixteen miles north-west of Madrid, while the *2a Escuadrilla de Chatos*, under Major Sergei Tarkhov (alias

'Antonio') was based at Alcalá de Henares, east of Madrid. The I-16s equipped the *1a Escuadrilla de Moscas*, under Major A. Tarasov at Campo XX, the *2a Escuadrilla de Moscas*, under Major S. P. Denisov at Alcalá, and the *3a Escuadrilla de Moscas*, under Major K. Koleshnikov, still working up at Albacete, where the Soviet chief aviation advisor, Colonel Yakov V. Shmushkevitch (alias 'General Douglas'), set up his air headquarters. In original theory the two fighter types were expected to complement each other, the I-16s primarily going after enemy bombers while the more tractable I-15s dealt with any fighter escort. They were also to escort bombers of their own, in the form of Tupolev SB-2s, known as *Katiuskas* to the Spaniards. Until sufficient numbers arrived to form separate air groups, the fighters and bombers were combined within a temporary organization called *Grupo 12*.

The bombers, led by Swiss-born *Major* Ernst Schacht, struck *Grupo 12*'s first blow against the Nationalists when they attacked Tablada airfield near Seville on 28 October. Bad weather and poor serviceability of their aircraft limited the activities of the Soviet fighter pilots to discreet flights on their side of the lines, familiarizing themselves with the terrain. Then, on 4 November, Rychagov led ten of the *2a Escuadrilla*'s I-15s on a mission to escort a squadron of SB-2s. As the *Chatos* descended through a cloud, they ran into a formation of six German-flown and six Spanish-flown Junkers Ju 52/3m bombers of *Hauptmann* Rudolf *Freiherr* von Moreau's *Kampfstaffel Moreau*, which were climbing to cross the Sierra de Guadarrama en route to bomb Republican targets north of Madrid. The Russians immediately attacked and shot down one of the German Junkers. They also damaged one of the Spanish-flown bombers, which was forced to land at Esquivas. Resuming their flight, the I-15s next encountered a flight of five IMAM Ro-37*bis* reconnaissance planes, escorted by two C.R.32s from the reorganized Italian *XVI Grupo de Caccia 'La Cucaracha'*. The *Chatos* promptly shot down both C.R.32s, also damaging one of the Ro-37s. The downed Fiat pilots were none other than early squadron leader *Capitano* Dequal, who parachuted to safety, and early scorer *Sergente* Magistrini, who was killed. In a third action of that eventful day, the *Chatos* jumped two more Fiats, which were badly damaged and subsequently crashed while trying to land at Torrijos airfield. No I-15s were lost in combat, but in the course of the patrol two Soviet pilots became disoriented and, when their fuel ran out, made emergency landings near Segovia, in Nationalist territory. In spite of the capture of the two wayward I-15 men, a report from the crew of the damaged Ro-37 of being attacked by American Curtiss fighters resulted in the *Chatos* being referred to as 'Curtisses' by the Nationalists for a long time to come.

The sudden appearance of advanced Soviet aircraft over Madrid gave the Nationalists, Italians and Germans an unpleasant shock, but it did not last long.

On the very next day nine C.R.32s were escorting Ro-37s to Casa del Campo when they were attacked over Leganés by sixteen I-15s that had been escorting three Potez 54 bombers. Five other patrolling Fiats joined in the swirling dogfight, the largest yet seen over Spain. Two Fiats were brought down and their Italian pilots, Picoli and Maccagno, captured, later to be exchanged for a Soviet prisoner, but one of the I-15s was also shot down by García Morato for his thirteenth victory.

Aerial encounters between the *Chirris* and *Chatos* continued on an almost daily basis. On Friday 13 November fourteen C.R.32s duelled with thirteen I-15s above the streets of Madrid. The claims of both sides—six fighters and an SB-2 bomber by the Nationalists, five fighters by the Republicans—were inflated, but two Italians, *Capitano* Mosca and *Tenente* Mariotti, were compelled to crash-land their shot-up Fiats at Talavera and were taken prisoner. García Morato claimed his fifteenth victory, while Salas and Salvador each achieved acedom with their fifth. Major Tarkhov was shot down by a Fiat and bailed out over Madrid, only to be mistaken for a German by angry members of the city's populace and so brutally treated that he died in hospital several days later. The incident led to the issuance by the Republican government of an order against the shooting of downed pilots, on the grounds that they might provide useful information—to say nothing of their possibly turning out not to be the enemy.

Friday the 13th also saw the first major clash between the Russian fighters and their German counterparts. The Germans already had a contingent of eager volunteers in Spain prior to the official formation of the *Legion Condor* in November 1936, and nine Heinkel He 51Bs had left their base at Avila to escort five Ju 52s and three Heinkel He 46s in an attack on Republican forces on the west bank of the Manzanares river when they encountered sixteen I-15s and eight I-16s. In the confused dogfight that followed, *Unteroffizier* Ernst Mratzek claimed to have downed an I-16 as it dived past him, though no such loss was acknowledged by the other side. *Oberleutnant* Oskar Henrici also claimed a Russian fighter before leading his *Kette* (flight) down through the clouds. *Oberleutnant* Herwig Knüppel, *Leutnant* Hennig Stümpel and *Oberleutnant* Dietrich von Bothmer also claimed I-15s, as did *Unteroffizier* Erwin Sawallisch, although the last came back with his tail riddled. Yet another I-15 fell victim to the German fighter unit's *Staffelführer*, *Oberleutnant* Krafft Eberhardt, but moments later he collided with his victim and was killed, while the Soviet pilot succeeded in bailing out. In a tragic finale to what the Germans would consider a 'Black Friday', Henrici, though shot in the lung, managed to land his He 51 in friendly territory, emerged from the cockpit, took a few steps from his plane and then collapsed and died. Later the Germans learned that the Republicans had claimed to have shot down four of their planes, for the loss of two I-15s.

After about a week of reticence the I-16 pilots finally joined the fighting in earnest at 3.30 in the afternoon of 15 November when two of them engaged a trio of C.R.32s over Villa del Navalcarnero, with inconclusive results for both sides. On the following day four I-16s were flying 'top cover' for nine I-15s of Rychagov's *1a Escuadrilla de Chatos* when the biplanes came under attack by '*Limonesi*' Dequal's Fiats. The unsuspecting C.R.32 pilots suddenly found themselves in turn being dived on by the new monoplanes, which claimed two of them. Three more Fiats were also claimed by the I-15 pilots, including two by Rychagov before he was himself shot down, bailing out and parachuting unharmed into Madrid's Paseo de la Castellana. On the other side, Enrico Loresco died in flames and another Italian was wounded but managed to make it back to his aerodrome.

The I-16 had at last been blooded, and quite successfully, but its pilots, like their I-15 counterparts, soon learned the folly of underestimating the Fiat. On 17 November I-16s of the *2a Esuadrilla de Moscas* were attacking an *escuadrilla* of Ju 52/3m bombers when they were pounced on by seven C.R.32s, led by Salas. Two I-16s were claimed and, for the first time, the loss of one was admitted by the Republicans.

The last major air battle of 1936 occurred when 50 Nationalist Ju 52s and S.81s dropped 40 tons of bombs on Madrid. The bombers' escort of nine Nationalist He 51s and sixteen C.R.32s engaged about an equal number of I-15s and I-16s, resulting in claims of four Republican fighters shot down. The Republicans acknowledged the loss of two I-16s while claiming three Ju 52s and three fighters.

Bad weather curtailed aerial operations for the rest of the year, and both sides took the time to reappraise the situation and develop tactics to compensate for their respective deficiencies. The Italians, intimidated by both the I-15 and the I-16, made it a policy seldom to go outside their lines and not to engage the Republican fighters unless they flew in formations of at least fifteen planes. The Spanish Nationalists, in contrast, continued to fly their *Chirris* aggressively against the *Chatos* and *Ratas*. García Morato took command of his own Spanish unit in May 1937; officially designated *Grupo 2-G-3*, it would become legendary as the *Patrulla Azul* (Blue Patrol).

One of the C.R.32 pilots' principal methods of dealing with the I-16s was to attack from above, using the Fiat's sturdy structure and high diving speed to advantage. Another popular tactic among the Italians was to engage the Republican fighters head-on, using the greater range and striking power of their 12.7mm Breda-SAFAT machine guns. Many Spanish pilots carried a combination of one 7.7mm and one 12.7mm gun on their C.R.32s, although García Morato preferred to keep both of the lighter 7.7s on his plane.

Chastened by their first losses, the I-16 pilots resolved to avoid being drawn into a turning dogfight with the Fiats, in which the C.R.32s were more manoeuvrable and the I-16s had proved to be less stable gun platforms. Whenever possible the I-16 pilots reverted to the formula that had brought them their first success on 15 November—flying their *Moscas* about 1,000 feet above the I-15s, making diving attacks on whatever enemy aircraft engaged the *Chatos* and then using the momentum of the dive to climb back up to the original attack altitude for another pass.

As for the German fighter pilots, the action of 13 November had painfully but decisively rammed home something that they already knew—that their He 51B fighters were barely enough to handle a NiD 52 and no match for an I-15, let alone the newer, faster I-16. Fortunately for them, a new fighter was on the way, of a design that represented an advance beyond the I-16—the Messerschmitt Bf 109.

The 'Great White Hope' of the *Legion Condor* in 1936 had begun as a 'dark horse' just a few years earlier. On 1 May 1933, 35-year-old Wilhelm Emil Messerschmitt was co-manager of the Bayerische Flugzeugwerke Allgemeine Gesellschaft (BFW), a firm that had been revived after being driven to bankruptcy through the cancellation of a contract with Deutsche Lufthansa two years earlier. BFW's future prospects still seemed bleak, however, because the National Socialist Party's Undersecretary of Aviation, Erhard Milch, had been Lufthansa's managing director—and one of Messerschmitt's chief detractors—back in 1931.

Messerschmitt was working on a light civil transport in the spring of 1934 when he learned that the German state technical office, or *C-Amt*, was holding a competition of aircraft designs. With little to lose, he rushed his project, the BFW M.37, to completion and entered it in the fourth *Challenge de Tourisme Internationale* as the Bf 108 *Taifun* (Typhoon). Although the Bf 108 did not win any of the events, its overall configuration and performance was impressive enough to land a production contract.

Even before the Bf 108 had made its first flight in the spring of 1934, Messerschmitt learned that the RLM (*Reichsluftfahrtministerium*, or Air Ministry) was about to issue a specification for a fighter, to be powered by a Junkers Jumo 210 engine and to be capable of at least 280 mph. Although most German aircraft manufacturers were invited to submit designs, only the established firms, like Arado, Heinkel, Fieseler and Focke-Wulf, could expect serious consideration. Given BFW's lack of experience in fighters and Milch's long-standing antagonism toward Messerschmitt, it seemed a waste of time and effort for Messerschmitt to enter such a competition. Milch had not even informed Messerschmitt of the competition, but his superior, Aviation Minister Hermann

Göring, did—in a confidential message requesting Messerschmitt to develop 'a lightning-fast courier plane which needs only to be a single-seater'.

Deducing just what Göring was hinting at, Messerschmitt and his design team at BFW's Augsburg factory—most notably Robert Lüsser, Richard Bauer and Hubert Bauer—set about incorporating the Bf 108's features into a low-wing monoplane fighter with retractable landing gear, an enclosed cockpit, leading-edge slots and trailing-edge flaps in the wings. While work proceeded on the *Versuchs* (prototype) Bf 109 fighter, Germany officially established the *Luftwaffe* on 1 March 1935 and Hitler publicly renounced the Treaty of Versailles' restrictions on German rearmament on 16 March.

The prototype Bf 109 V1 was completed in August 1935 and evaluation flights began at the RLM's test centre at Rechlin, initially using a 675 hp Rolls-Royce Kestrel engine in place of the Jumo. The Bf 109 V2, completed in October, introduced the 610 hp Jumo 210A as well as a strengthened undercarriage, and the Bf 109 V3, delivered in June 1936, was the first to be armed, with an engine-mounted 7.92mm MG17 machine gun.

In spite of its high wing loading, which limited its manoeuvrability at low speeds, the Bf 109 yielded such outstanding performance that the RLM quickly eliminated the Arado Ar 80 and Focke-Wulf Fw 159 from consideration, leaving only the Heinkel He 112 in contention. Ten pre-production Bf 109B-0s were ordered, at which point two events occurred that would alter the Bf 109's fate.

Coincident with the Bf 109 V3's appearance, June 1936 also saw the issuance by the Royal Air Force of production contracts for 600 Hawker Hurricane fighters and 310 Supermarine Spitfires, the latter of which, first flown on 5 March, had a similar performance to that of the Bf 109 V1. The potential threat posed by those British fighters added urgency to the German fighter's development, and the armament in the Bf 109 V4, introduced in November, was increased from two to three MG17s.

The other event of significance was, of course, the outbreak of the Spanish Civil War in July. Here was an opportunity to test the Bf 109 under combat conditions, developing not only the aircraft but also practical tactics for using it to the best effect—an idea lent an element of urgency by the appearance of the I-15 and I-16 over Madrid in November. In consequence the Germans rushed the Bf 109 V4 to Spain in December, to be followed by Bf 109B-1s, the first of which left the production line in February 1937.

The first operational unit in Spain, 2. *Staffel* of *Jagdgruppe 88* (*2./J 88*) under *Oberleutnant* Günther Lützow, began receiving its first Bf 109s in March. The high torque produced by the Jumo engine, combined with the narrow track of the new fighter's undercarriage, gave the aircraft an alarming tendency to drop its left wing during take-off and landing, causing a rash of accidents at first. Eventually, however, its pilots learned to compensate through liberal application of rudder to the right. Once they had overcome the Bf 109B's idiosyncrasies, they gained confidence in it and were ready to commence operations over the Brunete salient in July 1937.

The Messerschmitt drew first blood in the air on 8 July when *Leutnant* Rolf Pingel and *Unteroffizier* Guido Höness were credited with two SB-2s, although the Republicans attributed only one of their two losses that day to a Bf 109, the other having fallen victim to a C.R.32. The Republicans later credited Bozidar Bozko Petrovic, a Yugoslav communist serving in the *2a Escuadrilla de Chatos*, with shooting down the first Bf 109 for his fifth victory on 8 July, although the Germans recorded no such loss.

A series of air battles fought on 12 July resulted in the downing of two Aero A-101s by Höness, an SB-2 by Pingel and three I-16s by Pingel, *Feldwebel* Peter Boddem and *Feldwebel* Adolf Buhl. Höness, however, was shot down and killed while attacking another SB-2 that same day—the first of thousands of Messerschmitt pilots to die in combat over the next nine years. García Morato's *Grupo 2-G-3* was also active that day, in which the Nationalists claimed four *Moscas* and five *Chatos*, while the Republicans claimed eight C.R.32s and one He 51. Among the actual losses was *Capitán* Aleksandr Minaev, the commander of an *escuadrilla de Moscas*.

By that time the I-15s and I-16s had been proliferating, and the Russians had been gradually displaced by Spanish pilots as well as a number of airmen from other countries. The presence of the foreign volunteers was particularly evident during a sprawling dogfight on 13 July which lasted nearly an hour. Among the two Ro-37s, one Ju 52 and nine fighters claimed by the Republicans was a Bf 109 credited to *Teniente* Frank G. Tinker, an American pilot in *Capitán* Ivan A. Lakeev's *1a Escuadrilla de Moscas*, and a C.R.32 to Yugoslav volunteer Petrovic for his seventh and last accredited victory. Depending on the account, Petrovic was following his victim as it dived towards the ground when he was either shot down by two other Nationalist fighters or had the wings of his I-15 fold up. In either case he crashed to his death near his late opponent, who may have been *Capitán* Narisco Bermudez de Castro, a member of García Morato's *Patrulla Azul* who was killed in action that day. The Italians claimed two I-16s, but two of their own C.R.32s were lost after colliding in mid-air.

The Germans lost no Bf 109s on 13 July, although a subsequent confusion of dates caused Höness's death the day before to be matched to Tinker's claim. On the other hand, *Feldwebel* Boddem was credited with shooting down an I-15 whose pilot turned out to be another American, Harold Evans Dahl. Condemned to death by the Nationalists, 'Whitey' Dahl was the subject of a protracted appeal—including one by his showgirl wife, Edith Rogers—before Franco finally relented and rescinded his death sentence, and Dahl was finally released from Spanish captivity in 1940. *Feldwebel* Heinz Braunschweiger, assigned a Bf 109B marked '6-13' because nobody else in his *Staffel* wanted to fly a plane with such an unlucky number, shot down an I-16 in the 13 July mêlée and made a point of keeping the same plane thereafter.

The Bf 109B and its principal Republican rival, the I-16, were at first closely matched. The Bf 109B was faster in level flight and in a dive, while the I-16 had a better climb rate and superior manoeuvrability. Republican ace and fighter leader Andres Garcia Lacalle commented in his memoirs that the I-16 was superior to the Messerschmitt up to 3,000 metres (9,840 feet), but from that altitude upwards the Bf 109B's performance gave the German aircraft complete mastery.

During the second Ebro campaign, between July and October 1938, *Oberleutnant* Werner Mölders of *3./J 88* developed a fighter tactic of far-reaching significance. By combining two *Rotten*, the basic two-man elements within a *Staffel*, into a loose but mutually supportive team, he created an infinitely flexible offensive and defensive unit that he called the *Vierfingerschwarm* (four-finger formation). That fundamental concept would become the basis for numerous variations to the present time. Mölders himself emerged as the leading ace of the *Legion Condor* with fourteen victories and later became the first fighter pilot to pass the 100 mark on 15 July 1941. When he died in a transport plane crash on 22 November 1941 his score stood at 115.

Guided by lessons learned in Spain, Messerschmitt incorporated a rapid succession of improvements into his new fighter. The Bf 109C-1, with a fuel-injected Jumo 210Ga engine and four machine guns, arrived in Spain in the spring of 1938, followed by the Bf 109C-2 which mounted a fifth machine gun in the engine. The Bf 109D, five of which joined *3./J 88* in August, combined the Bf 109C-1's four-gun armament with the Bf 109B-1's carburettor-equipped Jumo 210Da engine. Meanwhile, Messerschmitt's experiments with the fuel-injected Daimler Benz DB600 and DB601 engines, largely handicapped by cooling problems, were ultimately solved by installing two radiators under the wings, leaving only an oil cooler under the fuselage. In addition, the DB 601A-powered Bf 109 V14 increased the armament to two MG 17 machine guns in the nose and two 20mm MG FF cannon in the wings, along with a three-blade, controllable-pitch VDM airscrew. The result was put into production in early 1939 as the Me 109E-1.

The fighter's revised designation, which has caused confusion and controversy among aviation historians for decades, reflected the complete acquisition of BFW stock by Willy Messerschmitt in late 1938. According to the *Luftwaffe*'s own historical record's, the old 'Bf' reference was retained for the Bf 108, the Bf 109B to D, and for the Bf 110A and B *Zerstörer* twin-engine fighter. All other Messerschmitt products, starting with the Me 109E and Me 110C, officially used the 'Me' prefix, although the issue would continue to be confused for years to come because of the appearance of the 'Bf' prefix on stamped plates on various Me 109 components as late as 1945.

The Germans wasted no time in sending three Me 109E-1s to La Cenia late in December 1938. Twenty of an eventual grand total of 44 Me 109Es—including the latest Me 109E-3s—were operational with the *Legion Condor*'s fighter arm in March 1939. By then, however, Nationalist air superiority was virtually absolute and the *Luftwaffe's* newest fighter saw relatively little action prior to 28 March 1939, when the last of the Republican forces capitulated. They would, however, have plenty to do on 1 September 1939, and in almost six years to follow.

The later careers of the three transitional fighters of the Spanish Civil War give insights into the conclusions drawn by the countries that built them. Having often overcome the performance handicaps of the C.R.32s by skill and adaptive tactics, the Italian pilots remained hard to convince that the days of the biplane fighter, let alone that of the lone dogfighter, were on the wane. Consequently the next important Fiat fighter, the C.R.42, would be another biplane with fixed landing gear and an open cockpit—even while that same company was producing a more advanced design with retractable landing gear and an enclosed canopy, the G.50.

The Fiat G.50 was built in response to specifications issued by the *Ministerio dell' Aeronautica* in 1936, calling for a lightly armed interceptor, a long-range escort fighter and a fighter-bomber. While other manufacturers submitted four designs to address each of those requirements, Fiat's Guiseppe Gabrielli designed his G.50 to satisfy all three. Built around the new new 840 hp Fiat A.74 twin-row, 14-cylinder radial engine, the G.50, which first flew on 26 February 1937, became the first Italian monoplane fighter with retractable landing gear to enter production, with an initial order for 45 machines. After the second prototype crashed in September, the G.50's competitor, the Macchi C.200, was judged the better fighter, but G.50 production continued as an insurance against any problems in getting the C.200 into operation.

During a visit to Italy, García Morato test-flew a G.50 at Guidonia in October 1937. The first G.50s entered *Regia Aeronautica* service at the end of 1938 and ten were promptly shipped to Spain, where they were formed into a *Gruppo Sperimentale de Caccia* (Experimental Fighter Group) under the command of *Maggiore* Mario Bonzano. The unit was based at Escalona alongside the C.R.32s of Bonzano's old unit, the *XXIII Gruppo*, and consequently some of the G.50s were marked with that group's '*Asso di Bastoni*' (Ace of Spades) emblem. Flying as escort to the C.R.32s at an altitude of 8,000 metres, the G.50s saw some service in the last fortnight of the war but encountered no aerial opposition. The principal operational evaluation consisted of pilot complaints about inadequate visibility from the enclosed cockpit, which resulted in the adoption of a traditional open cockpit for all subsequent production batches of the G.50.

Even after World War II broke out, the *Regia Aeronautica* was remarkably reticent in committing its Fiat G.50s to combat. During the Battle of Britain, for example, the *20o Gruppo*'s G.50s only flew discreet patrols over the English Channel while the *18o Gruppo*'s C.R.42 biplanes escorted Fiat B.R.20 bombers over Britain in November 1940—with predictably disastrous results when they encountered Hawker Hurricanes and Supermarine Spitfires. By that time, however, another country had been less shy about blooding the G.50 in combat.

After the Soviet Union attacked Finland on 30 November 1939, Italy—which, unlike Germany, had not signed a non-aggression pact with Stalin—shipped some of its G.50s to the beleaguered Finns. The first Fiats were organized into a *Koelentue* (test flight) under *Kapteeni* Erkki Olavi Ehrnrooth and were soon 'tested' in battle. On 13 January 1940 Ehrnrooth, appropriately flying a Fiat bearing the serial number FA-1, shot down an SB-2 bomber over Sisä-Suomi, followed by an Ilyushin DB-3 on 29 January. By February G.50s were actively serving in a regular squadron, *Lentolaivue 26*, and they added a few more Soviet aircraft to the butcher's bill before Finland finally capitulated on 13 March 1940. The Finnish Fiats would serve on in the Continuation War as well, with considerably more distinction than they achieved in *Regia Aeronautica* service.

The Red Army Air Force, or *Voyenno-Vozdushny Sili*, came away from the Spanish Civil War with mixed feelings about the monoplane as the fighter of the future. To hedge its bets, Polikarpov was ordered to manufacture a cleaner version of the I-15 with retractable landing gear. Built after the intrinsically more advanced I-16, the I-153 biplane was to be the second most numerous fighter in the V-VS at the time of the German invasion of the Soviet Union on 22 June 1941. However, neither the I-153 nor late-model variants of the I-16 would prove to be a match for the Me 109Es and Me 109Fs that served as the vanguard of the rampaging *Luftwaffe*.

While the Fiat C.R.32's and Polikarpov I-16's relatively brief careers were enough to earn them a place in aviation history, the Me 109 achieved an uncommon measure of longevity as well as immortality. After being adopted as the *Luftwaffe*'s principal fighter, it underwent a number of engine and airframe changes that kept it an adversary to be reckoned with right up to the fall of the Third Reich on 8 May 1945. By then at least 30,000 Me 109s of all models had been built, making it second only to the Soviet Ilyushin Il-2 *Shturmovik* as the most heavily produced aeroplane in history. Moreover, the ubiquitous Me 109 was credited with shooting down more enemy aircraft and producing more aces than any single fighter in the annals of aerial warfare—including the leading ace of all time, Erich Hartmann, with 352 victories. Even after the war, a Czech-built Jumo-engine version, the Avia S-199, had the ironic distinction of being the first fighter to serve in the Israel Defence Force/Air Force during that new nation's fight for survival in 1948–49.

The Me 109's operational career ended where it began—in Spain. In 1945 Hispano Aviación installed 1,300 hp Hispano Suiza 12-Z-89 engines in the airframes of the Me 109Gs it had imported from Germany and subsequently manufactured its own version. The final Spanish variant, the HA-1112-MIL *Buchon*, powered by a 1,400 hp Rolls-Royce Merlin 500/45 engine driving a Rotol four-blade propeller, was built until 1956 and soldiered on into the 1960s. As if using the same engine as its most famous enemy were not irony enough, in 1969 the Merlin-engine Me 109 represented its German forebear in a film re-creation of its earlier duels with the Spitfire—*The Battle of Britain*.

Chapter 7

FIRST SHOTS OF A
SECOND WORLD WAR

Czechoslovakian, Polish, German, French and Dutch Fighters, 1930–1940

Although World War II officially began with the German invasion of Poland on 1 September 1939, there had been conflict aplenty in Europe earlier that year. The spring of 1939 saw the Spanish Civil War winding down and the flare-up of a brief territorial struggle between Hungary and the newly formed republic of Slovakia. The latter conflict saw the less than auspicious combat debut of an Eastern European fighter that had earned a place alongside the classic biplanes of aviation's Golden Era—Czechoslovakia's Avia B.534.

The Czechoslovakian republic, formed after the disintegration of the Austro-Hungarian Empire on 28 October 1918, wasted no time in building up an army—along with an air force, the *Ceskoslovenské letectvo*, and its own aviation industry, sustained by talented designers and engineers who had gained previous experience in Austro-Hungarian service. One of its manufacturers, Avia, was established in 1920 and bought by the powerful Skoda armaments firm in 1926. In 1930 Avia designer Frantisek Novotný produced the B.33 fighter, followed by the B.34 in 1931. First trials of the B.34 were disappointing, but Novotný subjected it to a series of modifications and engine changes, ultimately leading to the use of a supercharged 775 hp Hispano-Suiza 12 Ybrs engine in the B.534/1. All the pilots who flew the B.534/1 in August and September 1933 were impressed not only by the aesthetically pleasing, well-balanced contours of the plane but also by its speed, climb and diving characteristics. On 17 July 1934 the Ministry of Defence decided to make the B.534 the standard fighter of the *Ceskoslovenské letectvo* and in the following month placed an order for 34 planes, which was later increased by another 147.

Avia B.534s came in several models, with open cockpits or plexiglass canopies and an armament ranging from two to four 7.62mm Model 28 or 30 synchronized machine guns. There was also the Bk.534, with a Swiss-built Oerlikon

FFS-20 20mm cannon cannon firing through the reduction gear shaft of its HS-12 Ycrs engine as well as two machine guns in the fuselage and racks for six 44-pound bombs under the wings.

The principal variant, the B.534-IV, had a maximum speed of 252.12 mph empty, but with its full armament of four machine guns and 220 pounds of bombs that speed dropped to 236 mph. During the 4th International Flying Meet held at Zürich-Dübendorf, Switzerland, between 23 July and 1 August 1938 the B.534 distinguished itself among the biplanes in almost every event, but almost invariably came off second best against Germany's new Messerschmitt Bf 109. Novotný responded by initiating work on a new monoplane fighter of his own, the B.35, but time was running out—both for Avia and for Czechoslovakia.

In spite of the build-up and modernization of the German armed forces, Czechoslovakians were prepared to fight when Hitler demanded that the Sudetenland, with its large German population, be incorporated into his *Reich* in 1938. As a result of the Munich Agreement of 30 September, however, Czechoslovakia had to cede the Sudetenland and its eastern borders. On 15 March 1939 the Germans occupied the entire country. All of the fighters in the occupied 'Protectorate of Bohemia and Moravia' were confiscated by the Germans, but some were given to the breakaway fascist state of Slovakia.

On 16 March another country with which Hitler was trying to ally himself, Hungary, annexed the Carpatho-Ukraine and made further claims on territory in southern Slovakia. As both nations mobilized for war, the Slovaks formed a new air arm, the *Slovenské Vzdusné Zbrane* or SVZ, mainly from the former Czechoslovakian 3rd *Letecký Pluk* (Air Regiment), which had been stationed at Piestany since 1938. Comprising 164 fighter, bomber and reconnaissance aircraft, the regiment was reorganized into specialized flights, including Fighter Flights (*Stíhacia letkou*) 37G, 38H, 39J, 45L and 49P, equipped with a total of 60 B.534s and one obsolete B.33. The Slovaks then hurriedly transferred their newly acquired warplanes to airfields at Spisská Nová Ves and Nizný Sebes (Sebastová), near Presov.

At 9.00 in the morning of 23 March 1939 Hungarian troops and armour crossed the Ung river and invaded Slovakia. Three B.534s of Flight 45L, led by Staff Sergeant Ján Hergott, took off to bomb and strafe the advancing Hungarian ground forces, followed at 9.14 by three Letov S.328s, escorted by three B.534s of Flight 49P. At 3.00 three B.534s of Flight 45L, flown by Hergott, Second Lieutenant Ján Svetlík and Corporal Martin Danihel, attacked a column of Hungarian tanks and armoured cars in the face of intense anti-aircraft fire. Svetlík was shot down and killed. Three more B.534s of the same flight, piloted by Hergott, Corporal Stefan Devan and Corporal C. Martis, attacked the Hungarian column an hour later. Devan was wounded and his plane crippled by machine-gun fire, and he crashed to his death while trying to force-land at Stakcin.

The first air-to-air combat of the conflict began at 5.30 the next morning when six B.534s of Flights 45L and 49P left Spisská Nová Ves. At the same time the 2nd Section of Hungarian *Vadasz Század* (Fighter Squadron) *1/1*, composed of three Fiat C.R.32s flown by First Lieutenant Aladár Negro and Sergeants Sandor Szoják and Arpád Kertész, took off from Uzhorod. Apparently the two elements of the Slovakian flight became separated, because Negro reported encountering only three Avias over Sobrance. The opposing fighters immediately engaged in a swirling dogfight—and the Slovaks took the worst of it. Badly wounded by Negro, Second Lieutenant Ján Prhácek, commander of Flight 45L, tried to make a forced landing but he was killed when one of the bombs that were still toggled under his wings exploded. Szoják put some bullets into Corporal Martis's engine, compelling him to force-land near Lúcky. Kertész hit the third Avia, though its pilot, Private Michal Karas, brought his damaged machine home. The other three B.534s strafed a column of Hungarian vehicles en route back to their airfield.

At 10.00 three B.534s, flown by First Lieutenant Ján Pálenícek, Hergott and Corporal Jósef Zachar, attacked Hungarian infantry and armour between Tibaya and Nizná Rybnica. Intense anti-aircraft fire wounded Pálenícek, who nevertheless made it to the Slovakian side of the battle line before force-landing his damaged plane. Zachar's B.534 was also slightly damaged, but as he tried to reach Slovakian territory he came under more Hungarian ground fire, which further damaged his plane and caused him to become disoriented. He finally came down in a field, where both he and his plane fell into Hungarian hands.

At 1.45 p.m. three S.328s of Flight 12D left Spisská Nová Ves, accompanied by three B.534s of Flight 45L. Again, they encountered nine C.R.32s of *Vadasz Század 1/1*, led by First Lieutenant Béla Czekme. The Hungarian formation was made up of three V-shaped elements, the first of which flew on into a cloud without noticing the Slovaks. First Lieutenant Lászlo Palkó and one of his wingmen, Second Lieutenant Matyás Pirithy, spotted the six Slovakian aircraft to their left and attacked. Just then the Slovakian fighters spotted Negro's 2nd Section and left the Avias to attack those Fiats—unwittingly leaving the Letovs vulnerable to Palkó's section.

Again the fight went badly for the Slovaks. Palkó accounted for a Letov, the pilot of which, Corporal Gustav Pazický, was killed. The observer, Second Lieutenant Ferdinand Svento, bailed out but was shot by Hungarian hussars who thought he was reaching into his jacket for a pistol—only to discover afterwards that he had only been reaching for his identification papers. First

Lieutenant Antal Békássy claimed another Avia, which was probably flown by Corporal Danihel, who made it back to his airfield. Negro brought down his second B.534 of the day and Pirithy downed another, corresponding to Ján Hergott and Master Sergeant Frantisek Hanovec, both of whom made forced landings and were taken prisoner. Hanovec later claimed that both he and Danihel shot down Fiats in the action, but none of the Hungarian fighters was even damaged that day. Kertész and Szoják were also credited with Avias in the fight, while Czekme was credited with a second Letov.

Meanwhile, during an interrogation of the captured Corporal Zachar, the Hungarians learned of the concentration of Slovakian aircraft at Spisská Nová Ves. At 4 p.m. nine Hungarian Junkers Ju 86K-1s bombed the airfield, damaging hangars and destroying ten S.328s, a B.534 and an Avia B.71 bomber. One S.328 pilot tried to take off but he was wounded by machine-gun fire and his observer was killed. One B.534 managed to take off but did not take part in the fighting.

The Slovaks assembled 28 aircraft for a retaliation raid on Miskolc the next day, but before it could be launched the Germans persuaded both sides to agree to an armistice, which came into effect on 25 March. Negotiations were concluded on 2 November 1939, Hungary being allowed to keep 4,200 square kilometres of the Slovakian territory it had occupied, along with the 1,000,000 people living therein. The Hungarians repaired and test-flew Zachar's captured B.534 against the C.R.32 and found the Avia to be faster and more manoeuvrable but more vulnerable to gunfire than the Fiat.

The Avia B.534 went on to a curious career throughout World War II. When the Germans invaded Poland on 1 September 1939, 35,000 Slovakian troops moved into the regions of Orava and Spis—Slovakian territories that had been taken by Poland in the wake of the 1938 Munich Agreement—and twenty B.534s participated in the invasion. Two were lost, but on 26 September Sergeant Viliam Grún scored the SVZ's first confirmed victory—and its only one of the campaign—when he brought down an RWD-8 liaison plane of the 13th *Eskadra Szkolna* near Presov. The Polish crew was taken prisoner but eventually escaped to Romania. The B.534 was still the SVZ's principal fighter when Slovakia committed its *Rychlá Divise* (Express Division) to support German Army Group South in the invasion of the Soviet Union on 22 June 1941. By June 1942, however, the B.534 was acknowledged as obsolete and was mainly used against Soviet Ukrainian partisans behind the lines while Slovakian fighter pilots switched to the Me 109E.

When elements of the Slovakian armed force rose up against the Germans on 29 August 1944 the insurgents operated a handful of aircraft, including two B.534-IVs and a Bk.534, from the airfield at Tri Duby (Three Oaks). The Germans had crushed the uprising by the end of October, but not before one of Tri Duby's defenders had added a curious footnote to history. On 31 August Warrant Officer Frantisek Cyprich took off in response to reports of an enemy plane south of the field and attacked what turned out to be a Hungarian Junkers Ju 52/3m transport flying from Budapest to Krakow with a load of mail and half a dozen military passengers. Cyprich killed a passenger and set the plane's right engine on fire on his second firing pass, and its pilot, György Gách, force-landed in a meadow near Radvan. As Gách and his passengers emerged to be taken prisoner by the villagers, Cyprich flew over and saw Gách throwing up his hands in dismay. Mistaking it for a friendlier gesture, Cyprich saluted before turning back for Tri Duby. He may as well have been waving a belated farewell to an era that most people thought had ended years earlier, for Cyprich had just scored the last aerial victory in a biplane fighter.

Avia B.534s were also used by the Royal Bulgarian Air Force, but by 1943 they were patently useless as fighters. After Bulgaria switched her allegiance from the Axis to the Allies in September 1944 about a dozen B.534s served as close-support planes in operations against the Germans until January 1945. For a biplane that had been obsolete before the war began, the B.534 had had a curiously long, if less than outstanding, fighting career.

While Czechoslovakia's Avia B.534 was destined to serve on the peripheries of World War II's decisive campaigns, a Polish fighter, the PZL P.11c, met the first one head-on. Built by the *Pánstwowe Zaklady Lotnicze* (National Aviation Establishment) and first flying in August 1931, the PZL P.11 was the descendant of a series of clean monoplanes designed by Zygmunt Pulawski, incorporating a unique gull wing that was its thickest near the point where four faired steel struts buttressed it from the fuselage sides. When the first PZL P.1 flew on 26 September 1929 it thrust Poland to the forefront of progressive fighter design. In 1933 Poland's air force, the *Lotnictwo Wojskowe*, became the first in the world to be fully equipped with all-metal monoplane fighters as the improved P.6 and P.7 equipped its *eskadry*. When the production P.11c, powered by a 645 hp Skoda-built Bristol Mercury VI.S2 9-cylinder radial engine, entered service in early 1935 it still rated as a modern fighter, with a maximum speed of 242 mph at 18,045 feet and a potent armament of four 7.7mm KM Wz 33 machine guns, although its open cockpit and fixed landing gear were soon to become outdated. By 1939 the P.11c was clearly obsolete, and efforts were already under way to develop a successor to replace it within the year. Poland did not have a year, however: on 1 September time ran out as German forces surged over her borders.

A morning fog over northern Poland thwarted the first German air operation as *Oberleutnant* Bruno Dilley led three Junkers Ju 87B-1 Stukas of *3 Staffel*,

Sturzkampfgeschwader 1 (*3./StG 1*) into the air at 4.26 a.m., flew over the border from East Prussia and at 4.34 a.m.—eleven minutes before Germany formally declared war—attacked selected detonation points in an attempt to prevent the destruction of two railway bridges on the Vistula river. The German attack failed to achieve its goal and the Poles blew up the bridges, denying German forces in East Prussia an easy entry into Tszew (Dirschau). The 'fog of war' also handicapped a follow-up attack on Tczew by Dornier Do 17Z bombers of *III Gruppe, Kampfgeschwader 3* (*III./KG 3*).

Weather conditions were better to the west, allowing *Luftflotte 4* to dispatch 60 Heinkel He 111s of *KG 4*, Ju 87Bs of *I Gruppe, StG 2*, and Do 17Es of *KG 77* on a series of more effective strikes against Polish air bases near Kraków at about 5.30 a.m., Rakowice field being the hardest hit. Assigned to escort the Heinkels was a squadron equipped with a new fighter of which *Luftwaffe Marschall* Hermann Göring expected great things—the Messerschmitt Me 110C-1 strategic fighter, or *Zerstörer*.

The Me 110 had evolved from a concept that had been explored during World War I but only put into practice successfully by the French with their Caudron 11.A3, a twin-engine, three-seat reconnaissance plane employed as an escort fighter in 1918. The strategic fighter idea was revived in 1934 with the development of the Polish PZL P.38 *Wilk* (Wolf), which inspired a variety of similar twin-engine fighter designs in France, Germany, Britain, the Netherlands and the United States.

Göring was particularly enthralled by what he dubbed the *Kampfzerstörer* (battle destroyer), and in 1934 he issued a specification for a heavily armed, twin-engine, multi-purpose fighter capable of escorting bombers, establishing air superiority deep in enemy territory, carrying out ground attack missions and intercepting enemy bombers. BFW, Focke-Wulf and Henschel submitted design proposals, but it was Willy Messerschmitt's sleek BFW Bf 110, which ignored the bombing requirement to concentrate on speed and cannon armament, that won out over the Fw 57 and the Hs 124. Powered by two Daimler Benz DB 600A engines, the Bf 110 V1 was first flown by Rudolf Opitz on 12 May 1936 and attained a speed of 314 mph, but the unreliability of its engines required a change to 680 hp Junkers Jumo 210Da engines when the pre-production Bf 110A-0 was completed in August 1937.

Although more sluggish than single-seat fighters, the Bf 110A-0 was fast for a twin-engine plane and its armament of four nose-mounted 7.9mm MG 17 machine guns and one flexible 7.9mm MG 15 gun aft was considered impressive. Prospective *Zerstörer* pilots were convinced that tactics could be devised to maximize its strengths and minimize its shortcomings, just as the British had done with the Bristol Fighter in 1917. The Bf 110B-1, which entered production in March 1938, was even more promising, with a more aerodynamically refined nose section housing a pair of 20mm MG FF cannon. Later in 1938 the 1,100 hp DB 601A-1 engine was finally certified for installation, and in late January 1939 the first Messerschmitt Me 110C-1s, powered by the DB 601A-1s and bearing a new prefix to mark Willy Messerschmitt's acquisition of BFW, entered service. By 1 September a total of 82 Me 110s were operating with *I(Z)./LG 1* and *I Gruppe, Zerstörergeschwader 1*, assigned to *Luftflotte 1*, and with *I./ZG 76*, attached to *Luftflotte 4* along the Polish/Czechoslovakian border.

Intensively trained for their multiple tasks, the *Zerstörer* pilots, like those flying the Stuka, had been indoctrinated to think of themselves as an elite force. Therefore the Me 110C-1 crewmen of the *2. Staffel* of *ZG 76* were as eager as Göring himself to see their mettle tested as they took off at 6 a.m. to escort *KG 4*'s He 111s. To the Germans' surprise and disappointment, however, they encountered no opposition over Kraków.

During the return flight *2./ZG 76*'s *Staffelführer, Oberleutnant* Wolfgang Falck, spotted a lone Heinkel He 46 army reconnaissance plane and flew down to offer it protection, only to be fired at by its nervous gunner. Minutes later Falck encountered another plane, which he identified as a PZL P.23 ground attack aircraft. Falck recalled:

> As I tried to gain some height he curved into the sun and as he did I caught a glimpse of red on his wing. As I turned into him I opened fire, but fortunately my marksmanship was no better than the reconnaissance gunner's had been, for as he banked to get away I saw it was a Stuka. I then realized that what I had thought was a red Polish insignia was actually a red E. I reported this immediately after landing and before long the coloured letters on wings of our aircraft were overpainted in black.

As the Stukas of *I./StG 2* were returning from their strike they passed over Balice airfield just as PZL fighters of the *III/2 Dywyzjon* (121st and 122nd *Eskadry*), attached to the Army of Kraków, were taking off. By sheer chance one of the Stuka pilots, *Leutnant* Frank Neubert, found himself in position to get a burst from his wing guns into the leading P.11c's cockpit, after which he reported that it 'suddenly exploded in mid-air, bursting apart like a huge fireball; the fragments literally flew around our ears'. Neubert's Stuka had scored the first air-to-air victory of World War II—and killed the commander of the *III/2 Dyon, Kapitan* Mieszyslaw Medwecki.

Medwecki's wingman, *Podporucznik* (Sub-Lieutenant) Wladyslaw Gnys of the 121st *Eskadra*, was more fortunate, managing to evade the bombs and bullets of the oncoming trio of Stukas and get clear of his beleaguered airfield. Minutes later he encountered two returning Do 17Es of *KG 77* over Olkusz and attacked. One went down in the village of Zurada, south of Olsusz, and Gnys was subsequently credited with the first Allied aerial victory of World War II. Shortly afterwards the wreckage of the other Do 17E was also found at Zurada and confirmed as Gnys' second victory.

In spite of the adverse weather that had spoilt its first missions, *Luftflotte 1* launched more bombing raids from East Prussia, including a probing attack on Okacie airfield outside Warsaw by 60 He 111Ps of *Lehrgeschwader 1* (Operational Training Wing 1), escorted by Me 110Cs of the wing's *I Zerstörergruppe (I(Z)./LG 1)*. As the Heinkels neared their target the Polish *Brygada Poscigowa* (Pursuit Brigade), on alert since dawn, was warned of the Germans' appoach by its observation posts and at 6.50 it ordered 30 PZL P.11s and P.7s of the 111th, 112th, 113th and 114th *Eskadry* up from their airfields at Zielnoka and Poniatów to intercept. Minutes later the Poles encountered scattered German formations and waded in, with *Kapral* Adrzej Niewara and *Porucznik* Aleksander Gabczewicz sharing in the destruction of the first He 111. Over the next hour the air battle took the form of numerous separate duels, during which *Kapitan* Adam Kowalczyk, commander of the *IV/I Dyon*, downed a Heinkel and *Porucznik* Hieronim Dudwal of the 113th *Eskadra* destroyed another.

The Me 110s pounced on the PZLs but the *Zerstörer* pilots found their nimble quarry to be most elusive targets. *Podporucznik* Jerzy Palusinski of the 111th *Eskadra* turned the tables on one of the *Zerstörer* and sent it out of the fight in a damaged state. Its wounded pilot was *Major* Walter Grabmann, a Spanish Civil War veteran of the *Legion Condor* and commander of *I(Z)./LG 1*.

In all, the Poles claimed six He 111s, while the German bombers were credited with four PZLs; their gunners had in fact brought down three. Once again Göring's vaunted *Zerstörer* crews returned to base empty-handed. When the Germans sent reconnaissance planes over the area to assess the bombing results at about noon, *Porucznik* Stefan Okrzejai of the 112th *Eskadra* caught one of the Do 17s and shot it down over the Warsaw suburbs.

As the weather improved *Luftflotte 1* struck again in even greater force as 200 German bombers attacked Okecie, Mokotow, Goclaw and bridges across the Vistula river. They were met by 30 P.11s and P.7s of the *Brygada Poscigowa*, which claimed two He 111Ps of *KG 27*, a Do 17 and a Ju 87 before the escorting Me 110Cs of *I(Z)./LG 1* descended on them. This time the *Zerstörer* finally drew blood, claiming five PZLs without loss. The Poles actually lost five of their elderly PZL P.7s. One Me 110 victim, *Porucznik* Feliks Szyszka, reported that the Germans attacked him as he parachuted to earth, putting seventeen bullets in his leg. The Me 110s also damaged the P.11c of Hieronim Dudwal, who landed with the fuselage just aft of the cockpit badly shot up. Two bare metal plates were crudely fixed in place over the damaged area but the plane was still not fully airworthy when the Germans overran his airfield.

For most of 1 September the Me 109s were confined to a defensive posture, save for a few strafing sorties. For the second bombing mission in the Warsaw area, however, *I Gruppe* of *JG 21* was ordered to take off from its forward field at Arys-Rostken and escort *KG 27*'s He 111s. The Me 109s rendezvoused with the bombers, only to be fired upon by their gunners. When the *Gruppenkommandeur*, *Hauptmann* Martin Mettig, tried to fire a recognition flare it malfunctioned, filling his cockpit with red and white fragments. Mettig, momentarily blinded and wounded in the hand and thigh, jettisoned his canopy—which broke off his radio mast—and turned back. Most of Mettig's pilots saw him head for base and, being unable to communicate with him by radio, they followed him. Only upon returning to their base did they learn what had happened.

Not all of the *Gruppe* had seen Mettig, however, and those pilots who continued the mission were rewarded by encountering a group of PZL fighters. In the wild dogfight that followed, the Germans claimed four of the P.11cs, including the first victory of an eventual 98 by *Leutnant* Gustav Rödel. The Poles claimed five Me 109s, including one each credited to *Podporuczniki* Jerzy Radomski and Jan Barowski of the 113th *Eskadra* and one to *Kapitan* Gustaw Sidorowicz of the 111th. *Podpolkovnik* (Lieutenant-Colonel) Leopold Pamula, already credited with an He 111P and a Ju 87B earlier that day, rammed one of the German fighters and then bailed out safely. *Porucznik* Gabszewicz was shot down by an Me 109 and, like Szyszka, subsequently claimed that the Germans had fired at him while he parachuted down.

In addition to challenging the waves of German bombers and escorts that would ultimately overwhelm them, PZL pilots took a toll on the army co-operation aircraft that were performing reconnaissance missions for the advancing panzer divisions. *Podporucznik* Waclaw S. Krol of the 121st *Eskadra* downed a Henschel Hs 126, while *Kapral* Jan Kremski shared in the destruction of another. After taking off on their second mission of the day to intercept a reported Do 17 formation at 3.21 p.m., *Porucznik* Marian Pisarek and *Kapral* Benedykt Mielczynski of the 141st *Eskadra* spotted an Hs 126, attacked it and sent it crashing to earth near Torun. Shortly afterwards two more P.11cs from a sister unit, the 142nd *Eskadra*, flew over the downed Henschel. One of the Poles, *Porucznik* Stanislaw Skalski, later described what occurred when he landed nearby to recover maps and other information from the cockpit:

The pilot, Friedrich Wimmer, was slightly wounded in the leg; his navigator, whose name was von Heymann, had nine bullets in his back and shoulder. I did what I could for them and stayed with them until an ambulance came. The prisoners were transferred to Warsaw. After the Soviet Union invaded Poland on 17 September, they became prisoners of the Russians, but were released at the end of October. When they were interrogated by the highest *Luftwaffe* authorities, Wimmer told them of my generosity. The Germans, who later learned that I had gone to Britain to fight on, said if I should became their prisoner, I would be honoured very highly.

The observer, von Heymann, died in 1988 . . . I tried to get in touch with the pilot for three years. The British air attaché and *Luftwaffe* archives helped me to contact Colonel Wimmer. I went to Bonn to meet him in March 1990, and the German ace Adolf Galland also came over at that time. In 1993, Polish television went with me, to make a film with Wimmer. Reporters asked why I did it—why I landed and helped the enemy, exposing my fighter and myself to enemy air attack. I was young, stupid and lucky. That is always my answer!

I came back late in the afternoon and I had to land on the road close to a forest—Torun aerodrome had been bombed already. I then gave Lt. Gen. W. Bortnowski, commander of the Pomeranian Army, the maps that I had captured from the Hs 126, which gave all the dispositions and attack plans of German divisions in Pomerania. He kissed me and said this was all the information his army needed.

On the following day Skalski came head-on at what he described as a 'cannon-armed' Do 17 in a circling formation of nine and shot it down, then claimed a second bomber minutes later. Dorniers were not armed with cannon but Me 110s were, and Skalski subsequently recalled that the Poles were completely unfamiliar with the *Zerstörer*—nobody had seen them in action until 1 September. Moreover, *I Gruppe* of *Zerstörergeschwader 1* lost an Me 110C-1 at that time, suggesting that Skalski was the first to destroy one of the twin-engine fighters in combat. Skalski's 'double' was the first of four and one shared victories with which he would be officially credited during the Polish campaign. Later flying with the Royal Air Force, he would bring his total up to $18^{11}/12$, making him the highest-scoring Polish ace of the war.

Although Poland was overrun in three weeks, its air force occasionally put up a magnificent fight, though its efforts were rendered inconsistent by poor communications and co-ordination. Polish fighters were credited with 129 aerial victories for the loss of 114 planes, and many of the pilots who scored them would fight on in the French *Armée de l'Air* and the Royal Air Force. The fall of Poland terminated the career of the PZL P.11c but only marked the beginning for the Me 110, which after a further run of success finally met its nemesis in the form of the Hurricane and Spitfire. Relegated to fighter-bomber and photo-reconnaissance duties after the Battle of Britain, the *Zerstörer* would undergo a remarkably productive revival as a night fighter.

Although France and Britain had let Hitler get away with his take-overs of Austria and Czechoslovakia, he overplayed his hand by invading Poland and by 3 September Germany found herself at war with both powers. Apart from an abortive French offensive into the Saar region, however, the armies on both sides of the Franco/German border spent months in a state of stalemate that was called the *Drôle de Guerre* by the French, the *Sitzkrieg* by the Germans and the Phoney War by the British. The opposing air arms were less shy about trading shots, however, and at 7.30 a.m. on 8 September a flight of six Curtiss H-75A Hawks of *Groupe de Chasse II/ 4*, led by *Adjudant-Chef* Cruchant, was on a mission to escort a reconnaissance plane over the Saar region when it came under heavy anti-aircraft fire and then was bounced by a four-plane *Schwarm* of Me 109E-1s. Using the superb manoeuvrability of their H-75As to advantage, the French managed to turn the tables on their attackers and claimed two of the Messerschmitts over Auterbahlscheidt—one jointly credited to Cruchant and *Adjudant* Pierre Villey and the other to Cruchant and *Sergent-Chef* Jean Casenobe.

The German protagonists in this first encounter over the Western Front were from *1. Staffel* of *JG 53* and in fact their only casualty occurred when the *Schwarmführer's* plane was hit in the engine and, as he tried to force-land in a field near Wölfersweiler, his wheels sank in the soft ground and his plane somersaulted on to its back. It took the combined effort of three burly farm labourers and members of a nearby *Flak* unit to free the pilot, *Oberleutnant* Werner Mölders, who had to spend the next few days in bed with a strained back.

On the same day two Me 109s on the German airfield at Saarbrücken were strafed by a Morane-Saulnier M.S.406 of *GC I/3*. Three more of the unit's M.S.406s attacked the same field on the following day, destroying several German planes on the ground, for which the French flight leader, *Lieutenant* Lacombe, was reprimanded by his superiors for having carried out an unauthorized mission. That marked the combat debut of France's principal indigenous fighter. Its precursor, the M.S.405, marked a departure from Morane-Saulnier's long line of parasol monoplanes when it was conceived in secret in 1934 and first flew on 8 August 1935. An improved version, the M.S.406, entered production on 8 February 1938 and went into service on 1 March 1939. Powered by an 860 hp Hispano-Suiza 12Y-31 V-12, liquid-cooled engine with a retractable ventral radiator, the M.S.406 had a maximum speed of 302 mph and was armed with a 20mm Hispano-Suiza HS-9 or HS 404 cannon firing through the propeller hub and two wing-mounted 7.5mm MAC 1934 machine guns. Most of the aeroplane was skinned with Plymax, a light alloy bonded to plywood, but the rear of the fuselage was fabric-covered. A total of 1,081 M.S.406s were built, and 1,074 had been delivered to ten *groupes de chasse* by 10 May 1940, making them the most numerous fighters in the *Armée de l'Air*. By then, however, the M.S.406 was seriously outclassed by its contemporaries, including the Curtiss H-75A, which a desperate France had ordered as a stop-gap measure until a better home-built successor, the Dewoitine D.520, became available.

After recovering from his minor back injury, Mölders eventually got his revenge—and his first victory of World War II—by downing one of two H-75As claimed by the Germans on 20 September. The French involved were from *GC II/ 5*—*Sergent* Péchaud force-landed near St Mihiel with 22 bullet holes in his plane while *Sergent* Quéquiner was shot down in flames and had to bail out, surviving with severe burns on his face and hands. *Sergent* André Legrand was credited with downing an Me 109 in the fight. On the following day Mölders was flying with *3./JG 53* when the *Staffel* became involved in the *Luftwaffe's* first air-to-air encounter with the M.S.406, which swiftly established the disparities between the two fighters. The lower wing loading and smooth responsiveness of the M.S.406 made it the more nimble of the two, but the Me 109E's perform-ance was superior in all other respects and the fight ended in the Germans' favour, with *Sergent* Baize of *GC I/3* falling victim to Mölders.

The M.S.406s scored their first victory the next day, 22 September, when air-craft of *GC III/2* brought down a Do 17, but on the same day one of the Moranes accidentally landed in German territory at Ensheim. The pilot had no time to destroy his plane, but French artillery was in range and did the job for him.

Another thirteen M.S.406s would be lost before the Germans launched their offensive in the West, though the Messerschmitts did not have things entirely their own way. In a long dogfight between seven fighters of *GC II/7* and nine Me 109Es of *I/JG 52* near Toul on 21 November, the M.S.406 pilots used their aircraft's manoeuvrability to maximum advantage, scoring two victories and one 'probable' without loss. *Groupe de Chasse II/6* repeated the feat on the following day, its M.S.406 pilots claiming four Me 109Es over Rémering-les-Puttelange and Wörth with shares in the destruction of two each going to future aces *Sous-Lieutenants* Léon Cuffaut (thirteen victories) and Émile Thierry (six). The cannier Messerschmitt pilots soon learned not to let themselves be enticed into traditional turning engagements with M.S.406s, however, and although the Morane-Saulnier pilots would claim a grand total of 191 confirmed victories and 93 'probables'—figures not borne out by German loss records—about 150 M.S.406s were lost in aerial combat and another 100 on the ground by the time France capitulated on 18 June 1940.

When the Germans finally launched their offensive in the West on 10 May 1940, two powerful new Allied fighters were ready to stand in their way, though there were not enough of either to do so for long. When the prototype of the Dutch-built Fokker G.I twin-engine fighter was first unveiled at the 1936 Paris Salon it caused a sensation. A twin-boom heavy fighter with a central nacelle that could be modified to fulfil a variety of tasks, the G.I made its first flight on 16 March 1937 and entered service with the Royal Netherlands Air Force in May 1938. The G.IA, powered by two 830 hp Bristol Mercury VIII 9-cylinder radial engines, had no fewer than eight 7.9mm FN-Browning M36 machine guns in the nose of the nacelle as well as a ninth gun in a rotating tail cone, in addition to which it could carry an internal bomb load of 880 pounds. The G.IB, twelve of which had been intended for use by the Spanish Republican forces before the Dutch government placed an embargo on their export, was powered by two 750 hp Pratt & Whitney R-1595-SB4-G Twin Wasp Junior 14-cylinder radials and had a nose armament of two 23mm Madsen cannon and two 7.9mm FN-Brownings.

The first duty of Dutch aircraft during the first months of the war was to guard the country's neutrality, and it was in that pursuit that the Fokker G.I first fired its guns in anger. At 11.05 during the night of 27 March 1940 Armstrong Whitworth Whitley Mk V N1357, call sign KN-H of No 77 Squadron, departed from Driffield on a nocturnal reconnaissance mission but later strayed into Dutch airspace and came under attack at 5.30 a.m. by a Fokker G.IA piloted by First Lieutenant P. Noomen of the *3e JachtVleigtuig Afdeling*. Set on fire, the Whitley came down on the Vondelingenweg at Pernis, the dock area of Rotterdam. The bomber's observer, Sergeant J. E. Miller, was killed and is believed to have fallen from the plane seconds before it crashed. The rest of the crew, Flying Officers T. J. Geach and W. P. Copinger, Leading Airman S. E. E. Caplin and Airman Second Class R. B. Barrie, were interned, but they were soon released and returned to Driffield by the Dutch, who may have little suspected that the unwelcome intruders Noomen had intercepted would be his allies just seven weeks later.

A total of 23 serviceable Fokker G.IAs and G.IBs were available to the Dutch—eleven with the *3e JaVA* at Waalhaven and twelve with the *4e JaVA* at Bergen—when the Germans invaded. At 3.50 p.m. on 10 May He 111s of *KG 4* carried out a surprise attack on Waalhaven and only two of *3e JaVA*'s G.IAs managed to get off the runway. One of them, No 311, was flown by Lieutenant Gerben Sonderman, an experienced G.I test pilot, and he quickly shot down the He 111 piloted by *Oberst* Martin Fiebig, a *Gruppenkommandeur*, who crashlanded and was taken prisoner, along with his crew, by troops of a nearby Dutch coastal battery. The other G.IA, No 312, flown by Lieutenant Noomen, brought down two more Heinkels before landing with one dead engine and two punctured fuel tanks.

Waalhaven airfield had been damaged and three of its G.IAs destroyed on the ground, but by 4 a.m. the runway had been sufficienty repaired and cleared for Lieutenant Jan Pieter Kuipers to scramble up in G.IA 302 and engage a second wave of attacking bombers. He had to abort his first attack when his radio operator, J. Venema, reported three German aircraft approaching from behind and to the left. Kuipers made a climbing turn to the left, found himself behind three He 111s and opened fire at 200 metres' distance.

The enemy gunners immediately responded [he reported]. The combat offered a fascinating spectacle: all the bullets that the antagonists served up were tracers. My first reaction had to be to try to put the machine-gunners out of action. For that effect, I fired successively on all three aeroplanes. During that action, the distance between the squadron and me finally came down to 25 to 50 metres.

As we flew over Rotterdam (Charlois quarter), the squadron turned south, all maintaining a tight formation. South-west of Waalhaven aeroport, the first bomber was finally forced to land on its belly east of Pernis; another Heinkel went into a pronounced turn and fell into a dive. I would not observe the result further because I had already thrown myself into the purusit of the third machine. However, my Fokker had not left the fight without harm, and at a given moment my left motor's power diminished and then it stopped completely. Force to make a half turn, it was only with great effort that I succeeded in landing at Waalhaven aeroport.

It was 4.10 as Kuipers and Venema scrambled out of their disabled plane and joined the ground forces defending the airfield. Kuipers assisted an anti-aircraft section at the north-east part of the field until Ju 88As of *KG 30* attacked them so vigorously that he was forced to take cover in a crater, miraculously emerging unhurt. Most of the anti-aircraft gunners were less fortunate. Only after the war did Kuipers learn that Venema was among those killed in the attack.

At that point German paratroopers were descending on Waalhaven, but Fokker G.IA No 311 had been refuelled and re-armed and it took off along with aircraft Nos 328 and 329, 315 and 319. G.IA 315 was already suffering from bomb damage, so its pilot simply flew to De Kooy airfield near Den Helder for temporary repairs. Aircraft No 319, piloted by Sergeant Jan Buwalda, had made its way to the far end of the cratered runway when he saw three unidentified single-engine planes approaching while the Dutch anti-aircraft gunners, equally uncertain of their nationality, held their fire. Then the trio—which turned out to be Me 109Es—began strafing the field. Throttling up his engine and slaloming between barrages of cannon shells and machine-gun bullets, Buwalda managed to get his plane airborne. As he fought for altitude his gunner, Sergeant Wagner, noticed German bombers coming, while two kilometres to the left flights of Junkers Ju 52/3ms were dropping paratroopers over the airfield:

The Germans destroyed Waalhaven aerodrome to assure their airborne operation [Buwalda recalled]. It was 4.00 in the morning, and, as the bombardment reached its paroxism, I succeeded in taking off and found myself in the middle of a packet of bombers flying at 150 metres. In my first attack, I downed a Heinkel . . . then I saw another and I got on his tail, my eight machine guns spitting three short volleys at a distance of 100 metres.

Buwalda was credited with the second plane, a Dornier Do 215, but then he came under attack by twelve Me 109Es. He dived with the enemy in pursuit, his gunner firing at each in turn, allegedly causing one to explode in the air and shooting down a second. 'Then they fired at us from above,' Buwalda said, 'hitting both motors and forcing me to the ground. I was unhurt, but Sergeant Wagner was wounded . . . my war had not lasted five minutes.'

The other three Fokkers fared somewhat better. Sonderman in No 311 claimed a Ju 52 and two fighters, bringing his score up to four in two sorties in less than an hour. Sergeant H. F. Soufrée in G.IA 328 claimed an He 111 and an Me 109E, while Lieutenant K. W. Woudenberg in 329 claimed a Junkers Ju 87B and a Ju 52. Unable to return to Waalhaven, the three planes landed on the beach near Oostvoorne, where they were hurriedly camouflaged. Amid the confusion of the German offensive, however, it was not until the morning of 14 May that Soufrée and his gunner, Sergeant J. C. de Man, managed to return to the beach with fuel, oil, ammunition and ground personnel for the three G.Is—only to discover that they had been strafed and set afire by Me 109Es just half an hour earlier.

At Bergen the *Luftwaffe* found all twelve Fokker G.IAs of the *4e JaVA* parked wing tip to wing tip when they attacked at 3.59 a.m. One Fokker was destroyed and ten damaged, leaving only aircraft No 321 to take off, with Lieutenant J. W. Thijsse at the controls, to intercept the next wave of bombers. As he did, however, he came under fire not only from enemy fighters but from Dutch anti-aircraft gunners, who were already assuming that anything in the air had to be German. Thijsse therefore gave up the idea of fighting and sought a safe haven at Schipol airfield—only to find it in flames. He then headed for the beach at Katvijk, where he found three newly landed Ju 52/3ms, which he strafed and set afire. After reconnoitring Ypernberg and Schipol airfields, he opted to return to Bergen, which was having a momentary respite from German attack, and landed at 6.20.

Considering the circumstances, the Fokker G.Is—of the *3e JaVA*, at least— gave an extraordinarily good account of themselves, shooting down not less than a dozen German aircraft in their first chaotic two hours of combat. Heavily armed and easy to fly, though too slow to compete with single-engine fighters, the G.IA had lived up to its nickname of *Le Faucheur* (The Grim Reaper), but it would only have four more days in which to fight before the Netherlands were overrun. After that, most surviving G.Is became part of a growing trove of war booty, to serve the Germans as trainers for their twin-engine fighter pilots.

Although numerically better prepared than Belgium or the Netherlands, by 1940 France found most of her fighters to be outclassed by the *Luftwaffe*'s Messerschmitt Me 109Es. In addition to the outdated M.S.406, the French had five *groupes de chasse* equipped with the Bloch M.B.152 on 10 May 1940, while another three groups were in the process of re-equipping with that new fighter. Originally conceived by Maurice Roussel in 1935 and developed as a private venture until finally accepted by the *Armée de l'Air*, the Bloch M.B.152 was powered by a 1,080 hp Gnome-Rhône 14N49 radial engine which gave it a maximum speed of 310 mph at 18,045 feet. The plane was powerfully armed with two 7.5mm machine guns and two 20mm HS 404 cannon mounted in the wings, though its first action was less than conclusive: on 13 May *Capitaine* Germain Coutaud and three of his pilots of *1e Escadrille, GC I/1*, claimed a Do 215 near Namur, only to have it counted as a 'probable'. Subsequent encounters with enemy fighters proved to be another matter, as one M.B.152 pilot, Pierre Courteville of *GC II/9*, later recalled:

> From our first mêlées with the Messerschmitt Me 109Es we were aware that our Bloch 152s needed two or three hundred more horsepower. Our opponent was faster and could outclimb us, and we had good cause to be grateful for the Bloch 152's small turning radius and ability to accept heavy punishment. Many a Bloch fighter staggered back to its airfield full of holes but with its pilot unscathed. We frequently complained to the Gnome-Rhône technical staff attached to our *groupe de chasse* that their 14N49 engine, admittedly reliable, was giving us insufficient power, but their answer was invariably the same: 'Just wait until the 14R engine comes along and then you will see something!'

Unfortunately for Courteville and his squadron colleagues, they could no longer wait.

It was a sad commentary on the state of France's military aircraft development that the best fighter available to the French at the start of 1940 was the Curtiss H-75A—ironically, imported from the United States, which in the previous war had had to purchase her fighters from France—and that too was outperformed by the Messerschmitt in all respects save manoeuvrability. The great exception was the Dewoitine D.520, an outstanding little fighter for its time but, unfortunately for France, a case of almost too late and decidedly too little.

Emile Dewoitine had built an innovative line of monoplane fighters with fixed undercarriages during the early 1930s, but in June 1936 he set up a new design bureau, headed by Robert Castello, with the intention of creating a new fighter with retractable landing gear to use the 900 hp Hispano-Suiza 12Y-21 engine to achieve a speed of 500 kph (311 mph). When the *Armée de l'Air* rejected his design following an upgraded speed specification of 520 kph (323 mph), Castello and staff redesigned the plane with a reduced wing span and an airframe to accommodate a newer 1,200 hp engine expected from Hispano-Suiza. Designated D.520 (in reference to the speed requirement), the new fighter was rejected in favour of the already chosen M.S.406, but Dewoitine perservered, building two prototypes at his own expense, and finally obtained a government contract on 3 April 1938. The D.520.01 prototype first flew on 2 October 1938, with Marcel Doret at the controls, and, after being modified with a single central radiator in place of the original twin underwing radiators, a new HS 12Y-29 engine and a three-blade metal propeller in place of the original two-blade, wooden one, it satisfied the speed requirement. After further alterations, the French authorities—who were at last coming to the realization that the quality of their fighter force was falling dangerously behind that of Britain and Germany—placed an order for 200 D.520s in April 1939.

The first production D.520, powered by an 850 hp HS 12Y-45 engine for a maximum speed of 332 mph and armed with one hub-firing 20mm HS 404 cannon and four wing-mounted 7.5mm MAC 1934 machine guns, did not fly until November 1939. The tempo of production rose slowly but steadily from there, and by 10 May 1940 36 D.520s were on the strength of *Groupe de Chasse I/3* at Cannes-Mandélieu, while *GC II/3*, *GC II/7* and *GC III/3* were engaged in conversion training in the new type. With the start of the German offensive, *GC I/3* was hastily moved to Wez-Thuisy in the Second Army's sector.

The D.520's first day of battle, 13 May, went encouragingly well. *Sous-Lieutenant* Georges Blanck was leading *Adjudant* Vinchon and *Sergent* Rigalleau on a mission to escort some Lioré-et-Olivier (LeO) 45 bombers when they encountered an Hs 126 and shot it down near Bras-de-la-Semois. *GC I/3*'s pilots claimed another two Hs 126s and an He 111 without loss that day. On 14 May the *groupe* fought over Sedan, downing four Me 110s, two Me 109s, two Do 17s and two He 111s for the loss of two pilots killed. Among the victorious pilots that day was *Sous-Lieutenant* Michel Madon, who downed an Me 110 over Brinon, and *Sergent* Marcel Albert, who teamed up with an M.S.406 pilot to bring down a Do 17 north of Suippes. Both Madon and Albert would become aces, Albert eventually flying Yakovlev fighters with the Normandie Regiment on the Eastern Front to become the leading French fighter pilot of the war, with a total of 23 victories. Blanck scored again on 15 May, sharing in the destruction of an Me 109 near Hastière á Meuse and then downing an He 111 northeast of Reims, while *Sous-Lieutenant* Émile Thierry accounted for a Do 17 north of Reims. On 17 May, however, the *Luftwaffe* struck back, attacking Wez-Thuisy in force and destroying seven D.520s on the ground, after which *GC I/3* was withdrawn to Meaux-Esbly.

GC II/3, based at Bouillancy, entered the fighting on 21 May, joined by *GC II/7* and *GC III/3* in June. At Le Luc airfield in southern France *GC III/6* received its first D.520 on 10 June—the day on which Italy declared war and invaded southern France. The unit put up a brief but creditable resistance, *Adjudant* Pierre Le Gloan of *GC III/6*'s *5ème Escadrille* adding three Fiat C.R.42s and three Fiat B.R.20s to the four German aircraft he had previously downed while flying M.S.406s.

A total of 437 D.520s had rolled off Dewoitine's assembly line at Toulouse by 25 June—demonstrating how much inertia can be overcome by a national emergency—but by then France had capitulated. The D.520s went on to curious careers in the wake of the Armistice, actively serving in such Axis air arms as Italy's, Romania's, Bulgaria's and that of Vichy France itself, engaging the

Royal Air Force over the Levant in 1941 and the US Navy and Army Air Forces over North Africa in 1942. The fortunes of the surviving D.520s would come full circle in the summer of 1944 as airmen of the *Forces Françaises de l'Interieur* formed their first fighter unit, commanded by former Dewoitine test pilot Marcel Doret, to participate in the liberation of their country.

One other fighter was produced by a country that had to face German invasion—Yugoslavia, which, after young officers overthrew her pro-Axis government on 27 March 1941 and refused to allow German troops through her territory to assist the Italians in their stalled invasion of Greece, became the target of *Unternehmen Strafgericht* (Operation 'Punishment') on the orders of an enraged Hitler on 6 April. Among the aircraft thrown up by the Royal Yugoslav Air Force (*Jugoslavensko Kraljevsko Ratno Vazduhoplovstvo*, or JKRV) during the brief but spirited struggle was the indigenously built IK-3.

The IK-3 was the brainchild of three engineers—Ljubomir Ilic, Kosta Sivcev and Slobodan Zrnic. Ilic was attending the national high school of aeronautics in Paris when he conceived of a new fighter to replace the Czechoslovakian-built Avia BH-33E, then the mainstay of the JKRV. At the same time he met Kosta Sivcev, a pilot and engineer who was then working with the Bréguet and Hispano-Suiza firms. The two friends returned to Yugoslavia in 1931 and, after overcoming scepticism at Air Force Headquarters, they got permission to build the IK-01, a high-wing monoplane with fixed, spatted undercarriage and a fully enclosed cockpit, powered by an 860 hp Hispano-Suiza 12Y-Crs engine and armed with one 20mm cannon firing through the propeller hub and two 7.9mm machine guns in the front upper fuselage. After assembly at the Ikarus factory in Zemun, the prototype flew for the first time on 24 April 1934 but crashed on its third flight. A new prototype, the IK-02, with wings covered with duralumin instead of fabric, was completed in June 1936 and displayed very good performance, with a maximum speed of 435 kph—15 kph higher than originally planned. During comparative tests held between 14 and 24 June 1937, the IK-02 proved not only to be faster than the Hawker Fury Mk I but to be more agile and to have a better rate of climb. Twelve IK-2s were produced, and seven were still operational in April 1941.

While they were working on the IK-01 in 1933 Ilic and Sivcev started on a new project. This time it would be a streamlined, low-wing aircraft with retractable landing gear and enough speed and power to intercept the latest generation of bombers. That project was also started as a private venture, when Slobodan Zrnic-Zrle, chief of the construction bureau of the aeroplane factory at Kraljevo, joined the team. Ilic worked on aerodynamic calculation, Sivcev on equipment, tail surfaces and ailerons and Zrnic on the airframe and engine installation.

The new aircraft was designated IK-3, again according to the first letters of the constructors' names—'3' standing in for the 'Z' in Cyrillic script, but later being transformed to the number '3' as a serial mark. Powered by a 980 hp Hispano-Suiza 12Y-29 engine, the prototype was completed in the Rogozarski factory in Belgrade, and after test-flying it in May 1938 Captain Milan Bjelanovic stated that the plane was very manoeuvrable and the control efficiency very good in all respects. Maximum speed was 527 kph, and the aircraft could climb to 5,000 metres in seven minutes. Armament comprised one Oerlikon 20mm cannon firing through the propeller hub and two 7.9mm Browning/FN machine guns in the upper front fuselage. Eighteen production IK-3s had been delivered by the end of July 1940. Rogozarski planned to produce 48 IK-3s in 1941 and 1942, but 25 aircraft were still under construction when the Germans struck.

Air raid sirens awoke Belgrade on the early morning of Sunday 6 April 1941, and at 6.50 the first German bombers flew over the capital. Outside the city at Zemun airport, less than ten minutes after the alert was sounded, sixteen fighters of the 51st *Grupa*, 6th *Istrebitelski Puk* (Fighter Wing), took off—six IK-3s of the 161st and 162nd *Eskadrili* leading ten German-built Messerschmitt Me 109E-3s of the 102nd *Eskadril*.

After taking off, the formation scattered in pairs and intercepted the Germans just as the latter arrived over Belgrade. *Potporucik* (Second Lieutenant) Dusan Borcic of the 161st *Eskadril* and his wingman, *Potporucik* Eduard Bamfic, separated over Senhak, one plane heading toward Romania while the second continued towards the old fortress at Kalamegdan. When Borcic reached an altitude of about 4,000 metres a formation of eighteen Do 17Zs appeared to the north. He turned his aircraft and closed on them from the rear. When he opened fire with his cannon and two machine guns the nearest German bomber shook, fell out of formation and plunged down to the banks of the Danube river, where it exploded.

Having scored the first aerial victory for the JKRV, Borcic continued flying north, where more German bombers were coming from Hungary. His IK-3 plunged head-on into the enemy formation but was soon caught by escorting Messerschmitt fighters in what the Yugoslavs called the 'Devil's Circle'. Borcic's short-lived moment of glory ended as his crippled IK-3 crashed on Sarajevska Street. Meanwhile his wingman, Bamfic, had been wounded and his plane damaged in a fight above the village of Batajnica. Bamfic broke off the action and tried to land but was attacked by two Me 109s, and although he evaded them for a while by a series of steep, banking turns, during which his wing tips almost touched the ground, he finally crash-landed on the airfield. His IK-3 was completely demolished, but Bamfic survived.

Kapetan (Captain) Sava Poljanec, commander of the 161st *Eskadril,* lost his wing-man, *Podnarednik* (Sergeant) Dusan Vujicic when the latter suffered engine problems. Climbing alone to 4,000 metres, Poljanec dived at a German formation he spotted over the village of Krnjaca, set the left engine of a German bomber on fire and saw the plane go down into the Pancevacki Rit. Its crew survived, to be taken prisoner. At that moment tracers shot past Poljanec's cockpit as about twenty yellow-nosed Me 109Es dived towards him. Poljanec, a flight instructor and one of the three best aerobatic pilots in Yugoslavia at that time, rolled and spun his aircraft but soon was caught in a Devil's Circle. One Messerschmitt made the mistake of passing in front of the IK-3, and Poljanec discharged his machine guns into it. Glycol vapour began trailing from the Me 109's fuselage as it fell into an erratic dive, suggesting that the pilot was dead. Poljanec tried to land at Zemun but his IK-3 was hit again, this time by an Me 110 that had been strafing the airfield. Upon landing, Poljanec jumped from the cockpit of his smoking plane. The Me 110 was chased away by *Podnarednik* Sava Vujovic of the 101st *Eskadril.*

In spite of the prominent yellow markings employed to distinguish them from their Yugoslav counterparts, German Me 109s were understandably reticent about engaging Yugoslav Messerschmitts; on the other hand, the IK-3s tended to attract their undivided attention. After another air battle with 100 German attackers at 10 a.m., *Major* Adum Romeo was relieved of command of the 162nd *Eskadril* by his brigade commander for insufficient air activity in the face of the enemy and replaced by *Kapetan* Todor Gogic. As another wave of 37 Ju 87B and 30 Me 109 attackers came on at 2 p.m., Gogic and *Podporucik* Veljko Vujicic attacked a Stuka formation, shot down one of the aircraft, then used up their fuel and ammunition in a fight with the escorting Messerschmitts before returning to base. A third IK-3, flown by *Podnarednik* Milislav Semiz, also downed a Ju 87 that day—the first of four victories credited to him in seventeen sorties before the brief campaign was over.

German bombers mounted a total of 484 sorties in four waves over Belgrade alone in the course of 6 April, and small groups or single bombers continued to make nuisance raids in the evening. According to the 6th *Puk*'s commander, *Potpukovnik* (Lieutenant-Colonel) Bozidar Kostic, a total of ten German aircraft were downed by pilots of the 51st *Grupa* on that first day. The Germans themselves recorded the loss of two Do 17s from *8./KG 3,* four Ju 87s of *II./StG 77,* one Me 109 of *Stab./JG 54* and five Me 110s of *I./ZG 26* in combat, as well as a sixth Me 110 that crashed on landing. Determining the Germans' claims over IK-3s is handicapped by their unfamiliarity with the fighter, which bore a superficial resemblance to the Hurricanes with which the Yugoslavs were also equipped, but a claim over a 'Dewoitine' by *Oberfeldwebel* Erwin Riehl of *III./JG 77* is one likely candidate.

German raids continued on 7 April, but with significantly smaller bombing formations. The Yugoslav fighters attacked in larger groups, breaking up formations and downing a substantial number of German aircraft, but their own losses were also heavy due to increased enemy fighter activity over Belgrade.

The old IK-2s also became involved in the fighting at 2 p.m. on 9 April 1941 when 27 Me 109Es of *III./JG 54* struck at the 4th *Puk*'s airfield at Nova Topola. *Podnarednik* Branko Jovanovic was landing when he came under attack by nine Me 109s, but he evaded them by pulling his IK-2 into a steep turn. Five of the 107th *Eskadril*'s IK-2s joined six Hurricanes taking off to defend the airfield, during which *Podnarednik* Zivorad Tomic claimed an Me 109, while *Kapetan* Dragisa Miljevic, commander of the Hurricane-equipped 106th *Eskadril*, claimed a 'probable' before being killed. One IK-2 and two Hurricanes were shot down, while a second IK-2, its pilot wounded, crash-landed. *Leutnant* Erwin Leykauf was credited with a Hurricane in the fight, while *Oberleutnante* Hans-Ekkehard Bob and Gerhard Koall of *9./JG 54* were credited with the IK-2s. Tomic's victim, *Gefreiter* F. Fabian, was listed as missing by *9./JG 54*, but he had survived and he re-joined the unit a few days later.

After several days of attrition, the remaining fighters of the 51st and 32nd Fighter Groups (three IK-3s and eleven Me 109Es) flew to the auxiliary airfield at Veliki Radinci near Ruma where they were burned on the night of 11 April to prevent their falling into German hands. Some of the remaining IK-2s were destroyed by their crews prior to the retreat, while three planes were captured by the Germans, who later turned them over to the air arm of the *Nezavisna Drzava Hrvatska* (Independent State of Croatia).

The German occupation of Yugoslavia did not bring an end to the story of the best pre-war Yugoslav aircraft. Blueprints for the IK-3 spent the war carefully hidden under the floor of Slobodan Zrnic's house in Belgrade. After the war relations between Yugoslavia and the Soviet Union gradually deteriorated because of Marshal Yosip Broz Tito's constant refusal to be under Josef Stalin's 'protection'. In 1948 the dispute culminated in Yugoslavia being under an economic blockade by all Socialist countries, and the design team of Ilic, Sivcev and Zrnic found themselves in business again. They built the Model 211 and 212 trainers, as well as the S-49A fighter, a direct modification of the IK-3. Forty-five of those fighters were produced, followed by 130 of the more powerful S-49C fighter-bomber, which would serve the Yugoslav Air Force until 1965.

Chapter 8

THE IMMORTALS

Hawker Hurricane and Supermarine Spitfire, 1939–1940

Britain was still in the process of modernizing her Royal Air Force when Germany invaded Poland on 1 September 1939, and nowhere was this transitional state more evident than in its fighter squadrons. Some still had the Gloster Gladiator, a biplane with fixed landing gear, on which the only concessions to modernity were an enclosed cockpit and a pair of extra guns that looked as though they had been stuck under the wings as an afterthought. A few squadrons, in marked contrast, had equipped with the new Vickers Supermarine Spitfire Mk I, a sleek, shapely thoroughbred with landing gear that retracted into remarkably thin wings for a cantilever monoplane. In between those extremes of old and new, filling out the majority of RAF squadrons, was the Hawker Hurricane Mk I.

The Hurricane's designer, Sydney Camm, had been a believer in monoplanes since he joined Harry G. Hawker's engineering company as a draughtsman in 1923. The RAF did not agree. Ever since the bad experiences that No 60 Squadron RFC had had with the Morane-Saulnier N in 1916, the senior officers of Britain's air arms had been set against monoplanes as a matter of principle. Consequently, after becoming Hawker's chief aircraft designer in 1925 Camm dutifully produced a series of high-quality single- and two-seat biplanes, with names like Fury, Hornet, Audax and Hotspur.

By 1933 Camm was so convinced that the biplane fighter had reached the logical zenith of its performance that he began conceiving a 'Fury monoplane'. At about that same time, at Vickers Aviation's Supermarine subsidiary, Reginald J. Mitchell was coming to the same conclusion and began working on a fighter based on his experience with a highly successful series of seaplane racers. On 30 January of that fateful year Adolf Hitler was elected Chancellor of Germany. Following the consolidation of his National Socialist Workers' Party in power, Hitler formally withdrew from the Disarmament Conference on 14 October and took Germany out of the League of Nations the following week.

If the prospect of German rearmament were not enough to stir the RAF's air marshals into reconsidering their prejudices against monoplanes, the fact that Hawker's Hart light bomber could outpace most fighters should have. Even so, Camm's and Mitchell's efforts over the next few years remained private ventures. Mitchell entered a monoplane with fixed, trousered landing gear and powered by a 660 hp Rolls-Royce Goshawk engine, the Type 224, in a fighter competition to satisfy the RAF's F.7/30 Specification, but it failed to find favour, the production contract ultimately going to the Gladiator biplane.

Meanwhile Camm forged ahead with his 'Fury monoplane,' later called simply the 'Monoplane Interceptor'. Rolls-Royce's new 900 hp PV12 engine was substituted for the Goshawk, its extra weight requiring the underwing radiator to be moved back to compensate. In so doing, Camm found room under the front of the thick cantilever wing for inward-retracting landing gear. Expecting higher speeds from his design, he also added a glazed sliding canopy for the pilot. By then, only the shape of the nose and tail surfaces remained to hint at the fighter's Hart and Fury ancestry.

During discussions on armament at the Air Ministry, Squadron Leader Ralph Sorley, a member of its Operational Requirement Branch, suggested that a monoplane would be capable of such speeds that a pilot would only be able to keep a bomber in his sights for two seconds and that an armament of eight guns would be necessary to bring the enemy down. Although Air Chief Marshal Sir Robert Brooke-Popham, commander of Britain's air defences, thought that 'eight guns was going a bit far', early in 1935 the Air Ministry at last issued a specification, F.5/34, for a monoplane fighter capable of a speed of 275 mph at 15,000 feet and of mounting eight 0.303-inch machine guns.

As far as Camm and Mitchell were concerned, the RAF had finally caught up with them. In fact, they were both so confident of exceeding the specification's expectations that the Air Ministry accommodated them by issuing a revised Specification F.36/34, raising the speed requirement from 275 to 330 mph.

Even before Camm submitted his plans to the Air Ministry on 4 September 1934 and displayed a wooden mock-up at Kingston on 10 January 1935, he had been optimistically forging ahead with his 'high-speed monoplane'. Consequently he was ready when the Air Ministry finally gave him an official contract on 12 February. On 6 November Flight Lieutenant P. W. S. Bulman took the prototype, K5083, for its first flight from Brooklands Aerodrome. After further flight-testing at Martlesham Heath, the RAF ordered 600 of the new fighter on 3 June 1936, officially christening it 'Hurricane' on 27 June. The first production Hurricane, L1547, flew on 12 October, and fifteen months later No 111 Squadron became the first RAF unit to be equipped exclusively with a monoplane fighter since 1916.

While the Hurricane and Spitfire were undergoing acceptance trials at Martlesham Heath, a visiting RAF group captain described them in memorable fashion. Passing a Spitfire, he remarked, 'There's a racehorse for you.' Then, as he approached a Hurricane, he declared, 'That's more like an aeroplane.'

The more sophisticated Spitfire may have been the better performer of the two, but the Hurricane's simpler construction allowed it to be mass-produced in greater quantities at a time when Britain had a lot of catching up to do. The thin wing that Mitchell had designed for the Spitfire was an aerodynamic marvel that proved capable of handling speeds approaching the sound barrier, but its distinctive elliptical shape, described by more than one pilot as the most graceful thing in the world with the possible exception of a nice pair of feminine legs, only served to complicate the manufacturing process. Consequently, by the time Britain declared war on Germany on 3 September 1939 she had a total of seventeen fully equipped Hurricane squadrons compared to nine equipped with the Spitfire.

Few military aircraft can be said to have had more embarrassing combat debuts than the Hurricane and Spitfire. Given the precedent set during World War I, the British were not unjustified in expecting German bombers to strike at their cities within hours of the declaration of the new war. Squadrons were put on alert and false alarms led to numerous abortive interception flights.

Then, on 6 September, two flights of Spitfires from No 74 (Trinidad) Squadron—'A' Flight, led by Flight Lieutenant Adolph Gysbert Malan, and 'B' Flight, under Flight Lieutenant W. P. F. Treacy—took off from the unit's base at Hornchurch, Essex, to intercept enemy aircraft reported to be moving up the Thames Estuary. Radar had detected the intruders, and soon afterwards anti-aircraft guns at Clacton reported that they were firing at enemy twin-engine bombers, one of which had been shot down.

With Malan in the lead, the two Spitfire flights sighted an oncoming fighter formation and rapidly closed to engage. Suddenly Malan realized that the approaching aircraft were not German and immediately turned away. Not all of his pilots followed his lead, however: Flying Officers Paddy Byrne and John Connell Freeborn opened fire and saw their two targets go down. After landing, the entire squadron was horrified to find their suspicions confirmed. Their 'opponents' had been Hurricanes of No 56 (Punjab) Squadron, which had taken off from North Weald to intercept the same imaginary enemy force that had brought No 74 Squadron on the scene.

It took almost an hour to sort everything out, but the final, sobering realization was that no German aircraft had come near the Thames Estuary that day. The origin of the 'Battle of Barking Creek', as it came to be called, lay with the Chain Home radar station at Canwedon near Southend, which had received echoes from aircraft to the west and, failing to filter them out, got the impression that aircraft were approaching from the east. As more and more British aircraft scrambled up to meet the reported threat, their echoes added to the confusion, making the supposed enemy force seem to grow progressively larger. As word of the attack spread and became fixed in the mind of the defenders, a case of mistaken identity, followed by the first shot from a trigger-happy anti-aircraft gunner that would set off a chain reaction of shooting from the ground and air, became inevitable. The whole affair would have been comical had it not been for the loss of a Bristol Blenheim of No 64 Squadron to the anti-aircraft gunners and the destruction of two of No 56 Squadron's Hurricanes and the death of one of their pilots, Pilot Officer Halton-Harrop, at the hands of the Spitfires.

Byrne and Freeborn were subsequently court-martialled but both were acquitted. A court of inquiry ultimately determined that the solution to such tragedies in future would be the development of Identification Friend or Foe (IFF) radar equipment for the aircraft, the production and installation of which was given highest priority.

Johnny Freeborn would later redeem himself during the Battle of Britain, shooting down eleven German aircraft and sharing in the destruction of two more. Paddy Byrne's misfortunes were not over, however. Leading a section of Malan's flight during a sortie over Dunkirk on 21 May 1940, he was downed by anti-aircraft fire, wounded in the leg and taken prisoner by the Germans. Byrne made several escape attempts—including the 'Great Escape' from *Stalag Luft III* on 24 March 1944—but was repeatedly recaptured and in the end was lucky just to have survived the war.

Both of RAF Fighter Command's principal weapons had got off to an inauspicious start, and were sorely in need of redemption. The opportunity would not be long in coming.

In spite of the Hurricanes' having been sent to France early on, where they would be closer to potential action, it was the stay-at-home Spitfires that would draw first blood from the *Luftwaffe*. On 16 October nine Junkers Ju 88A-1s of *I Gruppe, Kampfgeschwader 30*, led by *Hauptmann* Helmut C. W. Pohle, left their base at Westerland on the island of Sylt with orders to attack British warships in the Firth of Forth. Their principal victim was to be the battlecruiser *Hood*, which was reported to have been there, but only if she were in open waters; in that early stage of the war, the *Luftwaffe* High Command wanted to avoid inflicting civilian casualties.

The Germans did not expect serious opposition since their intelligence had stated that only obsolescent Gladiators had been committed to Scotland's defence. Unknown to them, a flight of Spitfires of No 602 (City of Glasgow) Squadron, Auxiliary Air Force, had arrived at Drem on 13 October. Nor could the Germans have known that a section from No 603 (City of Edinburgh) Squadron was refuelling at Turnhouse after unsuccessfully chasing a Heinkel He 111P of *KG 26* over the Lothians.

Serving in No 602 Squadron at that time was Flight Lieutenant George Pinkerton, a Renfrewshire farmer who typified the unit's local membership:

> Working on my farm, I used to see aeroplanes flying around and pilots being taught to fly. It interested me, so I went along and found that the Scottish Flying Club could teach me to fly at a cost of two pounds per hour. I applied to 602 and was granted a commission in 1933. The Auxiliary Air Force was really the same as the Territorial Army. The officers and the airmen were recruited from Glasgow. Among the officers were bank clerks, stockbrokers, a plasterer, a miner and a couple of lawyers. The airmen came from all walks of life, many of them out of engineering works and technical jobs in the city. When it really got serious we were mobilized on 24 August. We were put on a war footing and we armed the aeroplanes and manned them. Of course we were proud of our ability to operate and we didn't really think the regulars had anything on us at all.

So it was that, on that afternoon, Blue Section of No 602 Squadron, led by Pinkerton, and Yellow Section of No 603 Squadron, under Flight Lieutenant George Lovell Denholm, were up when unidentified aircraft were reported heading towards the Forth Bridge. Pinkerton was at 10,000 feet when he spotted the Ju 88s dive-bombing warships off Rosyth. The Germans had spotted *Hood*, but she was in the harbour and too close to a civilian area. In accordance with his rules of engagement, Pohle went after secondary targets outside the harbour instead. One of the Germans' bombs struck the light cruiser *Southampton* amidships but failed to explode, while the light cruiser *Edinburgh* and destroyer *Mohawk* suffered slight damage.

Pinkerton and his section attacked the leading bomber, which pulled out of its dive and fled over May Island:

> We got fleeting glimpses of him but not sufficient to be able to fire at him [Pinkerton reported]. And when we got to the edge of a bank of cloud, he emerged—with me sitting on his starboard side and my number two sitting on his port side. We came up astern of him and carried out an attack. His aeroplane lifted up in the air and then went down into a dive and I think I had probably injured him in some way. My number two came in and gave him some more, and then I came back to finish him off.

The Spitfires took turns attacking Pohle's Junkers, killing his flight engineer and rear gunner, mortally wounding his navigator and then disabling one of his engines. When the second engine was demolished in a hail of bullets, Pohle made for a trawler and crash-landed in the water nearby:

> We watched how he flew over a merchant ship and then crashed down in the sea about a mile away [wrote Pinkerton]. We were quite glad to see him in the sea because the last thing I wanted was to go back to my unit and say I hadn't shot him down!—considering that I had eight machine guns that could fire ammunition at the rate of 2,400 rounds a minute.

Pohle suffered facial injuries and a concussion, but minutes later the trawler crew recovered him from his sinking plane and he regained consciousness in a naval hospital at Port Edgar five days later. Pinkerton visited him and said that afterwards 'I sent him some sweets and cigarettes and he wrote a letter thanking me.' 'I thank you for your friendly conduct,' Pohle wrote, 'wish you the best and greet with you likewise, the other pilot. To all airmen, comradeship.'

Pinkerton's 'other pilot' to whom Pohle referred was Flying Officer Archibald Ashmore McKellar, a 5 foot 4 inch tall plasterer from Glasgow who had been serving in No 602 Squadron since 1936. Called into active service upon the declaration of war, he had just had his first fight and had scored the first of three shared victories. He would go on to become one of the heroes of the Battle of Britain, scoring an additional seventeen individual victories before being killed in action on 1 November 1940.

Meanwhile No 603's commander, Squadron Leader Ernest H. Stevens, led Red Section against an He 111P of *Stab./KG 26* which was observing the Ju 88s' mission over Dalkeith. Another section, led by Flight Lieutenant Pat Gifford, also joined the chase, which ended in the He 111's pilot being wounded and forced to crash-land—the first German aircraft to fall on British soil since 1918.

Three Spitfires of No 602 Squadron, led by its commander, Squadron Leader Andrew Douglas Farquhar—a Glasgow stockbroker before the war—arrived in time to pursue a Ju 88 retiring off Aberdour. Farquhar and one of his men, Pilot Officer Paul Clifford Webb—hitherto an employee of the National Bank of Scotland—sent it crashing into the sea off Crail, its entire crew being killed.

Four other Ju 88s were damaged in the fight. The pilot of one stricken Junkers, *Leutnant* Horst von Riesen, survived to describe how his starboard radiator was hit and erupted in a cloud of steam, forcing him to turn off the engine before it burst into flames. His speed went down to 112 mph and he could barely keep his Ju 88 above the waves, but at that point the Spitfires, at the limit of their range, broke off their pursuit and headed for home. With a four-hour flight ahead, one of Riesen's crew suggested they turn back and crash-land in Scotland, but he and the rest of his men decided to take their chances: 'We preferred to risk death from drowning or the cold, rather than have to face those Spitfires again.' As the Junkers's fuel was expended, it became lighter and gained altitude, allowing Riesen to reach his air base at Westerland. 'So it was that I survived my first encounter with Spitfires,' Riesen concluded. 'I would meet them again during the Battle of Britain, over the Mediterranean and during the battle of Sicily. It was not a pleasant experience.'

An hour later Farquhar and two other pilots damaged an He 111P over Rosyth, while Stevens sent another one crashing into the sea off Port Seton. One of the downed Heinkel's crew was killed, but three others were rescued, shaken but miraculously uninjured.

The Auxiliary Air Force had proved its worth—and so had the Spitfire. Not to be outdone, a Canadian Spitfire pilot of No 41 Squadron RAF, Flying Officer Howard Peter Blatchford, downed an He 111 twenty or thirty miles east of Whitby the next day.

Over in France, the Hurricane's first chance to fight came 11 a.m. on 15 October when Squadron Leader Patrick J. H. Halahan led five sections of No 1 Squadron, consisting of three fighters each, from the airfield at Étain and commenced a patrol of the Saarlautern sector. The British flew 40 miles into German territory, came under heavy anti-aircraft fire and saw their first Me 109s, but instead of accepting combat the latter dived away.

As with the Spitfire, the Hurricane first fired its guns in anger against coastal raiders. On 21 October nine Heinkel He 115A-1 twin-engine floatplanes of *1 Staffel, Küstenfliegergruppe 106*, went on a sweep of the Channel, looking for merchant ships to attack. It was they, however, not the ships, that would end up running the gauntlet. The Heinkels were about fifteen miles from Spurn Head off the Yorkshire coast when they encountered two Spitfires of No 72 Squadron, flown by Flight Lieutenants Thomas A. F. Elsdon and Desmond F. B. Sheen, who raked the formation and claimed to have inflicted fatal damage on two of the floatplanes before their fuel ran low and they had to break off the action. By then six Hurricanes of 'A' Flight, No 46 Squadron, had joined the fray and in a fifteen-mile chase they claimed five more of the fleeing He 115s, a share in the destruction of one going to Pilot Officer Peter W. Lefevre, who went on to score five personal and four more shared victories before being killed in action on 6 February 1944.

The Hawkers on the Continent finally drew their first blood on 30 October when a Dornier Do 17P of *2. Staffel (Foto)/Aufklärungsgruppe 123 (2.(F)/123)* crossed into French territory and Sergeant Peter William Olbert Mould, a resident of Hallaton, Uppingham, serving in No 1 Squadron, scrambled up to intercept the intruder in Hurricane L1842. He caught the Dornier ten miles west of Toul and shot it down in flames, for the first official RAF fighter victory over France since 1918. 'Boy' Mould was awarded the Distinguished Flying Cross for his success, and would later add six more German aircraft to his score, and a share in one other, before France's capitulation on 18 June 1940.

There would be further run-ins with the Germans over the next month, almost invariably involving quick dashes into Allied airspace by their reconnaissance planes. On 2 November Flight Lieutenant Robert Voase-Jeff of No 87 Squadron downed an He 111H of *2.(F)/122* near Hazebrouck, while one of his squadron pals, Flying Officer William D. David, damaged another half and hour later. David's quarry gave as good as it got, however: not only did its gunners damage his Hurricane but they shot up the fuel and oil lines of Pilot Officer C. C. D. Mackworth's plane, forcing him to land at Seclin, after which the Heinkel succeeded in returning to its airfield at Münster-Handorf.

A significant victory was scored on 8 November when a Hurricane of No 73 Squadron intercepted and shot down a Do 17P of *1.(F)/123* near Lubey, north-west of Metz. The pilot was Flying Officer Edgar James Kain from Hastings, New Zealand, and it was the first of at least sixteen enemy planes that he would destroy over France, making him the leading RAF ace prior to the Battle of Britain. With tragic irony, just after taking off for Britain on 7 June 1940, 'Cobber' Kain made a last slow roll over the field, his wing tip struck the ground and his Hurricane crashed, killing him.

German probes began to intensify later in November. On the 21st Flight Lieutenant Richard H. A. Lee of No 85 Squadron caught an He 111 of *Stab./KG 4* ten miles north of Cap Gris Nez and sent it crashing into the sea. Flight Lieutenant F. S. Brown and Flying Officer James W. E. Davies of No 79 Squadron teamed up to bring down a Do 17P of *3.(F)/122* east of Deal. No fewer than eight reconnaissance planes were downed on 23 November, including a Do 17 of *Stab./KG 2* by Flight Lieutenant John E. Scoular and a colleague of No 73 Squadron, and a Do 17P of *3.(F)/22* crashed near Conflans for 'Cobber' Kain's second victory. The principal honours of the day went to No 1 Squadron, with an He 111 falling to Squadron Leader Arthur V. Clowes north-east of Saarbrücken; an He 111 of *2.(F)/122* jointly credited to three Hurricanes of No 1 Squadron, three French M.S.406s of *Groupe de Chassse II/5* and Flying Officer Newell Orton of No 73 Squadron near Königsmacher; another Heinkel from the same unit brought down by Flying Officer George H. F. Plinston and two colleagues of No 1 Squadron; and yet another Heinkel, of *Stab./JG 53*, forced to land by 'Fanny' Orton. Flying Officer John Ignatius Kilmartin also teamed up with two fellow Hurricane pilots of No 1 Squadron to down a Do 17 over Menehould.

The most unusual action of the day took place when Flying Officers Cyril D. Palmer, Francis Soper and Mark H. Brown of No 1 Squadron took off from the field at Vassincourt to intercept yet another intruder. They caught the German, a Do 17P of *4.(F)/122*, as it was racing back towards the border and three sets of eight machine guns soon set one of its engines on fire, after which 'Pussy' Palmer saw its navigator and gunner take to their parachutes. Palmer's guns jammed at that point, but he noticed that the Dornier pilot was slumped over the controls and brought his Hurricane alongside the stricken machine to make sure that it was indeed going down for good. At that point, however, *Unteroffizier* Arno Frankenberger, who in fact had only been 'playing possum', suddenly came to life and throttled down both engines. Then, as a startled Palmer sped ahead of the plane, Frankenberger abandoned his controls, climbed into the empty navigator's seat, grabbed the MG 15 machine gun and fired a long burst into the Hurricane.

Palmer instinctively ducked and pushed his stick forward, but before his Hurricane nosed down a bullet whizzed past his head and smashed his windscreen, while other slugs struck his engine and his radiator. The engine stopped and, trailing a white plume of glycol, Palmer brought his aircraft down—only to find that his undercarriage was also damaged and would not extend. He belly-landed in a field and saw Frankenberger—who was unwilling to press his luck with two other Hurricanes closing on his tail—jump from his doomed plane, which crashed not far from Palmer's.

After parachuting to earth Frankenberger was taken prisoner by a squad of French soldiers and spent the night in jail, but on the following day pilots of No 1 Squadron came and, over the objections of French officials, had the German released into their custody for the evening. They then took Frankenberger to the upstairs room of a small inn near Vassincourt, which served as their officers' mess, and treated him to a tankard of beer and the best dinner locally available. The airmen compared notes on the action, and Frankenberger showed off photographs of his wife and baby and presented his hosts with an autographed picture of himself. It was well past midnight when, after a final toast to the universal fraternity of the air, the British wandered off to bed while their German guest was returned to French custody.

There was more to the incident than the chivalry of an earlier war, however. Palmer had been shot down and nearly killed largely because the Hurricane, though equipped with an armoured fuel tank and a bullet-proof windscreen, had no rear protection for the pilot. 'Bull' Halahan petitioned the Air Ministry for armour plate to be added behind the pilot's seat, only to have his request rejected on the grounds that it would upset the centre of gravity. Undaunted, he took removed armour plating from a Fairey Battle bomber, installed it behind the seat of one of his squadron's Hurricanes and then had one of his pilots demonstrate its effects on the plane's flying characteristics to visiting experts with a brilliant aerobatic show. Shortly afterwards armour plating behind the pilot's seat became a standard item for both Hurricanes and Spitfires.

Such, then, were the beginnings of two legends. In the years to come, Hurricane and Spitfire would be familiar names to friend and foe alike.

Chapter 9

ZERO HOUR

Japanese Fighters, 1937–1942

Although Japan was quick to appreciate the aeroplane's value as a weapon, Japanese aircraft of the 1920s and early 1930s were invariably dismissed by European observers as either outright imitations or second-rate variations on French or British designs. A case in point could be seen in an incident over the Chinese port of Shanghai on 22 February 1932 in which three Mitsubishi B1M3 three-seat biplane bombers from the aircraft carrier *Kaga* came under attack from a Boeing 212—a unique all-metal version of the P-12 that was being demonstrated for the Chinese by American pilot Robert Short. Short killed the lead plane's pilot, Lieutenant Susumu Kotani, and wounded his observer, Airman 1st Class Setsuro Sasaki, but the third crewman, Lieutenant (junior grade) Yoshiro Sakinago, managed to land the stricken B1M3 at Shanghai. Besides coming under fire from the other B1M3 gunners, however, Short was attacked and sent to his death in flames by three fighters flown by Lieutenant Nokiji Ikuta, Petty Officer 3rd Class Toshio Kuriowa and Seaman 1st Class Kazuo Takeo. The three Nakajima A1N2s that shared in the Imperial Japanese Navy's first aerial victory were, in fact, licence-built copies of the Gloster Gamecock biplane.

By the mid-1930s the backward nature of Japanese aviation and the inferiority of Japanese airmen had become virtually ingrained in European and American strategic thinking. That complacency was rudely shaken on 7 December 1941 when the carrier-launched Japanese aircraft that staged a surprise attack on the US Navy and Army bases at Pearl Harbor on the Hawaiian island of Oahu, and the Army aircraft that supported the Japanese invasion of British-held Malaya, proved to be not only equal but superior to their Western counterparts. In the vanguard of that first, devastating Japanese offensive was a fighter that would come to symbolize Japanese air supremacy in the first six months of the Pacific War—the Mitsubishi A6M2 Zero.

The Zero's performance seemed nothing short of phenomenal in 1941. Only a year before, Messerschmitt Me 109Es were handicapped by their inability to fight Supermarine Spitfires or Hawker Hurricanes for more than twenty minutes after crossing the English Channel. The Zero, in contrast, could fly as far as 1,930 miles with the aid of a drop tank, staying in the air several times as long as an Me 109, Spitfire or Hurricane. At a time when the structural reinforcement, deck-landing gear and navigational aids necessary for a carrier fighter intrinsically limited its performance, the A6M2, with its maximum speed of 331 mph, made history as the first carrier-based fighter capable of outperforming its land-based opponents.

At Allied headquarters, officers wondered how the Japanese could have kept such a wonder weapon secret for so long. The truth was that they had not—the Zero had been in combat over China since August 1940. Such was the mind-set in the British and American high commands about Japanese inferiority that even reports from their own military observers in China had been dismissed as fiction. Thousands of American, Dutch and British Commonwealth airmen would pay with their lives for that self-imposed ignorance.

While they had been manufacturing Western aircraft under licence in the 1920s, Japanese builders had been catching up on the fine points of aeronautical design. In the early 1930s they were ready to proceed with designs of their own.

In February 1934 Imperial Navy Air Headquarters issued a *9-shi* specification calling for a new single-seat fighter. Although carrier-based capability was virtually implicit in a Navy requirement, one of its chief architects, Lieutenant-Commander Hido Sawai, had deliberately avoided specific reference to such characteristics, fearing that it would inhibit the designers. In contrast to British and American naval aviation planners, Sawai wanted the manufacturers to produce a high-performance fighter that would bring Japan up to world standard; the matter of adapting and equipping it for operations from carrier decks would be dealt with afterwards. The specification called for a maximum speed of 350 kph (217 mph) at 3,000 metres (9,840 feet) and the ability to climb to 5,000 metres (16,405 feet) within 6.5 minutes. Armament was to consist of two 7.7mm machine guns; the wing span would not exceed 11 metres (36.08 feet) and length would no more than 8 metres (26.25 feet).

Among those who sought to meet the requirement was Mitsubishi's chief designer, Jiro Horikoshi. After giving cursory consideration to other configurations Horikoshi determined that the fighter must be a low-wing monoplane, with attention paid to the cleanest possible aerodynamics and the minimum possible weight. The airframe he designed used stressed-skin aluminium over a two-spar box-type wing structure of inverted gull form, which was later altered into a flat centre section with dihedral for the outer wing panels. After considering the possibility of incorporating retractable landing gear into his design, Horikoshi rejected it on the grounds that the ten per cent decrease in drag would result in only a three per cent increase in speed—not enough to justify the system's greater weight and complexity. Instead, his monoplane would have fixed gear, with streamlined fairings over the wheels.

The first Ka-14 prototype, powered by a 550 hp, 9-cylinder Nakajima Koto-buki 5 radial engine, was completed in January 1935, just eleven months after Mitsubishi received the *9-shi* specification. During its first flight tests in February it reached a speed of 444 kph (276 mph) at 10,500 feet, exceeding both the Navy's requirement and Horikoshi's own expectations. Nevertheless, the Ka-14 had a great obstacle to overcome when it competed with the Nakajima A4N1 biplane in the autumn of 1935 because of the almost insurmountable prejudice in favour of dogfighting capabilities over all others among senior JNAF officers. The Ka-14's low wing loading made it extremely agile for a monoplane, but it still could not match the manoeuvrability of the A4N1—until the rules of mock combat were altered to include climb-and-dive tactics. That change gave the Ka-14 such an overall edge that even Minoru Genda, one of the most ardent biplane partisans, was won over to the new type.

After further development—and an unsuccessful attempt to interest the Army in the design—Mitsubishi were able to put their monoplane into production as the A5M1 Model 96 carrier fighter in the autumn of 1936. An improved version with a 610 hp Kotobuki 2 KAI *3ko* engine, a longer-chord cowling and a three-blade propeller in place of the two-blade airscrew entered production in the late spring of 1937 as the A5M2-*ko*. The outbreak of war with China on 7 July 1937 lent urgency to the JNAF's efforts to hasten the A5M to operational units, and the newly formed 13th *Kokutai* (Air Group) got its first monoplanes just four days later.

Initially the Japanese Army advanced quickly, taking Peking and Tientsin, but resistance stiffened as it approached Shanghai, and at the same time Japan's regular arsenal of biplanes was proving unable to achieve a decisive degree of air superiority over the mixed bag of Chinese aircraft that opposed it. The land-based Japanese units were augmented by the air groups of the light carrier *Hosho* off Shanghai, which was joined on 15 August by the large carrier *Kaga*, both of which achieved a marginal degree of local air superiority with their ageing Nakajima A2N fighters. Then two A5M2s landed on *Kaga* and flew their first combat sortie on 22 August. Their first chance to test their mettle came on 4 September when Lieutenant Tadashi Nakajima and a companion encountered several Chinese Curtiss Hawk IIs and IIIs over Dahu Lake. In the ensuing fight the Japanese claimed three Hawks and returned to *Kaga* undamaged.

Five days later the 13th *Kokutai*, equipped with twelve A5M2 fighters and eighteen Aichi D1A and Yokosuka B4Y bombers, arrived at Gong Da airfield near Shanghai and commenced operations against the Chinese Army. Little contact was made with Chinese air elements until 19 September, when twelve of the 13th *Kokutai*'s A5M2s, led by Lieutenant Shichio Yamashita, flew escort for seventeen carrier bombers on a mission to Nanking and encountered a swarm of twenty Hawks and Boeing 248s.

The results, as they appeared in the *Asahi Shimbun* on the following morning, were spectacular. In what the newspaper dubbed the A5M's debut, the new Japanese fighters had destroyed 33 enemy planes without loss to themselves within fifteen minutes. The account was considerably exaggerated, but the truth could have stood on its own merits. The large-scale engagement had not marked the operational debut of the A5M2—that had already occurred more than two weeks before—but in a swirling dogfight that lasted for more than fifteen minutes the Japanese fighters did record fifteen victories, including three 'probables'. A second mission that same day brought Japanese claims up to 26, for the loss of three bombers, one reconnaissance plane and no fighters. The Chinese Air Force admitted to the loss of eleven aircraft and claimed only one Japanese plane in return.

Whatever the statistics, the A5M2 had had one of the most auspicious debuts of any fighter in history, and in the months to come it would all but drive the Chinese Air Force from the skies. Lieutenant Yamashita would not be around to see it, however. Just a week after leading the 13th *Kokutai* to instant glory over Nanking he was compelled to make a force-landing behind Chinese lines and was taken prisoner, dying shortly thereafter.

Curiously the Japanese Army Air Force (JAAF) was slower than the Navy in adopting more innovative and potent fighter designs. One reason was its longer adherence to the Japanese tendency to compare aerial combat to the swordsman's art of *Kendo*, involving dexterity of manoeuvre. Finally, in June 1935, the *Koku Hombu* (Army Headquarters) issued a requirement for an 'advanced fighter' to replace the Kawasaki Ki-10 biplane. The new fighter was to be capable of 280 mph in level flight and of reaching 16,405 feet (5,000 metres) in less than six minutes, but still mount two 7.7mm Type 89 machine guns.

Nakajima's design team, led by Tei Koyama and assisted by Minoru Ota and Hideo Itokawa, had already had some experience with externally braced monoplane designs when they learned of the new Army requirement. They went on to design a small cantilever monoplane around the Nakajima Kotobuki II-Kai 9-cylinder radial—a licence-built version of the Bristol Jupiter—using all-metal, stressed-skin construction. As with the A5M, fixed landing gear enclosed within two streamlined fairings was selected over the heavier and more complex retractable undercarriage, but an enclosed canopy was incorporated into the second prototype. Increased wing area and the incorporation of wing flaps kept the fighter manoeuvrable enough to satisfy the *Koku Hombu*, which chose it over its faster competitor, the Kawasaki Ki-28, following trials in the spring of 1937. Powered by an improved 710 hp Nakajima Ha-I-*otsu* engine driving a two-blade, all-metal, two-pitch (ground adjustable) Sumimoto PE propeller, the production version of the Nakajima Ki-27-Otsu Type 97 fighter had a maximum speed of 291 mph at 13,125 feet.

So confident were Nakajima in their new fighter that they were making production preparations at their new plant at Ota even before the Army's order became official on 27 December 1937. Even the most conservative pilots were delighted with the new fighter's manoeuvrability, as well as its higher performance.

Eager to blood the new fighter in combat, the Army dispatched three of the first planes to leave the assembly line to the 1st *Chutai* of the 2nd *Hiko-Daitai* (Air Battalion), which was then flying Ki-10s from Yanchow, northern China. Just one week after their arrival, on 10 April 1938, Captain Tateo Kato, commander of the 1st *Chutai*, flew his first combat sortie in the new fighter and came back claiming to have shot down no fewer than three Polikarpov I-15s. The *Daitai* commander, Major Tamiya Teranishi, flew one of the Ki-27s five days later when the K-27 trio joined the older Ki-10s in a dogfight with 30 Chinese I-15s over Shensi that resulted in 24 Japanese claims. Over the next few weeks the 2nd *Hiko-Daitai* supported the Army's Hsuchow campaign, intended to give the Japanese complete control of the Peking–Nanking railway. Chinese aerial opposition became infrequent, but on 20 May the 1st *Chutai's* Ki-10s and Ki-27s accounted for twelve enemy fighters.

The 2nd *Hiko Daitai* was still in the process of replacing its Ki-10s with Ki-27s in August 1938 when a restructuring of the JAAF resulted in its being redesignated the 64th *Sentai* (Air Regiment). Adoption of the Ki-27 proceeded rapidly thereafter, and the fighter went on to its most celebrated period during the undeclared conflict between Japan and the Soviet Union in the Nomonhan region of Mongolia and Manchuria in the summer of 1939.

Meanwhile the Imperial Navy, encouraged by the A5M's success but mindful of the rapid advances being made in Europe, issued a new specification for an even more advanced carrier fighter to representatives of the Mitsubishi and Nakajima firms during a meeting at the Yokosuka Naval Air Arsenal on 17 January 1938. Nakajima, convinced that it would be almost impossible to meet the Navy's requirements, immediately withdrew from the competition.

Mitsubishi's design team again accepted the challenge, but to meet the 12-*Shi* fighter requirement it had literally to build its aeroplane around an 875 hp 14-cylinder Mitsubishi Zuisei-13 twin-row radial engine. Again, weight reduction became the paramount consideration to compensate for every innovation incorporated in the new fighter. The wing was built around a one-piece spar of

Extra-Super Duralumin—the first use of that alloy in the main spar construction of an aeroplane—with the fuselage centre section integral with the wing. Horikoshi's team designed the fuselage to be as long, slim and streamlined as its radial engine would allow. The relatively long, narrow wing provided a high aspect ratio and a low enough wing loading to meet the Navy requirement for manoeuvrability equal to that of the A5M and, with the assistance of underwing flaps, a landing speed of less than 66 mph.

The most noteworthy advances in the 12-*Shi* fighter's design were the use of retractable landing gear and a considerably heavier armament. In addition to two fuselage-mounted Type 97 7.7mm machine guns, the aeroplane featured two wing-mounted Type 99 20mm cannon—licence-built versions of the Swiss Oerlikon gun manufactured by the Dai-Nihon Heiki Company, which were reliable and accurate although they were somewhat handicapped by a slow rate of fire and a low muzzle velocity.

The 12-*Shi* prototype emerged from the Mitsubishi plant in southern Nagoya on 16 March 1939 and testing commenced at Kagamigahara Airfield on 1 April. Teething troubles were minor. Engine vibration problems were eliminated after Horikoshi replaced the prototype's two-blade airscrew with a constant speed, three-blade propeller—the first of its kind to be used on a Japanese aeroplane. By 14 September Mitsubishi's new design had once again matched or exceeded the performance requirements that inspired its creation, and it was assigned the military designation A6M1 Type 0 carrier borne fighter—the '0' referring to the year 1940, in which it was expected to enter service, which on traditional Japanese calendars would be the year 2600. In Japanese parlance it was known as *Rei Shiki Sento Ki*, but pilots soon abbreviated that to *Rei-sen*. It would eventually achieve even wider notoriety by the English translation of that nickname—Zero Fighter.

The third Zero prototype was modified to use the more powerful 950 hp Nakajima Sakae-12 engine and was placed in production as the A6M2 Model 11, the first production machine leaving Mitsubishi's Nagoya plant in December 1939. First tested on 18 January 1940, the Sakae-12-powered Zero exceeded all of the original Navy specifications. By then word of the new fighter had reached pilots in China and they began clamouring for it. Overriding objections from Mitsubishi's engineers, the Navy ordered six pre-production A6M2s to be transferred from the Yokosuka *Kokutai* (Naval Air Group) to Wuhan, China, on 21 July 1940—ten days before the type was to be officially accepted into regular service. Those Zeros and nine more that followed them shortly thereafter were assigned to the 12th *Kokutai*, a new unit that had been formed the previous June, under the command of Captain Kiichi Hasegawa. On 19 August Lieutenant Tamotsu Yokoyama led twelve Zeros on their first operational mission, escorting 54 Mitsubishi G3M2s on a 1,150-mile round trip to bomb Chunking. The Japanese encountered no aerial opposition, nor did they on another mission the following day.

The first aerial contact occurred on 13 September when thirteen Zeros led by Lieutenant Saburo Shindo escorted 27 bombers and a Mitsubishi C5M1 reconnaissance plane to Hankow. After the bombing raid was carried out, the Japanese were about to head home when they spotted Chinese fighters converging over the smoking target area. Eager to test their new mounts, the Zero pilots climbed for height, then dived on the enemy—28 Polikarpov I-152 biplane fighters and nine I-16 monoplanes of the 4th Group, led by Colonel Cheng Shao-yu. A battle royal ensued, such as had not been seen over China in months—with results that revived the A5M's heyday with a vengeance.

Petty Officer 1st Class (PO1C) Saburo Kitahata, No 2 in Shindo's 1st *Shotai* (Flight) of the 1st *Chutai* (Squadron), claimed two enemy planes (his eventual score would be more than ten). He then strafed the Paishih railway station. Another Chinese fighter was claimed by PO2C Kihei Fujiwara, while PO3C Yoshio Oki scored no less than four.

The leader of the 2nd *Chutai's* 1st *Shotai*, Lieutenant (jg) Ayao Shirane, was having his first combat but he managed to down one of his adversaries. He would eventually be credited with eight more. The number two man in his *shotai*, Petty Officer 1st Class Masayuki Mitsumasa, accounted for two, as did the number three man, PO2C Tsutomu Iwai; Iwai's final wartime total would be eleven. PO1C Toraichi Takatsuka, leader of the 2nd *Chutai's* 2nd *Shotai*, claimed three enemy aircraft, while PO2C Kazuki Mikami got two and PO3C Masaharu Hiramoto accounted for one.

Among the three Zero pilots of the 1st *Chutai's* 2nd *Shotai*, PO2C Toshiyuki Sueda downed one enemy plane—the first of an eventual total of nine—and PO3C Hatsuyama Yamaya shot down two. The star performance of the day, however, was by their *shotai* leader, Warrant Officer Koshiro Yamashita, who accounted for five Chinese fighters, the last of which he fought down to an altitude of 50 metres before finally sending it crashing into a rice paddy. He then re-joined his two wingmen, performed a victory loop and led them in a strafing attack on the Paishih railway station.

The Japanese claimed 27 victories in all. Not one Zero had been touched. Chinese records showed that, on this occasion, the Japanese claims, though typically optimistic, were not that far off the mark so far as perception went. Thirteen Chinese fighters had actually been destroyed and another eleven had come down damaged. Ten pilots had been killed and eight wounded, including Colonel Cheng. Admiral Shigetaro Shimada, commander of the China Area Fleet, issued a special unit commendation to mark what he regarded—more rightly than he may have imagined—as a historic event.

By the end of 1940 the Zeros would have accounted for a total of 87 Chinese aircraft. The 12th *Kokutai*'s own losses remained nil until 20 May 1941, when PO1C Eichi Kimura was shot down and killed by anti-aircraft fire over central China. PO1C Kichiro Kobayashi suffered a similar fate over Lanchow on 23 June. These would be the only Zeros destroyed in action prior to 7 December. Their phenomenal performance did not go entirely unnoticed. Colonel Claire Lee Chennault, then engaged in organizing a force of American mercenary pilots for the Chinese Air Force, examined the remains of shot-down Zeros, prepared a report on the fighter's capabilities and sent it to Washington, DC—where it was completely ignored.

Then came 7 December 1941 and the Zero's first appearance over Pearl Harbor and the Philippines, taking the Americans completely by surprise. At the same time surviving Allied airmen over Malaya and China were also recording their shock at the sudden appearance and astonishing performance of the Zero. In most cases there, however, the Zero's name and mystique were being passed on to another Japanese 'mystery' fighter—an Army type that was even newer, yet not as good as the Mitsubishi A6M2.

Although the JAAF's Nakajima Ki-27 had been a great success, it was fundamentally little more than a refinement of Mitsubishi's A5M formula. The *Koku Hombu* was so pleased with it, however, that essentially the only concession to technological progress that it put in its specification for a Ki-27 successor in December 1937 was retractable landing gear, which was expected to bring the new fighter's speed up to 311 mph (an unambitious seven per cent increase over the Ki-27's speed). The *Koku Hombu*'s complacency was also reflected in its decision not to open its requirement to competition, leaving it to Nakajima designers Hideo Itokawa and Yasumi Koyama to improve on the Ki-27 formula without sacrificing its manoeuvrability. They responded, roughly as Horikoshi had done, by designing a slim, lightweight fuselage with a three-spar, one-piece wing around the new 990 hp Nakajima Ha-25 14-cylinder radial engine. The result, designated Ki-43, was completed on 12 December 1938, but during test flights in January 1939 it proved to be barely faster and far less nimble than its predecessor, while displaying unsatisfactory take-off and landing characteristics. Only the provision for overload tanks, for increased range, offered any real improvement over the Ki-27.

Disappointed, the *Koku Hombu* was about to suspend further development, but Itokawa won a reprieve by promising to redesign the plane. New, finer tail surfaces were incorporated, with a fuselage of reduced cross section on the first pre-production aircraft, which was completed in 1939 and displayed a promising improvement in speed and climb rate. Subsequent pre-production airframes were used in various engine and armament experiments, but it was the eighth, which introduced Fowler-type wing flaps to boost lift and manoeuvrability, that revived enthusiasm in the Army. The final pre-production Ki-43, completed in September 1940, incorporated the 'butterfly' combat flaps, had an uprated Ha-105 engine driving a two-blade, two-pitch metal propeller and featured twin Ho-103 12.7mm machine guns in the cowling. Its performance actually exceeded the *Koku Hombu*'s expectations and Nakajima were urged to begin production on the Type 1 Fighter Model 1-Ko *Hayabusa* (Peregrine Falcon) as soon as possible.

Although the *Hayabusa* was even smaller and lighter than the Zero, its performance was inferior to that of the carrier fighter, its maximum speed being no more than 308 mph. Moreover, the first Ki-43-I-Ko fighters retained the puny armament of two synchronized 7.7mm machine guns, although an interim Ki-43-I-Otsu with one 7.7mm and one 12.7mm weapon was put into parallel production pending the availability of more Ha-103 guns.

In August 1941 the first Ki-43s began replacing Ki-27s in the 59th and 64th *Sentai*s. During their training period in the new fighters the pilots reported an alarming rash of accidents due to wing structural failure during dives, indicative of just how much the Nakajima team had sacrificed in the name of weight reduction. The aircraft were returned to Tachikawa, where the wings underwent some hasty improvised strengthening. Then, as war clouds loomed in the Pacific, the 59th and 64th *Sentai*s were deployed, alongside the Ki-27-equipped 1st, 11th and 77th *Sentai*s, for the coming invasion of British-held Malaya.

Stationed at Duong Dong airfield on the island of Phu Quoc off the Cambodian coast, the 64th *Sentai* covered the landings of the Japanese Twenty-Fifth Army at Khota Bharu, Singora and Panati on 8 December 1941 (which, because of the International Date Line, actually occurred just before the Pearl Harbor raid). The previous evening Lieutenant Takeo Takayama led the 2nd *Chutai* of the 64th *Sentai* over the invasion fleet. The patrol was relieved at 5.30 p.m. by six *Hayabusa*s led by the regiment's veteran commander, Major Tateo Kato, but three planes of that second flight were lost when their pilots became disorientated amid darkness, bad weather and low cloud, eventually running out of fuel and going down in the Gulf of Siam.

The Ki-43's first combat mission took place when aircraft of the 64th *Sentai* left Duong Dong at 9.50 a.m. to escort Mitsubishi Ki-21 bombers of the 12th and 98th *Sentai*s on their second raid on Sungei Patani airfield, where the Brewster Buffaloes of No 21 Squadron Royal Australian Air Force were based. Two Buffaloes had been destroyed and five damaged in the earlier raid, and the bombers' second strike was followed up by *Hayabusa*s strafing the field, leaving the Australians only four serviceable fighters. Two of the Ki-43s also claimed their first aerial victory when they attacked a Bristol Blenheim Mk IV of No 34 Squadron that had been trying to bomb the Japanese beach-head and compelled it to force-land at Machang airstrip. One of the victorious pilots, Lieutenant Yohei Hinoki, would survive the war with twelve victories, the last of which was scored after he had lost a leg. On the way home a Ki-43 of the 3rd *Chutai* had to ditch in the sea off Phu Quoc after being hit by gunfire from a Japanese destroyer, and all the others landed at Duong Dong with their tanks nearly dry.

As other Blenheims were returning to Butterworth airfield to refuel they encountered Ki-43s of the 59th *Sentai*. Warrant Officer Takeomi Hayashi claimed two Blenheims but in reality only brought down one, piloted by New Zealander Sergeant J. E. Smith, who belly-landed his damaged bomber and suffered slight injuries, as did one of his crewmen, Australian Sergeant E. H. Brown. A second Blenheim, flown by Flying Officer N. N. H. Dunlop, was chased for twenty miles at tree-top level while his Australian gunner, Sergeant K. R. Burrill, stuck to his gun in spite of being wounded in the lower jaw. Although he was in great pain, Burrill's doggedness was rewarded by the sight of his attacker taking telling hits just as it was closing in for the kill, after which it crashed in the jungle. Dunlop landed safely at Butterworth, while the 59th *Sentai* recorded one pilot missing. Bad weather and disorientation, however, were responsible for the loss of two other 59th *Sentai* planes—twice as many as were lost in combat that day.

Seventeen Ki-43s of the 64th *Sentai* escorted 79 Ki-21s on a mission to the British airfield at Victoria Point on the following day, but, when thick cloud cover forced the bombers to turn back, the fighters landed at the newly captured field at Singora to refuel. They then went off on their own to strafe the airfields at Penang Island and Butterworth.

After the Japanese occupation of Thailand JAAF units were moved to air bases there, giving the British a few days' grace to re-form their ravaged squadrons to the south. The 64th resumed its duties on 11 December, escorting 41 Ki-21s of the 12th and 60th *Sentai*s on a raid against Penang. During the return flight two of the 64th's Ki-43s landed at Khota Bharu, where the Japanese found stocks of fuel in the tanks of abandoned British aircraft. The rest of the unit moved there on the 13th in preparation to support operations over Kuantan.

Thus far the Ki-43s had encountered little aerial opposition, the more numerous Ki-27s proving to be sufficient to establish air superiority. However, when Buffaloes of No 453 Squadron RAAF attacked Japanese bombers over Penang, shooting down two Kawasaki Ki-48s and two Mitsubishi Ki-51s, five *Hayabusas* of the 59th *Sentai* were dispatched to save the bombers. They arrived 30 minutes later to find the Buffaloes already gone and contented themselves with strafing

Butterworth. On the return trip, however, two of the Ki-43s collided, one of the two pilots killed being the 59th's commander, Major Reinosuke Tanimura.

By 17 December the JAAF had lost a total of ten Ki-43s, almost all to non-combat-related causes. As three *Hayabusa*s of the 59th *Sentai* were strafing Ipoh airfield that morning they were dived upon by three Buffaloes of No 453 Squadron. A lively dogfight followed, in which the Australians found themselves being quite handily outfought. One *Hayabusa* got on Sergeant V. A. Collyer's tail, and he escaped only by jinking away at tree-top height. Sergeants A. W. B. Clare and J. Summerton also survived, but both of their planes were badly shot up. Upon returning to base the Japanese reported tackling six Buffaloes and claimed two shot down, as well as seven bombers destroyed or damaged on the airfield.

The Japanese advance continued with such rapidity that they often found the airfields they occupied to have vast amounts of ammunition, fuel, equipment and provisions. One such 'Churchill aerodrome', as the Japanese wryly dubbed them, was Sungei Patani, which still had 1,500 drums of aviation fuel when the 27th and 59th *Sentai*s arrived on 20 December.

A dozen of the 59th *Sentai*'s Ki-43s were escorting fourteen Ki-48 and Ki-51 bombers to Kuala Lumpur on 21 December when they encountered two Buffaloes of No 453 Squadron—the only Allied fighter squadron left on the Malay mainland. Sergeant Eric A. Peterson went after the bombers, claiming one shot down, one 'probable' and one damaged before breaking off and landing safely. Sergeant K. R. Leys took on the fighter escort but was quickly overwhelmed, although he succeeded in bailing out and parachuting to earth in spite of the Japanese firing on him. The 59th pilots claimed four victories in the fight—two more than the total engaged—including one credited to Second Lieutenant Hiroshi Onozaki, who would go on to be the 59th *Sentai*'s leading ace with fourteen victories.

The *Hayabusa*s encountered their first sizeable aerial opposition on the following day when Major Kato led eighteen Ki-43s of the 64th *Sentai* on a mission to Kuala Lumpur. At 11.40 a.m. the regiment's 2nd *Chutai*, under Lieutenant Takayama, spotted a formation of fifteen Buffaloes, dived on them and subsequently claimed a total of eleven destroyed—three of which were credited to Takayama—as well as four damaged. Lieutenant Oizumi was credited with one Buffalo, and it is believed that others were credited to Major Kato, Lieutenants Hinoki and Shogo Takeuchi and Sergeants Yoshito Yasuda and Miyoshi Watanabe.

In actuality No 453 Squadron only had twelve planes up at that time, of which five were lost and four others damaged. After being shot up by six Ki-43s, Pilot Officer T. W. Livesey belly-landed at Kuala Lumpur with shrapnel wounds in both calves and one ankle. Pilot Officer R. W. Drury also crash-landed, but he hit the embankment at the end of the strip and died of his injuries minutes later. Sergeant H. H. Griffiths made it down with a wound to his left hand. Sergeant M. N. Read was killed, and was reported to have rammed or crashed into one of his opponents. Collyer was wounded in the right foot but managed to land at Sembawang, where he was taken to hospital. Sergeant S. G. Scrimgeour was involved in a head-on duel with a *Hayabusa* when his Buffalo burst into flames, burning his face, wrists and fingers before he was able to bail out. Although his parachute was shot up by his victorious adversary, Scrimgeour landed without further mishap.

Sergeant Gregory Richmond Board later recalled: 'Spotting a "Zero" below, I half rolled . . . before I could set up the fighter for the kill, all hell broke loose behind me . . . the instrument panel exploded and blew apart . . . brilliant fire gushed from the fuel tanks.' Board, managed to bail out and survive, but his summation of the experience spoke for most of his contemporaries: 'No one knew what the Zeros were, but they were not slow, ancient, fabric-covered biplanes.'

The Australians credited enemy fighters to Sergeants Griffiths, Read and Clare, the last of whom also claimed two Japanese probably shot down. Flight Lieutenant R. D. Vanderfield was also credited with a 'probable', as were Sergeants K. Gorringe, Collyer and Scrimgeour. In fact the only Japanese loss was Lieutenant Tatayama. The tail of his plane, which was found by Indian troops, revealed that he had taken some devastating hits from large-calibre bullets, but some of his squadron colleagues swore that they had seen his right wing collapse as he was pulling out of a dive. Moreover, an examination of the 64th's *Hayabusa*s upon their return to Kota Bharu revealed cracks in the wings of six other aircraft: clearly, the alterations they had undergone at Tachikawa had not been enough to cope with the stresses of aerial combat. More fundamental strengthening would be necessary on production Ki-43s, but the 59th and 64th *Sentai*s could not wait. For the time being their ground crews spent the night improvising their own field modifications to reinforce the wing structures, with which the *Hayabusa* pilots courageously made do.

The Australians had little time to rest before another air raid was called in. As the Buffaloes taxied to take off, four more Ki-43s, this time from the 59th *Sentai*, arrived and began shooting up the airfield. All of the Buffalo pilots stopped their planes and abandoned their cockpits except one—Eric Peterson, who got airborne only to find a *Hayabusa* on his tail, guns blazing. The Buffalo spun into the ground from 700 feet, killing Peterson. With only three serviceable aircraft, three others barely flyable and six fit pilots left, what remained of No 453 Squadron retired to Semwabang, to be amalgamated with No 21 Squadron, RAAF.

In spite of its somewhat premature introduction to combat, the Ki-43 did well in the early months of the Pacific War—rather better, in fact, than its intrinsic design deserved—partly due to the skill and elan of its experienced pilots and partly by riding on the coat-tails of the reputation of its Navy stablemate, the Zero. Even so, the *Hayabusa*'s fighting debut cannot be called an unqualified success and it was fortunate for its pilots that the Allies, in their stunned ignorance, did not learn of the early Ki-43's weaknesses and—with the notable exception of Chennault and his American Volunteer Group—take fuller advantage of them.

While the fighting continued, the *Hayabusa*'s flaws were ironed out, more powerful engines developed and more potent armament installed. It became as much the workhorse fighter of the JAAF as the Zero was for the JNAF, for much the same reasons—the Japanese committed themselves to it for too long and their industry was unable to produce enough improved successors to replace it completely it front-line service. As with the Zero, a great many *Hayabusa* pilots became aces in spite of its rapidly advancing obsolescence, getting by on individual skill and their sheer familiarity with its flying characteristics. For every one of those extraordinary paladins, however, there would be scores of other JAAF airmen who died in the cockpits of the fighter that the Allies came to code-name 'Oscar'.

On 25 December 25 Ki-43s of the 64th *Sentai*, led by Kato, escorted 27 Ki-21s from the 12th *Sentai* and 36 Ki-21s from the 60th *Sentai* to Rangoon. After the target had been bombed the Japanese were attacked by Buffaloes of No 67 Squadron RAF and Curtiss P-40s of Chennault's AVG. The 64th *Sentai* claimed ten victories but lost two fighters and their pilots, while the 12th *Sentai* lost three bombers, in addition to which a fourth damaged bomber had to force-land upon its return to base. Two Ki-27s were also lost by the 77th *Sentai*, which in turn claimed seven victories. The Allies, who lost two P-40s and four Buffaloes destroyed and two Buffaloes damaged, claimed a total of sixteen bombers and twelve fighters that day.

While that sprawling, confused, Christmas dogfight raged over Rangoon, four other Japanese fighters remained at the 12th and 64th *Sentais*' base at Don Muang. They were the only flyable examples left of a nine-plane detachment and their sole duty that day was to patrol over the airfield and prevent the other aircraft from being attacked while taking off or landing. Minor though their role was, however, the arrival of these fighters at the Front was not without significance. Bearing virtually no family resemblance to the Ki-27 or the Ki-43, they were prototypes of a new Nakajima fighter that represented a radical conceptual change in the *Koku Hombu*'s thinking.

The specification that brought the new fighter into existence stemmed from the undeclared 'Nomonhan Incident' between Japan and the Soviet Union in the summer of 1939. At first the Ki-27 pilots had enjoyed a field day against Soviet Polikarpov I-152 and I-153 biplanes that were barely able to match the Japanese in speed or manoeuvrability. The I-16 monoplane proved to be a different matter, however: it was faster than the Ki-27 and Soviet pilots soon learned to eschew dogfighting the Ki-27s in favour of hit-and-run tactics. In response to that disturbing trend the *Koku Hombu* began to reconsider its earlier dismissal of the fast, heavily armed fighters that were being developed in the West. The specification that it finally issued in 1939 called for an interceptor capable of 373 mph (600 kph) at 13,125 feet (4,000 metres) and a climb rate of 16,405 feet in less than five minutes. The armament was to consist of two 12.7mm and two 7.7mm machine guns—less potent than the Navy Zero's but heavy by Army standards. Since the aeroplane specified was officially classed as an interceptor, manoeuvrability was regarded to be of secondary importance.

Nakajima had already been experimenting with a more advanced fighter concept with retractable landing gear. Tohru Koyama's design team responded to the *Koku Hombu's* specification by designing the smallest possible fighter around a 1,185 hp Nakajima Ha-42 14-cylinder, twin-row, radial engine. The short-span, three-section, two-spar wing, designed largely at the suggestion of Professor Itokawa, had an area of only 161.46 feet, resulting in a wing loading of 30 pounds per square foot—very high by Japanese standards. The reduction in stability due to the wing's relatively small dihedral was to be compensated for by the substantial side area of the oval-section fuselage, and both climb and manoeuvrability in combat were to be enhanced by 'butterfly' wing flaps similar to those used on the Ki-43.

The first prototype of the Nakajima Ki-44 first flew from Ojima airfield, Ota, in August 1940, leaving Koyama and his team less than satisfied. Flying characteristics were acceptable, but the aircraft's weight was sixteen per cent higher than they had originally calculated, raising the wing loading to 34.8 pounds per square foot and consequently increasing the landing speed. Drag was also greater than anticipated, resulting in a maximum speed of only 342 mph at 13,125 feet and a climb rate of 16,405 feet in 5 minutes 54 seconds. Increasing the rigidity of the engine mount, recontouring the supercharger air intake and modifying the cowl flaps eventually brought the maximum speed up to 389 mph and the diving speed to 528 mph in 1941. At that point it was estimated that a fully armed Ki-44 would be capable of 360 mph and the *Koku Hombu* ordered the second and third prototypes to be modified accordingly, along with as seven more for evaluation purposes.

On 15 September 1941 a special evaluation unit, the 47th *Dokuritsu Hiko Chutai* (Independent Air Squadron), unofficially dubbed the 'Kingfisher' *Chutai*, was formed. The experienced airmen assigned to evaluate the new *Shoki*, or Demon, as the Ki-44 was christened, wasted little time in expressing their opinion that the name was appropriate—in regard to its malevolence towards its own pilots. They complained of poor forward visibility on the ground, the high landing speed and the excessive 3,280-foot run required for a safe landing, and of course they bewailed the high wing loading and consequent loss of the agility to which they were accustomed. As they became more familiar with the plane, however, they came to appreciate its fast roll rate, high diving speed and steadiness as a gun platform.

On 30 November the 47th *Chutai* was shipped off to Canton, China, to evaluate its fighters under combat conditions. When war broke out a week later three *shotais* (flights) of the 47th were attached to the 1st, 11th and 12th *Sentais*—the 1st *Shotai*, led by Captain Toshio Sakagawa, the 2nd, led by Captain Susumu Jimbo, and the 3rd, under Captain Yasuhiko Kuroe. During previous service in the 59th *Sentai* First Lieutenant Kuroe had fought over the Nomonhan plateau, where he was credited with two Soviet I-152s in September 1939. He had then served as a flight instructor at the Army Officers' Flight Academy, where he was promoted to Captain in May 1941 and assigned to the 47th *Chutai* four months later.

In late December 1941 the JAAF diverted its efforts from Malaya to Burma in response to reconnaissance reports that large numbers of Allied aircraft were gathering at the airfields of Mingaladon and Toungoo. On 24 December the 12th and 64th *Sentais* and the 47th *Dokuritsu Hiko Chutai* moved to Don Muang airfield in preparation for the Christmas raid. During the move, however, three of the Ki-44s had to force-land, including that of the *Chutai* commander. Only four *Shokis* were combat-ready the next day and in consequence they were kept close to home, serving only to cover the airfield.

By January 1942, while Nakajima was putting the Ki-44-I into production, the nine prototype and evaluation aircraft were being put through their paces over Singapore. On the 15th sixteen bombers attacked Tengah and Sembawang, while the 59th *Sentai*'s *Hayabusas* claimed six Buffaloes that tried to interfere and Ki-27s of the 1st *Sentai* claimed seven more Buffaloes. Also ordered to participate in the Singapore mission were Kuroe and Jimbo in their Ki-44s. Kuroe went after a Buffalo over Tengah, and when his first pass failed to bring it down it was engaged by Jimbo. Kuroe then came at the Buffalo again and, as he reported afterwards, 'after five bursts it fell to the ground'. The *Shoki* had been blooded, and it would be again on 18 January when Ki-44s of the 47th *Chutai* claimed another Buffalo during a further sortie over Singapore.

On 26 January a British force of Lockheed Hudson bombers and Vickers Vildebeest biplane torpedo-bombers, escorted by Buffaloes and Hawker Hurricanes, left Singapore to attack a Japanese invasion force approaching Endau when they were set upon by nineteen Nakajima Ki-27s of the 1st and 11th *Sentai*s. Five Vildebeests were shot down, while four Hudsons and several Buffaloes returned with damage. Although the Commonwealth pilots claimed numerous 'Zeros' and 'Navy Type 96 fighters' shot down, only one Ki-27 of the 1st *Sentai* was actually lost and its pilot bailed out safely. Also present was Kuroe and his Ki-44, but on this occasion he stayed discreetly above the fight, merely observing and reporting results. Although the costly British attack on Endau inflicted slight damage to the troopship *Kanbara Maru*, it failed to deter the Japanese landing.

A second strike was duly launched from Singapore, consisting of nine Vildebeests and three Fairey Albacore biplane torpedo-bombers, escorted by seven Hurricanes and four Buffaloes. The motley force arrived over Endau at 5.30 p.m. and immediately came under attack from ten Ki-27s of the 1st *Sentai*, which shot down six Vildebeests and two Albacores. When Hurricanes of No 232 Squadron tried to intervene, two Ki-44s of the 47th *Chutai*, flown by Kuroe and Jimbo, plunged through their formation. The *Shoki* pilots were subsequently credited with a Hurricane each, although only one was actually shot down, Jimbo being the more likely victor. Canadian-born Sergeant John P. Fleming reported:

> On this last trip of the day I immediately attacked three fixed-undercarriage Japs attacking a Vildebeest who was making a bomb run on one of the ships—I think a freighter. The three scattered and I saw a bomb strike at the waterline of the ship—as I broke away from this attack I was struck by fire from a 'Zero' I think. Oil pressure collapsed—managed to fly south for about 20 miles before the engine seized, abandoning the aircraft at low level over the beach just north of Mersing.

The Hurricane pilots claimed three or four Ki-27s in the fight, corresponding to the 1st *Sentai*'s logging several aircraft damaged, though none was lost.

On 28 January four Boeing B-17Es of the American 19th Bomb Group, operating from Java, bombed Kuala Lumpur airfield, setting one Japanese fighter on fire, badly damaging three others and causing lesser damage to another six. The 11th *Sentai* was reduced to only one combat-ready *Chutai*, while the 47th *Dokuritsu Hiko Chutai*'s local detachment was left with only one operational Ki-44.

The 47th *Chutai* continued to serve throughout the early months of 1942. Three of its *Shoki*s participated in a large fighter sweep over Mingaladon in Burma on 25 February and they claimed two Allied planes during a wild fight with Hurricanes of No 17 Squadron RAF and P-40s of the AVG. Both sides, in fact, made extravagant claims that day, but one of the Ki-44s' misperceived victims may have been Sergeant J. F. Barrick, an American serving in No 17 Squadron, who described his lone fight with fifteen enemy fighters:

I attacked and shot down one 'Army 97' [Ki-27] and was then jumped from above by a 'Zero' [undoubtedly a Ki-44]. I went into a tight turn which caused one of the gun panels to fly open. This made the aircraft 'flick' and probably saved my life, because the 'Zero' was in an excellent position behind me. As it was my plane was not hit.

Four of the 47th's Ki-44s may also have been the so-called 'Zeros' that attacked four Blenheims over the Sittang area on 4 March, shooting down one plane from No 45 Squadron. By 20 March the unit's quartet of Ki-44s had joined the 32 Ki-27s of Headquarters *Shotai*, 12th *Hiko-Daitai*, and of the 1st and 11th *Sentai*s at the newly taken airfield at Pegu, as components of the 5th Air Division during the continuing Japanese offensive into Burma.

On 21 April Captain Kuroe left the 47th *Chutai* to take command of the 3rd *Chutai* of the 64th *Sentai*, succeeding Captain Katsumi Anma, who had been killed on 8 April. Four days later the 47th *Chutai* was recalled to Japan and turned its Ki-44s over to the 64th *Sentai*. In spite of the three victories credited to him while flying the *Shoki*, Kuroe reported that it did not live up to his expectations. By then, however, Nakajima had committed the new interceptor to production and it was accepted for JAAF service. Eventually identified by Allied intelligence and given the code-name 'Tojo', the Ki-44 was nevertheless to be frequently misidentified as a 'Zero' in Allied combat reports in China for years to come. Its speed and rate of climb were soon overtaken by newer Allied fighters, but the Ki-44 *Shoki* would soldier on throughout the war, its pilots often managing to distinguish themselves as late as 1945 in its original role of interceptor, defending their homeland against Boeing B-29s. More importantly, it set a precedent that roused the JAAF from its obsession with manoeuvrability for its own sake, leading to a generation of more potent fighters. Unfortunately for the Japanese, the latter still came out too little and too late: even as the Pacific War neared its end in 1945, they never fully replaced the Navy Zeros and Army *Hayabusa*s with which they had started it.

Chapter 10

UNDER FOREIGN MANAGEMENT

1939–1942

Not all of the famous fighters of World War II started out serving the countries that built them. The most obvious examples would come from the United States, which did not officially enter the conflict until 7 December 1941 but which provided aircraft to several of the combatants prior to that date. Two other cases, however, can be found in two of the war's most famous flying anachronisms, built by Britain and Italy but first used in combat by two other air arms entirely.

Incredibly, the Gloster Gladiator was still in first-line service with several Royal Air Force squadrons when Britain entered the war, even though low-winged monoplane fighters with retractable landing gear had been making their way into the RAF since 1936. Developed by Harry P. Folland in 1934, the Gloster S.S.37 was first flown by Flight Lieutenant P. E. G. Sayer on 12 September 1934 and entered production, with an 830 hp Bristol Mercury IX engine, on 1 July 1935 under the official designation 'Gladiator'. A compact but conventional biplane, the Gladiator looked more modern than its Italian contemporary, the Fiat C.R.42, only in that it had an enclosed sliding canopy and two 0.303-inch machine guns under the wings in addition to the usual two in the fuselage—touches that, to the retrospective eye, only look quaintly out of place on an aircraft that should have been retired within a year of being committed to production.

Tangmere-based No 72 Squadron began replacing its Bristol Bulldogs with Gladiators on 22 February 1937, the first of an eventual nine squadrons to get the type. Rough running of the Mercury IX engine with a two-blade airscrew led to the decision to use a three-blade Fairey-Reed propeller in July 1937. The resultant improvement was standardized, along with a Mercury VIII or VIIIAS engine, as the Gladiator Mk II.

The 1938 Munich Crisis led to increased production of all available fighter types for the RAF, and the Gladiator II was among those mass-produced for use by the Auxiliary Air Force. At the same time foreign orders for the Gladiator I came from Latvia, Sweden, Norway, Greece and China. The Royal Navy, too, wanted a replacement for its ageing Hawker Nimrods, for which Gloster developed the Sea Gladiator, with a naval TR.9 radio, an airspeed indicator calibrated in knots and provision for an arrester hook. By September 1939 Gladiators and Sea Gladiators were serving actively with the RAF and thirteen other air arms. Long before World War II, however, it was the Chinese who had the distinction of first blooding the type in combat.

Early in 1938 the Chinese Central Government ordered 36 Gladiators, which were accompanied to Kai Tak airfield, Hong Kong, by a Gloster test pilot and a small party of riggers and technicians. From there the crated fighters had to be transported by rail and junk up the Pearl river to Canton. As each plane was assembled at Tien Ho airfield it was flown by the Gloster test pilot and then by a Chinese pilot—who more often than not would prang the tricky biplane while taxying or in a heavy-handed stall upon take-off.

Some of the Gladiators' earliest combats were flown by American citizens of Chinese descent who had volunteered to defend their ancestral homeland from the Japanese invaders. Wong Sun-shui, also known as John Wong, was born on 15 March 1914 in Los Angeles, California, which was also where he earned his pilot's licence. He subsequently went to China, and after training at the Gwangdung Air Force Academy he became deputy commander of the 17th Squadron, which was originally equipped with Boeing 248s—export versions of the P-26 Peashooter monoplane fighter. 'Buffalo' Wong, as he was nicknamed, was credited with two victories in the Boeings before being wounded over Nanking during a disastrous encounter with new Mitsubishi A5M2 fighters of the Japanese 13th *Kokutai* on 19 September 1937 which cost the Chinese eleven planes.

When Wong returned to combat he learned that the 17th Squadron's Boeings had been virtually annihilated while defending Nanking in December. He was given command of the 29th Squadron, newly equipped with Gladiators, and it was in one of the British biplanes that Wong re-opened his account over Gwangzhou on 24 February 1938, shooting down two Nakajima A4N fighters and sharing in the destruction of a third with a squadron colleague. On the following day Wong, flying Gladiator No 2905, downed an A5M over Gwangzhou, his late opponent being either Lieutenant Shigeo Takuma or Petty Officer 1st Class Hisao Ochi of the 13th *Kokutai*, both of whom were killed in action that day. Wong scored three more victories during an air battle with aircraft from the carrier *Kaga* on 13 April, bringing his account up to 8½. He was later promoted to the rank of Major, and on 15 November 1940 he was put in command of the 5th Fighter Group, with which unit he flew Polikarpov I-152s. On 14 March 1941 Wong was wounded during a dogfight with Mitsubishi A6M2 Zeros, and he died of his wounds two days later.

Another early exponent of the Gladiator was Chin Shui-tin, also known as Arthur Chin, from Portland, Oregon. Born on 23 October 1913, Chin became one of fifteen Sino-American volunteers who trained at Al Greenwood's flying school in Portland before joining the Cantonese Air Force on 1 December 1932. In 1936 Chin was sent to Germany for additional training, then returned to become executive officer (XO) of the 28th Squadron of the 5th Group, Chinese Air Force. First flying the Curtiss Hawk III biplane fighter, Chin opened his account with a Mitsubishi G3M2 on 16 August 1937. The squadron re-equipped with Gladiators in the spring of 1938, and on 13 April Louie Yim-qun, another American volunteer from Seattle, Washington, downed an A4N and shared in another over Gwangzhou. Chin used a Gladiator to down a Nakajima E8N floatplane over Hukou, Kiangsi, on 31 May. On 1 June 1938 he was promoted to Captain and placed in command of the 28th Squadron, with Louie as his XO.

On 16 June Chin downed a Mitsubishi Ki-21 as well as damaging another bomber over Shaokuan, near Canton, while Louie and a Chinese Gladiator pilot teamed up to bring down a third. Also active that day was Wong Pan-yang of the 17th Squadron, who downed a Ki-21 and shared in the destruction of three others over Namsung. Like Chin, Wong Pan-yang, who came from Seattle, Washington, had gained a private pilot's licence in Portland before going to China and had scored two victories in Boeing 248s with the 17th Squadron in August 1937.

That the Gladiator's days were numbered became evident on 3 August 1938 when Chin's 28th Squadron tangled with A5M2s over Liang Chia-Tien in Hupei province. Chin, flying Gladiator No 2809, managed to damage one of the swift monoplane fighters and then, out of sheer desperation, rammed a second and succeeded in bailing out. Louie and a Chinese comrade also claimed an A5M, and at least one more was also forced down, for the 15th *Kokutai* recorded the deaths of Lieutenant (jg) Shinjo Naoshisa and PO2C Hitoshi Fukosawa, while PO3C Namitaro Matsushima was brought down as a prisoner of war. Chin went on to destroy two more A5Ms and share in the destruction of two others before being badly burned in combat on 27 December 1940. Returning to the United States, he died in 1997.

The Gladiator was still in Chinese use in 1939 but by then it was hopelessly outclassed by the A5M. Had anyone in Europe been paying serious attention to what was going on in China, the Gladiator would probably have been retired before 10 May 1940 when the Germans launched their offensive in the West. As it was, desperate circumstances often bought the biplanes to the forefront over Finland, Norway, Belgium, France, the Western Desert, Greece and Malta, and heroic deeds were performed in the Gladiators before the last of them were withdrawn from RAF service in 1942.

If ever there were an aeroplane that was obsolete before its wheels left the runway, the Italian Fiat C.R.42 *Falco* (Falcon) would be the all-time champion. The last of a successful series of biplane fighters designed by Celestino Rosatelli, the C.R.42 had a robust airframe of light alloy and steel, and its wings were braced by the same sturdy Warren truss structure as its predecessors. Its engine was a reliable 840 hp Fiat A74R.1C.38, neatly cowled and driving a three-blade, constant-speed Fiat 3D41 propeller. The armament comprised one 7.7mm and one 12.7mm Breda-SAFAT machine gun in the upper fuselage decking, which was later wisely upgraded to two 12.7mm weapons. The prototype displayed the same excellent manoeuvrability as the earlier C.R.32 but could go much faster at 274 mph. Moreover, its development proceeded so smoothly that it first flew, went into production and began squadron service in the same year. Unfortunately for Italy, that year was 1939.

When Italy entered the war on 10 June 1940 the C.R.42 was numerically the *Regia Aeronautica*'s principal fighter. Arguably it represented the ultimate development of the old World War I formula of a biplane fighter with fixed landing gear and an open cockpit, but that could not make up for the fact that that configuration was long obsolete.

The C.R.42 joined the Italian Army in its fourteen-day invasion of southern France, beginning with strafing attacks on the air bases at Fayence and Hyères and the escort of Fiat B.R.20 bombers over Toulon harbor on 13 June. More than a month before Italy's entry into the conflict, however, the fighter had already seen some action—and drawn a few drops of blood—in the hands of Belgian pilots.

Belgium had undergone a fitful rearmament in the face of the growing threat from a resurgent Nazi Germany during the late 1930s. Fully roused by the German invasion of Poland in September 1939, the Belgian military began sending out feelers with a view to acquiring more modern aircraft for the woefully inadequate *Aéronautique Militaire*. One of the most desperate such actions was the purchase of 34 Fiat C.R.42s that month. The first of them was delivered in March 1940, and by May there were enough to equip the *3ème* and *4ème Escadrilles* of *Groupe de Chasse II*. While Italian fighter pilots may have still favoured the 'seat-of-the-pants' atmosphere of the Fiat's open cockpit, the Belgians were less nostalgic. So low was their opinion of their new mounts that the two *escadrille* commanders were said to have flipped a coin to see who would test-fly the biplane first—with that distinction going to the loser.

By May 1940 Belgium had a total of 180 aircraft at her disposal, of which only eleven Hawker Hurricanes of the *2ème Escadrille* could be considered up to contemporary standards. In addition to the two C.R.42 squadrons, the *1ère Escadrille* was operating the Gladiator, which in the coming year would be better known for duelling the Fiats than for fighting alongside them. Still, the C.R.42s and Gladiators seemed more likely to survive in the air than the fighters with which the *5ème* and *6ème Escadrilles* were equipped. Those two squadrons were still using the Fairey Fox VIC, a Hispano-Suiza-engine version of the British-built reconnaissance and training two-seater, converted to a single-seat interceptor by the Belgians pending the arrival of 40 replacement Brewster B-239s (export versions of the F2A Buffalo).

Such was the situation when the C.R.42's true combat debut came on 10 May 1940, as *Luftwaffe* aircraft heralded the end of the 'Phoney War' and the beginning of the German offensive in the West—with Belgium and the Netherlands among the initial stepping-stones on the road to Paris. Junkers Ju 87B Stukas caught most of the Belgian aircraft on the ground, thirteen of the Fiats being destroyed alongside most of the *Aéronautique Militaire*.

Among the few Belgian aircraft to get into the air on that disastrous first day was a C.R.42 flown by *Sergent* Jean Henri Marie Offenberg. Born at Laeken near Brussels on 3 July 1916, 'Peike' Offenberg had joined *Capitaine* Jean de Gallatay's *4éme Escadrille* at Nivelles in March 1939 just as it was exchanging its Fox biplanes for the barely more up-to-date Fiats.

In his autobiography Offenberg describes how he was awakened at 1 a.m. on 10 May by his squadron colleague, *Sergent* Alexis Jottard, who told him that war had broken out with Germany. Knowing that German aircraft would be likely to attack the airfield, *GC.4/II*'s pilots took off shortly after 4.30 and flew to the emergency airstrip at Brusthem near Saint-Trond. Upon arriving there the Belgians learned that Nivelles had indeed been dive-bombed just minutes after they had left. For some time they waited for reports of German aircraft coming their way, then Offenberg asked his group commander if he could fly a patrol with two wingmen, *Sergents* Jottard and Maes, if only to avoid being caught on the ground. Permission was granted and the trio took off at 7.05 a.m.

As they circled up over Saint-Trond Offenberg noticed what a slow rate of climb the C.R.42 had:

> Then [he wrote], a plane passed to port, a very elongated twin-engined aircraft with two tail units and black crosses surrounded by a thin white border—a Hun, my first Hun. My heart beat faster and I managed to wave to my two comrades. But they had seen him too and Maes, without waiting for orders, had broken away. I caught sight of his Fiat's belly against a cloudless sky the moment he dived on the Dornier 17. Why had he done it? Why hadn't he waited for my orders? For a thousandth of a second I thought of our fighting instructions. I could not reflect for long, for Jottard pointed to a spot on the horizon and I suddenly saw a ragged formation of planes staged at various altitudes. Messerschmitts . . . Instinctively I went into a spin, while the two German fighters on my port beam broke formation. And then I cannot remember . . . I do recall diving between two Messerschmitts on a bomber whose rear gunner fired at me. I fired my first burst and then a second . . . My starboard machine gun jammed and I pulled out of the dive.

As he did, Offenberg found himself alone in the sky over Diest. It was 6.45 and he had descended 5,000 feet. As he prepared to set course for Saint-Trond he spotted another twin-engine bomber below him. Offenberg pursued it in a shallow dive but was too far away to fire and too slow to catch up with the German. 'Above Maastricht I gave up the chase,' he wrote. 'Passing a finger across my lips I noticed a little dark patch on my glove. I had bitten my lower lip without knowing it.'

After glancing down at Saint-Trond airfield, Offenberg followed the main road towards Brussels, then spotted another Do 17 approaching from his left:

> A dive, followed by an Immelmann turn, and I was in position above him [Offenberg continued]. I had learned a great deal in the past few minutes. Unless I was well above him the speed of my Fiat would not allow me to close in on him without a dive. He passed on a level with me. His turret revolved. I waded in and opened fire just as tracers bore down on me from all sides like scarlet beads. The old Fiat vibrated and bucked from the recoil of the machine gun. I did not know quite what to do so I went on firing. Spirals of black smoke began to pour from his port engine. He banked just as I pulled on the stick to avoid a red stream of tracers. Below me the Dornier was rapidly losing height.

Offenberg landed at Brusthem at 7.45, where he was credited with his first victory and was 'happy to be still alive'.

At 3 p.m. the Germans found Brusthem and five Me 109Es strafed the Fiats of *GC.II*, which were, in Offenberg's words, 'lined up like strings of onions— not dispersed enough for my taste'. The Germans accomplished little, and Offenberg was commenting to Jottard that 'I still think it would be better to get out of here and to get all that junk airborne before they return' when Ju 87s arrived. The Belgians took what cover they could as bombs fell on the C.R.42s. When the Stukas departed not one of the *3ème Escadrille*'s fifteen fighters remained operational. In contrast, none of the *4ème Escadrille*'s Fiats had been seriously damaged. Word arrived, however, that earlier in the day one of the unit's pilots, *Sergent* Delannay, had been shot down by an Me 109 while trying to intercept a Do 17, had come down with a bullet through his lung and had died in the ambulance on the way to the hospital. Another battle-damaged plane crashed on landing. 'I felt like weeping,' Offenberg recalled. 'All our airfields have been bombed and shot up by machine guns. Fort Eben-Emael has been put out of action by German parachutists. Night fell mercifully on our grief . . .'

Somehow, Offenberg survived the swift destruction of the *Aéronautique Militaire* with one enemy plane to his credit, and two other C.R.42 pilots claimed victories as well. Few Belgian pilots, not even those flying the more modern Hawker Hurricane, were so fortunate. After that the remaining seven Fiats of *Escadrille 4/II* redeployed to Nieukerke, where they claimed two more enemy aircraft for the loss of another C.R.42 before 16 May when, with Belgium about to be overrun, Offenberg and his comrades were ordered to withdraw to Chartres, France.

When France fell a month later, Offenberg and his squadron chum *Sergent* Jottard commandeered two Caudron Simouns and flew to Montpelier, then made their way across the Channel to England. There Offenberg enlisted in the RAF, joining No 145 Squadron on 17 August. After flying Hurricanes in the Battle of Britain and later switching to Spitfire IIBs, 'Pyker' Offenberg, as he was known to his RAF comrades, became the first Belgian to be awarded the Distinguished Flying Cross in June 1941, and on the 27th of that month he joined No 609 Squadron. He subsequently commanded a Belgian flight within the squadron, but during a training flight on 22 January 1942 he was killed in a mid-air collision with a Spitfire from No 92 Squadron. At the time of his death Offenberg had added four victories, plus two shared, to that first one he had scored while flying the Fiat C.R.42. At that same time the *Falco*, though finally eclipsed by monoplanes as a first-line fighter, was still soldiering on as a fighter-bomber and night fighter in the *Regia Aeronautica* as well as the Royal Hungarian Air Force (*Magyár Kiraly Honved Légierö*) and, later, even the *Luftwaffe*.

At about the same time Belgium was struggling in vain to slow the German onslaught, the Netherlands was also fighting a losing battle against the *Luftwaffe*. The principal Dutch fighter at that time was the Fokker D.XXI, a low-wing monoplane with an enclosed cockpit and fixed, spatted landing gear. Before the Dutch commenced their gallant but doomed fight against the Germans, however, Fokker D.XXIs had been blooded in another war against equally daunting odds, yet with far greater success.

Designed in 1936, the Fokker D.XXI was a reasonably advanced if unexceptional plane for its time, with a 760 hp Bristol Mercury VIII 9-cylinder radial engine that gave it a maximum speed of 286 mph and an armament of four 0.30-calibre machine guns. The D.XXI gave Fokker's *Nederlandsche Vliegtuigenfabriek*, which had suffered during the economic depression and recession of the 1930s, a new lease on life. In addition to orders from the Royal Netherlands Air Force, the firm sold rights for the licence manufacture of ten D.XXIs by Denmark and 38 by Finland in 1937. By May 1940, however, the D.XXI was becoming obsolescent and only 39 were operational in the Royal Netherlands Air Force. Small wonder, then, that the Germans overran the Netherlands in a matter of days. Long before that, however, the Finnish Fokkers had already drawn blood of their own—and lots of it.

Taking advantage of the Nazi-Soviet pact of August 1939 while Hitler's attention was on Britain and France to the west, Josef Stalin sought to secure his country's northern flank by occupying part of Finland's Karelia isthmus.

When the Finns refused to give up that territory the Soviets commenced hostilities with a bombing attack on Helsinki on 30 November 1939.

The Finns were astonished that war had actually broken out in so sudden a fashion, but they got over their shock quickly. The army was mobilized and soon managed to stall the Red Army's invasion in the Finnish forests while inflicting tremendous casualties on its personnel.

Although numerically no match for the Soviet Army Air Force, the *Ilmavoimat* had done its best to compensate through intense training. 'The younger pilots got additional training in aerial combat and gunnery,' recalled then-Warrant Officer Eino Ilmari Juutilainen of *Lentolaivue* (Flying Squadron) *24*. 'During bad weather we indulged in sports, pistol shooting and discussions about fighter tactics. Our *esprit de corps* was high despite the fact that we would be up against heavy odds. We were ready.'

Thus when unescorted Soviet bombers returned on 1 December the Fokker pilots of *LeLv 24*, led by Captain Gustaf Erik Magnusson, were up and waiting for them over Kannas. In short order Lieutenant Eino A. Luukanen downed an Ilyushin DB-3, while Tupolev SB-2s fell to Magnusson, Lieutenant Pekka J. Kokko, Second Lieutenant Lauri V. Nissinen and Sergeant J. T. Virta.

It was only the beginning of a disastrous mismatch between the overwhelming quantity of Soviet aircraft and the outstanding quality of Finnish pilots. Fighting alongside more aged types such as Gloster Gladiators and even Bristol Bulldogs, the Fokkers were credited with 120 victories by the time Finland capitulated on 13 March 1940, making *LeLv 24* the top-scoring unit of the Winter War. Five of the squadron's pilots became aces, and a good many future ones opened their accounts in the D.XXI. Juutilainen, who shot down a DB-3 and a Polikarpov I-16 and joined five other pilots in downing an SB-2, compared the Fokker D.XXI with its principal adversary:

> It was our best fighter in 1939, but the Soviet Polikarpov I-16 was faster, had better agility and also had protective armour for the pilot. I flew a war booty I-16, and it did 215 knots at low level and turned around on a dime. I liked that plane. In comparison the Fokker could make about 175 [knots]. The D.XXI also lacked armour, but it had good diving characteristics and it was a steady shooting platform. I think that our gunnery training made the Fokker such a winner in the Winter War.

The Fokker D.XXI's most successful exponent was a relative latecomer, Lieutenant Jorma Sarvanto, who opened his account on 23 December with two SB-2s over Kannas. Flying the same plane, FR-97, on 6 January, he encountered a formation of DB-3s over Kannas and shot down six of them in less than five minutes. He went on to down four more Soviet planes and share in the destruction of two others before the Winter War ended, making him the leading ace of the conflict.

In addition to seven D.XXIs bought from Fokker and the 38 that it was licensed to produce, the Finnish State Aircraft Factory, or *Valtion Lentokonetehdas* (VL), built 60 more, incorporating such modifications as a 1,050 hp Pratt & Whitney R-1535 Twin Wasp Junior engine, enlarged vertical control surfaces, the transfer of the two fuselage guns to the wings and more canopy glazing for better visibility. VL also built one experimental version with inward-retracting landing gear. Although the careers of the Dutch and Danish Fokkers were extremely brief, the Fokker D.XXI steadfastly served Finland throughout the Continuation War until September 1944.

By 1940 the Gladiator had been eclipsed in RAF service by a number of British-built monoplane fighters, supplemented amid the exigencies of war by several types imported from the United States through the Lend-Lease programme. As a result of that arrangement, three famous American fighters first fired their guns in anger in British or Commonwealth service.

Arguably the best-known fighter in the US Army Air Forces (USAAF) in the first year of direct American participation in the war was the Curtiss P-40. Designed by Donovan Reese Berlin, the prototype XP-40 was more evolutionary than revolutionary in concept, being nothing more than the tenth production airframe of Berlin's P-36A Hawk fighter with an Allison V-1710 liquid-cooled inline engine substituted for the P-36's 875 hp Wright GR-1820-G3 Cyclone air-cooled radial.

Donovan's original monoplane design dated to 1934. He designated it the Curtiss Model 75, reflecting his obsession with that number, while the emotive nickname 'Hawk', already famous from an earlier generation of Curtiss biplane fighters, was revived for the new monoplane. Although the Hawk 75 first flew in 1935, engine problems delayed its development until 7 July 1937, when the Army Air Corps gave Curtiss the largest American peacetime production order up to that time—210 P-36s, as the Army called them, for $4,113,550. Hawk 75s, built with retractable landing gear or with fixed, spatted undercarriage—depending on whether speed or simplicity was the customer's main priority—were also sold to numerous foreign air arms. The first to employ them in combat were the Chinese in 1939, but the poor training of their pilots rendered the P-36s' combat debut less than stellar.

Although its performance was eclipsed by that of other types by 1940, the Hawk 75 was fondly remembered by its pilots for its easy handling and excellent manoeuvrability. Export Hawk 75As, powered by 950 hp Pratt and Whitney Twin Wasp engines, became the best fighters available in quantity to the French in May 1940 and were credited with more enemy planes shot down than any French-built fighter. Thailand purchased Hawk 75Ns with fixed landing gear and used them during its war against the French in Indo-China in January

1941 as well as during its equally brief resistance to invading Japanese forces in December 1941. The US Army Air Corps still had P-36Cs on strength when Pearl Harbor was attacked on 7 December 1941 and they scored some of the first American air-to-air victories that day. The exiled Royal Netherlands Air Force used Cyclone-engine P-36s in the East Indies, where they became easy prey for the Japanese Zero. The RAF also used P-36s, which it called Mohawks, as stop-gap fighters, most notably in Burma in 1942. Vichy French pilots flew Hawk 75As against the British and Americans during their invasion of North Africa in November 1942 and other French H-75As, shipped to Finland by the Germans, fought the Soviets until September 1944. Although neither as modern nor as famous as the P-40 that succeeded it, the P-36 can lay claim to greater ubiquity and the rare—if dubious—distinction of having fought on both sides during World War II.

The Allison-engine XP-40 first flew on 14 October 1938 and competed against the Lockheed XP-38, Bell XP-39 and Seversky AP-4 at Wright Field, near Dayton, Ohio, on 25 January 1939. The XP-40 emerged the winner and in April Curtiss was rewarded with what was touted as 'the largest contract since World War I'—for 543 P-40s.

Although outclassed by the Zero, P-40s soldiered on as best they could, starting with the very first Japanese attack on Pearl Harbor. In the months that followed, the P-40 pilots fought desperately and often heroically, with decidedly mixed fortunes. They were ultimately annihilated in the Philippines and the Dutch East Indies, but in the hands of master tactician Colonel Claire L. Chennault and his American Volunteer Group in China the Hawk 81 (as the export version of the P-40 was known) did a disproportionate amount of damage and became one of the war's legendary fighters.

More than six months before the United States entered the war, however, P-40s had already fought over terrain that could not have been farther removed from Pearl Harbor, the mountains of China or the jungles of South-East Asia. Even while it was filling the Army Air Corps' orders for P-36s and P-40s, Curtiss were marketing both the Hawk 75 and 81 to overseas customers. Although not used quite as widely as the Hawk 75, the Hawk 81 saw considerable Chinese use—first by the American mercenaries of the AVG and later by Chinese pilots—as well as service in the Soviet army and naval air arms, the RAF and the Royal Australian Air Force (RAAF). It was, in fact, in British service that the 'Hawk' designator probably got more use in reference to the P-40 than it ever did by the fighter's American pilots. The earliest models were called 'Tomahawks' by the British while the later ones were christened 'Kittyhawks'.

The first major action in which Tomahawks figured prominently was a sideshow that nevertheless serves as a reminder of just how global a conflict World

War II was. On 2 May 1941 British forces in Iraq came under attack by Iraqi forces, directed by the anti-British, pro-German chief of the National Defence Government, Rashid Ali el Ghailani. The revolt was quickly crushed and Rashid Ali fled the country on 30 May, but not before a number of Axis aircraft had been committed to his cause. Sixty-two German transport aircraft carried *matériel* to the Iraqis, making refuelling stops at airfields in Syria and Lebanon, then mandates of Vichy France. The Germans and Italians had also sent fighters and bombers, which, hastily adorned in Iraqi markings, had made their way into the country from the French air bases. Amid the British counter-attack, at 4.50 p.m. on 14 May two Tomahawk Mk IIBs of No 250 Squadron, flown by Flying Officers G. A. Wolsey and F. J. S. Aldridge, carried out the first P-40 combat mission when they escorted three Bristol Blenheims in an attack on suspected German and Italian aircraft staging at Palmyra in Syria.

In allowing Axis planes to stage from their territory, the French-mandated Levant presented a threat to British security in Palestine and Egypt at a time when *Generalleutnant* Erwin Rommel's *Afrika Korps* was starting to make its presence felt in North Africa. On 15 May British aircraft attacked French air bases at Palmyra, Rayack, Damascus, Homs, Tripoli and Beirut. The Vichy government responded by dispatching *Groupe de Chasse III/6* to Rayak with a complement of top-of-the-line Dewoitine D.520 fighters. In addition to those, *Général* Jean Jannkeyn, commander of the *Armée de l'Air* in the Levant, had *GC I/7*, equipped with Morane Saulnier M.S.406 fighters, *Groupe de Bombardment II/39* with American-built Glenn Martin 167F twin-engine bombers, *GC III/39* with antiquated Bloch 200s, *Groupe de Reconnaissance (GR) II/39* and Flight *GAO 583* with Potez 63-IIs and a multitude of less effective Army and Navy planes at his disposal, for a total of 90.

By the end of May the British had decided to seize the Levant. General Archibald Wavell organized an invasion force by pulling the Australian 7th Division, less one brigade, from its defensive position at Mersa Matruh and combining it with with the 5th Brigade of the Indian 4th Division, elements of the 1st Cavalry Division, a commando unit from Cyprus, a squadron of armoured cars and a cavalry regiment. The scratch force was to receive some offshore support from the Royal Navy and air support from 60 aircraft of the RAF and the RAAF. The latter included Tomahawk Mk IIBs of No 3 Squadron RAAF, based at Jenin, Palestine, in place of No 250 Squadron's Tomahawks, which had been transferred to Egypt.

The three-pronged invasion commenced from Palestine and Trans-Jordan at 2 a.m. on 8 June. The British and accompanying Gaullist French forces had hoped that the 35,000 Vichy troops in Syria would be loath to fight their former allies but they were in for a disappointment. Anticipating Allied propaganda appeals based on the idea of saving Syria from German domination, Vichy High Commissioner *Général* Henri-Fernand Dentz saw to it that all signs of German presence were removed throughout the country. The *Luftwaffe*, too, had discreetly evacuated all of its aircraft, aircrews and technicians from the Syrian airfields forty-eight hours ahead of the expected invasion. In consequence the Allied propaganda fell on deaf ears, the French officers defending Syria refused to deal with their Gaullist compatriots and the Allied invasion force found itself with a fight on its hands.

On the day of the invasion, 8 June 1941, Hurricanes of Nos 80, 108 and 260 Squadrons and five Tomahawks of No 3 Squadron RAAF carried out pre-emptive attacks on the French airfields. Among other targets the Hurricanes and Tomahawks strafed *GC III/6*'s fighters on the ground at Rayak, burning a D.520 and damaging seven others. On this occasion the Tomahawks drew relatively little fire from French ground gunners, who mistook the unfamiliar new fighters for their own D.520s. Elsewhere on the same day two Tomahawks of No 250 Squadron RAF shot down an intruding Cant Z.1007*bis* reconnaissance-bomber of the Italian *211a Squadriglia* five miles north-west of Alexandria.

As Vichy France rushed reinforcements to the Levant, the Germans and Italians put airstrips in newly conquered Greece at their disposal, allowing the swift ferrying of Lioré et Olivier LeO 451 bombers of *GB I/31*, *I/14* and *I/25*, D.520s of *GC II/3* and Martin 167s of the *4e Flotille* of the *Aéronavale* to Syria by 17 June.

French bombers attacked Admiral Sir Andrew Cunningham's naval force off Saida on 9 June, damaging two ships. Eight German Junkers Ju 88As of *II Gruppe*, *Lehrgeschwader 1*, operating from Crete, also turned up to harass the fleet on 12 June, but they were intercepted by Tomahawks of No 3 Squadron. Squadron Leader Peter Jeffrey shot down one of the attackers and Flight Lieutenants John R. 'Jock' Perrin and John H. Saunders claimed two others, while Flight Lieutenant Robert H. Gibbes caught a fourth bomber right over the fleet and claimed it as a 'probable'. In fact two Ju 88s failed to return—one from *4. Staffel* piloted by *Leutnant* H. Dickjobst and one from *5. Staffel* flown by *Leutnant* R. Bennewitz.

Three days later the Australians turned their attention to the Vichy French as Jeffrey and Flight Lieutenant Peter St George B. Turnbull each accounted for a Martin 167F of *GB I/39* in the area of Sheik Meskine. On 19 June Turnbull damaged another Martin bomber over Saida and Pilot Officer Alan C. Rawlinson damaged two others near Tezzine. Damascus fell to the Allied forces on 21 June. In an encounter between Tomahawks and D.520s of *GC III/6* two days later, *Capitaine* Léon Richard, commander of the *6e Escadrille*, was credited with shooting down a Tomahawk south of Zahle—probably Turnbull, who crashed his damaged Tomahawk upon returning to Jenin. The starboard wing of Sergeant F. B. Reid's Tomahawk was also damaged by 20mm shells, but the French took the worst of the fight. *Sous-Lieutenant* Pierre Le Gloan was forced to beat a hasty retreat when his D.520 began to burn, probably after being hit by Flying Officer R. Bothwell, who also sent *Lieutenant* Marcel Steunou, a five-victory ace, down in flames near Zahle and killed *Sergent* Savinel between Ablah and Malakaa. Flying Officer L. E. S. Knowles claimed to have shot the wing tip off another Dewoitine, which was credited to him as damaged.

Among the toughest Vichy strongpoints was Palmyra, a fortified air base surrounded by concrete pillboxes, anti-tank ditches, observation posts and snipers' nests. When 'Habforce', a composite invasion group drawn from British and Arab troops occupying Iraq, crossed the border and moved on Palmyra on 20 June, it came under heavy and very effective bombing and strafing attacks by the base's aircraft. Habforce's advance ground to a halt for about a week. Then, on 25 June, appeals for air support by Habforce's commander, Major-General George Clark, were finally answered as Commonwealth aircraft arrived, including No 3 Squadron's Tomahawks. In an aerial engagement fifteen miles southwest of Palmyra, Saunders, Flying Officers John F. Jackson and W. E. Jewell and Sergeant Alan C. Cameron each claimed a LeO 451 of *GB I/12*—though only three such bombers were in fact present and all were lost, along with the lives of five of their twelve crewmen. When six Martin 167s of *Flotille 4F* sallied out of Palmyra to attack Habforce again on 28 June they were intercepted by No 3 Squadron's Tomahawks and six were promptly shot down in sight of the British ground troops, Rawlinson accounting for three of them, Turnbull downing one and Sergeant Rex K. Wilson destroying another. 'From that moment,' Clark commented, 'things began to look up.' The only downturn of the day occurred after the Tomahawks had refuelled and were returning to Jenin: Sergeant Randall's plane suffered engine failure and he was killed in the crash.

Ultimately the Allied forces prevailed, launching their final thrust on Beirut on 7 July. Amid fierce but hopeless resistance High Commissioner Dentz passed a note to Cornelius Engert, the US Consul-General in Beirut, expressing his willingness to discuss surrender terms with the British but absolutely not with the Gaullist French.

Negotations dragged on for sixty hours, during which fighting continued and the Tomahawks had one more occasion to test their mettle against the D.520 in the air. On 10 June seven Tomahawks of No 3 Squadron RAAF went to cover twelve Bristol Blenheims of No 45 Squadron which were to bomb an ammunition dump near Hamana south of Beirut. The Blenheims bombed the target but the explosions drew the attention of five D.520s of *Aéronavale* Flight *1AC* which had been transferred to the Lebanon six days earlier and were escorting

Martin bombers on a mission. Attacking from head-on and below, the French quickly shot down three, riddled a fourth so badly that it subsequently had to crash-land and damaged six others.

Diving to the belated rescue, the Tomahawk pilots claimed all five of the Dewoitines—two by Turnbull and one each by Jackson, Pilot Officer E. Lane and Sergeant G. E. Hiller. In actuality only two French fighers were lost: *Premier Maître* Ancyon was mortally wounded, dying a few days later, while *Premier Maître* Goffeny bailed out of his burning D.520 over the Bekaa valley with slight wounds, subsequently claiming that his pursuer had crashed into a mountain while trying to follow his evasive manoeuvres. The other three French pilots returned, *Enseigne de Vaisseau* Du Merle being credited with two bombers, *Premier Maître* Benezet being credited with another and *Lieutenant de Vaisseau* Pirel sharing in the destruction of the fourth Blenheim with Goffeny—who was also credited (wrongly) with the 'crashed' Tomahawk.

On the following day *Lieutenant* Lèté of *GC II/3*, lagging behind his formation on account of engine trouble, spotted three Tomahawks and attacked, shooting down Flying Officer F. Fisher. Lèté was one of only two Frenchmen to shoot down a Tomahawk during the campaign but he had little time to exalt in the distinction for, moments later, Flight Lieutenant Robert Gibbes got on his tail and claimed to have sent him down in flames. In fact Lèté survived his crash-landing—as did Fisher, who, after hiding from the French in an Arab village, re-joined No 3 Squadron after hostilities ceased. The squadron lost one other Tomahawk to anti-aircraft fire over Djebel Mazar that day, Flying Officer Knowles crash-landing near Yafour, ten miles from Damascus.

At 12.01 a.m. on 12 July a cease-fire finally went into effect, ending the 34-day Syrian campaign. A formal armistice was signed at St Jean d'Acre on 14 July. The Tomahawks of No 3 Squadron RAAF were transferred to the Western Desert, where their colleagues in RAF and South African Air squadrons were already battling the *Luftwaffe* and *Regia Aeronautica*. Among other early successes over the Western desert, Pilot Officer Thomas G. Paxton of No 250 Squadron, who had shared in the Cant Z.1007*bis* on 8 June, added an Me 109E to his growing score south of Tobruk on 26 June, while on 30 June one of Paxton's squadron friends, Sergeant Robert J. C. Whittle, shared in the destruction of an Me 110, damaged an Me 109 and probably downed an Italian aircraft.

And so the Curtiss P-40 had its baptism of fire in the Middle East. Although its principal virtue in 1941 was its ready availability, great things would be done in the P-40 and a series of improved models kept the Curtiss fighter in production for five years, a total of 13,737 being produced.

Another American workhorse that gave good, if less extensively publicized, service for the British was the Grumman F4F, dubbed 'Wildcat' by its builder but known in Royal Navy circles—at least initially—as the Martlet. Originally conceived as a biplane successor to Grumman's F3F series, the F4F prototype had evolved into a mid-wing monoplane with retractable landing gear by the time the XF4F-2 appeared in 1937. In the course of development the rounded wings and control surfaces became more square in shape and the machine guns were moved from the fuselage to the wings.

Soon after entering production the F4F-3 attracted orders from the French and Royal Navies. The French ordered 81 G-36As, as the export F4F-3 was called, to be fitted upon arrival with two fuselage and four wing-mounted 7.5mm Darne machine guns. The first of the French G-36As, with a Wright R-1820-G205A engine, was tested at the Grumman factory on 11 May 1940 but by then Germany had launched its offensive in the West. With the capitulation of France in June the export order was transferred to Britain, augmenting a British order for 100 G-36Bs with 1,200 hp Pratt & Whitney S3C4-G single-stage supercharged engines. The first F4Fs were designated Martlet Mk Is by the British and later arrivals with folding wings were called Martlet IIs. In all cases the British armed their Grummans with four wing-mounted 0.50-inch Colt-Browning machine guns.

The first Martlet Is reached Prestwick in August 1940, replacing the Sea Gladiators of 804 Naval Air Squadron, while the first Martlet II flew in October. The first aerial victory for the F4F was scored under circumstances curiously similar to those of the Supermarine Spitfire's first success. On Christmas Day 1940 two of 804 Squadron's Martlet Is, BJ515 and BJ562, flown respectively by Lieutenant L. N. Carver and Sub-Lieutenant A. Parke, intercepted a Ju 88A as it tried to enter the Royal Navy's anchorage at Scapa Flow and shot it down. It was a modest beginning for a corpulent little fighter that would soon become legendary in US Navy service at the Battles of the Coral Sea, Midway, Eastern Solomons and Santa Cruz and with the Marines at places such as Wake Island and Guadalcanal.

One of World War II's enduring ironies is that the war's best all-round fighter owed its very creation to a British order—and its status among the war's immortals to the subsequent substitution of a British engine for the American one with which it was originally powered. First flown on 26 October 1940, the prototype North American NA-73X had been developed to satisfy an order from the British Purchasing Commission earlier that year in response to the imminent German invasion threat. By the time production on the Mustang Mk I began, however, the Battle of Britain had been won and the need for a complementary fighter to the Hurricane and Spitfire was less pressing.

The first Mustang Mk Is reached Britain in October 1941. The aircraft impressed its RAF pilots with its strong construction, good flying characteristics, eight-gun armament (six in the wings and two alongside the engine crank-case) and, above all, its four-hour endurance (twice that of a Spitfire), but its unsupercharged Allison V-1710 engine performed poorly above 25,000 feet. For the high-altitude combat that dominated the Battle of Britain and the subsequent duels over the Channel the Mustang was clearly outclassed by the Spitfire Mk V as well as by its most likely opponents, the Messerschmitt Me 109F and Focke-Wulf Fw 190A. It was therefore relegated to Army Co-operation Command, for which role the Mustang pilots spent most of their time training in England for the inevitable Allied counter-invasion of Hitler's *Festung Europa*.

The first Mustang I unit, No 26 Squadron at Gatwick, Sussex, began con-verting to the type in January 1942. Among the tasks envisaged for the close-support Mustang was high-speed photo-reconnaissance using a single F24 camera installed behind the pilot's seat. After some testing it was determined that the Mustangs could get the best results from an altitude of 9,000 feet, hold-ing the aeroplane in a bank and aligning the camera with a mark made on the wing trailing edge.

In May 1942 No 26 Squadron began participating in 'Rhubarb' raids, cross-ing the Channel to strafe German targets in France, at the same time carrying out reconnaissance sorties over targets of potential interest along the French coast. As the RAF and the newly arriving bomber squadrons of the United States Army Air Forces (USAAF) began planning operations against industrial centres in German-occupied Europe, the Mustangs were also committed to the photo-reconnaissance role. On 27 July 1942—three weeks before the American Eighth Air Force was to dispatch its first daylight attack with Boeing B-17s—sixteen RAF Mustangs flew their first photo mission over the Dortmund–Ems Canal, leading into the Ruhr Valley and its vital industrial centres.

The first enemy aircraft officially credited to a Mustang was brought down by a member of No 414 Squdron Royal Canadian Air Force. Curiously but appropriately, however, the pilot was an American. Born in Baxter, Iowa, on 25 March 1915, Hollis Harry Hills had been a civilian flier during the 1930s before slipping across the border into Canada and enlisting in the RCAF on 5 September 1940. Flying Officer Hills was posted to No 414 Squadron, then equipped with Tomahawks, on 12 October 1941.

Hills's first air-to-air fight took place during Operation 'Jubilee', the RAF's effort to support the Anglo-Canadian landing at Dieppe on 19 August 1942. By then fifteen RAF squadrons were equipped with Mustang Mk Is, of which four—Nos 26, 239, 400 and 414, making up No 35 Wing at Gatwick—were committed to low-level reconnaissance missions over the Dieppe area, primarily to scout for German motorized activity.

Hills took off early in the morning to accompany Flight Lieutenant Freddie Clark on a low-level road reconnaissance from Abbeville to Dieppe, checking for movements of German armour. The two lost one another in the darkness and returned to their base at Gatwick with nothing to report. They flew a second such mission later in the day and Hills described what happened in an account in the summer 1990 edition of the US Navy's aviation journal *The Hook*:

> The weather was sunny, not a cloud in the sky. As we approached the French coast, the sky was full of fighters in one massive dogfight from sea level to the contrail level. In hurried glances, I counted seven parachutes in the air at one time. A couple of miles short of landfall I spotted four Fw 190s off to our right at about 1,500 feet. Their course and speed were going to put them directly overhead when we crossed the beach. I called Freddie twice with a 'tally ho' but there was no response. He did not hear the warnings and apparently did not see the Fw 190s. When Freddie turned right to intercept our recce road at Abbeville, we were in an ideal position for the FWs to attack. I swung very wide to Freddie's left during the turn, dusting the Abbeville chimney tops. That kept me beneath the FWs and I believe they lost sight of me.
>
> My plan was to cut off the lead Fw 190 before he could open fire on Freddie, but my timing went to pot when a crashing Spitfire forced me to turn to avoid a collision. That gave the lead FW pilot time to get into firing position and he hit Freddie's Mustang with the first burst. I got a long-range shot at the FW leader but had to break right when his number two man had a go at me. Number two missed and made the big mistake of sliding to my left side ahead of me. It was an easy shot and I hit him hard. His engine caught fire, and soon after it started smoking the canopy came off. I hit him again and he was a goner, falling off to the right into the trees.

The second *Rotte* of Fw 190s had disappeared so Hills went looking for Clark and found him heading for Dieppe harbour at 1,000 feet, streaming glycol and still being pursued by the leading Fw 190. Hills fired a short high-deflection burst, just to distract the German from finishing Clark, and saw the enemy plane break into a tight left-hand turn to engage him. Hills found that he could outmanoeuvre the Fw 190, but whenever he tried to press his advantage the Fw 190 pilot would break away, using his superior speed to get clear of the Mustang and fly inland, only to turn back and attack Hills when he tried to retire over the Channel. At one point in the long duel Hills had to dodge a falling Me 109 and the Focke-Wulf pilot got his best chance at a shot, but missed. 'My opponent was a highly competent pilot and I was ready to call a draw as soon as I could,' remarked Hills.

Finally, during one of the Focke-Wulf's breakaways Hills made a break toward Dieppe at maximum speed and was relieved to find the German fighter no longer in pursuit. As he crossed the Channel, Hills passed under some Ju 88s and Me 109s returning from a raid on Southampton but they all kept going. The American returned without further incident but was saddened to learn that Clark had not come back. His squadron was not alone in suffering a loss during Operation 'Jubilee'—No 26 Squadron had lost no fewer than five of its Mustangs to anti-aircraft fire or enemy fighters while No 239 had lost two and No 400 one.

At about 5.00 the following morning, however, Hills was rudely awakened as his door burst open. He recalled:

> I was grabbed in a bear hug by what smelled like a huge clump of seaweed. It was Freddie. He'd ditched his Mustang in the Dieppe harbour and was rescued unconscious by a brave soldier of the amphibious forces. With Freddie as witness, the Fw 190 shoot-down was confirmed for me and RCAF No 414 Squadron—the first Mustang victory.

Later, of course, the Mustang would have its Allison engine replaced with the Rolls-Royce Merlin and reach its full potential as the best fighter of the war. Scores of Allied pilots would become aces in Mustangs, but 'Holly' Hills would not be one of them.

As the USAAF began establishing bases in Britain, Hills was pressured to transfer to his own country's air arm. He was willing to do so provided he got to fly Spitfires with the 4th Fighter Group, then being created from the three volunteer Eagle Squadrons of the RAF, Nos 71, 121 and 133. Instead he was offered a slot in a squadron equipped with twin-engine Lockheed P-38s. Hills refused to go, transferring instead into the US Navy on 9 November. After returning to the United States and training on Grumman fighters, Lieutenant (jg) Hills was assigned to fighter squadron VF-32 on 28 May 1943 and returned to action in the Pacific aboard the light carrier *Langley* in October. It was in that unit, flying Grumman F6F Hellcats, that he added significantly to his tally by downing three Zeros and damaging a fourth over Truk on 29 April 1944. Another Zero over Manila on 21 September made Lieutenant Hills an ace. On the following day he was shot down by anti-aircraft fire over Subic Bay, but, like Freddie Clark, he was pulled from the water by crewmen of the submarine *Haddo*.

There was one other American fighter that had an auspicious combat debut in the hands of foreign pilots during World War II—the Brewster B-239, an export version of the F2A-1 that was known to its RAF pilots as the Buffalo. Designed in 1935 and entering service with VF-3 aboard the carrier *Saratoga* late in 1938, the F2A-1 has a place in history as the US Navy's first monoplane fighter with retractable landing gear and an enclosed canopy. It also acquired a less than flattering reputation during the early months of Japanese expansion in South-East Asia and the Pacific when Buffaloes of the RAF and RAAF, B-239s of the Royal Netherlands East Indies Air Force and US Marine F2A-1s based on Midway Island suffered terribly against nimbler, more heavily armed and usually more numerous Japanese fighters like the A6M2 Zero and Nakajima Ki-43 *Hayabusa*. Survivors of the débâcles in Malaya, Singapore, Burma and

Right, upper: Roland Garros's Morane-Saulnier L, modified into a single-seater with the machine gun deflectors devised by himself and his mechanic, Jules Hue, in April 1915, (Musée de l'Air et l'Espace)

Right, lower: Anthony Fokker poses before one of his *Eindeckers*. The aircraft is fitted with a synchronized machine gun. (Johan Visser Collection)

Below: Eugène Gilbert prepares to undertake an offensive patrol in *Le Vengeur*, his Morane-Saulnier N equipped with a machine gun and deflectors. (Service Historique de l'Armée de l'Air)

Left, upper: *Adjudant* André Borde of *Escadrille N.65* stands beside his Nieuport 11 *Bébé*, which has an early Lewis gun mounting (note the extended pistol grip). (Service Historique de l'Armée de l'Air)

Left, lower: *Sergent* Georges Guynemer prepares to take off in his modified single-seat Nieuport 10 with upper wing machine gun mounting. (Service Historique de l'Armée de l'Air)

Below: *Lieutenant* Armand de Turenne of *N.48* poses beside an early Nieuport 17.C1 with synchronized Vickers gun. The aircraft is marked with the pilot's family coat-of-arms. (Service Historique de l'Armée de l'Air)

Right, upper: *Leutnant* Kurt Wintgens, the first to use the Fokker E.I in combat, stands beside a Halberstadt D.II. He was shot down and killed on 25 September 1916, shortly after this photograph was taken. (IWM)

Right, lower: *Leutnant* Ernst Udet of *Jasta 15* with his new Albatros D.III, 1914/16, at Habsheim on 1 January 1916, His mechanics are pouring hot water into the radiator. (Greg van Wyngarden)

Below: An early Albatros D.V, with Albatros D.IIIs in the background. Adapting the Nieuport 17's sesquiplane wing arrangement to a heavier, inline-engine fighter proved to be a mistake. (IWM)

Left, upper: *Capitaine* Georges Guynemer (third from right), Louis Béchereau of the *Société anonyme pour l'Aviation et ses Dérivés* and *Capitaine* Albert Deullin examine a newly delivered Spad 13.C1 (probably S.504) at *Spa.3*'s aerodrome at St Pol-sur-Mer in August 1917. (Louis Risacher Album via Jon Guttman)

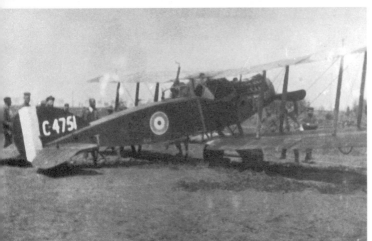

Left, lower: Even at its peak of development, the Bristol Fighter was not invincible. F.2B C4651 of No 62 Squadron was brought down by *Leutnant der Reserve* Rudolf Stark of *Jasta 34b* on 19 May 1918. Lieutenant Frank Atkinson and Sergeant Charles Brammer were taken prisoner. (H. H. Hauprich)

Below: Captain Albert Ball of No 56 Squadron in S.E.5 A4850, following his improvements to what he considered to be 'a rotten machine'. (IWM)

Right, upper: Sopwith Pup N6172 *Black Tulip* of No 3 Squadron Royal Naval Air Service, flown by Flight Commander Robin G. Mack, after being brought down on 22 April 1917 by *Hauptmann* Hennig von Osterroht of *Jasta 12*. (Peter M. Grosz via Jon Guttman)

Right, lower: The unappreciated Bristol M.1C, which was banished to the Middle East and Macedonia. (IWM)

Below: Fokker F.I 103/17, the second Fokker triplane to see combat, was flown by *Leutnant* Werner Voss of *Jasta 10* to death and glory on 23 September 1917. Next to it is an early Pfalz D.III. (IWM)

Left: *Leutnant der Reserve* Rudolf Windisch of *Jasta 66* in the cockpit of his new Fokker D.VII—in which he was brought down on 27 May 1918. (Jon Guttman)

Below: First Lieutenant Douglas Campbell, the first American-trained fighter pilot to score an aerial victory (on 14 April 1918), poses with a Nieuport 28.C1 of the 94th Aero Squadron. (Douglas Campbell via Jon Guttman)

Right, upper: *Caporal* Walter John Shaffer, an American volunteer in *MSP.156*, climbs—with some difficulty—into his new Morane-Saulnier 27.C1 (single-gun variant of the AI). (Walter J. Shaffer Album via Jon Guttman)

Right, lower: A Fokker E.V in the markings of *Jasta 6*, which used the aircraft—briefly—in August 1918. (IWM)

Below: A Fiat C.R.32*bis*, powered by the improved Fiat A-30RA*bis* engine, carried two wing-mounted 7.7mm machine guns as well as two 12.7mm weapons in the fuselage. Some of the 100 built were given operational evaluation over Spain, where, the italians determined, the plane's greater weight had an adverse effect on performance. (IWM)

Top: An early Messerschmitt Bf 109B. The aircraft would quickly be committed to combat over Spain. (National Air & Space Museum)
Above: A late-model Polikarpov I-16 of the *Voyenno-Vozdushny Sili* in 1942. In seven years the fighter had passed from innovation to obsolescence. (IWM)
Below: An Avia B.534-IV. The Slovak fighters still bore Czechoslovakian markings when they were committed to battle against the Hungarians on 23 March 1939. (Radko Vasicek)
Right, top: The Polish PZL P.11c, in which many Battle of Britain pilots obtained their first

combat experience on 1 September 1939. (IWM)
Right, centre: Fokker G.IA No 302 lies derelict at Waalhaven aeroport after Lieutenant Jan Pieter Kuipers and J. Venema used it to bring down two Heinkel He 111s on 10 May 1940. The crew then landed their damaged plane, which was destroyed on the ground. (Courtesy of Brian Schultz)
Right, bottom: A line-up of Morane-Saulnier M.S.406C1s—France's principal fighter—faces a Fairey Battle of No 88 Squadron RAF at Auberive-sur-Suippes in April 1940. (IWM)

Above: A Supermarine Spitfire Mk I of No 19 Squadron RAF—the first unit to receive the new fighter but not the first to fire its eight guns in anger. (IWM)

Below: Hawker Hurricane Mk Is of No 73 Squadron—only one of the aircraft carrying the unit letters 'TP'—fly a patrol over France, 19 April 1940. P2569/D, on the right, was flown by Flight Lieutenant Eric Lovett, who downed three German aircraft before being killed in action on 7 September 1940. (IWM)

Right, top: Mitsubishi A5M2s from an early production batch warm up their engines for a mission over China in 1937. (US National Archives)

Right, centre: A Mitsubishi A6M2 Model 11 *Reisen* (Zero Fighter), 3-182 of the 12th *Kokutai*, photographed over China in the autumn of 1940. The aircraft has an unusual light grey/whitish grey finish and a yellow fuselage band for *Shotai* (Flight) identification. (IWM)

Right, bottom: The Nakajima Ki-43-IIb *Hayabusa*—an attempt to improve a nimble but flawed Army fighter whose early successes were largely won on the Navy Zero's coat-tails. (IWM)

Left, top: Grumman F4F-3 Wildcats of VF-3 from the carrier *Lexington* off Hawaii, 10 April 1942. 'F-1' (BuNo 3976) is flown by Lieutenant John S. ('Jimmy') Thach (six victories), while 'F-13' (BuNo 3986) is piloted by Lieutenant Edward H. ('Butch') O'Hare (a Medal of Honor recipient whose score stood at seven when he was killed in action on 27 November 1943). (IWM)

Left, centre: Lockheed YP-38s, P-38-LOs and P-38Ds of the 1st Pursuit Group undergo training in 1940. The Group saw its first action off the coast of Iceland on 14 August 1942. (IWM)

Left, bottom: The Republic P-47D introduced a more powerful engine than the P-47C and streamlined underwing hardpoints for extra fuel tanks. In this form the aircraft began to retrieve its pilots' confidence, which had been eroded in its first few weeks with the 4th Fighter Group. (IWM)

Right, top: Mikoyan-Gurevich MiG-3s of the 120th *Istrebitelnye Aviatsye Polk*, 6th *Istrebitelnye Aviatsye Korpus*, outside Moscow in the winter of 1941/42. By that time the disappointing fighter had found its niche as an interceptor. (IWM)

Right, centre: A Lavochkin-Gorbunov-Gudkov LaGG-3 of the first production series, identifiable by the balance weights above and below the rudder. (IWM)

Right, bottom: A Fairey Firefly Mk I in markings for the European Theatre. The fighter first saw action over Norway but scored its first air-to-air success over Sumatra. (IWM)

Top: Vought F4U-1 Corsairs of US Navy squadron VF-17, whose entry into combat was postponed because of the aircraft's poor carrier landing characteristics. The type made its combat debut with Marine squadron VMF-124 instead. (IWM)
Above: Westland Whirlwind F Mk I P6969 of No 263 Squadron RAF, in which Pilot Officer K. A. G. Graham scored the fighter's first victory, over an Arado Ar 196A—at the cost of his plane and his life—on 8 February 1941. (IWM)
Below: A Bristol Blenheim Mk IF of No 248 Squadron, which was formed at Hendon in October 1939. (IWM)

Top: Bristol Beaufighter Mk VI night fighters, equipped with air intercept Mk IV radar. (IWM)
Above: One of the fourteen de Havilland D.H.98 Mosquito NF Mk IIs that entered service in March 1942. The new fighters flew their first combat sorties on the night of 27 April in response to the *Luftwaffe's* 'Baedeker' raids. (IWM)

Below: Boulton Paul Defiant Mk Is of No 264 Squadron on patrol in March 1940. N1535 (PS-A) wears the commander's fuselage pennant of Squadron Leader Philip A. Hunter, who, with his gunner Sergeant F. H. King, claimed a Junkers Ju 88A for the Defiant's first victory on 12 May 1940. (IWM)

Above: Curtiss-Wright CW-21Bs of the 2nd *Jachtafdeling, Vliegtuig Groep IV*, at Andir, Java, in January 1942. (RNethAF)

Below: A Messerschmitt Me 262A-1a: a case of 'too little, too late'—much to the good fortune of the RAF and USAAF. (IWM)

Bottom: The Gloster Meteor Mk III was a significant improvement over the Mk I and entered service in time to fight with No 616 Squadron RAF. (IWM)

the East Indies would never have believed it, but, almost six months before their ordeals began in December 1941, export derivatives of the F2A were enjoying incredible success—over Finland.

During the Winter War Finland had desperately sought new aircraft to replace the obsolescent machines with which its air arm had to defend the country. In spite of the official ban on the export of all military material issued by the US Government at the start of World War II, on 16 December 1939 Finnish representatives managed to order 44 fighters from the Brewster Aeronautical Corporation, a cost of $55,404 each, since deliveries of the aircraft to the US Navy had been delayed and the planes were still technically Brewster's property. The Finnish order was made up of 38 F2A-1s intended for the US Navy and six B-239Bs scheduled for delivery to Belgium, all standardized to basic B-239 configuration. In the case of the F2A-1s, all US Navy property was removed, including guns, instruments and carrier deck landing equipment, resulting in a significant reduction in weight. The F2A-1's 950 hp Wright Cyclone R-1820-34 9-cylinder radial engine was replaced by a civilian version of equal output, the Cyclone R-1820-G5.

After being shipped to Stavanger, Norway, the Brewsters were transported by train to Trollhättan, Sweden, where they were assembled and armed with two synchronized machine guns—one 7.62mm and one 12.7mm—and two wing-mounted 12.7mm Colt-Browning weapons. From there they were flown to Finland, the first four arriving on 1 March 1940.

The first six B-239s were hurriedly assigned to *LeLv 22*, commanded by Captain Erkki Heinila and based in southern Finland. Flying from a frozen lake at Säkylä in western Finland, they made one uneventful sortie before the Finns and Soviets agreed on a truce, ending hostilities on 13 March 1940. A month later, on 19 April, the Brewsters were all reassigned to Major Gustaf Magnusson's *LeLv 24*, based at Helsinki-Malmi airport. Pleased just to have a replacement for their ageing Fokker D.XXIs, *LeLv 24*'s experienced pilots enthusiastically strove to master the new Brewsters and to develop flexible tactics for using them in combat. The squadron lost two aircraft and pilots in the course of fourteen months, but that intensive training would soon pay off.

When Germany launched *Unternehmen 'Barbarossa'*, her invasion of the Soviet Union, on 22 June 1941, Finland tried to avoid becoming involved, though at the same time she kept her military forces on alert on the assumption that involvement might be unavoidable. The Soviets seem to have harboured similar notions, and in the morning of 25 June they chose to strike first, dispatching 150 unescorted bombers to neutralize Finnish defensive installations.

They should have known better. Alert Finnish patrols spotted the oncoming first wave and soon fighters were scrambling up to intercept them. The Finns had not been as well prepared for trouble as they should have been—only 24 fighters of the 125 in the *Lentolaivues*' operational inventory actually engaged the bombers, but they wrought havoc aplenty on them. First blood was drawn when six Fokker D.XXIs of the 1st *Lentueessa* (Flight) of *LeLv 32* intercepted a wave of DB-3s near the railway junction at Riihimäki and Lieutenant Vekko Arvid Evinen managed to shoot down two of them. *Lentolaivue 26*, flying its Fiat G.50s over eastern central Finland, shot down thirteen SB-2s while Flight Sergeant Antti Johannes Tani, flying a Morane-Saulnier M.S.406 of *LeLv 28*, downed another in the same area.

Making their fighting debut alongside those fighters were seven B-239s of *LeLv 24*'s 2nd Flight, which took off at 7.15 a.m. led by Lieutenant Jorma Sarvanto. The flight split into two divisions, both of which ran into waves of unescorted Tupolev SBs. Warrant Officer Eero Aulis Kinnunen downed no fewer than four SB-2s and shared in the destruction of a fifth with Sergeant Heimo Olavi Lampi, who personally accounted for two more, while Sarvanto added one more to his Winter War account. Meanwhile a Brewster of *LeLv 24*'s 1st Flight, flown by Warrant Officer Yryö Olava Turkka, was vectored to another sector and downed two more SB-2s. The second division landed, refuelled, re-armed and took off again at 10.50 a.m. They met more SB bombers, and Warrant Officer Eero Aulis Kinnunen destroyed another two of them.

In total the 24 Finnish fighters that took off accounted for 26 bombers. The incident gave the Finnish Government cause to declare war on the Soviet Union. The Continuation War was on.

By the time Finland accepted Soviet terms for an armistice on 8 September 1944 its Brewsters had accounted for 496 enemy aircraft for the loss of only nineteen in aerial combat. Most of Finland's leading aces flew the type, including Sarvanto, who used it to add four victories to the $12^5/6$ with which he had been credited during the Winter War, and Ilmari Juutilainen, whose total of $94^1/6$ was the highest confirmed fighter pilots' score outside the *Luftwaffe*. Finland's second-ranking ace, Hans Henrik Wind, scored 39 of his 75-victory total while flying the Brewster—a record that none of its American, Dutch or Commonwealth pilots would have found easy to believe.

Chapter 11

THE TIDE-TURNING GENERATION

American Fighters, 1941–1943

When the Japanese surprise attack on Pearl Harbor abruptly plunged the United States into the war in official earnest on 7 December 1941, the Americans had only one fighter that was intrinsically comparable to its opposition—the Grumman F4F-3 Wildcat. The Curtiss P-40E had arrived in the Philippines and the Brewster F2A-1 Buffalo and Bell P-39D Airacobra were in full production, but they would all prove disappointing when matched against the astonishing speed, climb, manoeuvrability, range and firepower of Japan's Mitsubishi A6M2 Zero.

Better designs were waiting in the wings. The twin-engine, twin-boom Lockheed P-38E Lightning and the inverted gull-wing Vought F4U-1 Corsair had entered production, but they were not yet available for front-line use. The Wildcat was, and although its performance was generally inferior to the Zero's it was the closest thing the Americans had to a fighter that could face it on even terms.

The Grumman Martlet, to use its British designation, had already seen action with the Fleet Air Arm a year before the first American Wildcat fired its guns in anger. The Pearl Harbor strike caught half of Marine squadron VMF-211's complement of F4F-3s on the ground at Ewa Field on the island of Oahu, destroying nine out of twelve. The other twelve Wildcats of VMF-211 had been delivered on 4 December to Wake Atoll, America's farthest Pacific outpost, lying 1,025 miles from Midway and 1,300 from Guam. It was also just 764 miles from Japanese-held Marcus Island and 620 miles from Roi and Namur in the Japanese-mandated Marshall Islands. Wake's garrison, too, was taken by surprise when 36 Mitsubishi G4M1s departed Roi and Namur, slipped past a patrol under the fortuitous cover of a rain squall and bombed the airfield, destroying seven Wildcats and demolishing the auxiliary fuel tank in the sole plane that remained in one piece. To make the day complete, one of the four returning F4Fs was damaged when it ran into a bomb crater on the runway.

In spite of that disastrous beginning, Wake's garrison put up a heroic defence in the air and on the ground. Cannibalizing parts from the wrecks to keep two to four Wildcats flying at a time, the Marines were credited with shooting down nine enemy aircraft in two weeks. Two bombers were downed on 10 December by Captain Henry T. Elrod, who also used an improvised rig to drop a 100-pound bomb among the depth charges on the Japanese destroyer *Kisaragi* on 11 December, causing it to blow up and sink with all hands.

After suffering the ignominy of having launched the only amphibious assault to be repulsed by shore batteries in World War II—with the loss of the destroyer *Hayate* to Wake's 5-inch guns as well as that of *Kisaragi* to Elrod's air attack—the Japanese assembled a more powerful invasion force at Kwajalein. The aircraft carriers *Soryu* and *Hiryu*, then on the way home from the Pearl Harbor raid, were diverted to support the renewed effort. When a planned sortie by the US Navy to relieve Wake was cancelled, the island's ultimate fate was sealed. The carrier planes attacked on 21 December, and during another air strike the next day Wake's last two airworthy F4Fs rose to challenge them. Attacking a formation of enemy planes head-on, Captain Herbert C. Freuler claimed two Zeros—the first such victories credited to the Wildcat—but his victims were, in fact, Nakajima B5N2 torpedo-bombers from *Soryu*. One of *Hiryu*'s Zero pilots, Petty Officer 3rd Class Isao Tahara, then shot up Freuler's plane, which had to crash-land, and Tahara was subsequently credited with downing the other F4F, killing Lieutenant Carl R. Davidson.

With the last of their planes gone, the twenty surviving pilots and maintenance crewmen of VMF-211 joined the Marines on the ground as the Japanese landed in the morning of 23 December. Wake's naval commander, Commander Winfield Scott Cunningham, finally judged the situation hopeless and surrendered that afternoon. Elrod, who had died while manning a machine gun position on 23 December, was posthumously awarded the Medal of Honor.

The F4F's Pacific combat debut in the defence of Wake would have been enough in itself to assure the rotund little scrapper a place in military aviation annals, but it had many more names still to add to its laurels, and seven more Navy and Marine Wildcat pilots would be awarded the Medal of Honor for courage above and beyond the call of duty.

As would be the case with the P-40—particularly as used by Colonel Claire Chennault's American Volunteer Group over China—the Wildcat pilots had to develop tactics that would exploit the Zero's weaknesses to the fullest degree while minimizing their own. Since the F4F-3 was almost as fast as an A6M2 in level flight and slightly faster in the dive, the best tactic was to start the engagement from a higher altitude, hit hard and dive away. Another tactic by which the F4Fs were able to 'hold the line' against the Zero in 1942 was the development of a US Navy variation on Werner Mölders' 'finger four' concept of flexible teamwork. Called the 'Thach Weave' after Commander John S.

'Jimmy' Thach of VF-2 from the aircraft carrier *Lexington*, it involved constant co-ordinated weaving by two-man teams during a dogfight, each pilot ready to cover his partner's tail if an enemy plane got on it. The Japanese airmen, individually skilled though they were, seldom became as proficient in that technique as their well-drilled US Navy and Marine counterparts—a factor that resulted in the deaths of numerous veteran Zero pilots to the guns of prowling Wildcats.

While the Wildcat had seen service with the British prior to Pearl Harbor, another Lend-Lease American fighter, the Bell P-39 Airacobra, saw action with its own air arm before its British counterpart did—mainly because the British did not want to use it at all. Conceived by Lawrence Dale Bell and made practicable by his gifted chief engineer Robert J. Woods, the P-39 emerged from two ideas for fighters that sought to improve manoeuvrability by locating the engine near the centre of gravity, using a 10-foot shaft to connect it to the propeller. The Bell Model 3, with the cockpit placed far aft behind the engine, afforded poor visibility for the pilot, so the Model 4, with the pilot sitting just ahead of the engine, was selected for development, using an Allison V-1710-E4 engine with a B5 turbo-supercharger. Never a man to stop at one novel approach when a second or third would be even better, Bell also proposed installing a 25mm cannon to fire through the propeller shaft, and a tricycle landing gear arrangement. His proposal was approved on 7 October 1939, and the first XP-39 was completed in March 1939, with the cannon's calibre increased to 37mm at the Army Air Corps' request, along with two synchronized 0.50-calibre machine guns in the nose.

The prototype was flown under a veil of secrecy on 6 April with James Taylor at the controls and produced a speed of 390 mph at 20,000 feet. Severe cooling problems were encountered, so the oil cooler scoops on the fuselage sides were enlarged. As the promising design made the transition from testing to acceptance, the Army abandoned the supercharger, a measure that facilitated production and maintenance but sacrificed a critical amount of performance. The oil cooler intakes were relocated from the fuselage sides to the wing roots, a carburettor intake was installed behind the canopy and covers were added over the main wheels. Two additional 0.30-calibre machine guns were also installed in the fuselage.

While the turbo-supercharger had been removed, the extensive modifications that the Army Air Corps had had made to the P-39 raised its empty weight from about 4,000 to more than 5,600 pounds. Its maximum speed was reduced to 375 mph at 15,000 feet, but the Army Air Corps was satisfied and ordered 80 P-45s, as the revised fighters were initially called, although that designation was later changed back to P-39C. After twenty P-39Cs had been built, a small dorsal fillet was added to the vertical stabilizer and the gun arrangement was changed to one 37mm cannon and two 0.50-calibre machine guns in the nose and four 0.30-calibre machine guns in the wings. In that form the remaining 60 planes—and 369 in a follow-up order—were designated P-39D. In addition to the American order, on 8 May 1940 the British Purchasing Commission ordered 675 of the fighters under the name 'Caribou', later changed to 'Airacobra Mk I'. Export Airacobras were to use a 20mm cannon in place of the 37mm, and 175 of them were repossessed by the US Army Air Forces in December 1941, being given the designation P-400.

The only operational British unit equipped with Airacobras was No 601 (County of London) Squadron of the Auxiliary Air Force, which received its new planes in August 1941. The squadron flew its first desultory low-level strafing mission, or 'Rhubarb', on 9 October when two planes left Manston airfield, crossed the Channel and attacked a German trawler, although the vessel's ultimate fate went unrecorded. Two more Airacobras flew over the same area the next day but found nothing and returned without firing a shot. On 11 October two Airacobras attacked German barges near Gravelines and Calais while three planes scouted the area around Ostend.

Those four missions in three days marked the entirety of the Airacobra's fighting career in the RAF. Problems with the plane's compass was the official reason for grounding No 601 Squadron's fighters, but in spite of the superior manoeuvrability displayed by the Airacobra when pitted against a captured Messerschmitt Me 109E its rate of climb was inferior to that of both the Me 109E and the Spitfire Mk VB and it was clearly no match for the new Me 109Fs and Focke-Wulf Fw 190As that it would be more likely to encounter. 'Iron Dog' became the third British term for the P-400, courtesy of its disgusted pilots, as No 601 Squadron stood down until it was re-equipped with Spitfire VBs in March 1942.

While the Channel Front had stabilized enough for Britain to afford to hold off using its Airacobras in earnest, the situation in the South Pacific in early 1942 offered no such luxury. In March the American 8th Pursuit Group was shipped to Australia. From there, in early April, it moved to Port Morseby, New Guinea, which had been under increasing pressure from units of the Japanese Naval Air Force, operating from bases at Lae and Salamaua, since 3 February. The P-39s drew first blood during an engagement on 6 April when two of the 8th Group's pilots scored hits on Japanese aircraft.

A more typical foretaste of things to come occurred on 11 April when A6M2s of the Tainan *Kokutai*, completing a sweep of the Coral Sea, swung over Port Moresby and encountered four P-39s flying in two pairs 300 yards apart. One of the Zero pilots, PO1C Saburo Sakai, signalled their presence to his *shotai* (flight) leader, Lieutenant (jg) Junichi Sasai, who gestured in reply for Sakai to attack while he covered him. Sakai, with his two wingmen following in close attendance, dived on the unsuspecting Americans and closed to 50 yards' distance from the rearmost pair:

> I jammed down on the cannon button, and in a second the first Airacobra was done for [wrote Sakai]. The shells converged in the centre of the fuselage; pieces of metal broke off and flipped away. A fountain of smoke and flame belched outward.
>
> I skidded and brought the guns to bear on the second P-39. Again the shells went directly home, exploding inside and tearing the fighter to bits. Both Airacobras plummeted out of control.

Sakai then turned to deal with the remaining two P-39s but saw that they were already descending in smoke and flames, ambushed by two other paladins of his air group, PO1Cs Hiroyoshi Nishizawa and Toshio Ota.

Over the next six months Sakai, Nishizawa and Ota would amass personal scores that would rank them among the leading Japanese fighter pilots of the war. A significant share of their victories would be over P-39s.

Sporadic fighting continued throughout the month until 30 April, when Lieutenant-Colonel Boyd D. Wagner, commander of V Fighter Command, led 26 P-39Ds of the 35th and 36th Squadrons on their first major sweep. Twelve of them surprised the Japanese at Lae, heavily damaging nine bombers and three fighters on the ground. The Tainan *Kokutai* scrambled up after the departing Airacobras and managed to shoot down two. In fact three P-39s failed to return, but the Americans claimed four Zeros, three of which were credited to 'Buzz' Wagner, a veteran of fighting over the Philippines with five victories already to his credit. The Tainan *Kokutai*'s only recorded loss in the action was PO2C Hideo Izumi, killed in action.

In the month that followed, the 8th Pursuit Group claimed 40 Japanese planes destroyed but at a cost of 25 of their own in combat, eight in forced landings and three destroyed on the ground. The group was relieved by the 35th Pursuit Group shortly thereafter, but that outfit was to fare no better with its P-39Ds and P-400s, the latter of which was derisively referred to by its crews as 'a P-39 with a Zero on its tail'.

By July 1942 the USAAF had issued orders that P-39 pilots were not to engage enemy aircraft in air-to-air combat over any front unless circumstances compelled them to do so. In spite of the appalling losses they suffered, the American Airacobra pilots did their best to hold the line in the Pacific until the arrival of better fighters made it possible for them to relegate their planes to the fighter-bomber and reconnaissance roles. The RAF had already abandoned the Airacobra, but Free French pilots flew P-39s over North Africa and the Mediterranean when there was nothing else available, and so did members of the *Regia Aeronautica* after Italy had changed over to the Allied side in September 1943. Soviet pilots flew Lend-Lease Airacobras as ground-attack planes, bomber interceptors and low-level fighters—and, surprisingly, liked them very much. Second-ranking Soviet ace Aleksandr Pokryshkin accounted for a sizeable share of his 59 credited victories at the controls of a P-39, as did Grigori Rechkalov and a good number of other notable Russian fighter pilots.

The most successful fighter design available to the US Army Air Forces in the first year of the Pacific War had its origin in a 1936 Army Air Corps requirement for an interceptor capable of 360 mph at 20,000 feet and of staying at least an hour at that altitude. Lockheed designers H. L. Hibbard and Clarence L. Johnson worked to fill that unusual specification by going through an assortment of twin-engine arrangements before settling on twin booms attached to a long tailplane, with the pilot and armament located in a central nacelle. Using a pair of Allison V-1710-11/15 engines fitted with General Electric turbosuperchargers, the Model 22 had a projected top speed of 417 mph at 20,000 feet—far exceeding the Army's expectations—and on 23 June 1937 Lockheed were awarded a contract to build a prototype.

The first XP-38, serial number 37-457, made its first flight from March Field, California, on 27 January 1939. Aside from the failure of a flap linkage, the strange-looking plane functioned perfectly. As a result of that encouraging start the XP-38 was flown by First Lieutenant B. S. Kelsey from March to Mitchell Field with the intention of breaking the transcontinental speed record. Unfortunately Kelsey became overtired and after he missed his first approach, and then applied power too quickly to go around for a second try, one of the engines faltered and he had to crash-land. Nevertheless, the XP-38 had demonstrated its potential, and the Army Air Corps ordered thirteen pre-production YP-38s on 27 April 1939, followed by a full production order on 10 August.

As with the Spitfire, the P-38 was a sophisticated, complex piece of machinery resulting in a long process of tooling up for production. The first P-38, with a 37mm cannon and four 0.50-calibre machine guns in the nacelle, was not delivered until June 1941. By then the type had been undergoing further development and the first P-38D, with self-sealing fuel tanks and a 23mm Madsen cannon in place of the 37mm gun, came out in August, followed by the P-38E, with a 20mm cannon, in October. All three types were assigned to the 1st Pursuit Group at Selfridge Field, Michigan, followed by the 14th Pursuit Group at March Field.

The Lockheed P-38E was first deployed in a combat zone to defend American soil—with the 54th Fighter Squadron, with flights stationed at Elmendorf, Thornborough and Cape airfields in the territory of Alaska. The Lightning was a logical choice to patrol the treacherous skies over the Alaskan coast and the Aleutian Islands since its twin 1,325 hp Allison V-1710-49 liquid cooled engines gave its pilots a greater feeling of security than did a single engine. Its range of 1,500–2,000 miles also suited it for the long distances that it would have to fly.

The pilots, by and large, were as new as the planes they flew. As they searched for the Japanese fleet on 5 June, one flight of Lightnings saw a ship below and promptly attacked it. Fortunately nobody aboard was hurt, for it turned out to be Russian. As one of the planes was landing at Cape Field its pilot accidentally pressed the gun button on his control yoke and sent a stream of 0.50-calibre and 20mm shells down the runway.

The P-38 pilots had much to learn and little time in which to do so for a more tangible threat was coming. On 7 June Commander Sukemitsu Ito's Yokohama-based Toko Seaplane Squadron arrived at newly occupied Kiska Island with six four-engine Kawanishi H6K4 flying boats, code-named 'Mavis' by the Allies, which the Japanese secured to buoys that the US Navy had originally installed there to handle Consolidated PBYs. Normally used for maritime reconnaissance, the H6K4s could also carry torpedoes and bombs, and on 20 July three of the big boats tried to bomb the seaplane tender *Gillis* in Kuluk Bay, Adak. Although *Gillis* was not hit, the Americans withdrew her from that advanced island base and the P-38s were ordered to fly regular combat air patrols over Nazan Bay in case the 'Mavises' returned.

The first two such patrols were flown on 4 August, with a bomber from Colonel William O. Eareckson's 28th Composite Group providing navigation support to each two-plane P-38 flight. The third flight of the day was manned by Lieutenants Kenneth Ambrose and Stanley Long and led by Lieutenant Major H. McWilliams in a Boeing B-17. Once the Lightnings arrived over Nazan Bay they began circling over the two seaplane tenders anchored there while McWilliams flew on toward Kiska. Soon afterwards McWilliams spotted three 'Mavises' flying toward Atka Island and radioed that information to Ambrose and Long.

The fighters climbed to 22,000 feet in order to be in a better position to intercept the intruders, and Long was the first to see the H6Ks flying along the south coast of Atka in a V formation, approaching Nazan Bay at an altitude of 7,000 feet. As the two P-38s dived on them the Japanese broke formation and fled to the west, trying to seek cover in a sea fog that rose some 1,500 feet above the ocean. Overhauling their targets, Ambrose and Long began circling around to attack from the front or sides since the H6K4 was armed with a formidable 20mm cannon in the tail position. Long was the first to achieve success: as he made a firing pass at close range on two of the boats, he saw the canopy on one disintegrate. As the two Lightnings climbed away, Ambrose congratulated Long, then said, 'Let's concentrate on the outside one.' They then dived for another firing pass, during which Ambrose set the 'Mavis''s left wing on fire. It was last seen descending out of control into the overcast while the third H6K escaped.

Since they still had enough fuel, Ambrose and Long headed for Kiska hoping to catch another enemy plane. After flying about 150 miles they were rewarded by the sight of another H6K emerging from a cloud. As the Japanese took frantic evasive action Ambrose made a frontal attack while Long attacked from the side and raked it from nose to tail before it disappeared into the clouds again.

Upon their return to Cape Field at 1 p.m. the B-17 and two Lightnings buzzed the runway at low altitude. As he taxied into his revetment Ambrose held up two fingers and shouted, 'We got two of them!' Long, who had scored the first P-38 victory of the war, was nevertheless chided by one of his comrades for leaving his ejection door open and losing all his machine gun casings, which should have been saved for the war effort. 'I really couldn't have cared less,' Long remarked afterwards. 'I was more interested in getting some strength back into my weakened legs so that I could stand up after all the excitement.'

Long and Ambrose were credited with one 'Mavis' apiece and the effect of their interception was indeed felt on the other side of the Aleutian chain. Commander Ito launched no more offensive operations, and on 17 August he and the remainder of his Toko Seaplane Squadron withdrew to Paramushiro Naval Base in the Kurile Islands. Left with only fighter and reconnaissance seaplanes, Kiska had little or no further offensive capabilities.

Later in that same month of August 1942 another P-38 scored the first victory for the type against the Germans, under similarly unlikely circumstances. The unit involved, the 1st Pursuit Group, spent the first months of the war defending the Continental United States from what some people thought to be an imminent Japanese invasion. After the initial panic subsided, the unit was redesignated the 1st Fighter Group and went on to record several 'firsts', including the first fighter unit to fly the North Atlantic ferry route and the first P-38 unit to arrive in England.

During Operation 'Bolero' as the transatlantic ferry flights to Britain were called, the 1st Group's 27th Fighter Squadron spent several boring weeks in Iceland, the midway point of the route. Flying weather was extremely rare, but on 14 August 1942 First Lieutenant Elza Shahan of the 27th was taking advantage of one of those few occasions to patrol when he encountered a Focke-Wulf Fw 200C Condor, a four-engine maritime reconnaissance bomber that was on the prowl for Allied convoys. This time the Germans got more than they bargained for as Shahan's P-38F, joined by a Curtiss P-40E flown by First Lieutenant Joseph Shafer of the 33rd Fighter Squadron, attacked the Fw 200 and shot it down for the USAAF's first aerial victory in the European Theatre.

Later, on 1 September, the 1st Fighter Group flew the first P-38 combat sortie over German-occupied territory—an uneventful sweep over France by the 71st and 94th Squadrons—and went on to become the first such unit to be deployed to North Africa, commencing operations from Tafaroui, Algeria, on 13 November.

The P-38 went on to live up to much of its promise in North Africa and Europe, although its record there would be greatly outshone by its accomplishments over Asia and the Pacific. There the Fifth Air Force's Lightning pilots would include the first- and second-ranking American aces, Richard I. Bong with 40 victories and Thomas G. McGuire with 38. One of the many aces of the Thirteenth Air Force, Rex A. Barber, was credited with only five victories, but one of them was the G4M2 bomber-transport carrying the mastermind of the Imperial Japanese Navy, Admiral Isoroku Yamamoto, when he was killed on 18 April 1943.

Unquestionably the most heavily armed single-engine fighter in the USAAF's arsenal was the Republic P-47 Thunderbolt. The P-47D weighed 13,800 pounds, its bulk compensated for with an equally monstrous 2,300 hp Pratt & Whitney R-2800-21 radial engine. Its armament consisted of eight wing-mounted 0.50-calibre machine guns. Its size, weight and the raw power required to yank it into the air lent the Thunderbolt the look of an ugly, oversized juggernaut, which its pilots soon abbreviated into the sobriquet 'Jug'.

The P-47's ancestor was the SEV-1XP, a single-seat fighter built by expatriot Russian World War I naval ace Alexander P. de Seversky to compete against the Curtiss Hawk 75 and the Northrop 3-A for a USAAC fighter contact in August 1935. Seversky was given an order for 77 P-35s on 16 June 1936, but his aircraft was essentially intended to tide things over for the Army Air Corps until problems with the Hawk 75's engine could be worked out. Meanwhile Seversky's chief designer, a fellow Russian exile named Alexander Kartveli, set to work on improving the already less than state-of-the-art P-35. One of Kartveli's principal improvements was to replace the P-35's landing gear, which retracted backwards behind two underwing fairings, with an undercarriage that retracted inwards, flush with the wing undersides. The aircraft was also powered by a 1,200 hp Pratt & Whitney R-1830-19 radial engine with a two-stage supercharger. Designated the XP-41, it produced a maximum speed of 313 mph at 15,000 feet—an improvement over the P-35 but not impressive enough to ensure acceptance.

In spite of some brisk export sales Seversky was unable to overcome his financial difficulties and his firm had to undergo a reorganisation in 1938. In June 1939 the company was renamed the Republic Aviation Corporation. Seversky had left, but Kartveli remained as Republic's chief designer.

When the USAAC held a new fighter competition at Wright Field, Ohio, in January 1939 Kartveli entered not only his XP-41 but also an improved version, with an R-1830-31 engine and a turbo-supercharger in the central fuselage and an air intake in the left wing root, called the AP-4. The USAAC accepted the Curtiss XP-40 but kept its options open on 12 May by ordering thirteen test versions of the AP-4, which received the Army designation YP-43 Lancer. Powered by a 1,200 hp R-1830-35 Twin Wasp engine, the Lancer had two 0.50-calibre machine guns in the cowling and two 0.30-calibre weapons in the wings and could reach 351 mph at 20,000 feet.

In spite of the fact that inline, water-cooled engines seemed to be favoured by the USAAC (as seen in the production contracts granted to the P-40, P-39 and P-38), Kartveli remained a believer in the power and easier installation of the radial and considered that its principal disadvantage, drag, could be overcome by careful design (a theory that, unknown to Kartveli, Japanese designer Jiro Horikoshi was already proving with his Zero fighter). He proposed refined versions of the P-43, the AP-4J, to be powered by a 1,400 hp R-1800-1, and the AP-4L, using a 2,000 hp R-2800-7 Double Wasp. The USAAC showed an interest in the former and at the end of 1939 Karveli set to work on a mock-up for what would be designated the P-44. In August, however, Republic submitted proposals for an AP-4 variant using a 1,150 hp Allison V-1710-39 inline engine. The USAAC was interested but suggested that it be enlarged to carry an increased armament of four 0.30-calibre wing guns in addition to the 0.50-calibre machine guns in the fuselage. Republic got a contract to build two prototypes—the XP-47 built to their specifications and a lighter version, the XP-47A.

It soon became apparent to Kartveli that neither version of the XP-47 would be able to produce the performance he had originally envisaged while taking on the added weight of armament and internal protection that the Army Air Corps required. In June 1940, therefore, he proposed a further modification, inspired by the passed-over AP-4L, using the Pratt & Whitney XR-2800 engine with turbo-supercharger, which could produce 2,000 hp at 27,800 feet. He promised that the higher power produced by the new engine would give his enlarged fighter a speed of 400 mph, the ability to reach 15,000 feet in five minutes and the ability to carry eight machine guns and a greater quantity of fuel for long-range missions. Within two months the USAAC agreed, and on 6 September 1940 the contract was altered to order a single XP-47B using the new Double Wasp engine. Plans to produce the P-44 were amended on 13 September, Republic instead being ordered to produce 54 P-43s, 80 P-43As and 125 P-43A-1s. The Lancer order was made primarily to keep Republic's assembly lines active until the P-47B was ready to enter production; most were shipped off to serve in the Chinese Air Force.

The first prototype XP-47B flew on 6 May 1942 with Lowry L. Brabham in the cockpit. Poorly sealed joints in the exhaust ducts resulted in smoke and fumes filling the cockpit, but Brabham managed to make an emergency landing at Mitchell Field, New York. The hinged canopy was subsequently replaced by a sliding canopy and eventually the plane lived up to its promise, with a speed of 412 mph at 25,800 feet and a service ceiling of 38,000 feet. An order for 171 P-47Bs was placed in March 1942 and Republic delivered the last of that order six months later. That was followed in September 1942 by the first of 602 P-47Cs with an eight-inch extension of the fuselage forward of the firewall, improving the centre of gravity and allowing the installation of a shackle under the fuselage for a drop tank or a 500-pound bomb. The P-47C also replaced the P-47B's forward-sloping radio mast with an upright one and had revised elevator balance systems.

The first P-47Bs were allocated to the 56th Fighter Group, still being organized in the United States, and the 78th Fighter Group subsequently got P-47s after the P-38s originally assigned to it were diverted to North Africa to replace losses there. The first unit to fly combat missions in the new type, however, was the 4th Fighter Group, already operational with the Eighth Air Force, which started receiving its P-47Cs in January 1943.

On the face of it, the 4th was a logical choice to blood the new fighter: its three squadrons had been formed directly from the three Eagle Squadrons, Nos 71, 121 and 133, consisting of American volunteers in the RAF. The one fly in the ointment was that their experience was in the Spitfire, a finely balanced instrument of aerial warfare that hardly prepared them for a brute like the P-47. One of the flight leaders nominated to try out the new plane, Lieutenant Richard L. Alexander, spoke for most of his colleagues: 'Sitting in a P-47 after having flown Spitfires was like coming out of a small office at the end of a gymnasium and walking into the playing area. It was awfully big.' Indeed, it was apparently the 4th Group pilots who first began to coin the then-derogatory sobriquet 'Jug' for their new mounts. 'The "Repulsive Scatterbolt", we called it,' added former Spitfire ace William R. Dunn. 'It had a lot of nicknames, most of them nasty . . . The first time I saw one of them, I asked, "Where's the other engine?" This klunk weighed almost twice as much as the Spitfire.'

The RAF was not ready for the P-47 either. In February 1943 four of the 4th Group's new planes were fired upon by Spitfire and Hawker Typhoon pilots, and by ground gunners, who mistook them for Focke-Wulf Fw 190As. Late in the month the noses and tails of the P-47s were painted with white bands as an identification measure.

After accumulating about 50 flying hours in the Thunderbolts, eleven of the 4th Group's pilots left their air base at Debden on their first combat mission on 10 March. They flew over Flushing in the Netherlands, then turned inland and swept over Dunkirk before returning home. In addition to complications with the turbo-supercharger system, the pilots experienced problems with the radios, making inter-aircraft communication virtually impossible. Anti-aircraft guns threw some shells their way, but the 'Jugs' encountered no aerial opposition. 'A lot of Germans were up there, but they just stood off and looked at us,' recalled Lieutenant Don D. Nee. 'They hadn't seen Thunderbolts before, and were wary.' Upon their return to Debden, Lieutenant-Colonel Chesley G. Peterson, one of the most prominent of the group's 'old Eagles', indicated that he was relieved at the German fighters' reticence. 'I don't mind telling you,' he said, 'I was scared.'

A rash of accidents continued to plague the 4th Group before its pilots got the measure of their big fighters. On 3 April Lieutenant Frank Smolinsky's plane caught fire and he was killed while attempting an emergency landing at Sawbridgeworth. A similar accident befell Lieutenant Oscar Coen, but he safely bailed out of his burning machine. The 334th Fighter Squadron, which was flying the bulk of the 4th Group's early P-47 missions, was soon being referred to as the 'Suicide Squadron'.

A second sweep by 24 P-47Cs over the Pas de Calais on 8 April was uneventful, but during the next mission over St Omer by 36 Thunderbolts of the 4th and 78th Groups on 13 April one plane developed engine trouble and its pilot had to bail out over the Channel, resulting in the first operational loss. On a further patrol that evening another 'Jug' suffered from engine trouble, and when it passed by a British coastal battery off Deal, Kent, it was mistaken for an Fw 190 and hit, the pilot being forced to ditch his plane off the coast.

Anxiety about the P-47's prospects against the Fw 190 were not totally alleviated when a P-47C was flown in mock combat against a captured Fw 190A-4/U8. Although the Thunderbolt was able to hold its own at 20,000 feet and higher, its supercharged engine gave it no advantage at 15,000 feet, where the Fw 190 proved to be the better fighter.

April 15 saw the first shooting encounter with Fw 190s. Major Donald J. M. Blakeslee was leading ten Thunderbolts of the 335th Squadron on a sweep over Ostend when they spotted three Fw 190As at 23,000 feet. Blakeslee led his men in a diving attack and fired into one of the enemy fighters. According to Blakeslee the German pilot descended to 500 feet, then tried to bail out but was too low and fell to his death in the back yard of a house in Ostend. Later Blakeslee was congratulated on his victory and for proving that the P-47 could out-dive the Fw 190. 'By God, it ought to dive,' he retorted. 'It certainly won't climb.'

Lieutenant-Colonel Chesley Peterson and Lieutenant Douglas Booth were also credited with downing Fw 190s:

It was our first tangle with the Fw 190 [Peterson recalled]. I knew the P-47 could out-turn and out-dive the 190, and I knew it could not out-climb it. When we mixed it up, the 190 made the mistake of trying to dive away. It was really duck soup for me, and this became the first 190 to be shot down by a P-47.

Postwar German records told a rather different story. The Focke-Wulfs that the Americans encountered were from *II Gruppe* of *Jagdgeschwader 1*, patrolling some-what further west than it usually did. Its pilots claimed two of what they had by then identified as P-47s and suffered no losses whatsoever. Their own claims, on the other hand, were substantiated by the deaths of Captains Stanley M. Ander-son and Richard D. McMinn. Chesley Peterson's plane was also lost in that mis-sion, under different circumstances that he at least lived to describe, although he later said that, from the standpoint of terror, it was his worst day of flying:

As I shot the 190 down and pulled away to get back up to altitude, the engine blew up. A couple or three cylinders in front just let go.

I tried my best to glide back across the Channel to England, but the engine finally froze up. I was determined not to be taken prisoner: that would have to be the last thing that would happen to me. I got about five miles off the coast and was at very low altitude. I thought about coming down in the water, but knew the P-47 probably would not ditch suc-cessfully. I made my up mind to bail out.

The altimeter registered 500 feet when I rolled the plane over on its back, with my straps undone and the canopy open, still losing altitude. I fell out at around 300 feet and pulled the ripcord. The chute just streamed; it never did open.

I made a beautiful swan dive into the Channel—a swan dive so absolutely perfect that the impact did not knock me out. I went down in the water 35 or 40 feet. The silk kept me from going too deep . . .

Somehow I managed to get into my dinghy, and I sat in the water for a couple or three hours. Finally a wonderful old [Supermarine] Walrus airplane from the RAF Air–Sea Rescue practically flew into the Ostend harbor and picked me up.

On 4 May the 'Jugs' flew their first bomber escort mission, accompanying B-17s to Antwerp. By the end of May P-47 pilots had logged a total of 2,279 sorties and claimed ten enemy planes destroyed along with seven 'probables' and eighteen damaged. In that same time, however, eighteen P-47s had been lost on combat operations, five of which were attributable to engine failure.

In 1943 the P-47C's deficiencies were ironed out and the plane soon proved its worth. Not only could it overhaul both the Fw 190A and the Me 109G in level flight, it could outmanoeuvre them both at altitudes above 15,000 feet. And, if the worst came to the worst, neither German fighter had a chance of catching a Thunderbolt if it resorted to diving away.

While the North American P-51 Mustang, with its greater range, was the better overall performer, the rugged and heavily armed P-47 gained a solid following, particularly in the 56th Fighter Group, the only one in the Eighth Air Force to fly Thunderbolts throughout the war. Nineteen of the top 25 aces in VIII Fighter Command flew P-47s at some time during their careers, and the two leading American aces over Europe, Francis S. Gabreski with 28 victories and Robert S. Johnson with 27, both flew P-47s exclusively with the 56th Group. Fifty years later—and right up to his death on 27 December 1998—Bob Johnson still swore by the Jug:

> In the Thunderbolt, I could beat the crap out of a P-51 anytime I wanted to, and I did, many times, in mock dogfights. The P-47 would hold together no matter what you did, while the P-51 would break under many circumstances. We used to joke that in the P-47, if you couldn't outfly them, you'd run through them.

Chapter 12

ILLUSTRIOUS BEGINNINGS

Fairey Fulmar and Firefly, 1940–1944

While the United States and Japan were developing single-seat shipboard fighters during the 1930s Britain retained a fixation on the need for a navigator to help the pilot of a long-range carrier-based fighter find his way to his target and back to his ship. With that in mind the Admiralty issued Specification O.8/38 calling for a two-seat naval fighter. As was so often the case with carrier fighters of the time, that requirement imposed built-in restrictions on the aeroplane's performance, yet the plane that was ultimately built to satisfy it, the Fairey Fulmar, proved to be remarkably successful.

The Fulmar really began with an attempt to improve the performance of the Fairey Battle, a single-engine monoplane bomber that was pleasant to fly but overweight, underpowered and doomed to failure in the early months of World War II. Designed by Marcel Lobelle, the Fairey P.4/34 light bomber was much smaller and cleaner than the Battle and was built to withstand the stresses of dive-bombing. When O.8/38 came out it proved fairly easy to modify the second prototype of the light bomber into a two-seat fighter capable of absorbing the punishment of carrier landings. Among the changes involved were provision for wing folding, catapult points, arrester gear, an uprated 1,080 hp Rolls-Royce Merlin VIII 12-cylinder engine and eight 0.303-inch Browning machine guns mounted in the wings. Besides the need to house the navigator, a relatively large aeroplane was necessary to accommodate the fuel required for more than four hours' endurance.

After examining a mock-up based on the P.4/34 the Admiralty told Fairey to proceed with their carrier fighter on 5 May 1938. Just twenty months later, on 4 January 1940, Fairey test pilot Duncan Menzies took the first true Fulmar prototype up for its first test flight from Ringway airfield. By the time the second Fulmar flew at Boscombe Down on 4 April 1940 approval of the new fighter was all but a foregone conclusion—by June, ten Fulmars had been delivered to 806 Naval Air Squadron, which began training on them for use aboard *Illustrious*, a new carrier equipped with radar and an armour-plated flight deck.

With a maximum level speed of 256 mph the Fulmar was hardly a world-beater by 1940 standards, but it was pleasant to fly, easy to operate from carrier decks and capable of absorbing considerable punishment. For the Admiralty it at least represented the long-overdue introduction of a modern monoplane fighter with retractable landing gear to the Royal Navy's arsenal. It was also a classic case of the right plane coming at the right time, for on 10 June 1940 Italy invaded France, thereby entering the war as a German ally and threatening such British holdings in the Mediterranean as Gibraltar and Malta. Indeed, British and Italian warships had already had some indecisive engagements, and aircraft of the *Regia Aeronautica* had been attacking Malta-bound convoys, when *Illustrious* arrived at Gibraltar with her complement of brand-new Fulmars on 29 August.

On the following day *Illustrious*, with the battleship *Valiant* and anti-aircraft cruisers *Coventry* and *Calcutta*, departed to reinforce Admiral Sir Andrew Cunningham's fleet at Alexandria, Egypt, as part of a multi-pronged manoeuvre called Operation 'Hats'. While naval units under Vice-Admiral Sir James Somerville feinted and raided to divert Italian attention from Force F, as the reinforcing vessels were called, *Illustrious* kept six-plane patrols up to cover the little fleet.

The Fulmars fired their guns in anger for the first time on 1 September but, tragically, the aeroplane they attacked was not one of the enemy's. As Force F approached the Sicilian Narrows some of *Illustrious*'s Blackburn Skua dive-bombers spotted an unidentified aircraft approaching eighteen miles to the south-east and went to investigate. As they closed, the Skua leader recognized the plane as a Lockheed Hudson from Malta and exchanged signals with its pilot. At that point three Fulmars came up from below and opened fire on the Hudson, causing considerable damage before signal flares fired from the Skua and their victim caused them to break off their attack. The Hudson's pilot, Flying Officer G. W. Vincent Davies of No 233 Squadron, headed for the nearest landfall, the Cap Bon peninsula in Vichy French Tunisia, and managed to crash-land on El Aouina airfield at Tunis. Two of his crew were injured and taken to hospital while Davies and his other crewman were interned at Le Kef. There they would remain until their liberation in the wake of the British and American invasions of North Africa in November 1942.

The Fulmars that attacked Davies were led by 806 Naval Air Squadron's commander, Lieutenant-Commander Charles L. S. Evans, but the pilot who actually shot at the Hudson was 43-year-old Leiutenant-Commander Robin A. Kilroy, the former commander of the Fairey Swordfish-equipped 815 Squadron, who was on his way to take command of the Royal Naval Air Station at Dekheila outside Alexandria. He had offered to assist in flight duties, but in his first combat patrol in the Fulmar he mistook the twin-engine Hudson for a Junkers Ju 88 until he saw the roundel on the fuselage.

While Somerville approached Malta from the west, Cunningham, flying his flag from the battleship *Warspite*, left Alexandria to rendezvous with his reinforcements. There were some brushes with Italian aircraft and search planes from the carrier *Eagle* reported an Italian battle fleet to be coming out to intercept Cunningham on 30 August, but the next day a Malta-based flying boat reported the Italian warships as retiring into the Gulf of Taranto. At 9 a.m. on 2 September Cunningham's look-outs spotted Force F.

The two naval units were also being observed by a Cant Z.501 *Gabbiano* flying boat, which spotted them 35 miles west of Malta. Evans was leading three Fulmars on patrol, however, and by means of some primitive Morse code transmission he, Kilroy and Sub-Lieutenant I. L. F. Lowe were directed towards the shadower at 11.20 a.m. Cunningham himself described the effect on morale as the Fulmars attacked the Z.501 from astern at 500 feet altitude and sent it flaming into the sea:

> . . . to loud cheers of the ships' companies, who had had just about as much as they could stand of being bombed without retaliation. The tremendous effect of this incident upon everyone in the fleet, and upon the Commander-in-Chief as much as anyone, was indescribable.

The Italian air crew had managed to get off a transmission before going down, however, and at 2.15 p.m. nine SIAI-Marchetti S.79 *Sparviero* tri-motor bombers of the *36o Stormo Bombardimento Terrestre*, followed by nine more from the *41o Stormo BT* , set out to destroy the British fleet. Only the *41o Stormo*'s S.79s found their target and made for *Illustrious*. Again, however, two sections of Fulmars, led by Lieutenant William L. Barnes and Sub-Lieutenant Stanley G. Orr, were up, and as they went to intercept the bombers two more sections were catapulted from *Illustrious*'s flight deck. The Italians had been expecting nothing more potent than Sea Gladiators to bar their way and two of the attackers jettisoned their bomb loads and fled. The remaining seven were made of sterner stuff and pressed on.

Now the Fulmars truly earned their keep, riddling the bomber formation before it could reach *Illustrious*. Barnes downed an S.79 in flames and damaged two others:

> From that moment [Cunningham said], whenever an armoured carrier was in company, we had command of the air over the fleet. By that I do not mean that bombing ceased. Far from it. But we felt we now had a weapon which enabled us to give back as good as we were getting.'

The *41o Stormo* made another appearance later that afternoon with six S.79s of the *235a Squadriglia, 59o Gruppo BT*, trying to strike at *Illustrious* when they were intercepted by Barnes's section at 5.15 p.m. Barnes downed his second

S.79 of the day and damaged another, which was subsequently finished by anti-aircraft fire from the ships. The Fulmar team of Sub-Lieutenant G. R. Golden and Leading Airman Harry Phillips claimed one S.79 shot down and a second damaged, while Sub-Lieutenant Alfred Jack Sewell was credited with two more. The perspective of Sewell's observer, Leading Airman Denis J. Tribe, suggests the relative helplessness of the Fulmar's unarmed 'back-seater' in aerial combat:

> We claimed two shot down but in the action caught up with fire from the enemy. From the rear seat it was difficult to see except for tracers coming at us—a row of holes in my perspex cover; the glycol coolant pouring into my cockpit. Also the intercom was damaged and out of action. I thought I was badly hit as whenever I moved I could see blood. I was greatly relieved to find it was coming from a flesh wound under my right forearm. Although Jackie Sewell had armour-plated glass in front of him I thought he must have been hit because the plane seemed out of control. I could not communicate owing to the damage and I could not open my sliding cover. Fortunately he regained control and with damaged engine we made quite a good landing at Hal Far—guided by Lt. Barnes who also landed at Hal Far. I had first aid locally and in the early evening we were picked up by one of the Swordfish from *Illustrious*.

Italian Junkers Ju 87B Stukas dive-bombed the fleet that evening but little damage was done by them or to them by the carrier fighters and anti-aircraft guns that tried to stop them. Cunningham then steamed into the Aegean to raid the island of Rhodes, with two flights of six Fulmars providing fighter cover for the carriers while Swordfish from *Illustrious* and *Eagle* bombed the airfields at Callato, Maritza and Gadurra in the morning of 4 September. The *163a Squadriglia Autonoma*, comprising Fiat C.R.32s and C.R.42s and Meridionali biplanes, scrambled up from Maritza and shot down four of the Swordfish while losing three of their own—including a C.R.32 and C.R.42 that collided during take-off.

Four S.79s of the *39o Stormo* were able to get off the ground at Gadurra and approached the British fleet at 10.30 a.m. but they were intercepted, shot up and chased off by Barnes and Sewell. When two more S.79s of the *201a Squadriglia, 92o Gruppo BT*, showed up, Barnes shot one down in flames, killing *Tenente* Nicola Dell'Olio and his crew, and damaged another. Sub-Lieutenant I. P. Godfrey and Leading Airman Phillips attacked another S.79 and scored damaging hits on its port engine. Two other S.79s were also damaged by the Fulmars, returning with two of their crewmen dead and five wounded.

Elsewhere, at 10.05 Lieutenant-Commander Kilroy and Sub-Lieutenant Orr were vectored over to investigate a tri-motor aircraft identified as a Caproni Ca.133 bomber-transport which was about to land and they sent it crashing into the sea. Two crewmen were seen to bail out of what apparently was an SIAI-Marchetti S.81 *Pipistrello* of the *233a Squadriglia BT*. At 1.45 that afternoon a Fulmar section led by Lieutenant O. J. Nichols encountered two S.79s 50 miles south of Castello Point and pounced. Nichols thought he saw pieces fly off the starboard wing of the plane he attacked, but neither enemy aircraft was shot down.

Three Fulmars intercepted another Cant Z.501 at 11 a.m. on 17 September. Stanley Orr attacked and thought he killed the pilot because the flying boat started to climb before slowly spinning into the sea. On the 29th Sub-Lieutenant Graham Angus Hogg's section caught another of the shadowing flying boats flying at 8,000 feet between Alexandria and Malta. Hogg sent it spiralling down in flames, but not before its return fire had disabled the Fulmar of Sub-Lieutenant Lowe, who had to ditch five miles astern of the Australian destroyer *Stuart*, which turned about and rescued him and his observer, Leading Airman P. Douet. Three hours later Orr's section caught another Z.501 at 10,000 feet and he sent it down in flames as well. As the fleet headed back to Alexandria on 1 October it surprised the surfaced Italian submarine *Berillo*, whose crew surrendered and were taken off, after which the boat was sunk. At 11.15 a.m. Evans caught a Cant Z.506B *Airone* tri-motor floatplane at 4,000 feet and sent it crashing into the sea with its right engine on fire. The body of an Italian airman identified as A. Girondola was found by a British ship five days later; he may have been one of the Z.506's crewmen.

The Italians came out in force again as *Illustrious* was making her way back from Malta to Gibraltar on 12 October, only to run afoul of 806 Squadron's Fulmars once more. Sewell and Sub-Lieutenant J. M. L. Roberts intercepted a shadowing Cant Z.501 at 11.45 a.m. and pursued it from 3,000 feet until it finally ditched in the sea, after which they strafed it. Lieutenant Nichols's section encountered twelve S.79s at 12.30 and he sprayed their second flight with bullets before latching on to a lone plane. Attacking from astern, he reported white smoke pouring from its starboard engine, but it was not confirmed as shot down. Evans, Hogg and Lowe ran into five more S.79s of the *36o Stormo* at 1.50 p.m. and made beam attacks on them. Evans and Hogg sent one of the Italians down in flames and compelled a second to ditch, corresponding to the losses of aircraft piloted by *Tenente* Alberto Soldato of the *108o Gruppo BT* and *Tenente* Francesco Tempra of the *109o Gruppo*. Barnes claimed a third S.79, which could either have been a plane that returned to Sicily damaged with one dead and two wounded crewmen aboard or another damaged machine, flown by *Tenente* Giorgio Pieri of the *109o Gruppo*, which flew into a mountainside and was destroyed.

By 14 October the Fulmars of 806 Squadron had accounted for a total of ten Italian bombers. *Illustrious* returned to the Mediterranean on 11 November to launch a raid against the Italian naval base at Taranto, in which its Swordfish torpedoed and sank the battleships *Caio Duilio, Italia* and *Giulio Cesare*—the last-named for the duration of the war. The strike accomplished much in proportion to the type and number of aircraft involved, but the material damage the Swordfish meted out was far exceeded by the psychological crippling they inflicted on the *Regia Marina*.

While the Swordfish were so engaged, *Illustrious*'s Fulmars continued to protect the carrier, downing several shadowers before they could send accurate reports to their superiors. Sub-Lieutenants Orr and W. H. Clisby claimed a Z.501 in flames at 11.55 a.m.; Evans and Lowe sent another *Gabbiano* down in flames ten minutes later. Half an hour after that Evans found a Z.506B at 7,000 feet and after two attacks saw it go down in flames. One of the victims reportedly fell alongside the battleship *Warspite*, flagship of the task force. As a result of the Fulmars' efforts, no Italian counter-attack materialized following the Taranto raid. Orr and Hogg teamed up against one more Z.506B at 3.30 the following afternoon, expending all their ammunition on it and then seeing it catch fire and descend after they broke off their attack.

All in all the Fairey Fulmar had truly got off to an illustrious start, and over the next few years it would perform yeoman service for the Fleet Air Arm as a fighter, reconnaissance plane and night fighter. Although the Fulmar was intrinsically no match for the Me 109, the Macchi C.200 or the Mitsubishi A6M2 Zero, its pilots often gave a good account of themselves even against those single-seat foes. Eventually the Fulmar's performance was eclipsed, but Fairey already had a successor on the way—curiously similar in basic layout but destined for a more distinguished and much longer career.

Following its acceptance of the Fulmar, the Admiralty persisted with its rationale that two sets of eyes were better than one. In 1939, therefore, it issued two specifications around the new Rolls-Royce Griffon engine—N.8/39, armed with eight 0.303-inch machine guns, and N.9/39, to use a power-operated four-gun turret as employed on the Boulton Paul Defiant and the Blackburn Roc. Fairey's design team, supervised by L. Massey Hilton and led by H. E. Champlin, concluded early on that no amount of ingenuity would compensate for the weight and drag of the power turret and therefore concentrated on satisfying specification N.8/39. The brutishly handsome aeroplane they came up with bore a clear family resemblance to the more elegant-looking Fulmar, and although it was slightly smaller in dimensions its empty weight almost matched that of a fully loaded Fulmar. As with the Fulmar, the new reconnaissance fighter was quick to gain Admiralty approval—in fact, with the completion of the mock-up on 6 June 1940 it was given a new specification number, 5/40, and a 200-plane order was placed virtually off the drawing-board. On 22 December 1941 C. S. Staniland flew the first hand-built Fairey Firefly off the grass airfield at Heston.

Besides its 1,735 hp Griffon IIB V-12 engine, the Firefly differed from the Fulmar in having a fuselage built in two halves, joined along the vertical centre-line and deriving its strength from a series of heavy U-shaped frames and the outer skin rather than from longitudinal stringers. The engine was mounted in a quickly detachable 'power egg' and the wings featured innovative, hydraulically operated Youngman flaps which could not only be angled to slow the plane for landing or reduce its turning circle in a dogfight but also extended aft to increase the wing area for cruising—an early form of variable geometry.

By the time the second Firefly prototype had been delivered to Heston for flight-testing in March 1942 the machine gun armament had been replaced by four wing-mounted 20mm Hispano cannon. Capable of a maximum speed of 316 mph, the first production Firefly F Mk I was delivered to the Royal Navy on 4 March 1943.

After trails and training, the first Firefly unit, 1770 Naval Air Squadron, was formed at Yeovilton on 1 October 1943, followed by 1771 Squadron on 1 February 1944. Assigned aboard the new aircraft carrier *Indefatigable*, 1770 Squadron blooded the Firefly in battle for the first time on 17 July 1944 when it participated in Operation 'Mascot', a raid against the German battleship *Tirpitz* in Altenfjord, Norway.

Earlier, during Operation 'Tungsten' on 3 April, British carrier planes had scored some 1,000-pound bomb hits that damaged *Tirpitz*'s guns and radar, but by mid-July her repairs were nearing completion, resurrecting her status as a threat to Allied convoys to the Soviet Union via the Arctic. As a participant in the follow-up raid, 1770 Squadron had as its duties primarily to reconnoitre Altenfjord and strafe anti-aircraft gun positions during the attack. A German smokescreen foiled the first strike and natural fog contributed to the failure of the second. Two more carrier raids on 22 and 29 August also failed to inflict serious damage on *Tirpitz*, but the information gathered by the Fireflies proved useful for later air attacks until Avro Lancasters, dropping 12,000-pound 'Tall-boy' bombs finally succeeded in sinking the great ship in Tromsø Fjord on 12 November.

Engaged in reconnaissance and anti-shipping sorties along the Norwegian coast, the Fireflies of 1770 Squadron, joined in October by 1771 aboard HMS *Implacable*, seldom encountered aerial opposition in 1944. The two-seaters finally got their chance to engage enemy aircraft half a world away, however, when *Indefatigable* was transferred to the Indian Ocean. The vindictive eagerness of the Firefly crews to test their mettle against the Japanese was bolstered by confidence after a Firefly repeatedly won out in mock dogfights with a Grumman F6F Hellcat at the US Navy test centre at Patuxent River. On 1 January 1945 the carriers *Indomitable, Illustrious, Victorious* and *Indefatigable*, commanded by

Rear-Admiral Sir Philip Vian, launched their aircraft for the first of a week-long series of strikes on the Pangkalan Brandan oil refinery on Sumatra, during which 1770 Squadron's Fireflies, led by Major Teddy Cheesman, contributed to the carnage with wing-mounted rockets. On 4 January the Japanese Army Air Force came up to fight, though the principal fighter encountered by the Fireflies was a slightly improved version of the same Nakajima Ki-43, or 'Oscar,' that the British had first encountered back in 1941. Grumman Hellcats of 1839 and 1844 Squadrons based aboard HMS *Indomitable* downed three of the 'Oscars', while Vought Corsairs of *Victorious*'s 1834 Squadron accounted for five Ki-43s, a Mitsubishi Ki-21 bomber and a Mitsubishi Ki-46 reconnaissance plane. During one of 1770 Squadron's encounters with the enemy Lieutenant P. Levitt drew first blood by downing a Ki-43 while Sub-Lieutenants Redding and John Philip Stott shared in the destruction of a second. The British lost only one Grumman Avenger in the day's fighting.

The Pangkalan Pradan raid was only a dress rehearsal for a greater strike. Moving from Trincomalee to Sydney, Australia, the carrier force launched Operation 'Meridian One' and 'Two', a pair of massive strikes on the ex-Shell refineries at Pladjoe near Palembang, on 24 and 29 January. The Japanese defended the precious oil facilities with heavy anti-aircraft fire, barrage balloons, Ki-43s, Nakajima Ki-44s and Kawasaki Ki-45 twin-engine fighters. Roaring through flak and past the barrage balloons, *Indefatigable*'s Fireflies again sub-jected the refinery to a deluge of rockets. As they left the targets and flak behind, Cheesman's pilots spotted a flight of Avengers under attack by enemy fighters and engaged the Japanese until Corsairs and Hellcats arrived to drive them off. During the fight the Fireflies downed two more Ki-43s, Stott sharing in both victories. Total British losses amounted to three Avengers, three Corsairs and two Hellcats.

The job was only half done, however, and on 29 January the carriers struck Palembang again, this time seeking out the Soengei Gerong refinery. None too astonishingly, the flak and aerial opposition were more intense than before. Four more Avengers went down, and the four fighters lost included 1770 Squadron's first Firefly. Stott paid the enemy back in kind by shooting down three Ki-43s.

When Vian's force returned to Fremantle, Australia, on 4 February, it had lost sixteen aircraft in combat and 25 from other causes while claiming the destruc-tion of 34 Japanese aircraft in the air and 38 on the ground. More importantly, it had reduced Pladjoe's production by half and put the Soengei Gerong refin-ery completely out of operation for six months.

So ended the Firefly's fighting debut, with almost six months elapsing between its first operation and its first air-to-air combat. Such a protracted blooding may have been appropriate, however. For the British Pacific Fleet, soon to be redesignated Task Force 57, the Okinawa campaign still lay ahead. On 10 July 1945 Fireflies of 1771 Squadron from *Implacable* would make history as the first British aircraft to fly over Japan—and, on 24 July, Fireflies would be the first British planes to fly over Tokyo. And after all that, the end of World War II would be just the beginning for the remarkably versatile Fairey Firefly which, through a series of progressive improvements, would fight again over Korea and during the Suez Crisis, and serve the Fleet Air Arm into the mid-1960s.

Chapter 13

THE AXIS STRIKES BACK

Axis Fighters, 1941–1944

For the first two years of World War II 'Messerschmitt Me 109' was syn-onymous with 'German fighter'—there simply was nothing else. Then, amid the cross-Channel aerial jousting between the Royal Air Force and the *Luftwaffe* that characterized the autumn of 1941, a new challenger entered the lists on the German side. Sharing the Messerschmitt's businesslike angularity but replacing its sharp nose with the pugnacious, blunt snout of a radial-engine fighter, this new combatant was the Focke-Wulf Fw 190.

Stemming from a 1937 contract from the *Reichsluftfahrtministerium* (RLM) for a new single-seat fighter, the Fw 190 was designed by Focke-Wulf's chief engineer Kurt Tank in two forms, one using the water-cooled inline Daimler-Benz DB-601 engine and one using the BMW 139 air-cooled radial. The latter was selected for development in the summer of 1938 and the first prototype, the Fw 190 V1, took off for the first time on 1 June 1939. With the fan-cooled 1,550 hp BMW 139 giving it a promising speed of 370 mph, the Fw 190 V1 originally used a ducted spinner, but cooling problems led to a more conventional cowling and spin-ner arrangement. As the prototype was refined, the BMW 139 was replaced by the newer BMW 801 which, while heavier, had greater development potential. Although the engine gave trouble, the Fw 190 displayed excellent handling char-acteristics and outstanding manoeuvrability while its wide undercarriage track made take-offs and landings far less tricky than they were for the Me 109. Eigh-teen pre-production Fw 190A-0s were ordered, the first seven of which had wing-spans of 31 feet 2 inches; the rest used wings 34 feet 5½ inches in span, which improved manoeuvrability. After pre-service trials at Rechlin-Rogenthin the larger wings were incorporated into the Fw 190A-1 *Würger* (Butcher-Bird, or Shrike), which went into production in Bremen and Hamburg, the first 100 being com-pleted in the later spring of 1941. Powered by a 1,600 hp BMW 801C engine, the Fw 190A-1 was armed with four wing-mounted 7.9mm MG17 machine guns.

In March 1941 thirty pilots were detached from *II Gruppe, Jagdgeschwader 26 'Schlageter'*, and brought to Rechlin to test-fly the new fighter. Designated the *Erprobungsstaffel* (Operational Test Squadron), the detachment was commanded by *Oberleutnant* Otto Behrens, a prewar *Luftwaffe* mechanic whose technical knowledge would be as handy as his proficiency as a veteran fighter pilot.

One of *Erprobungsstaffel 190*'s members, *Oberleutnant* Karl Borris, recalled his first impressions of the Focke-Wulf:

> From the first take-off we were convinced of the robustness and the excellent flying qualities of the new aircraft. However, the BMW 801 engine, a new twin-row, 14-cylinder, air-cooled radial design, gave us nothing but misery. Whatever could possibly go wrong with it, did. We hardly dared leave the immediate vicinity of the airfield with our six prototype machines. Oil lines ruptured. The heavily armoured oil cooler ring in front of the engine broke often. The bottom cylinder of the rear row seized again and again, since the oil pump and the cooling surfaces were too small. Leaking fuel lines left the pilots in a dazed state from the fumes, unable to climb out of their aircraft unaided. The constant-speed propeller often failed to work properly . . . *Professor* Tank tried to meet our demands in the most direct manner, avoiding the bureaucracy. The RLM propeller specialists and the Rechlin test pilots could only shake their heads when we soared across the field, smoking and stinking. An RLM commission . . . wanted to scratch the Fw 190 from consideration for active service. We protested vehemently, because the airframe itself was truly outstanding.

Behrens' strictly professional, constructive criticism of the new plane is often credited with saving the Fw 190 project from cancellation. Eventually its flaws were sufficiently corrected for the type to be cleared for service in July 1941. Tank also responded to the *Luftwaffe* pilots' complaints that the Fw 190A-1's armament was inadequate by replacing the inboard MG 17s with two 20mm MG FF cannon and redesignating the modified fighter Fw 190A-2.

The *Erprobungsstaffel* moved to Le Bourget airfield outside Paris and began training pilots of *II./JG 26* on the newly arrived production Fw 190A-2, starting with the *Gruppenführer, Hauptmann* Walter Adolph. *Oberleutnant* Walter Schneider's *6. Staffel* was the first squadron fully equipped with the new type, followed by *Oberleutnant* Kurt Ebersberger's *4.* and *Oberleutnant* Wolfgang Kosse's *5. Staffeln*. By 1 September the entire *II. Gruppe* was ready, *Erprobungsstaffel 190* had been dissolved and the group had moved up to front-line bases at Moorsele and Wevelghem in western Belgium.

Problems were still cropping up in the Fw 190A-2's BMW 801C-1 engine but *II./JG 26*'s training casualties only amounted to one pilot injured until 29 August, when German flak downed one of the unfamiliar-looking machines near Dunkirk, causing the first, tragically ironic Fw 190 fatality with the death of its pilot, *Leutnant* Hans Schenck. *II. Gruppe* was cautious about committing its new fighter to the unforgiving environment of the Channel Front, but while eight of its Fw 190s were covering a large tanker on 18 September the ship came under attack off Blankenberge by three Bristol Blenheims of No 88 Squadron RAF. The Germans engaged the bombers, shooting down two before getting into a lively dogfight with their escorts, Spitfire Mk VBs of No 41

Squadron. When the German flight reassembled and returned to Moorsele, its leader, *Hauptmann* Adolph, was absent. His body was washed up on the beach at Knokke, Belgium, three weeks later. The first combat fatality in an Fw 190, Adolph had by then been credited with 28 victories while flying Me 109Es and was a holder of the *Ritterkreuz*. Since the British had no idea of what an Fw 190 was at the time, it is very likely that Adolph's plane was identified as a 'Curtiss Hawk' credited to Flying Officer Cyril Babbage.

On the day following Adolph's disappearance *Oberleutnant* Joachim Münche-berg, then leader of 7. *Staffel* and victor over some 50 Allied aircraft, was promoted to *Hauptmann* and put in charge of *II. Gruppe*. Two days later, on 21 September, *Oberleutnant* Walter Schneider's 6. *Staffel* demonstrated the Fw 190A-1's potential with a vengeance when it engaged Spitfires of No 315 Squadron over Boulogne and claimed four of the vaunted British fighters without loss. (The Polish unit had in fact lost two planes, with one pilot killed and one taken prisoner.) These were but the first of thousands of Allied aircraft that would be destroyed or damaged by the *Würger* over the next four years.

The introduction of the new radial-engine German fighter took the RAF entirely unawares, and early descriptions of it were even discounted by British Intelligence, in spite of mounting losses throughout October 1941 to *JG 26*'s Fw 190 pilots, whose confidence and aggressiveness were growing. On 13 October Circus 108A, an attack on the ship lift at Arques by six Blenheims of No 139 Squadron, came under attack from below by *JG 26*'s *Geschwaderkommandeur, Major* Adolf Galland, who sent one of the bombers down in flames. Galland's wingman, *Leutnant* Peter Göring—a nephew of *Reichsmarschall* Hermann Göring—was less fortunate, being struck by return fire from a Blenheim turret gunner and crashing to his death. Elsewhere Me 109s of *I./JG 26* and Fw 190s of *2./JG 26* picked off five Spitfires from the bombers' escort, again suffering no losses. The returning British aircraft, however, carried clear gun-camera evidence of the Fw 190A's existence: at last the RAF airmen were believed.

October also saw the conversion of *Major* Gerhard Schöpfel's *III./JG 26* to the Fw 190, during which time the *Gruppe*'s technical officer, *Obleutnant* Rudolf Schroedter, discovered that by simply re-routing the exhaust system he eliminated the tendency of the BMW 801's lower rear cylinder to overheat. With more widespread modification the Fw 190's Achilles' heel could be remedied.

Barring the early engine troubles, the Fw 190A-2 showed a marked superiority to the Spitfire V, but worse was to come for the RAF. In response to complaints about the engine and the slow-firing, low-velocity MG FF cannon, Focke-Wulf began producing the Fw 190A-3 in the autumn of 1941. Powered by the improved 1,700 hp BMW 801Dg radial, the A-3 was armed not only with four faster-firing MG 151 cannon in the wings but also with two 7.9mm MG 17s in the fuselage.

From that time on the see-saw struggle for air superiority between Spitfire and *Würger* would be matched behind the lines as Supermarine and Focke-Wulf came up with progressively improved models of their superlative designs.

While the Fw 190A served as a worthy complement to the Me 109F in the *Luftwaffe's* fighter arsenal, Italy's *Regia Aeronautica* was in desperate need of a new fighter just to restore parity with such British counterparts as the Hurricane and Spitfire. The most numerous Italian fighter in 1939 had been the Fiat C.R.42 biplane, essentially a refined World War I fighter. The Fiat G.50, Italy's first monoplane fighter, could barely outperform the C.R.42 let alone its contemporary opposition.

Aeronautica Macchi's designer, Mario Castoldi, had already tried to redress these consequences of shortsightedness on the part of the *Regia Aeronautica*. His C.200 *Saetta* (Thunderbolt), which first flew on 24 December 1937, was a monoplane with retractable landing gear that strove to incorporate the aerodynamic refinements of Castoldi's Schneider Trophy racers, much as Reginald Mitchell had done with his Spitfire. Unlike the Spitfire, however, the C.200 suffered from compromises. It had a humped upper fuselage to provide the pilot with a good field of vision, enhanced by the later omission of its enclosed canopy at the behest of conservative 'seat-of-the-pants' pilots. Most telling, both from the standpoint of performance and from that of aesthetics, was the installation of an 870 hp Fiat A74 RC.38 14-cylinder, double-row radial engine on the airframe. Looking as if it had been stuck on as an afterthought, the radial obscured the C.200's Schneider Trophy pedigree and added an inordinate amount of drag.

C.R.42s were the only fighters committed to Italy's invasion of France on 10 June 1940, but on the following day the C.200 joined battle over another target entirely—the British-held island of Malta. As successive flights of SIAI-Marchetti S.79 tri-motor bombers of the *34o, 11o* and *41o Stormi BT* left their Sicilian air bases for Malta, eighteen *Saettas*, drawn in equal part from the *79a* and *88a Squadriglie* of *Tenente Colonello* Armando Francois's *6o Gruppo Caccia Terrestre*, took off from Comiso, Sicily, to provide escort. Malta's lone radar picked up the attacking formations and the island's fighter defences—three Gloster Gladiator biplanes led by Flight Lieutenant George Burges—rose to intercept them. The Italians were already bombing Valletta harbour and Hal Far airfield when the Gladiators split up to attack as many of the enemy as they could—with little damage inflicted by either side. It was the third Gladiator, flown by Flying Officer W. J. Woods, that caught the attention of one of the escorting C.200s, flown by *Tenente* Guiseppe Pesola of the *79a Squadriglia*. 'Timber' Woods had just completed his second attack on a five-plane bomber formation when he heard machine-gun fire behind him, immediately went into a steep left-hand turn and then saw the enemy fighter diving at him:

For quite three minutes I circled as tightly as possible and got the enemy in my sight [Woods said afterwards]. I got in a good burst, full deflection shot, and he went down in a steep dive with black smoke pouring from his tail. I could not follow him down, but he appeared to go into the sea.

Pesola, who had fired 125 rounds at the Gladiator before having the tables turned on him, was credited to Woods as the first aerial victory to be scored in the long aerial siege of Malta—but in fact he brought his Macchi back to Comiso undamaged. For neither the first nor the last time in the war a pilot and other witnesses had mistaken the black exhaust smoke from a fighter diving away with its throttle suddenly opened for a burning adversary.

The C.200's inconclusive first combat showed that it was nimble enough to dogfight with a biplane but otherwise said little for the monoplane's merits. Over the next three years *Saettas* would soldier on over Malta, North Africa and the Soviet Union with sometimes creditable but never spectacular results. Although a sufficient improvement over the Fiat C.R.42 and G.50 to have warranted production as a stop-gap fighter, the *Saetta* was barely a match for the Hurricane and no match for the Spitfire. A closer examination of the C.200's airframe, however, revealed an essentially clean design with an excellent combination of stability and manoeuvrability. All it needed was a better engine.

With this in mind Castoldi privately approached the Daimler-Benz AG and purchased a 12-cylinder, air-cooled DB 601Aa engine. He then commenced work on an aerodynamically refined adaptation of the C.200 airframe to accept the German engine, at the same time abandoning the C.201, another project to re-engine the *Saetta*. The result of his efforts, which took to the air at Varese on 10 August 1940, restored the racy appearance of the Castoldi floatplanes to the basic C.200 design as well as its performance potential. So successful were its tests that the *Ministerio dell'Aeronautica* immediately ordered the new fighter into series production—not only at Macchi's Varese factory but also at Breda's plant at Sesto San Gionvanni near Milan. While more DB 601Aas were ordered to power the first production batch, Alfa Romeo acquired a licence to manufacture the engine as the R.A.1000R.C.41-Io *Monsone* (Monsoon), which was rated at 1,040 hp at 2,400 rpm. The Macchi C.202 *Folgore* (Lightning), as the new fighter was designated, had a maximum speed of 372 mph at 18,370 feet and featured self-sealing fuel tanks, a moulded armour-plate pilot's seat and an enclosed canopy, although it lacked an armour-glass windscreen. Armament was initially the same as the C.200's—two synchronized 12.7mm Breda-SAFAT machine guns—but ammunition capacity was increased from 370 to 400 rounds per gun. Later-production series *Folgores* added two 7.7mm Breda-SAFAT guns in the wings.

The first C.202s were delivered to the *4o Stormo CT* at Gorizia in July 1941. After accustoming themselves to the new fighter, pilots of the wing's *9o Gruppo*, made up of the *73a Squadriglia (Fotoricognitiori)*, and the *96a* and *97a Squadriglie Caccia Terrestra*, commenced operations against Malta from their base at Comiso on 29 September 1941. The following afternoon Italy's new lightning bolt struck for the first time when five Hurricane fighter-bombers of No 185 Squadron, escorted by six other Hurricanes, attacked Comiso. Three C.202s of the *97a Squadriglia* scrambled up to intercept them and, in the running fight that followed, *Tenente* Jacopo Frigerio shot down Pilot Officer Donald W. Lintern, who was last seen bailing out near the island of Gozo.

After returning to their base to refuel, five of the Hurricanes accompanied a Fairey Fulmar of the Kalafrana Rescue Flight in a search for Lintern. They never found him, but they did come under attack by the C.202s. *Tenente* Luigi Tessari and *Sergente* Rafaello Novelli were jointly credited with downing an enemy fighter, which they reported to have fallen into the sea and blown up ten kilometres south of Cap Scaramia. Their victim was the Fulmar, but it ditched relatively intact and its crew, Lieutenant D. E .C. Eyres and Sub-Lieutenant B. Furlong, were subsequently rescued by a Fairey Swordfish floatplane of their flight. One of the Hurricane pilots, Flight Lieutenant C. G. St D. Jeffries, claimed to have probably downed one of the unidentified enemy fighters, while Pilot Officer P. J. B. Veitch and Sergeant A. W. Jolly each claimed to have damaged one. Tessari returned with numerous holes in his fuselage.

The *9o Gruppo* carried the fight back to Malta in the morning of 1 October as *Capitano* Mario Pluda led seven C.202s to escort a bombing raid on the island. At 11.50 eight Hurricane Mk IIAs of No 185 Squadron took off to intercept, but as they reached an altitude of 24,000 feet thirty miles north-east of the embattled island they were jumped by the Macchis. *Capitano* Carlo Ivaldi, *Tenente* Pietro Bonfatti and *Sergente Maggiore* Enrico Dallari claimed two Hurricanes shot down and two 'probables' in their first pass, but only one Hurricane was actually lost along with its pilot, Squadron Leader P. W. B. Mould—the same 'Boy' Mould who, as a member of No 1 Squadron, had scored the first confirmed Hurricane victory in France on 30 October 1939. Mould's total account stood at eight, plus one shared, when he became one of the C.202's earliest victims. The Italians did not get off scot-free, however. Sergeant E. G. Knight scored hits on Ivaldi's main fuel tank and the Italian only just made it to Sicily before the last of his fuel drained away and he force-landed on the beach near Pozzallo.

The *Folgore* quickly demonstrated its inherent mastery over the Hurricane and by the end of 1941 at least one of the *9o Gruppo*'s pilots, Teresio Martinoli, had been credited with the first five of an eventual personal total of 23 victories (one of them German, while flying for the Allies in Italy's Co-Belligerent Air Force). The C.202's numbers were too small to have a decisive impact over

Malta in the late months of 1941, however. By the time the aircraft was available in significant quantities in 1942 Spitfire Mk Vs had arrived to engage the Italian fighters on roughly equal terms. Nevertheless the C.202 gave a much-needed boost to the confidence of Italian fighter pilots and became the *Regia Aeronautica*'s fighter mainstay until Italy capitulated on 8 September 1943. A more potent variant with a licence-produced version of the DB 605 engine and increased armament, the C.205 *Veltro* (Greyhound), would continue to be a formidable fighter thereafter in the hands of both Allied Co-Belligerent pilots and the die-hard *Fascisti* of the *Aeronautica Nazionale Repubblicana*.

Aeronautica Macchi was not the only Axis aircraft manufacturer to benefit by installing the Me 109's powerplant in one of its airframes. The Kawasaki Kogyo KK of Japan obtained similar results with a series of inline-engine fighter projects that culminated in the Ki-61 *Hien* (Swallow). As a result of its experience against the Soviets over Nomonhan in 1939 the Japanese Army Air Force (JAAF) began to reconsider its obsession with manoeuvrability as the paramount asset in a fighter. One result was the beginning of a general trend among Japanese manufacturers to develop aircraft with higher speed and a heavier armament. Like Macchi, Kawasaki, the Japanese aircraft builder that had had the most experience with water-cooled inline engines, looked into the idea of building two fighter types around the DB 601A. One, given the *kitai* (body) number Ki-60, was to be a cannon-armed specialized interceptor. The other, the Ki-61, was to be a lighter, general-purpose fighter. Work began in February 1940, with chief engineer Takeo Doi and his deputy, Shin Owada, being instructed to place the higher priority on the Ki-60.

Armed with two wing-mounted Mauser MG 151 cannon and two 12.7mm machine guns in the fuselage, the Ki-60 had three wing spars and an unusually high wing loading by Japanese standards. The first of three prototypes was completed at Kagamigahara in March 1941, but during flight-testing the controls proved to be excessively heavy, Kawasaki's chief test pilot declaring, 'I have flown more manoeuvrable heavy bombers!' Overall performance was also disappointing, the top speed of 340 mph being almost nine per cent below that called for in the type specification.

The Ki-60 project was abandoned, but in December 1940 Doi and Owada began work on the Ki-61, employing a high aspect ratio wing with greater area than that of the Ki-60. The fuselage was longer and less deep than the Ki-60's, resulting in reduced drag. At the same time preparations were made for licence-production of the DB 601A at Kawasaki's Akashi plant. Designated Ha-40 Army Type 2, the engine entered production in November and the first Ki-61 emerged from Kawasaki's Kagamigahara factory in the second week of December. Early tests proved—to nobody's surprise—that the Ki-61 was no match for the Nakajima Ki-43 *Hayabusa* in a dogfight, but Doi and his design team were more than content with the acceptable handling qualities that it did display, as well as its considerably greater speed of 367 mph.

A strange twist of fate decreed that the Ki-61 would first fire its guns in anger during an early stage of its evaluation programme. Lieutenant Umekawa had just taken off in a prototype Ki-61 to perform firing trials at the Mito Army Flying School's target range on 18 April 1942 when he received a radio message to intercept enemy bombers that had appeared over the mainland of Honshu. It was an unprecedented order, but the aircraft in question were North American B-25B Mitchell medium bombers led by Lieutenant-Colonel James H. Doolittle which, unknown to the Japanese at the time, had been launched from the aircraft carrier *Hornet*. Umekawa spotted at least one of the raiders and after a long chase managed to get just close enough to fire one long-range, utterly ineffective burst before a shortage of fuel compelled him to turn back for home.

In the summer of 1942 two prototype Ki-61s were put through comparative trials against an imported Me 109E-4, a captured Curtiss P-40E, a LaGG-3 acquired when a Soviet pilot defected to Manchuria, a pre-production Naka-jima Ki-44 *Shoki* interceptor and a production Ki-43. Aside from its inferior manoeuvrability in comparison to the *Hayabusa*'s, the Ki-61 proved to be super-ior to all of its counterparts in every respect. After further testing, the first full production models of the Ki-61 Type 3 *Hien* began to leave the assembly line in September 1942. Early Ki-61-I-ko models retained the two fuselage-mounted 12.7mm Ho-103 and two wing-mounted 7.7mm Type 89 machine guns used in the prototypes, whereas the Ki-61-I-otsu featured four 12.7mm weapons. In addition to a sturdier airframe and heavier armament, the Ki-61 was the first production JAAF fighter to feature self-sealing fuel tanks and armour protection for the pilot.

The first Japanese unit to convert to the Ki-61 was the 23rd *Dokuritsu Hiko Chutai*, an independent squadron based at Chofu for the purpose of training JAAF pilots on the new fighter, in February 1943. The first operational *sentai*s (regiments) to exchange their old Nakajima Ki-27s for Ki-61s were the 68th and 78th, in May. On 14 June the 68th *Sentai* arrived at Wewak on the north-eastern coast of New Guinea while the 78th was deployed to Rabaul. The 68th flew its first combat patrol on 16 June.

By then the Japanese were on the defensive in the South Pacific and New Guinea in particular was gaining a reputation among the Japanese similar to that of Stalingrad among the Germans—a miserable meatgrinder of a place, from which few expected to come back alive. The heat and humidity, com-bined with the poor quality of fuel available, resulted in frequent overheating and mechanical failure in the Ki-61's relatively sophisticated engine. When the plane did work, however, it outperformed most of its early opposition—and certainly surprised the Allied pilots who first encountered so radical a departure from the light, nimble but fragile radial-engine fighters they had fought up to that time. American pilots mistook the Ki-61 for an Me 109 at first, while British Commonwealth airmen, many of whom were veterans of North Africa and the Mediterranean, thought the needle-nosed machine resembled a Macchi C.202. The latter opinion probably led to the adoption of 'Tony' as the Ki-61's Allied code name.

The first clash occurred on 18 July 1943 when elements of the 78th *Sentai* ran into Lockheed P-38s of the 39th Fighter Squadron between Lae and Salamaua. First Lieutenant Gene Duncan claimed to have damaged a plane that 'resembled a Me 109', while other members of his squadron claimed to have shot down two, probably destroyed four and damaged two. The 78th *Sentai* recorded no losses, and in turn claimed its first victory, credited to First Lieutenant Fujishima.

The 68th *Sentai* blooded its *Hien*s on 20 July, during an attack on Allied positions at Benabena. Captain Shogo Takeuchi of the regiment's 2nd *Chutai* spotted a Consolidated B-24 and led his five-plane element to attack and shoot down the four-engine bomber. On the following day B-25s attacked the Japanese base at Bogadjim, and when Ki-61s of both the 68th and 78th *Sentai*s rose to intercept them along with a unit of Ki-43s they in turn came under attack from escorting P-38s of the 39th and 80th Fighter Squadrons. The Americans claimed no fewer than 22 Japanese fighters in the swirling dogfight that ensued between the Ramu valley and Madang, but only four Japanese fighters were actually lost, two of which were Ki-61s of the 78th. The Japanese claimed two of the Americans but the latter, in fact, suffered no losses at all.

The *Hien* was a swallow that was destined to enjoy but a short summer. By the autumn of 1943 new-generation Allied fighters like the P-38 and the Republic P-47D Thunderbolt were taking the place of P-39s and P-40s over New Guinea and generally dominating the Ki-61s. Arguably the *Hien*'s most notable exponent, and reputedly the top-scoring JAAF ace over New Guinea, Shogo Takeuchi, was credited with at least 30 Allied aircraft there, in addition to the three Hawker Hurricanes he had downed in a single fight over Singapore on 31 January 1942 while flying a Ki-43 in the 64th *Sentai*. On 15 December 1944 Takeuchi's unit took on P-47s over the Arawe peninsula and, after allegedly downing one Thunderbolt (not matched by any loss in American records) and driving another off the tail of his *sentai* commander, Major Kiyoshi Kimura, Takeuchi himself was hit. As he tried to land at Hansa airfield his engine seized and the *Hien* crashed in the trees. Takeuchi was extricated from the wreck but he died of his injuries three hours later.

By 25 July 1944 the 68th and 78th, as well as the Ki-43-equipped 77th and 248th *Sentai*s, had been virtually annihilated and were officially disbanded, never to be re-formed. The Kawasaki Ki-61 would fight on, often heroically, in defence of the Japanese home islands against Boeing B-29s until the end of the war, but its period of aerial supremacy had been disappointingly brief.

A more formidable product of Japan's change of heart regarding the future of lightweight, general-purpose fighters would come from the builder of the Ki-43 *Hayabusa*. In November 1941—a month before the Ki-43's combat debut—the *Koku Hombu* asked Nakajima to design its successor. Anticipating an improved generation of Allied fighters, the *Koku Hombu* wanted a plane that would combine the Ki-43's manoeuvrability with the speed and climb of Nakajima's specialized interceptor, the Ki-44 *Shoki*. Powered by an Army version of the Navy's new Nakajima NK9A Homare 18-cylinder, twin-row, direct fuel-injection radial engine, the new fighter was expected to have a maximum speed of 400–420 mph. Like the Ki-61, it was also to incorporate a heavy armament, armour protection and self-sealing fuel tanks.

Early in 1942 Yasumi Koyama and the Nakajima design team began work on the new Ki-84 fighter. Their design was approved on 27 May, and such was the priority placed on the project that the first prototype emerged from Nakajima's Ota plant in March 1943. The Ki-84 was much sturdier than the Ki-43, its windscreen had 65mm of armour glass and the pilot's seat had 13mm of head and back armour. The armament comprised two synchronized 12.7mm Ho-103 machine guns in the fuselage and two wing-mounted 20mm Ho-5 cannon. Racks under the wings could carry either two 44-gallon drop tanks or up to 550 pounds of bombs. The first production example of the Army Type 4 Fighter Model I-ko *Hayate* (Gale) left the Ota plant in April 1944. The Army called for 2,565 Ki-84-I-kos by the end of the year, but continuing development problems with the Ha-45 engines held up production until April 1944 when a rate of 100 engines per month was finally achieved.

Using an 1,860 hp Ha-45 Model 21 engine driving a four-blade propeller, the Ki-84-I-ko had a maximum speed of 388 mph at 21,325 feet, a normal cruising speed of 236 mph and an initial climb rate of 3,790 feet per minute. Service ceiling was 36,090 feet and the 780-mile range at normal cruising speed could be increased to 1,410 miles with two drop tanks. Intrinsically the *Hayate* was the Allies' worst nightmare—a Japanese Army fighter with all the virtues of the nimble Ki-43 but none of its faults, such as inferior level and diving speed, weak armament and vulnerability to battle damage.

The *Hayate*'s debut was calculated for maximum effect. On 5 March 1944 the 22nd *Sentai* was formed at Fussa, Yokota, with 40 Ki-84-I-kos and a pilot cadre drawn from the *chutai* that had been evaluating the plane since October 1943.

The new regiment's commander, Major Jyozo Iwahashi, was a veteran of the 1939 Nomonhan incident and already had twenty victories to his credit. It was not until 24 August 1944, however, that the new fighter made its first appearance—at Hankow, China, at a time when Major-General Claire Chennault's Fourteenth Air Force had nearly half of its combat strength committed in Burma and the rest was supporting Chinese and American efforts to halt a Japanese offensive toward the Yangtze River.

The 22nd had its first fight on 29 August when it engaged a large force of Curtiss P-40Ns of the Chinese-American Composite Wing (CACW), the 118th Tactical Reconnaissance Squadron of the 23rd Fighter Group and the 51st Fighter Group, which were engaged in an attack on the railway yards at Yochow. As the Americans were returning from the target area First Lieutenant Robert S. Peterson chased what he identified as a Zero off First Lieutenant James A. Bosserman's tail while First Lieutenant Forrest F. Parham claimed to have shot down one 'Hamp' (Zero), probably downed a second and damaged a third. Lieutenant James Focht claimed to have damaged an 'Oscar', a 'Tojo' and a 'Hamp'.

Clearly the Americans had no idea of what aircraft the Japanese were flying, but, whatever they were, they had proved to be difficult opponents. On the Japanese side, Iwahashi was credited with a P-40N (possibly Bosserman's, though he did, in fact, return safely to base) for the 22nd *Sentai*'s first victory.

Over the next five weeks the 22nd *Sentai* ran roughshod over the best opposition the Allies could offer and also attacked China-based Boeing B-29 Superfortresses of the Twentieth Air Force's XX Bomber Command as they flew missions to Japan. Iwahashi was leading a strafing attack at Xian airfield on 21 September when his plane was hit by ground fire. Apparently deciding that he could not make it back, the 22nd's commander dived his *Hayate* into the ground; according to some witnesses, he tried to crash into an enemy fighter parked on the field.

On that same day twelve P-40Ns of the 75th Squadron set out on an offensive sweep against Ninsiang and Sinshih. One plane turned back because of engine trouble but the rest dive-bombed two Japanese anti-aircraft positions. First Lieutenant Bosserman—ironically, the pilot who most likely had been over-optimistically claimed by Iwahashi on 29 August—radioed that he was low on fuel and was heading home. Soon afterwards he reported that he was having to bail out over Sinshih. He was never seen again.

The 22nd *Sentai*'s rampage over China abruptly ended in October 1944 when it was transferred to Leyte to counter the imminent American invasion of the Philippines. By September another China-based *sentai*, the 85th, had begun to supplement its Ki-44s with new Ki-84s, and its pilots would make the *Hayate*'s presence felt in the coming months.

Most notable among these was Captain Yukiyoshi Wakamatsu, commander of the 2nd *Chutai* of the 85th *Sentai*, based at Canton. Although he had served in the JAAF since 1939, Wakamatsu did not come into his stride until 24 July 1943 when he shot down two P-40s of the 23rd Fighter Group's 74th Squadron over Kweilin while flying a Ki-44. He accounted for eleven more Allied aircraft while flying the *Shoki*. Just days after converting to the *Hayate*, he downed two North American P-51B Mustangs of the 23rd Groups' 76th Squadron over Wuchow on 4 October 1944, raising his score to fifteen.

Although the Americans had been hearing about a new Japanese Army fighter since early in 1944 and had given it the codename 'Frank', the Ki-84 came as something of a surprise to them and its resemblance to a cross between the Ki-43 and the Ki-44 probably resulted in its being frequently misidentified in their combat reports as either an 'Oscar' or a 'Tojo'. Captain David L. 'Tex' Hill, a former ace of Chennault's original AVG who still fought on in the Fourteenth Air Force, described a bombing raid over Hong Kong on 16 October that must have involved Wakamatsu and his squadron of *Hayate*s:

> We arrived down in the Hong Kong area and the first thing I know I see three enemy aircraft up there that I couldn't identify. I knew they were Japs but I'd never seen the type before. We called them out and turned into them, and as we pulled up into them, why they went straight up and I could see we were going to stall out and so I bent it over. These guys came right down on top of us and shot down the three guys who were with me, and they chased me all the way down to eight thousand feet, which was the altitude I needed to get back over some hills.
>
> I swear I believe this Jap was trying to overrun me in a dive [Hill continued]. His tracers were really going by my head. When I got back I talked to the Old Man, telling him about this new type Japanese fighter, which was later identified as a Zeke 52 or Tojo, which was another term I think they used for them. I told him, 'Well, I don't know, there's a new type here. I don't know if we're going to beat these guys in the air.' And Chennault thought awhile and very characteristically—he had an easy solution for everything—he said, 'Well, Tex, don't worry about that. Get them on the ground, then you don't have to fight them in the air.' So this was a strategy that was actually used. Some of the guys went up to the airfield around Tientsin where these airplanes were congregated and just cleaned them out right on the ground.

Of the three Mustangs Hill thought he saw shot down, two actually made it to friendly territory. The pilot of the third, First Lieutenant Robert Colbert, was wounded in the leg but managed to bail out and was eventually smuggled back to Allied lines by the Chinese.

Chennault launched his biggest counter-strike of the year on 18 December, co-ordinating his efforts for the first—and only—time with the Twentieth Air Force. While 84 of XX Command's B-29s dropped 511 tons of bombs on Hankow the Fourteenth Air Force's B-24 and B-25 bombers added to the destruction and fighters of the 23rd Group and the CACW flew interdiction strikes against known JAAF air bases.

The Japanese had anticipated the attack and Wakamatsu's 2nd *Chutai* had moved to the satellite airfield outside Wuchang to reinforce the 85th *Sentai*'s 1st *Chutai* at Hankow. Reports of oncoming B-29s sent Wakamatsu scrambling up to intercept, but he had just taken off and retracted his landing gear when he was attacked by ten of his old enemies, Mustangs of the 23rd Fighter Group's 74th Squadron, and was quickly shot down. He was probably the victim of Captains Philip G. Chapman and John C. 'Pappy' Herbst, both of whom claimed an 'Oscar' over Wuchang. At the time of his death Wakamatsu had at least eighteen enemy aircraft to his credit, half of them allegedly P-51s.

*Hayate*s would frequently give good accounts of themselves throughout the last year of the war but they could not stave off Japan's inevitable defeat. They were invariably outnumbered, on top of which the attrition of war was rapidly thinning out Japanese Army's pool of trained, experienced pilots whereas the number of proficient airmen on the American side was growing exponentially. Moreover, the Ki-84's merits were often handicapped by the lax production standards that attended its rush into service, which resulted in chronic hydraulic malfunctions, brake failures, broken landing gear legs and a general maintenance nightmare for the ground crews.

Only after Japan's surrender on 1 September 1945 did the Americans realize just how much deadlier an adversary their pilots could have faced. In 1946 a Ki-84-I-ko of the 11th *Sentai*'s 2nd *Chutai* that had been captured intact at Clark Field, Luzon, was test-flown at Wright Field, outside Dayton, Ohio. Its evaluators concluded that the

> . . . Hayate was essentially a good fighter which compared favorably with the P-51H Mustang and the P-47N Thunderbolt. It could outclimb and outmaneuver both fighters, turning inside them with ease, but both P-51H and P-47N enjoyed higher diving speeds and marginally higher top speeds.

That the earliest model of Ki-84 had compared so well with the latest models of P-47 and P-51 spoke volumes about the soundness of its basic design. Of equal significance, however, was the fact that the captured aircraft was using 100-octane fuel for probably the first time in its flying career: the *Hayate*s that the Americans had met in combat used lower-grade, 80-octane fuel, often mixed with dirt, water and the odd tropical insect.

After being passed on to the Smithsonian Institution's National Air Museum and the Ontario Air Museum at Claremont, California, the last surviving Ki-84 was acquired in 1973 by Morinao Gokan, president of the Japanese Owner Pilots' Association, who brought the *Hayate* home.

Chapter 14

RED RESURGENCE

Soviet Fighters, 1941–1944

The non-aggression pact between Adolf Hitler and Josef Stalin was rudely terminated on 22 June 1941 when German forces launched *Unternehmen 'Barbarossa'*, the invasion of the Union of Soviet Socialist Republics. Equally rude was the awakening for the *Voyenno-Vozdushny Sili*, or Soviet Air Forces. Most V-VS aircraft were caught and destroyed on the ground. The majority of those that were able to get into the sky were soon shot out of it by German fighters flown by airmen whose superiority was by that time based as much on experience as it was on training.

Numerically, the most important fighter in the V-VS arsenal at the time was still the Polikarpov I-16—revolutionary in 1935 but obsolescent in 1941. The second most numerous Soviet fighter, the I-153, was essentially a refined I-15 biplane with retractable landing gear, designed in 1937—after the I-16—because Nikolai N. Polikarpov, concerned that the higher wing loading of monoplanes reduced climb rate and agility, still thought the biplane might have a future. Powered by an 850 hp Schvetsov M-62 9-cylinder radial engine, the I-153 had a fair turn of speed for a biplane—280 mph at 15,090 feet. Armament consisted of four fuselage-mounted 7.62mm ShKAS machine guns, which would later be supplemented by underwing racks for up to four 55-pound bombs or six 82mm RS-82 rockets.

The new biplane entered service in the spring of 1939 and was soon committed to combat in the Khalkin-Gol region at the border of Mongolia and Japanese-controlled Manchuria, where an undeclared war had been raging since 4 May—and where Nakajima Ki-27s of the Japanese Army Air Force were outmanoeuvring the I-16s and outrunning the older I-152 biplanes. Twenty I-153s, fresh off the assembly line, were shipped by road across the Soviet Union and assigned to a squadron of the 70th IAP (*Istrebitelsky Aviatsy Polk*, or Fighter Air Regiment) commanded by Major Sergei I. Gritsevets, a veteran of the Spanish Civil War with 30 enemy planes already to his credit as well as two Gold Stars of a Hero of the Soviet Union (HSU).

The I-153's fighting debut came at 11 a.m. on 25 July when Gritsevets took nine of the planes into the sky, divided into three-plane *zveno*s (flights) led by himself and two other veteran pilots, Nikolai Viktorov and Aleksandr Niko-layev. Within seconds of noting a white marker in one of the foothills of the Khamardaba, indicating the forwardmost position of friendly troops on the ground, Gritsevets' deputy waggled his wings to attract his attention and then pointed toward the Uzur Nur, a lake on the Japanese side of the lines. There, about 5,000 feet above the lake and climbing toward the Soviets, was a gaggle of Ki-27s.

To the surprise of his pilots, Gritsevets turned a few degrees away from the Japanese and led them off at a leisurely speed. It soon dawned on them, however, that he was trying the draw the Japanese into Soviet territory, at the same time presenting an angle that would conceal the retractable landing gear of the I-153 from their view so that they would think they were dealing with I-152s—relatively easy prey. As the Japanese eagerly closed in on them the Soviet pilots cocked their gun triggers into the 'fire' position; then, once the Japanese had closed to 2,200 yards, Gritsevets made a circling gesture over his head. Gunning their engines to full boost, the Soviets broke formation and turned on their pursuers.

The wild dogfight that followed only lasted five minutes but it certainly left the Soviet pilots satisfied as all of them returned to their base and reported seeing one Nakajima break up in the air, a second spiral down trailing smoke and two others plunge down to the steppe below before the rest retreated over the lines. Their perception proved to be somewhat exaggerated—the enemy unit involved, the 24th *Sentai*, recorded the loss of only two planes—but it was far more conservative than the Japanese account of their fight with the I-153 which appeared in the newspaper *Yomiuri* a few days later, stating that 'although flown by veritable devils it had been bested by fighters of the Imperial Japanese Army which had accounted for no fewer than eleven of this new warplane'. In fact only two of the nine I-153s that returned even had bullet holes in their fabric skins to indicate that they had been in combat.

In spite of that promising start the I-153 soon lost its fleeting ascendancy over the Ki-27. Allegedly some Soviet pilots would fly with their landing gear down in the hope of convincing Japanese pilots that they were flying I-152s rather than I-153s, and retracting their undercarriage as the enemy closed in on them—no mean feat, since the I-153's landing gear had to be hand-cranked. More often, however, the I-153s took the worst of it against the Ki-27s and only proved effective if used in concert with a higher element of I-16s, just as the older I-15s had done over Spain. Its leading exponent, Gritsevets, added a total of twelve Japanese planes to his Spanish Civil War tally, but his wealth of experience was to be denied his comrades later, when it would have been needed most. Appointed a regiment commander just before the Soviet invasion of Poland on 17 September 1939, he was taxying for take-off on the preceding day when another plane coming in for a landing, flown by Major P. I. Khara, suddenly stalled and crashed on top of Gritsevets's machine, killing him.

The overall success of the Khalkin-Gol campaign did not blind the Soviet high command, or *Stavka*, to the shortcomings displayed by its standard fighters, but by then Polikarpov was committed to production of the I-153; 3,437 were completed by the time production finally ceased in early 1940. The embarrassing showing that the V-VS displayed during the 1939/40 Winter War against Finland reinforced the need for a major modernization of its arsenal, and, indeed, by that time Soviet designers were already developing a generation of aeroplanes to bring the V-VS back up to world standard. These newer types were only entering service, however, when the Germans struck in June 1941. In consequence the first line of Soviet fighters, and the men who flew them, would have to buy time for production of the more advanced types to reach full tempo—time for which they paid in blood.

In January 1939 Stalin and the Commissariat of the People for the Aviation Industry issued a specification for a new general-purpose fighter to compete with the Messerschmitt Me 109. Ten design bureaux took part in the resulting competition, including Aleksandr S. Yakovlev, Semyon A. Lavochkin and Nikolai Polikarpov. One of Polikarpov's proposals, more of a high-speed interceptor than a front-line fighter, was to be powered by the new 1,400 hp Mikulin AM-37 engine, which was expected to give it a normal maximum speed of 416 mph and briefly boost it to 445 mph by means of two turbo-superchargers.

The I-200 project was adopted for development in December 1939, but since Polkarpov was then engaged in developing his I-180—essentially a refined I-16—the Commissariat set up a special design department to proceed with the I-200, headed by Artyom I. Mikoyan, a talented engineer who was the younger brother of Anastas Mikoyan, National Commissar of Foreign Trade and Vice-Chairman of the Council of National Commissars of the USSR. Among Mikoyan's deputies were Mikhail Y. Gurevich and V. Romodin. When work on the AM-37 engine was abandoned, Mikoyan's team proceeded using the 1,200 hp AM-35A and produced a sleek fighter of mixed metal and wooden construction that made its first flight, with A. N. Yekatov at the controls, on 5 April 1940. Engine overheating problems were eventually overcome by redesigning the radiator and, after overflying Moscow in the May Day Parade, the I-200 was ordered into production on 25 May as the MiG-1. An improved version, the MiG-3, was flown by Yekatov in February 1941. Its maximum speed was 397 mph at its normal service ceiling of 25,500 feet, but during a test flight on 13 March 1941 the supercharger impeller suffered damage and the prototype went down out of control, killing Yekatov. In spite of that and subsequent crashes, the MiG-3 was also put into hasty production, resulting in operational aircraft of such crude manufacture that performance almost invariably fell below the intrinsic specification and the armament was not properly harmonized. The MiG-3 also suffered from increased weight, most of which shifted its centre of gravity aft, making it a difficult plane to fly and land.

By mid-1941, 1,289 MiG-3s had been delivered to V-VS units. Pyotr Stefanovsky, a MiG test pilot sent to convert the 4th and 55th IAPs of the 20th Mixed Air Division, later recalled:

> The division had two complete sets of fighters—aged I-16s and I-153s and modern MiG-3s. Nobody wanted to fly the MiG-3s, which was surprising. I decided to show them the capabilities of the MiG-3, and I squeezed all I could out of the aircraft and then a bit more. When I landed, the attitude to the new aircraft had changed sharply. The conversion was very intensive, flights being conducted from early morning until darkness.

One of the more talented pilots who managed to master the MiG-3's idiosyncrasies was Senior Lieutenant Aleksandr Ivanovich Pokryshkin of the 55th IAP, who after flying I-16s said that the MiGs' 'aerodynamic configuration captivated me at once'. He later said: 'It could be compared to a frisky, fiery horse—in experienced hands it rushed along like an arrow, but if you lost control you could end up beneath its hooves.'

The 4th IAP, stationed at Kishinyov near the Romanian border, claimed to have brought down three Romanian aircraft that had intruded into Soviet airspace prior to the German invasion. It was the 124th IAP, however, that would first blood the MiG-3 in earnest on 22 June 1941. As with most units in the Western Special Military District, most of its planes were caught on the ground when the *Luftwaffe* attacked, but its deputy commander, Captain Kruglov, managed to get airborne and forced down an enemy plane at 4.15 a.m. Fifteen minutes later Lieutenant Dmitri V. Kokorev destroyed a Junkers Ju 88 by ramming it—the first but by no means last time that a Soviet fighter pilot would resort to that tactic, eight other such aerial rammings being recorded on that first day alone.

The 4th IAP's sister unit, the 55th based at Beltsy to the north-west, also managed to get some MiG-3s into the air that morning, intercepting twenty Heinkel He 111s escorted by eighteen Me 109s. The flight returned claiming two Heinkels and a Messerschmitt, while three MiGs were damaged. Additional sorties were flown throughout the day, resulting in seven more claims, including a Henschel Hs 126 by Lieutenant Mironov and a Ju 88 by A. Surov. A more dubious combat debut was made by Pokryshkin, who attacked a bomber and forced it to land before discovering that it was a Soviet Sukhoi Su-2. 'Sasha' Pokryshkin swiftly redeemed himself, however, managing to shoot down an Me 109 on the following day and subsequently downing two Hs 126s in one sortie. More important than these aerial victories, however, were the lessons Pokryshkin was learning, which he would later convert into something the V-VS pilots needed even more than new fighters—an effective tactical fighting doctrine. Pokryshkin proved to be a great teacher and leader as well as the second-ranking Allied ace of World War II with a final tally of 59 victories. He would also be one of only two Soviet pilots to be awarded the HSU three times.

The successes enjoyed by a handful of MiG pilots could not offset the general malaise that pervaded the V-VS units on 22 June. At Tarnovo, near the Polish border, the 129th IAP had 57 MiG-3s, 52 I-153s and only 40 combat-ready pilots. Many of the MiGs were not airworthy, and so few of its pilots had accustomed themselves to their flying characteristics that, given the choice, most of them flew the old biplanes. The unit's commissar, Anatoly M. Sokolov, was still engaged in converting pilots from I-153s to MiG-3s when the Germans struck. Commissars already had an unsavoury reputation for being more politically reliable than competent, but when the chips were down on 22 June Sokolov proved to be an exception, hurling his MiG-3 at the enemy and managing to claim an Me 109. Inspired by his example more than they ever could have been by words, his comrades brought down another five German aircraft while losing only one of their own.

The badly mauled 129th IAP was forced to withdraw to Balbasovo four days later but it would go on to greater things. Sokolov was credited with eight enemy planes and earned an HSU before being shot down and killed by enemy fighters on 25 January 1942. Later equipped with Lavochkin LaGG-3s, La-5s and finally La-7s, the 129th IAP produced a number of outstanding aces—the highest-scoring of whom, Vitaly I. Popkov, was credited with 41 victories—and on 6 December 1941 was given an honorary *Gvardiya* (Guards) redesignation as the 5th GIAP. By the end of the war, on 8 May 1945, the 5th GIAP had been credited with 739 aerial victories—the highest score of any fighter regiment in the V-VS—as well as the destruction of 1,832 military vehicles and 283 artillery emplacements.

On the morning of 22 June V-VS commander General Pavel F. Zhigarev ordered 99 new fighters to be rushed to the Front but the chaos of the German advance made that impossible. There were no new fighters to oppose the *Luftwaffe* by 24 June, but 200 new fighters arrived the next day and after that a new regiment reached the Front almost daily. Prominent among the aircraft were MiG-3s, but they never fully measured up to original expectations and were eventually relegated to the defence of Moscow and other cities and to the high-speed reconnaissance role. Overall the design team of Mikoyan and Gurevich was not a particularly successful one during World War II, though the postwar jet age would make their names world-famous.

Ironically the MiG's high-altitude performance gave it no advantage as the kind of 'frontal fighter' that the V-VS needed to establish air superiority over the battlefield. Fortunately for the Soviets there was another type arriving at the Front that would—the Yakovlev Yak-1.

Conceived in May 1939 and completed eight months later, Aleksandr Yakovlev's fighter began as the I-26, a low-wing monoplane of mixed construction with a steel-truss forward fuselage structure skinned in duralumin, a fabric-covered after fuselage, wooden wings and duralumin ailerons and flaps. Powered by a Klimov M-105 12-cylinder, inline, water-cooled engine, the I-26 first flew on 13 January 1940, reaching the promising speed of 360 mph before its flight had to be curtailed owing to a dangerous rise in oil temperature. By the autumn of 1940 the production version of the I-26 was entering service as the Yak-1.

Although praised for its handling characteristics and overall performance—which was certainly an improvement over that of the I-16—the Yak-1 had gained considerable weight in the course of its development. Consequently the 1,250 hp M-105PF engine used in the production machine gave it a maximum speed of 358 mph, which was barely competitive with an Me 109E let alone the new Me 109F and the Focke-Wulf Fw 190A. Armament comprised one 20mm ShVAK cannon firing through the propeller hub and two synchronized 7.62mm ShKAS machine guns.

The 11th IAP received the first 62 Yak-1s in mid-May 1941 and became something of a training/conversion centre for subsequent Yak-1 units, such as the 20th, 45th, 123rd, 158th and 91st IAPs, all of which had some on hand prior to Operation 'Barbarossa'. Most of the aircraft were kept around Moscow but 105 Yak-1s had been sent to the Western Military Districts when hostilities commenced. Only 36 pilots of the 20th IAP, based at Sambora in the Kiev Special Military District, had mastered the new fighters when war began. In other units only regimental and squadron commanders were flying Yak-1s.

The first Yak victory actually preceded the German invasion. On 4 June 1941 a naval pilot, Lieutenant Y. Shitov of the 9th IAP of the Black Sea Fleet, shot down a Romanian reconnaissance plane. Among the first Yak-1s to see combat on the first day of the German invasion was that of Major B. N. Surin, commander of the I-153-equipped 123rd IAP based at Imenin. Responding to *Luftwaffe* attacks on Fourth Army headquarters at Kobrin, Surin led four missions on 22 June, during which he personally accounted for three German aircraft before failing to return from his last sortie. Members of his regiment, most of whom still flew the I-153, carried out as many as seventeen sorties on that first day and were credited with anything from 20 to 30 enemy planes for the loss of nine aircraft, including Surin's.

On 23 June Lieutenant Andrej V. Chirkov of the 158th IAP, already a veteran of the Winter War, downed an He 111 near Pskov for the first aerial victory over the Leningrad front. Two days later he downed a second Heinkel and damaged another, and although badly wounded by return fire he managed to bring his crippled Yak back to the airfield. Chirkov went on to survive the war with the rank of Major, command of the 196th IAP, a total of 29 victories and an HSU.

Such successes were minuscule in the face of the overall disaster that attended the German invasion, however. Within ten hours of the commencement of Operation 'Barbarossa' the *Luftwaffe* had attacked 66 airfields and destroyed more than 800 aircraft on the ground as well as shooting down almost 400 more. Although the handful of skilled pilots trained to fly the Yak-1s acquitted themselves comparatively well, their aircraft suffered from the maintenance problems attendant on a new and hastily manufactured design. At Leningrad, for example, it was discovered that there were twice as many faulty Yak-1s on hand as there were operational ones, compelling the 158th to give its aircraft over to the 123rd IAP and retire to the rear to pick up more fighters. As the airframe and engine defects were remedied, however, the basic soundness of the Yak-1's design became evident—even to its opponents, as expressed in a *Luftwaffe* assessment in 1942:

> Apparently the Yak is the best Soviet fighter. Its speed and rate of climb exceed those of the MiG-3. The fighter was similar in performance to the Me 109F, but was inferior to it in speed. The Yak-1 was harder to attack from the rear than the MiG-3. It had a good rate of climb to 6,000m (19,700 feet), but its manoevrability deteriorated at that height. That is why pilots dived from high altitude when going into action.

While little more was done with the MiG-3, the Yak-1 was only the first of a progressively improving line of fighters. There were, in fact, two divergent lines of development based on the original Yak-1 configuration. *Tyazhely*, or heavy fighters, designed for maximum range, armament and protection, included the Yak-7 and the superb Yak-9, which would be one of the most prolific fighters in history and respected even by German pilots as one of their most formidable adversaries at the end of the war. A line of *legky* (lightweight) interceptors based on the Yak-1 airframe began with the Yak-1M and culminated in the little Yak-3, equally feared by the Germans for its scintillating performance and indisputably the most successful lightweight fighter of the war.

A third contender in the 1939 competition had originally been proposed in 1938 by Semyon A. Lavochkin and Vladimir P. Gorbunov in the form of a fighter of all-wooden construction, to alleviate possible shortages of aluminium and other strategic alloys. 'Even if only one small grove of trees is left in Russia,' Gorbunov grandly declared, 'even then we shall be able to build fighters.' Stalin accepted their idea and in May 1938 a design team was placed under the supervision of Lavochkin, Gorbunov and Mikhail I. Gudkov. The fighter they laboured to develop was initially designated the I-22.

The principal element in the I-22's construction was delta wood, a plasticized composite of birch strips pressed together in cross-grained fashion and impregnated with bakelite. Working under a daunting time constraint, designers managed to have their first prototype ready for its first test flight on 30 March 1940. Powered by a 1,050 hp Klimov M-105P engine, the I-22 suffered its share of initial problems and at least one crash, but development continued and an improved prototype, the I-301, underwent state acceptance trails on 14 June 1940, during which it achieved a speed of 376 mph at 16,404 feet—faster than the Yakovlev I-26 even though the wooden fighter was heavier. Although it displayed several disadvantages, including stiff ailerons and elevators, on 29 July 1940 the I-301 was cleared for mass-production as the LaGG-3. Armament consisted of two Berezin UBS 12.7mm machine guns in the upper fuselage decking and a third firing through the propeller hub.

Tests of the production LaGG-3 conducted near Moscow in May 1941 showed that its performance had fallen rather short of the prototype's, with a maximum speed of 357 mph and a rate of climb (2,412 feet per minute) that was inferior to that of the I-16 it was meant to replace. Elevator control response was found to be so poor that horn balance weights were added to the control surfaces in later production series.

Only 322 LaGG-3s had been built when the German invasion occurred, and few were available to oppose the *Luftwaffe*, all operational aircraft having been assigned to units in the Far East. Only when Stalin was certain that the Japanese would respect the neutrality pact they had signed with the USSR on 13 April 1941 did he authorize the LaGG-3s' transfer to the West.

The 21st IAP was one of the few LaGG-3 units in sufficient shape to oppose the Germans on 22 June when it rose to intercept bombers en route to attack its home base at Riga. The regiment claimed nine victories in the course of that first day, including two by Lieutenant Kuzma D. Garkusha and Lieutenant Komissarov, and by August the unit had flown 2,366 sorties to destroy 87 aircraft, 42 tanks and 46 other vehicles. The 21st suffered heavy casualties of its own, however—to enemy fighters, to ground fire in the course of incessant strafing missions and to the unreliability of its own LaGG-3s. A more typical fate for Soviet units on 22 June attended the 166th IAP's first day of combat, in which it sadly logged four LaGG-3s destroyed and another ten damaged.

Another LaGG-3-equipped unit that entered the fray in June 1941 was the 5th IAP of the Baltic Fleet (KBF), which was soon engaged in the defence of Leningrad, during which Lieutenant Igor A. Kaberov scored the first of eight victories, plus eighteen shared. Lieutenants Ivan I. Tsapov (fifteen victories), Semyon I. Lvov (six, plus shares in 22 others) and Dmitri M. Tatarenko (sixteen) also opened their accounts with the unit at that time, the latter acquiring a reputation for striking his opponents on the first pass which earned him the nickname 'Rubaka' (Broadsword). Yet another member of the 5th, Lieutenant Georgy D. Kostylev, used a LaGG-3 to score the first of his eleven personal and 32 shared victories on 15 July when he downed an Me 110 over Samro Lake, south of Leningrad. By the end of August the 5th IAP-KBF had 57 enemy planes to its credit, which rose to 105 in 5,899 sorties by 18 January 1942 when the unit was given *Gvardiya* status as the 3rd GIAP-KBF. With a final total of 500 aerial victories plus seventeen planes, 71 armoured vehicles and 750 other vehicles destroyed in ground attacks, the 3rd GIAP-KBF was the highest-scoring Soviet naval regiment of the war.

The LaGG-3 underwent 66 production series by the time the 6,528th and last machine arrived at a V-VS unit in the summer of 1942, with improvements and refinements introduced in at least seven of them. Lavochkin often went to the Front to listen to pilots' complaints and then do what he could to remedy them within the constraints of a desperate production schedule that would tolerate no delays. He also brought with him Konstantin A. Gruzdev and Aleksei Grinchik, two highly skilled test pilots who had both enjoyed early successes in the LaGG-3 and who tried to show the demoralized front-line pilots the means of wringing out the best performance from their machines. Gruzdev, who scored nineteen victories before being killed in a flying accident on 2 February 1943, recommended 15 degrees of flap to tighten the fighter's turn in a dogfight. Grinchik's most notable experience in the LaGG-3 was hardly typical: hit in the engine by Me 109s, he was gliding down to a forced landing when one of his attackers miscalculated his firing pass and flew right in front of Grinchik's gunsight, at which point Grinchik opened fire and saw the German go down.

Most LaGG-3 pilots were not that skilled, however, and few of the biplane pilots were accustomed to a monoplane with such high wing loading, mated to an engine of such inadequate power. It had a habit of going into a sudden, vicious spin amid a steep banking turn, and during the landing approach it would suddenly nose-up and then stall. The landing gear was weak and the inadequate view from the cockpit was further impaired by the insufficient clarity of the plexiglass canopy of early versions, compelling most pilots to fly with it open or to discard it entirely, at the sacrifice of more than 9 mph to the added drag. At least one disparaging song was written about the LaGG-3, also known as the 'Mortician's Mate,' and many pilots swore that the wooden fighter's acronym really stood for *Lakirovanny Garantirovanny Grob* (Varnished Guaranteed Coffin).

While the Yak-1's fundamentally sound airframe lent itself to progressive improvements which culminated in the superb Yak-3 and Yak-9, it took a more radical step to turn the LaGG-3 into something more than a deathtrap—the replacement of its inline engine with Arkady Shvetsov's M-82 radial. Ironically, other Soviet designers had experimented with the radial on their existing airframes, such as Mikhail Gudkov's Gu-82, Mikoyan's MiG-9 and Yakovlev's Yak-7 M-82, while Lavochkin hesitated. By early 1942 only the Sukhoi Su-2 short-range bomber was using the M-82 when Lavochkin and Shvetsov were called in to a conference of the People's Commissariat of the Aircraft Industry in Moscow. In essence Lavochkin was told that reports on his LaGG-3 were so unsatisfactory that if something significant was not done soon production of the fighter would have to be cancelled. And since hundreds of unwanted M-82s were piling up at Shvetsov's Plant No 19 in Perm, Lavochkin was strongly urged to try fitting the radial in his plane.

Lavochkin objected: modifying the LaGG-3 airframe to take an air-cooled radial that was 18 inches greater in cross section and 551 pounds heavier than the inline M-105P would be complicated by a shift in the centre of gravity and the need to compensate for the M-82's inability to take a 20mm cannon through the propeller shaft, and Lavochkin feared that production would cease before he and his design team could effect such complex alterations. There was already a precedent for such a fighter, however. As early as March 1941 Gudkov had lifted an M-82 directly from an Su-2 and worked out a way of mounting it on a LaGG-3 airframe, and on 12 October the Commissariat announced a willingness to put his Gu-82 into production at the Gorky plant instead of the LaGG-3. Gudkov's attention was then diverted by a project to mount a 37mm cannon to fire through the LaGG-3's propeller hub, and the more resolute Aleksandr Yakovlev secured a contract to produce his new Yak-7B fighter at Gorky.

News that LaGG-3 production at Plant No 31 in Tblisi was to be halted in April gave Lavochkin some added incentive to intensify his efforts. The LaGG-3's fuselage mid-section was widened and the engine mount re-worked. Two variable flaps on the fuselage sides and altered air baffles provided uniform cooling. Two 20mm ShVAK cannon were mounted above the engine. The machine was completed in February 1942 and Lavochkin anxiously awaited the results of it first evaluation. 'The aircraft is good, pleasant to control and responsive, but the cylinder heads became hot,' reported test pilot G. Mishchenko. 'Measures should be taken.' He also reported that level speed was ten per cent greater than that of the LaGG-3. Encouraged, Lavochkin and his team did further work on the prototype, which got its first official evaluation from 9 to 14 May 1942. Cooling and controllability problems were encountered, but with a speed of 372.8 mph at its service ceiling of 21,000 feet, a climb rate of 16,400 feet in six minutes and manoeuvrability that was superior to that of foreign as well as indigenous designs, the LaGG-3 M-82 was good enough to reverse Lavochkin's shaky fortunes completely. Since Gorbunov had left the design team by then, the new fighter was designated the LaG-5 and ordered into production, the first example rolling out of Gorky's Plant No 21 on 20 June. Gudkov also parted company with Lavochkin soon afterwards, and from September 1942 the radial-engine fighters were officially referred to simply as 'La-5s'.

In August 1942 the first operational LaG-5s were assigned to Colonel Stefan P. Danilov's 287th *Istrebitelnaya Aviatsionnaya Diviziya* (IAD), attached to the First Air Army near the embattled city of Stalingrad. There were 57 LaG-5s attached to four regiments of the 287th IAD when the type was first committed to combat on 20 August 1942, but they bore the unmistakable signs of hasty production, only two-thirds of them being combat-capable. One plane crashed during takeoff while two others collided while taxying due to poor visibility from the cockpit. Again, impaired visibility compelled the pilots to fly with their canopies open, and cooling problems and a lack of confidence in the retractable tailwheel resulted in flying with the cowling side flaps fully opened and the tailwheel down, all contributing to an 18.6–24.8 mph reduction in speed. In the first three days of fighting the LaG-5 pilots claimed eight German fighters and three bombers but lost seven of their own planes—including three to Soviet anti-aircraft gunners who mistook them for German Fw 190As. In the course of flying their first 180 sorties LaG-5 pilots of the 49th IAP claimed sixteen German aircraft in seventeen combats. The regiment lost ten planes, however, and five of its pilots were killed in action.

The LaG-5's debut yielded mixed results at best. Pilots of the 287th IAD's 27th IAP concluded that their planes were inferior to the Me 109F-4 and even more so to the newer Me 109G-2 in speed and vertical manoeuvrability. 'We have to engage only in defensive actions,' they reported. 'The enemy is superior in altitude and, therefore, has a more favourable position from which to attack.' Concentrating on German bombers for a time, the LaG-5 pilots downed 57 of them within a month but continued to suffer heavy losses whenever they encountered enemy fighters.

Again, Semyon Lavochkin was eager to read and respond to the criticisms levelled at his fighters. Aerodynamic improvements, lightening of the airframe and the introduction of the new supercharged M-82F engine resulted in a better fighter, which entered production in January 1943 as the La-5F (for *Forsirovanny*, or 'boosted'). In addition, the ninth production La-5 batch, produced in November 1942, had control surfaces of reduced area, redesigned trim tabs and larger flaps which improved both controllability and manoeuvrability. The after part of the dorsal fuselage was also lowered and a new teardrop-shaped canopy of armoured glass was installed, greatly improving visibility from the cockpit. With the subsequent introduction of the fuel-injected M-82FN engine, which boosted take-off power from 1,700 to 1,850 hp, in the La-5FN during the Battle of Kursk in July 1943, the curious transition of Lavochkin's wooden 'grand pianos' from 'mortician's mates' to instruments of ultimate Soviet victory was nearly complete. As the tide of war turned in favour of the Red Army, production standards could improve. Lavochkin continued to refine his now-proven design, culminating in late 1943 with the La-7, one of the cleanest radial-engine fighters of its time.

Amid the heady successes that attended Operation 'Barbarossa', it may have been difficult for *Luftwaffe* pilots to imagine the V-VS recovering at all from the initial blow dealt it, let alone do so sufficiently to replace the obsolescent or flawed new fighters that they had first encountered. It would have been even harder for even the Soviet airmen to imagine that the unpromising LaGG-3, or even the less than world-beating LaG-5, was a step on the way to one of the great fighters of World War II. Nevertheless, the La-5FN and La-7, which were at their best at low altitudes, did much to clear the skies over the battlefield for the Red Army's resurgent ground forces. It might be added that the leading Allied ace of the war, Ivan Nikitovich Kozhedub, scored all 62 of his victories—including one Messerschmitt Me 262 jet—exclusively in Lavochkin fighters, from the La-5 to the La-7 that currently stands on display at the Air Force Museum at Monino.

Chapter 15

AERIAL SUPREMACY OVER THE ISLANDS

Vought F4U Corsair and Grumman F6F Hellcat, 1943

The Japanese pilots were momentarily puzzled as they peered down at the remarkably mixed bag of American planes that had come to bomb their ships in the Buin–Shortland area of the Solomon Islands on 14 February 1943. Nine of the intruders were four-engine bombers—Consolidated PB4Y-1s, naval versions of the B-24 Liberator, from bomber squadron VB-101—and ten of their escorts were Lockheed P-38F Lightnings of the 339th Fighter Squadron, Thirteenth Air Force. Twelve other American fighters, however, were large, single-engine monoplanes with inverted gull wings, of a type the Japanese had never seen before. Nevertheless, at that moment aces Isamu Miyazaki, Bunji Nakajima and 25 other Mitsubishi A6M2 Zero pilots of the 252nd *Kokutai* had more important matters than recognition with which to concern themselves. Registering the strange new fighters in their minds as either Bell P-39 Airacobras or Curtiss P-40 Warhawks, the Zero pilots plunged into the American fighter formations, while fifteen Nakajima A6M2-N and Mitsubishi F1M2 floatplane fighters of the 802nd *Kokutai* went after the bombers.

The Japanese had been expecting trouble that day. In the morning of 13 February the Americans had launched a similar raid from Henderson Field on the newly secured island of Guadalcanal. It had involved six B-24Ds of the 424th Squadron, 307th Bomb Group, escorted by four P-38s of the 339th Fighter Squadron and seven P-40Fs of the 44th Fighter Squadron, as well as nine PB4Ys of VB-101 escorted by four P-38s of the 339th Squadron and eleven of the new bent-wing fighters. The Navy PB4Ys did not encounter enemy fighters on this, their first mission, but none of their bombs struck their targets and the Japanese did not even notice their escorts. The Army B-24s scored one 1,000-pound bomb hit on a cargo vessel in Buin harbour but lost two of their number to the ships' anti-aircraft fire. Afterwards, in a fifty-minute running fight with Zero fighters, another B-24 was set on fire, but it managed to reach

211

Choiseul before ditching off the north coast of the island, while two P-40s and a P-38 were shot down and a second P-38 had to ditch offshore. Six Zeros were credited to the US Army Air Forces fighters, including two Zeros and a 'probable' to First Lieutenant Robert P. Rist before his P-38 was shot down. In reality the Japanese lost two Zeros and their pilots, Leading Seaman Hifumi Yamamoto of the 204th *Kokutai* and PO2C Takano Kotaro of the 252nd.

The new fighters whose presence had gone unnoticed by the Japanese on 13 February, and which accompanied the renewed effort on the 14th, were Vought F4U-1 Corsairs. Designed as carrier fighters, they were, nevertheless making their debut with a land-based US Marine fighter squadron, VMF-124, because the Navy did not want them.

Chance M. Vought built his first Navy fighter—a conversion from his VE-7 trainer—shortly after World War I ended. Although he produced a number of successful naval aircraft in the subsequent two decades, his attempts to produce an outstanding naval fighter had been in vain until February 1938, when his design bureau, headed by chief engineer Rex Biesel, set out to fulfil a Navy specification for a high-speed, high-altitude fighter. Built around an 1,800 hp Pratt & Whitney XR-2800-2 Double Wasp 18-cylinder, air-cooled radial engine, the XF4U-1 Corsair featured an all-aluminium fuselage that was spot-welded to reduce surface drag. Another drag-reducing measure was to assemble the wing at as close to a 90-degree angle to the fuselage as possible. Since the 13-foot Hamilton Standard propeller used on the XF4U-1 made the optimum mid-wing attachment impractical, Biesel's design team attached the wing at an angle to the lower part of the fuselage and gave it an inverted gull configuration, thus allowing for a shorter, sturdier undercarriage. The armament originally consisted of two synchronized 0.30-calibre machine guns in the fuselage and two 0.50-calibre guns in the wings, but this was later revised to six wing-mounted 0.50-calibre weapons.

First test-flown by Lyman Bullard on 29 May 1940, the XF4U-1 immediately demonstrated its potential. The first single-seat fighter to exceed 400 mph in level flight—reaching a record 405 mph in October 1940—the XF4U-1 also had an outstanding roll rate. The Navy was impressed and ordered the Corsair into production, but the new fighter soon showed problems as well as promise. The narrow canopy was confining and forward visibility was reduced even further when the cockpit of the production F4U-1 was situated almost three feet further aft to accommodate a 237-gallon self-sealing fuel tank in the fuselage, the original wing tanks having been replaced by the six 0.50-calibre machine guns. On top of that the port wing had a tendency to drop at low landing speeds. Vought later remedied the visibility problem somewhat by devising a more rounded canopy with reduced metal framing for the F4U-1A and F4U-1D models, and the eventual installation of a small triangular wedge on the leading edge of the starboard wing just outboard of the guns alleviated the wing-dropping problem. When the first F4U-1s were delivered to Navy squadrons VF-12 and VF-17 in October 1942, however, their landing characteristics were found to be too dangerous for carrier operations. VF-12 would eventually go into combat with Grumman F6F-3 Hellcats. VF-17, originally scheduled to serve aboard the new carrier *Bunker Hill,* was instead assigned to land bases in the Solomons, where its Corsairs established an outstanding record. Other production Corsairs were assigned to the Marines, starting with VMF-124, commanded by Major William E. Gise.

The Marines were accustomed to receiving Navy cast-offs but they soon found the Corsair to be a serendipitous case of the Navy's loss being their gain. Powered by a 2,000 hp Pratt & Whitney R-2800-8 engine and capable of 425 mph, the production F4U-1 was the 'hottest' plane they had yet flown. And with a range of 1,015 miles—twice that of the F4F-4 Wildcat—the Corsair gave the Marines a fighter capable of escorting bombers as well as defending their island air bases. When VMF-124's 24 planes were shipped to Guadalcanal in January 1943, however, its 29 pilots had only had an average of twenty hours' flight training, including one high-altitude flight, one gunnery exercise and one night flight, before being rushed to the Front. One hour after the first seventeen Corsairs arrived at Henderson Field on 12 February they flew their first mission, escorting a Consolidated PBY Catalina flying boat to Kolombangara, where it picked up two downed Marine Wildcat pilots, Lieutenant Jefferson DeBlanc (who would subsequently receive the Medal of Honor for outstanding valour in the action in which he had been brought down) and Staff Sergeant James A. Feliton, as well as an Army P-38 pilot who had ditched off the south coast of New Georgia. Although they came within 50 miles of a Japanese air base, the twelve F4U-1 pilots encountered no enemy planes on that sortie, nor did they during their escort mission on the following day. On 14 February, however, Japanese coast-watchers reported the oncoming Americans, and by the time the latter reached Buin the enemy were ready for them.

Ten P-38s, arranged in two three-plane sections and a four-plane flight, were providing top cover for the bombers when the 252nd *Kokutai*'s A6M2s tore into them. Captain J. A. Geyer, leader of the four-plane flight, claimed two Zeros shot down, while First Lieutenant William M. Griffith sent another crashing into the sea, but two other P-38s of that flight were lost. Two further P-38s from the three-plane sections were also lost, though the pilot of one ditched near the Russell Islands and was subsequently rescued. Two P-40s were also shot down by the Zeros.

Below the dogfight the bombers scored several hits on one cargo ship and near-misses on two others but came under attack by the floatplanes and Zeros that broke through the American fighter scrimmage. One of the A6M2-Ns scored a hit in a PB4Y's cockpit and it went down near Shortland Island. A second bomber, already damaged by anti-aircraft fire, was pursued by the aggressive floatplanes until it was forced to ditch in the sea twelve miles from New Georgia.

The Marines tried to defend the bombers, Captain Joseph Quilty and First Lieutenant James English being credited with downing a Zero and an F1M2 floatplane, but most of the Corsair pilots discovered that they had a lot to learn about fighting Zeros. First Lieutenant Howard J. Finn left his formation to pursue a lone Zero, only to find several others on his tail. He ended up seeking shelter under a PB4Y, the gunners of which claimed one of the Zeros and sent Army Intelligence officers to Henderson the next day asking Finn to confirm their kill. 'Some big hero,' Finn later remarked sarcastically of his performance in this first fight, although he would be credited with the destruction of six enemy planes in the months to come. At least he lived to learn from his experience. Lieutenant Stewart of VMF-124 was shot down and killed, while Second Lieutenant Gordon Lee Lyon Jr died in a head-on collision with another Zero.

Upon their return to Henderson Field the Americans claimed a total of fifteen enemy planes, including three by VMF-124 and no fewer than nine by VB-115's gunners. In actuality one F1M2 had come down damaged and three Zeros had been shot down, but only one Japanese pilot, PO2C Yoshio Yoshida of the 252nd *Kokutai*, was killed—probably in the mid-air collision with Lyon.

The raid went down in American records as the 'Saint Valentine's Day Massacre'. Given the losses it had suffered on 13 and 14 February, VB-101 cancelled further daylight bombing missions and flew night raids for some time thereafter. As for VMF-124, it had given the F4U a less than glorious baptism of fire. One of its chastened pilots, Second Lieutenant Kenneth Ambrose Walsh, later admitted: 'Being the first unit to go out in the Corsair, we didn't know exactly how to employ it, so we had to establish a doctrine.' When Walsh asked one of Guadalcanal's veteran Marine Wildcat aces about how to deal with the Zero, his only answer was, 'You've gotta go after them.' 'Well,' said Walsh, 'we knew it would take more than that!'

Ultimately Walsh and his comrades learned that having the advantage of altitude was the key to success. He also discovered that the Corsair could outfight the Zero at high speeds, although it was suicide to be caught by one in a slow climb or to try to outmanoeuvre it at low speeds. As with most other American fighters, the Corsair could take much more punishment than the Zero, which the F4U's six 0.50-calibre guns had little difficulty in setting afire.

Ken Walsh's next opportunity for a re-match with the Japanese came on 1 April 1943 when Admiral Isoroku Yamamoto launched Operation 'I', an all-out aerial counter-offensive against Allied forces in the Solomons. As 58 Zeros from the 204th and 253rd *Kokutais* swept down on Guadalcanal, 28 Wildcats, eight Corsairs and six Lightnings scrambled up from Henderson Field to inter-cept them. At about noon F4U-1s of VMF-124 and P-38Gs of the 12th Fighter Squadron got into a fight with A6M3s of the 204th *Kokutai* between the Russell Islands and Baroku. One of the P-38s was lost, but the 12th Squadron's com-mander, Major Paul S. Bechtel, claimed a Zero. Of the Marines, First Lieuten-ant Dean Raymond sent a Zero down in flames while Walsh accounted for two Zeros and an Aichi D3A1 dive-bomber. The 204th *Kokutai* lost two Zero pilots that day—Lieutenant (jg) Shigeto Kawahara and PO2C Eichi Sugiyama. In addition to the results of that fight, fifteen other Zeros were claimed by Navy and Marine pilots in the course of three hours of combat, for the loss of five aircraft. Besides the 204th's losses, the 253rd *Kokutai* lost five pilots on 1 April.

VMF-124 had got the measure of its adversary by 13 May when it was involved in another battle royal with 54 Zeros over the Russells, during which Walsh claimed no fewer than three Zeros to become the first Corsair ace. War-rant Officer Nayato Noda and PO2C Yuhi Kariya of the 204th *Kokutai* and PO2C Shogo Sasaki of the 582nd were killed in the fight. However, VMF-124 lost Major Gise, probably killed by one of the 204th *Kokutai*'s best pilots, War-rant Officer Ryoji Ohara, who downed a Corsair in his first diving attack. Ohara then became separated from his flight and was attacked by two Cor-sairs, which chased him half-way to New Georgia before he suddenly turned on his pursuers and put three cannon shells through the F4U-1 of First Lieu-tenant William Cannon. Although his Zero sustained 38 hits, Ohara managed to reach Kolombangara, where he force-landed and was subsequently credited with downing Cannon's Corsair as well as Gise's. Once again the Japanese had overestimated the damage they had done—Cannon made it back to Henderson Field.

By the time Walsh's first tour ended on 7 September he had been awarded the Medal of Honor and had twenty victories to his credit—of which sixteen were Zeros—to which he would add one more Zero while commanding VMF-222 in June 1945. VMF-124 downed a total of 68 enemy planes during its first deploy-ment, but paid for its growing font of experience with the loss of 30 aircraft and eleven pilots, including its commander, Gise. Walsh himself was shot down three times and crash-landed two other F4Us as a result of combat as well as bringing back about a dozen shot-up aircraft. Nevertheless, he noted that, by the time more F4U squadrons arrived in the Solomons, 'I had a lot more to tell them about than just "you gotta go after them".'

Britain's Fleet Air Arm was also receiving Corsairs, and its pilots were as appalled as their American colleagues at how such an excellent fighter could be such a dreadful carrier plane. In spite of numerous shipboard crashes, one of which resulted in the death of a squadron commander aboard the carrier *Illustrious*, the British managed to devise a landing technique—coming in out of a turn so that the pilot could see ahead until the last few seconds—which made it possible to operate their Corsairs from carriers. Their plight was somewhat alleviated later in 1943 when the F4U-1A, with its improved canopy, joined the FAA as the Corsair Mk II. On 3 April 1944 Corsair IIs of 1834 and 1836 Naval Air Squadrons from HMS *Victorious* became the first of their breed to participate in a full-scale carrier strike, Operation 'Tungsten', when they escorted bombers against the German battleship *Tirpitz*. US Navy and Marine squadrons began operating Corsairs from carriers later that year, and the F4U eventually replaced the F6F Hellcat as the standard Navy fighter. Some 11,000 Corsairs were built— more than any other US Navy fighter—and they would continue to serve with distinction in the Korean and Indo-Chinese wars and the 1956 Suez Crisis. The US Navy did not retire its last F4Us until August 1957, the French Navy used them until 1964, and Corsairs saw their last aerial combats during the brief war between El Salvador and Honduras in 1969. From its inauspicious combat debut and its initial rejection as a carrier plane, the Vought Corsair ultimately emerged as one of the most successful combat planes ever built.

By the autumn of 1943 the Japanese were fighting a losing battle over the Solomons against Allied aircraft that were both improving in quality and increasing in quantity. In addition to the P-38 Lightning and the F4U Corsair, that new generation included a formidable carrier fighter—the Grumman F6F Hellcat. Co-designed by Leroy R. Grumman and William T. Schwendler as a larger, more powerful replacement for the stalwart F4F Wildcat, the F6F embodied progressive improvements to increase survivability for the pilot, being sturdier and more heavily armoured than the Wildcat. As was the case with the US Army Air Forces' P-38 and the Marines' F4U, the main question facing the F6F was how it would fare against its principal Japanese opponent, the Mitsubishi A6M Zero, or 'Zeke', as the Allies had officially code-named it.

Contrary to popular myth, the Hellcat was not designed on the basis of data gathered from a downed A6M2 that had been recovered intact at Akutan Island in June 1942: the XF6F-1 prototype first flew on the 26th of that very month. Moreover, the two fighters were diametrically opposed in concept: the Zero had sacrificed all except armament in order to accommodate its 9-cylinder, 925 hp Nakajima Sakae 12 radial engine within the sleekest, lightest airframe possible, whereas the Hellcat was a brutish heavyweight that relied on a 2,000 hp Pratt & Whitney R-2800-10 Double Wasp 18-cylinder radial to haul its loaded weight of more than six tons at a maximum speed of 375 mph, and the largest wing area of any single-engine American fighter (334 square feet) to endow it with a surprising degree of agility. Test-flying the Zero, however, provided the F6F pilots with invaluable information on its performance, from which they could formulate tactics to cancel the Japanese fighter's strengths—primarily its superior manoeuvrability—and take full advantage of its weaknesses, which included slower level and diving speeds and a complete lack of protection for its pilot and fuel tank.

Production of the Hellcat coincided with a general build-up in US Navy carrier strength. The nucleus of the new fleet was the 27,000-ton *Essex* class fleet carrier, larger and more heavily armed successors to the *Yorktown* class, of which only one, *Enterprise*, remained (very much) operational after the costly battles of 1942. Supplementing the *Essex*es were the 11,000-ton *Independence* class light carriers, built on the hulls of *Cleveland* class light cruisers. Crowding the decks of those carriers like vengeful birds of prey were veteran Grumman TBF-1 Avenger torpedo-bombers and Douglas SBD-5 dive-bombers, as well as newer Curtiss SB2C-1 dive-bombers and F6F-3 Hellcat fighters, all manned by air crews that had been intensely trained by their combat-experienced forebears.

As his fleet's strength grew, the American commander-in-chief in the Pacific (CINCPAC), Admiral Chester W. Nimitz, formulated a plan to advance on Japan by a more direct route than was being carried out through the South Pacific. Except for some early retaliatory raids by US Navy carriers between February and April 1942, the great naval confrontation at Midway Island in June and a diversionary attack by US Marine Raiders in the Gilbert Islands in August, the Central Pacific had seen relatively little activity, while the main contest for the initiative in the Pacific went on in New Guinea and the Solomons. Now, however, Nimitz planned to seize strategic Japanese-held island groups in the Central Pacific one by one, while at the same time eliminating the main Japanese air and naval base in that region, Truk Atoll in the Carolines. First, however, he wished to blood his new task forces with some minor raids, to give their personnel experience and confidence.

The first such raid took place on 31 August 1943 when Task Force 15.5, built around the carriers *Yorktown, Essex* and *Independence* and commanded by Rear-Admiral Charles A. Pownall, launched its aircraft against Marcus Island, 1,568 miles from Midway and less than 1,000 miles from Tokyo. In the course of six strikes totalling 275 sorties the Americans destroyed several Mitsubishi G4M2 bombers (code-named 'Betty' by the Allies) on the ground for the loss of three Hellcats and one Avenger to anti-aircraft fire.

The first aerial victory for the Hellcat was scored on the following day when Lieutenant (jg) Richard L. Loesch and Ensign A. W. Nyquist of VF-6, attached to the light carrier *Princeton*, teamed up to shoot down a snooping Kawanishi

H8K2 four-engine flying boat (code-named 'Emily' by the Allies) near How-
land Island. Two days later Lieutenant (jg) Thaddeus T. Coleman of VF-6
was flying a patrol about 50 miles south-south-west of Baker Island when he
spotted another 'Emily' at 1.03 p.m. A 30-mile chase ensued, ending at 1.25
when Coleman finally sent his quarry crashing into the sea. Coleman's feat
was repeated on 8 September while *Princeton* was prowling around the Gilbert
Islands and encountered another H8K. On that occasion Lieutenant Harold N.
Funk, executive officer of VF-23, teamed up with Lieutenant (jg) Leslie H. Kerr
Jr to dispatch the 'Emily'.

Later Pownall led another force, built around carriers *Lexington*, *Princeton* and
Belleau Wood, on a raid in the Gilberts. Between 18 and 19 September seven
strikes were made on Tarawa and Makin. Again, four American aircraft were
lost, but half of the eighteen Japanese planes present on Tarawa were destroyed
on the ground, another four planes were destroyed on the ground at Makin
and Hellcats of Princeton's VF-23 shot down a G4M2. The Japanese 'Water
Defence Section' in the Gilberts (three picket boats and minecraft) was wiped
out and a transport ship was sunk in the lagoon. More important was a set
of low oblique photos taken by *Lexington*'s planes of the lagoon side of Betio
Island, which would prove to be useful for planning for the assault on Tarawa
two months later.

Apart from the snooping flying boats, the American carrier air groups had
met little aerial opposition thus far, leaving the Hellcat pilots still anxious to see
how they would fare against the Zero. Unknown to them, however, that question had already been answered, back in the Solomons, where a unit of land-
based Hellcats had already come to grips with the notorious Mitsubishis.

Commissioned at Espiritu Santo on 15 August 1943, VF-33, under the command of Lieutenant-Commander H. B. Russell, began its first tour of duty
from Henderson Field on 30 August. The unit had its first conclusive encounter
with Zeros while escorting bombers over Morgusaia Island on 6 September,
one of the enemy fighters being credited to Ensign James A. Warren of Sparta,
Michigan. Japanese records do not show a pilot lost as a result of that fight, nor
for a subsequent scrap between the Shortlands and Choiseul in which Lieutenant (jg) James J. Kinsella claimed a probable victory over an A6M.

VF-33 had its first real air battle on 14 September as part of a mixed force
of about 200 Thirteenth Air Force and Navy bombers, with an escort of Navy
F6Fs, Marine F4Us and P-38s of the Thirteenth Air Force, which was opposed
by 258 Zeros. The statistics that emerged from the day's series of confusing
mêlées were inevitably inflated on both sides, the Americans claiming 29 Japanese aircraft (eight by VF-33) while the Japanese 201st *Kokutai* alone claimed 60,
including six 'probables'.

One of the earliest American claims for the day came from a Marine F4U-1A pilot of VMF-222, Major Donald H. Sapp, who downed two Zeros fifteen miles south-east of Ballale at 9.16 a.m. The Navy's contribution consisted of 72 SBDs and TBFs, escorted by sixteen F6Fs, which left Munda to bomb Ballale. Their arrival stirred up a hornet's nest of A6M3 Zeros at 1.15 p.m. and ten of VF-33's Hellcats became embroiled in a running dogfight between Ballale and Kahili. Ensign Jack O. Watson downed one of the Japanese, Ensign Frank E. Schneider accounted for another and Lieutenant Carlos K. Hildebrandt was credited with three.

'Ken' Hildebrandt's first opponent was attacking one of the retiring Dauntlesses when he got on the Zero's tail. He reported afterwards:

> I poured lead into him and he rolled over on his back smoking, at 200 feet. Tracers went by me then, so I pulled up sharply and collected 7.7mm slugs through the cockpit enclosure. They went into my jungle pack and my back. The Zero turned away as I turned into [Ensign Jack] Fruitt who had another one following him. Firing from 100 yards, I continued through his pullout and roll. He went in when his port wing was shot off.
>
> Then I was jumped at 100 feet by a Zero. Using the hand lever to dump my flaps, I saw the Jap go by and pull up in a turn. I just held the trigger down until he blew up. Suddenly the sky was empty. Fruitt was nowhere to be seen and I headed home.

Actual Japanese losses for the day totalled five Zeros in the air and another nine aircraft destroyed on the ground. Three of the Zeros were from the 201st *Kokutai*, which recorded the deaths of PO2Cs Eiji Nishida and Hiroshi Mure. The 204th *Kokutai* lost the other two Zeros along with both of their pilots— PO2Cs Makato Terao and Tokuji Yoshizaki. The top Japanese scorer was Chief Petty Officer Takeo Okumura of the 201st *Kokutai*, who flew three sorties in the course of the day and was credited with one SBD and a share in the destruction of one B-24, an F4U, two P-40s and five of the new Hellcats—a one-day Pacific War record for a Japanese pilot. In fact all of VF-33's planes returned to Munda, although two pilots were wounded and their F6Fs so badly damaged that they had to be written off. In addition to those, Okumura was probably credited with Hildebrandt and Fruitt, whose stricken planes may have given the impression of being in more trouble than they actually were. This was by no means the last time that a Japanese pilot underestimated the rugged Hellcat's ability to bring its pilot home.

On the following day, 15 September, Schneider downed another Zero over Ballale for the fourth of an eventual total of seven victories. By then a second Hellcat squadron had joined the fray—VF-38, which had been formed in June and subsequently joined VF-33 at Henderson Field. At 11.15 a.m. on 15 September Lieutenant Oscar Chenoweth Jr downed a Zero five miles north-west of Ballale, and between 2.15 and 3 p.m. on the following day Lieutenant (jg)

Leland B. Cornell of VF-38 was credited with two Zeros and one 'probable' north of Ballale.

By the time VF-33 had been withdrawn from its first tour on 21 September it had claimed a total of 21 Japanese aircraft for the loss of two pilots killed and two injured. James Warren was with the squadron when it resumed operations from Segi Point and later Ondonga on the island of New Georgia, but before he could add to his score he was shot down over New Guinea while flying his 40th mission on 23 December. On the following day he was taken to a prison camp run by the notorious *Kempei Tai* (Military Intelligence), where he and 61 other Allied soldiers subsequently died—through execution, torture, mistreatment or neglect.

Two days after VF-33 had been withdrawn, a carrier unit, VF-12 from *Saratoga*, was stationed at Henderson Field. On 25 September Lieutenant John Magda, a VF-12 pilot who had seen previous combat during the Battle of Midway, shot down a Zero over Barakoma on the island of Bougainville. Technically Magda was the first pilot from a shipboard Hellcat unit to be credited with a Zero although he was not operating from a carrier at the time—VF-12 was reassigned to *Saratoga*'s decks on 29 September.

While VF-33 was ending its first tour in the Solomons the US Navy had assembled its largest carrier force to date—Task Force 14, composed of the carriers *Essex, Yorktown, Lexington, Cowpens, Independence* and *Belleau Wood*, under Rear-Admiral Alfred E. Montgomery. Their next target was Wake Island.

As a result of the increase in American naval activity in the Central Pacific, Wake's air defences had recently been bolstered by a detachment of Zeros from the 252nd *Kokutai*—the same unit that had drawn first blood in combat with the F4U Corsair back in February. After establishing its headquarters at Roi in the Marshall Islands, the 252nd distributed its 60 fighters among air bases at Wake, Nauru and Taroa on Maloelap Atoll. Although the Japanese had introduced a more powerful and aerodynamically refined version of the Zero, the A6M3, the veteran pilots of the 252nd *Kokutai* still preferred to use the older A6M2, desperately clinging to its lighter weight and consequent better manoeuvrability as their only hope against the newer Allied fighters that had taken their measure over the Solomons.

In addition to the 252nd *Kokutai*'s 26-plane fighter detachment led by Lieutenant Motonori Suho, a veteran credited with eleven victories in China and another four over the Solomons, the 22nd *Koku Sentai* (Air Flotilla) had placed a contingent of 25 medium bombers of the 755th *Kokutai* on Wake, consisting mainly of G4M2s but including a few older Mitsubishi G3M3s, known to the Allies as 'Nells'.

The Americans launched their first strike before dawn on 5 October. 'It was not only black dark,' exclaimed one pilot later. 'There was also one hell of a storm. Every time I thought of a couple of hundred planes rendezvousing in that mess, my teeth chattered. I had to kick myself in the pants to get going—and I was fighter skipper!'

The early launch resulted in the first operational losses when several aircraft crashed while trying to form up after take-off, but it failed to surprise Wake's Japanese defenders completely: they had been warned either by a picket boat or by radar. By the time the American planes arrived they were greeted by heavy anti-aircraft fire, while Japanese troops manned their trenches as though expecting an invasion. The 252nd *Kokutai* had 23 of its fighters up by 5.40 a.m., and the carrier-based Hellcat pilots finally got their first opportunity to duel with their Zero-flying counterparts.

The first combat of the day involved Ensign Robert Duncan of *Yorktown*'s VF-5, who was flying as wingman to Lieutenant-Commander Melvin C. Hoffman when he encountered a Zero at 5.47 a.m., sent a burst of fire into its cockpit and saw it go down. He then intercepted another Zero in the act of attacking a Hellcat just ahead of him. Turning his attention to Duncan, the Zero pilot pulled up sharply, winged over and started boring in on Duncan upside-down. As he drew close Duncan could hear the Zero's bullets striking his plane, but he was too busy to be scared. 'Maybe it's the old adrenalin,' he said, 'Maybe it's the instinct of self-preservation. Anyway, the Zero turned and pulled up into a loop . . . You hang a second in the top of a loop. Well, just there he turned—I turned—I followed—I fired. He went spinning in on fire. The pilot didn't bail out.'

The first of an eventual seven victories for Duncan may have ended the career of a Japanese ace. Warrant Officer Toshiyuki Sueda had been credited with one of the first Zero victories as well as an additional five over China and three during the Pacific War when he took off on the first flight to intercept the Americans. He did not return and was presumed killed in the first fight.

'Boogie' Hoffman accounted for a Zero of his own, while VF-5's squadron leader, Lieutenant-Commander Edward M. Owen, downed another Zero about half an hour later. Yet another 'Zeke' kill in the first dawn encounter was claimed by Lieutenant George C. Bullard, a veteran of the desperate carrier battles of 1942 who was now leading a twelve-plane detachment of VF-6 from the light carrier *Cowpens*.

Lieutenant-Commander Phil Torrey's VF-9 from the carrier *Essex* encountered enemy fighters at about 6 a.m. First blood for that unit was drawn by Lieutenant (jg) Hamilton McWhorter III of Athens, Georgia, in a display of tactics that led to his being known as 'One Slug' for the rest of his naval career. He reported:

> Suddenly, I was aware of Zekes all around me. There must have been twenty. I didn't see any of my gang so I headed to join up with three planes from another carrier. Just then it

happened: there he was, sitting in my sights. So I just let go. Just one burst. That was all. And I had my first Zeke. It was almost funny . . . you just sat back, pressed the button and he blew up and wasn't there any more.

McWhorter was credited with one Zero destroyed and one probably shot down. Another VF-9 pilot, Lieutenant (jg) Mayo A. Hadden Jr, was a little less fortunate, shooting down a Zero but being wounded in the fight, though he did manage to return to *Lexington* for treatment.

The Hellcats of *Lexington*'s VF-16, commanded by Lieutenant-Commander Paul D. Buie, ran into its first aerial opposition at 6.10. Buie himself shared in the destruction of one Zero while Lieutenant (jg) Alfred L. Frendberg destroyed one and damaged another. Lieutenant William E. Burkhalter got another Zero, while Ensign John W. Bartol destroyed one in flames after a head-on gun duel.

By the end of the first morning raids the first and second waves of American fighters were claiming to have encountered 33 Zeros and to have downed 27 of them, while Task Force 14 analysts stated that none of the American aircraft lost in that first strike had been downed in air-to-air combat. Such claims were exaggerated, but the truth stood on its own merits to mark a most auspicious debut for the carrier-based Hellcats. Of the 23 Zeros it sent up, the 252nd *Kokutai* lost fifteen, and three of the eight pilots who returned were wounded. Strafing and bombing eliminated eight more Zeros on the ground, as well as nineteen of the 755th *Kokutai*'s 25 G4M2s and G3M3s, virtually removing that unit as a threat to the carriers. The jubilant Americans predicted 'no further opposition from Wake-based planes', but that boast would prove to be somewhat premature.

Independence launched her first combat air patrol (CAP) of the day at 6.15, while Rear-Admiral Ernest G. Small's Southern Bombardment Group—comprising the heavy cruisers *Minneapolis, New Orleans* and *San Francisco* and three destroyers—left the task force to punish the Japanese further with their guns. A second flight of eight F6Fs of VF-6 left *Independence* at 9.15 with orders to cover Small's group until relieved, then strafe targets of opportunity on Wake before returning.

The cruisers were about to take up station off the southern coast of the island at 11.45 when *Minneapolis*'s radar detected several 'bogeys' (unidentified aircraft) 29 miles to the west, climbing as if they had just taken off from Wake. The cruiser's fighter director officer, Lieutenant (jg) Nelson H. Layman, relayed the information to the VF-6 leader, Lieutenant-Commander Edward H. O'Hare, and he led his Hellcats to investigate.

'Butch' O'Hare was already a US Navy legend, becoming its first ace in dramatic fashion by hurtling into a formation of G4M1s that were on their way to attack his carrier, *Lexington*, on 20 February 1942 and shooting down five

222

of them in as many minutes. O'Hare was awarded the Medal of Honor and toured the United States to raise public morale before returning to duty training—and inspiring—a new generation of Navy fighter pilots. Ill at ease about resting on his laurels, he was glad to be back in the combat zone as commander of VF-6 and eager to resume the job he had enlisted to do—that of a fighter pilot.

As Layman continued to direct the eight Hellcats towards their quarry, O'Hare's keen eyes spotted the bogeys at 12.05—three brownish-green 'Zekes' in a loose V-formation, heading back towards Wake. The hapless trio had been sent up at 11.30 and consisted of three survivors of the morning fracas, all wingmen and petty officers second class—Yasuo Matsumoto, leading Magoichi Kosaka and Kazuo Tobita.

As O'Hare led his wingman, Ensign Henry T. Landry, into position for a quick hit-and-run ambush of the 'Zekes' he was closely followed by Lieutenant (jg) Alexander Vraciu, whose radio was malfunctioning, and Vraciu's wingman, Ensign Allie W. Callan Jr. Lieutenant Cy E. Mendenhall, leading three other VF-6 Hellcats, also watched O'Hare intently since his radio was also not working. Making a diving turn to catch his target from above and to the right, O'Hare sent a stream of 0.50-calibre bullets into the cowling and cockpit of Kosaka's Zero. Kosaka, either wounded or killed in that first pass, slumped forward and his smoking plane nosed downwards. O'Hare then turned slightly to nail the lead Zero, but Matsumoto had been alerted by the sudden sight of tracers whizzing through his formation and took violent evasive action. O'Hare tried to follow but his F6F-3 was going 50 mph faster than the A6M2. Unable to stay with Matsumoto's turn, O'Hare wisely climbed to position himself for another pass at the Zero while his inexperienced wingman, Hank Landry, unwisely continued to pursue Kosaka's descending Zero.

Meanwhile Vraciu had attacked Tobita's Zero from above and to the right. The Zero's engine smoked, then burst into flames, and Vraciu had to pull up hard to avoid a mid-air collision. Suppressing his elation, Vraciu climbed to re-join O'Hare but lost track of Willie Callan, who like Landry was probably attacking Kosaka's already doomed plane. Mendenhall, following Callan, also got on the tail of a burning Zero—Vraciu's victim—and noticed another one on fire when Matsumoto's Zero suddenly flashed by in a wingover and disappeared into a cloud. Mendenhall then briefly flew alongside Kosaka's Zero before seeing it go into a shallow dive, with flames streaming from the engine.

Thinking his firing pass had accounted for the Zero, Callan later said that he was 'ready to shoot anything that moved', and went after a fighter he saw below him. He put one bullet hole through its rudder before he realized to his horror that it was Mendenhall's Hellcat. Once they had re-established themselves as mutual 'friendlies', Mendenhall and Callan climbed to find the remaining Zero, but in the meantime Matsumoto had discovered Landry's F6F and dived on it. Landry reacted with an evasive roll, causing Matsumoto to overshoot and recover in front of him. Landry then opened fire and saw the Zero roll over on its back and go into what the American thought to be a fatal dive. Moments later Landry again found tracers coming at him from above, some of which struck his rear fuselage behind the cockpit. As he turned and pulled up to engage his antagonist Landry was astonished to discover it to be an equally shocked Butch O'Hare.

Callan had re-joined Vraciu when the latter noticed a 'Zeke' racing towards Wake. Both men roared down and chased the enemy fighter all the way down to the runway. Matsumoto managed to land, and as soon as his plane had sufficiently slowed down he taxied off the runway on to the sand and hastily exited the cockpit—bare moments before Vraciu set his Zero ablaze. Vraciu then noticed a 'Betty' on the ground and he and Callan came around to destroy that too before heading north, back to *Independence*. O'Hare and Landry, also diving in pursuit of Matsumoto, contented themselves with shooting up ground installations and riddling another 'Betty' on the field. They then returned to their station over the cruisers, with O'Hare reporting to Layman: 'Tally ho, shot down two, other one not sure.'

The day was not yet over for O'Hare. At 12.20 *New Orleans*'s radar picked up a large bogey 95 miles to the south-east and Layman dispatched O'Hare and Landry to intercept it. About twenty miles south of Wake, Butch recognized the now-familiar profile of a 'Betty' and attacked it head-on. Only one of his guns was working, but it scored hits on an engine and the wing root. Landry let the G4M pass, then turned to make a high-side pass at one of its engines—only to end up directly behind the bomber, trading shots with its rear gunner, who was armed with a 20mm cannon. O'Hare, meanwhile, had climbed back into an attacking position and made a second pass, finishing off the bomber. Then, while the cruisers began bombarding Wake, he and Landry, their fuel and ammunition nearly exhausted, returned to *Independence*. O'Hare's victim was one of two G4M2s of the 755th *Kokutai*, piloted by Warrant Officer Godai Kawano and Chief Petty Officer Nobukichi Wakizara, which had left Maloelap that morning to search for the American task force. Neither plane made it to Wake, the other bomber apparently falling victim to Lieutenants John R. Behr and James H. McConnell and Lieutenants (jg) James A. Bryce and Donald C. Stanley of *Independence*-based VF-22 at 1.54.

During the debriefing O'Hare determined that he and Callan had mistaken Landry's and Mendenhall's F6Fs for Japanese aircraft because of the recent overpainting of the upper right and lower left insignias on the wings of all of

VF-6's planes, leaving nearly circular blotches of shiny paint that looked like red *hinomaru*s when the sun glared off them at a certain angle. O'Hare also asked to share his 'Betty' with Landry, despite his wingman's protests that he had contributed nothing to its destruction. Ultimately O'Hare was given sole credit for the victory—his seventh—and was awarded the Distinguished Flying Cross for his activities that day. For Alex Vraciu, Tobita's Zero was the first of an eventual nineteen victories, including six on 19 June 1944, that would make him the US Navy's fourth-ranking ace.

Another, more serious case of mistaken identity may have resulted in the loss of a Curtiss SOC Seagull floatplane from *New Orleans*, which was shot down at 1.12 p.m. by two fighters. Its crew, Lieutenant Alford M. Robertson and Aviation Radioman First Class George W. McCarthy, bailed out, and although strafed and wounded as they parachuted seaward both airmen were rescued by the destroyer *Schroeder*—which was fortunate indeed when a postwar examination of Japanese records revealed that the crippled 252nd *Kokutai* had no Zeros in the air at that time. At 1.30 p.m. Lieutenant Clement M. Craig of *Independence*'s VF-22 was leading a sweep north-east of Wake when he reported encountering a 'Dave'—the Allied designation for the Nakajima E8N1, an obsolescent reconnaissance float biplane. Thus the first of an eventual wartime total of 11¾ victories for Craig was probably over an American plane.

With Wake under attack, the 22nd *Koku Sentai* dispatched reinforcements from Maloelap made up of seven G4M2s of the 755th *Kokutai* led by Lieutenant-Commander Kaoru Ishihara and an escort of seven Zeros of the 252nd *Kokutai* led by Lieutenant Yuzo Tsukamoto. After a gruelling 600-mile flight the Japanese were about 40 miles south of their goal when they were attacked at 3.15 by four F6F-3s from VF-6's *Belleau Wood*-based contingent led by Lieutenant (jg) Harvey G. Odenbrett. Tearing through the bomber formation, the Hellcat pilots claimed one of them but lost Ensign Edward L. Philippe.

Meanwhile other American fighters were up dealing with what little air activity remained around Wake. Ensign Cyrus J. Chambers, joined by two colleagues of VF-6 from *Cowpens*, accounted for a G3M3 at 2.56. At 3.05 O'Hare led three F6Fs from *Independence* and, upon learning of the Japanese reinforcements coming from the Marshalls, tried to join the running fight. After much searching, however, he made a positive sighting only at 3.56—three Zeros, fleeing westward at 18,000 feet and too far away to overtake.

Judging it impossible to get through to Wake, Ishihara ordered his bombers to turn back for Maloelap. He wanted the Zeros to land on Wake but he could not communicate with them because their pilots had discarded their radios to lighten their planes. The retiring flight was about 100 miles away from the island at 4.20 when it was attacked by eight more Hellcats from *Belleau Wood*.

The Americans claimed three 'Bettys' and three 'Zekes'; in fact, they downed two of each. The two slain Zero pilots included Chief Petty Officer Bunkichi Nakajima, a veteran of numerous actions in the Solomons who was credited with sixteen American aircraft. The remaining Japanese bombers returned to the Marshalls in various shot-up states that evening, one being forced to ditch offshore, as was one of the Zeros. Tsukamoto managed to lead four Zeros to Wake through the cordon of American fighters, landing at 5.30 and taxying carefully down a runway pock-marked with bomb craters. Another Zero managed to make it back alone; its lucky pilot, CPO Isamu Miyazaki, would survive the war with thirteen victories to his credit.

The carriers struck at Wake again at 6.40 in the morning of 6 October, during which Lieutenant (jg) Eugene A. Valencia of *Essex*'s VF-9 damaged a Zero. It was not confirmed as shot down, but Valencia would subsequently be credited with 23, making him the third-ranking US Navy ace. The Americans flew two more follow-up strikes on Wake, adding greatly to the destruction inflicted on the previous day. The only unusual event occurred when *Independence*'s catapult malfunctioned, throwing Cy Mendenhall's Hellcat into the drink in front of the carrier. Mendenhall managed to get out of the sinking plane and was rescued by the destroyer *Schroeder*.

Wake also saw the first successful use by the US Navy of submarines to rescue downed airmen. Prior to the raid Rear-Admiral Pownall had asked Vice-Admiral Charles A. Lockwood, Commander Submarines Pacific Fleet (COM-SUBPAC) for the use of some of his vessels for lifeguard duty. As a result *Snook* had stood off Marcus on 1 September and *Steelhead* had lain off Tarawa on 20 September, but American losses had been few during both raids and neither submarine got a chance to perform its assigned task.

At dawn on 5 October *Skate*, under Commander E. B. McKinney, surfaced off Wake to support Task Force 14's strike. She was attacked several times by Japanese aircraft and shore batteries and one of her officers, Lieutenant (jg) W. E. Maxon, was mortally wounded, but she rescued six downed airmen and proved the value of submarine 'lifeguarding', which became standard doctrine for carrier strikes beyond the range of rescue planes. The effect her activities had on the morale of the carrier air crews was summed up in a radio message that McKinney subsequently received from *Lexington*'s Captain Felix B. Stump: 'Anything in *Lexington* is yours for the asking. If it is too big to carry away, we will cut it up in small parts!'

As Task Force 14 retired to the north-west in the evening of 6 October Admiral Montgomery felt satisfied with its results. Over the past two days his force had made six strikes totalling 758 sorties which had landed 340 tons of bombs on Wake—three times as much as had been dropped on Marcus—as well as

520 tons of shells. A force of **PB4Y** bombers also contributed to the carnage. The overall result was extensive damage to the island's fuel, water and ammunition storage facilities and the destruction of some 60 or 70 buildings. A gasoline-loaded tanker was also blown up in the lagoon.

As to Japanese planes, 22 (out of 65 claimed) were destroyed. Among the 252nd *Kokutai*'s losses were two aces: Sueda—who was posthumously promoted to the commissioned rank of Ensign—and Nakajima. Other Japanese fatalities included CPOs Yukuo Miyauchi, Hisashi Hide and Kazuo Tobita; PO1Cs Saburo Fujiyama, Tomotsu Okabayashi and Soyo Shibata; and PO2Cs Katsunobu Shiba, Yoshio Shiode, Kiyoshi Takei and Kazuyoshi Tokuhara. The Japanese, in turn, claimed fourteen American aircraft shot down. In fact Task Force 14 lost ten Hellcats and two Avengers, but the majority of them had fallen to anti-aircraft fire or accidents rather than in aerial combat.

After the Americans departed, Suho and Wake's other surviving Zero pilots flew back to Roi aboard a bomber. With only twelve flyable aircraft left on Wake the Japanese had to send fresh reinforcements from the Marshalls. They would need all they could muster in the ensuing months, for the Wake raid was only a harbinger of what was to come. On 23 November 1943 the Americans would return to the Central Pacific—not to raid its far-flung island bases but to begin the series of invasions that would eventually carry them to the very heart of the Japanese empire.

In the vanguard of that advance would be the Grumman Hellcat which, having achieved an ascendancy over the Zero in its first combats, would continue to wrest and maintain air superiority for the US Navy, often in spectacular fashion, during all the island campaigns to follow. By the time the Japanese formally surrendered on 2 September 1945, Hellcats had been credited with 5,200 Japanese aircraft and had produced 307 aces—the most for any single American fighter type.

Chapter 16

HEAVY HITTERS

Cannon-Armed Fighters, 1940–1944

The French first made the cannon a practical aerial weapon in 1917 when their Spad 12.Ca1 successfully fired a 37mm gun through the hollow propeller shaft of its geared Hispano-Suiza engine. Although its effectiveness was limited by the fact that its weapon had to be reloaded by hand after each shot, the basic arrangement that the Spad 12 pioneered was later used more successfully in fighters that mounted rapid-fire cannon through their propeller shafts, such as the Messerschmitt Me 109 and Bell P-39. Cannon were also installed on twin-engine fighters such as the Messerschmitt Me 110 and the Lockheed P-38, and advances in cantilever structure allowed them to be mounted in the wings of fighters such as the Supermarine Spitfire Mk IIB and Mitsubishi A6M2 Zero.

As such armament became practical, the urge inevitably arose to see how much 'punch' could be packed into a single aeroplane. The Hawker Hurricane Mk IIC mounted no fewer than four 20mm cannon in its wings but their weight handicapped the performance of a fighter that was already becoming outdated, though Hurricane IICs did yeoman service in the night intruder and ground attack roles. Meanwhile the Royal Air Force had been working apace on more specialized and, it was hoped, more advanced cannon-armed fighters.

The first such aeroplane had, in fact, sprung from Specification F.37/35, issued by the Air Ministry for a fighter to mount four 20mm cannon in 1935, just a year after F.5/34 had requested a fighter armed with eight 0.303-inch machine guns. One of the companies that strove to meet the requirement was Westland, seeking a chance to produce its first fighter for the RAF. William Edward Willoughby Petter directed the design team that settled on a twin-engine format with all guns in the nose, using then-new V-12, 860 hp Rolls-Royce Peregrine I engines. To reduce drag Petter decided to place the radiators in the wing inboard of the two streamlined engine nacelles. The slim monocoque fuselage was skinned aft of the cockpit with magnesium sheet, which had a better strength-to-weight ratio than aluminium, and the plane's one-piece, rearward-sliding glazed cockpit canopy was also ahead of its time. Fowler flaps extended under the fuselage and even included the rear fairings of the engine nacelles. A twin-tailed arrangement was originally envisaged for the aircraft, but wind-tunnel testing resulted in a single fin and rudder with a distinctive, high-mounted tailplane.

Completed in the late summer of 1938, the Westland P.9, soon christened the Whirlwind, had its first flight on 11 October. So radical an aeroplane mated to so new an engine inevitably suffered from development problems, but in January 1939 an order for 200 Whirlwinds was placed, the first machine being delivered in June 1940. The early aircraft were earmarked for a night fighter unit, No 25 Squadron, but then the Air Ministry decided that the experience of that unit's air crews suited them better for the Bristol Beaufighter. Instead the Whirlwinds were delivered to No 263 Squadron, which had lost all its aircraft when the carrier *Glorious* was sunk on 8 June and was in the process of reorganization. In July the squadron commenced training at North Weald and Drem—much of the time being spent wrestling with numerous difficulties with both the Hispano Mk I cannon and the Peregrine engines—then moved to Exeter and resumed combat operations.

The new cannon-armed fighter did not show much hint of fulfilling its promise until 12 January 1941, when two Whirlwinds, operating from St Eval in Cornwall, attacked a Junkers Ju 88A south-west of the Scilly Isles. After silencing its rear gun, Pilot Officer Stein and Sergeant Mason saw the bomber go into a spiral dive into the clouds. However, they were unable to witness its demise and it entered No 263 Squadron's records as a 'probable'. On the following day the Whirlwinds encountered a Heinkel He 111 and pursued it until they ran out of fuel.

The next opportunity came at 9 a.m. on 8 February when two Whirlwinds encountered an Arado Ar 196A of *Bordfliegerstaffel 5./196* about twelve miles south of Start Point. The first Whirlwind pilot, Sergeant Rudland, came down on the floatplane's tail but then thought he saw British roundels on the fuselage and broke off his attack, actually flying alongside the other plane until it vanished in a cloud. The floatplane turned up again and was attacked by the second Whirlwind pilot, Flying Officer Hughes, who closed to 200 yards but failed to achieve a hit. Meanwhile Flight Lieutenant David A. C. Crooks (a Canadian in RAF service) and Pilot Officer K. A. G. Graham had taken off from St Eval at 9.06 and began patrolling south of Dedman Point, only to lose contact with one another in the clouds. Crooks saw Graham pass below him, heading west, but by the time he turned Graham had disappeared again. Crooks then saw an enemy plane emerge from the cloud, descending to the north-east until it hit the water. Overflying the crash scene, Crooks noticed two floats and a piece of wing marked with a black cross. British Coast Guard observers subsequently reported seeing two aircraft, the first of which was in flames, plummet into the sea three miles offshore at 9.50. Graham was credited with the Arado but No 263 Squadron's first confirmed victory had come at a grim price: Graham, who had been flying the fourth production Whirlwind (P6969 HE-V), was also killed, either in a head-on gun duel or a as a result of a collision in the cloud.

Whirlwinds damaged Ju 88As on 1 and 5 March, but on the 11th Pilot Officer H. H. Kitchener was wounded in a fight with a Ju 88 south of the Lizard, after which he crash-landed, seriously injuring himself and burning up his plane. The *Luftwaffe* struck back at St Eval at 8.55 p.m. on 12 March when an He 111 dropped four bombs on the field and succeeded in damaging seven Whirlwinds and seven Hurricanes—three of the latter being write-offs. Ill-fortune continued to attend No 263 Squadron on 14 March as Pilot Officer Patric Glynn Thornton-Brown crashed Whirlwind P6973 upon landing. On 1 April Squadron Leader Arthur Hay Donaldson and Flight Lieutenant Crooks attacked a Do 215 five miles north of Preddannack, but as Crooks moved in to finish off the fleeing bomber its gunner scored a telling hit on his Whirlwind, P6989, which crashed in flames near Helston. Although damaged, the Dornier escaped

Soon after this No 263 Squadron's pilots were told that in order to take the most advantage of their armament their Whirlwinds would be used primarily to make pinpoint attacks on German airfields on the other side of the Channel—a somewhat ironic reprisal for what the *Luftwaffe* had already done to them. The first such mission was launched on 14 June against two Me 109 bases at Maupertus and Querqueville on the Cherbourg peninsula, but poor visibility prevented this from being any more auspicious a start than that of the Whirlwind as a day fighter. Further attacks, called 'Warheads', were more successful in July and August, and in the latter month Whirlwinds escorted a daylight bombing mission to Cologne.

In late September members of No 263 Squadron were withdrawn to form the nucleus of a second Whirlwind unit, No 137 Squadron, at Colerne. The two squadrons spent the rest of their fighting careers in the low-level strike role, particularly against German shipping in the Channel. Their destructive efforts were aided by the later provision of underwing racks for two 250-pound or 500-pound bombs, in which form their planes were designated Whirwind Mk IAs or, unofficially, 'Whirlibombers'.

Although liked by its pilots and a reasonably good fighter at low altitude, the Whirlwind was found to fare worse at altitudes above 15,000 feet, where its speed peaked at 360 mph. In spite of its generous flaps, the Whirlwind's landing speed remained a 'hot' 80 mph, handicapping its ability to operate from grass airstrips. Its main problem, however, was the RAF's pressing need for Rolls-Royce Merlin engines, production of which was being interfered with by the parallel production of Peregrines. Moreover, by the time the Whirlwind finally became operational, cannon-armed fighters such as the Hurricane Mk IIC and Typhoon Mk IB were available to do its job with just one engine. In consequence only 112 Whirlwinds were built before the original 400-plane order was cancelled. In June 1943 No 137 Squadron was re-equipped with Hurricane Mk IVs, and No 263 relinquished its last Whirlwinds for Typhoons in November.

The Typhoon's genesis began before the end of 1935, when the Air Ministry's Specification F.37/35 was followed by another, F.18/37, calling for a single-engine fighter armed with four cannon. Hawker's Sydney Camm, who had already proposed such an armament, needed no prodding to get the project under way, though the principal obstacle to making such an arrangement work on what was essentially an enlarged Hurricane was finding a sufficiently powerful engine. Prototypes were built to use several new engines that promised 2,000 hp, with two water-cooled powerplants being selected for final consideration—the 24-cylinder Rolls-Royce Vulture (essentially two Peregrines arranged in 'X' form around a common crankshaft) powering the Hawker Tornado and the 24-cylinder, flat-H, sleeve-valve Napier Sabre installed in the Typhoon.

The Tornado first took to the air on 6 October 1939 but exhibited a high rise in drag at speeds above 400 mph. This was traced to uneven airflow around its ventral radiator, which was repositioned directly under the engine cowling. The first Typhoon, powered by a Sabre I, made its first flight on 24 February 1940. By then the exigencies of war gave the Air Ministry impetus to order 1,000 of both new fighters, but problems with both the Sabre and Vulture engines held up development. By early 1941 persistent failures of the Vulture's connecting rod bolts led to its abandonment, along with the Tornado, while work proceeded apace on both the Sabre engine and the Typhoon. Since Hawker was still committed to producing the proven and still much needed Hurricane, Gloster Aircraft was selected to build the Typhoon Mk IA, armed with twelve 0.303-inch machine guns in the wings, and the Mk IB, with four 20mm Hispano cannon.

After six difficult months of further development, in September 1941 the first Typhoons began to leave Gloster's assembly line and were delivered to the Air Fighting Development Unit and No 56 Squadron at Duxford. Operational evaluation revealed the new fighter to be still far from ready for action, however. The view from the cockpit was poor, carbon monoxide seeped in through the engine firewall and the cannon feed mechanism was unreliable. Hawker had projected a maximum speed of 464 mph for the new machine, but the early aircraft barely achieved 400—though they did have the distinction of being the first production fighters in the RAF to achieve that speed—and at its best the Typhoon never exceeded 412 mph. On top of all that, the thick wing section and high wing loading of the Typhoon gave it a poor rate of climb and performance dropped off at high altitude. Tailplane flutter and structural weakness in the fuselage just forward of the tail also plagued the early Typhoons. There was a growing wave of opinion within the RAF that the whole Typhoon programme should be abandoned, but Hawker laboured on to rectify the shortcomings of its 'ugly-looking beast' while RAF Fighter Command put No 56 Squadron's planes, along with those delivered to No 266 and 609 Squadrons, to work patrolling the Channel against tip-and-run *Jagdbomber* or 'Jabo' raids by Me 109s and Focke-Wulf Fw 190s.

The first squadron-size operation by the Typhoons commenced at 3.15 p.m. on 20 June 1942 as Wing Commander Denys E. Gillam led Typhoons of Nos 56 and 266 Squadrons from Duxford, accompanied by the station commander, Group Captain John Grandy. Climbing to 20,000 feet, the Typhoons crossed the French coast at Gravelines at 3.38 and turned south, sweeping the coast from Calais to Boulogne in the hope of encountering German fighters. Some unidentified planes were seen in the distance south of Boulogne, but no contact was made and all fighters had returned to Duxford by 4.45, the only problem being that encountered by Sergeant N. J. Lucas, who had to land almost immediately owing to hydraulic trouble. Eight Fw 190s were encountered during the next offensive sweep on 23 June but the Germans chose not to engage the new fighters.

Patrols continued to be fruitless until 9 August, when Pilot Officers I. M. Munro and N. J. Lucas of No 266 Squadron, engaged in a sea patrol, spotted an aircraft approaching at 8.45 p.m. and, as it passed under them, identified it as a Ju 88. The Typhoon pilots turned to engage, Munro lining himself astern of the German and Lucas approaching from the port side. The German gunners opened up with inaccurate fire while their pilot started weaving, which only brought the plane dead ahead of Lucas. Munro opened fire, saw his cannon shells strike the water, closed to 200 yards and fired another three-second burst. Lucas, his plane belching black smoke as he gave it full boost, also fired short bursts at 600 and 400 yards, then loosed a longer one as he closed to 200 yards. At that point, flames appeared inboard of both the Ju 88's engine nacelles. A German crewman tried to bail out but was caught in the gunfire that was still being directed at his plane, and slumped back into the cabin. The Ju 88 bounced in the sea, dropped a wing and then went straight into the water. Lucas and Munro were credited with shares in the first confirmed Typhoon victory.

At 8.15 p.m. on 13 August Flight Lieutenant A. C. Johnston, Sergeant G. G. Osborne and Pilot Officers J. D. Miller and W. J. A. Wilson of No 266 Squadron were flying another sea patrol 50 miles north-east of Southwold when they encountered another twin-engine enemy plane. A running fight ensued during which Johnston, Osborne and Wilson all got shots into the fleeing machine, but Johnston was judged to have landed the fatal shot that set its engines on fire. At least one crewman was seen to bail out and Johnston orbited the crash site to pinpoint it for a Supermarine Walrus flying boat before returning to Duxford. Johnston was credited with a Ju 88 but his late adversary had more likely been a new Messerschmitt Me 210, VN+AV of *Erprobungsgruppe 210*, whose pilot, *Leutnant* H. Manger, was killed but whose observer, *Unteroffizier* E. Rudolf, was indeed rescued and taken prisoner.

Thus far the Typhoons had been engaged in what Denys Gillam described as 'sweeps on the fringe of things', but on 19 August his Wing, by then joined by No 609 Squadron under Group Captain Paul H. M. Richey, became involved in a *bona fide* air battle as Operation 'Jubilee', the landing at Dieppe, got under way. At 2 p.m. Gillam led all three squadrons from West Malling, with No 609 in the lead and Nos 56 and 266 flying 'top cover'. As they arrived 16,000 feet over Le Tréport, north-east of Dieppe, the Wing received word that enemy bombers were heading for the Channel, and shortly afterwards No 266, led by Squadron Leader Charles L. Green, spotted three Do 217s with some Fw 190s in attendance. Green ordered Flight Lieutenant R. H. L. Dawson and Pilot Officers W. S. Smithyman and I. M. Munro to peel off after the Dorniers. Minutes later Smithyman was heard on the radio reporting to have seen one Dornier crash, which Roland Dawson subsequently claimed as his victory. Munro dived on another bomber, fired one 100-shell burst as he closed the range from 300 to 50 feet and then reported seeing his opponent descend in a steep dive with smoke issuing from the port engine and fuselage, although it was credited to him only as a 'probable'. Diving to the deck and pulling out over the coast, Munro saw another Typhoon and upon re-joining it he found it was Dawson's.

Meanwhile another flight of No 266 Squadron Typhoons, led by Flight Lieutenant A. C. Johnston, went after ten Fw 190s, eight of which broke to port and two of which kept diving straight ahead. Johnston went after the latter pair, caught up with one and fired a series of short bursts between 600 and 400 yards, after which he and Pilot Officer J. D. Miller saw white smoke issue from the Focke-Wulf and its dive steepen to near-vertical. At that point Johnston's speed was 480 mph and he thought it prudent to pull out. Due to low ground haze his Fw 190 had to be recorded as 'probably destroyed'.

Dawson and Munro were about half-way across the Channel and hastening to re-join their now-retiring sections when they saw a squadron of Spitfires approaching fast on the starboard quarter. Suspecting trouble, the Typhoon pilots boosted their engines to get clear and weaved as the Spitfires closed in, but Dawson and Munro turned head-on at the ones approaching them. One of the Spitfires opened fire and Munro saw pieces fly off Dawson's plane, which half-rolled up to 100 feet and then plunged into the sea.

The remaining Typhoon pilots returned to West Malling, all complaining of the Spitfires that had attacked them, though Dawson's was the only case in which one actually fired. They later learned that the Spitfires were from No 331 (Norwegian) Squadron, led by Major Helge O. Mehre, who explained—as if the Typhoon pilots didn't have enough woes—that his pilots had mistaken their planes for Fw 190s. Both Gillam and Munro claimed to have damaged Fw 190s in the course of the patrol but Smithyman never returned and it was presumed that he had been shot down in the first fight with the Do 217s.

Gillam led another sweep at 5 p.m., but when his gun mounting came open he turned back—followed by No 609 Squadron, who were not on the correct radio frequency. Squadron Leader Green took charge of the remaining Typhoons and led the sweep from the coast just north of the Somme river to Cap Gris Nez. Cloud cover resulted in no enemy aircraft and no Flak, and the British landed at Duxford without further incident. A final sweep of the day, flown from Fernes to Dunkirk, came under extremely accurate Flak but no aircraft were damaged, and while two Fw 190s dived on the formation they did not press home an attack. So ended the Typhoon's participation over Dieppe, with only one enemy bomber confirmed as destroyed for the loss of two planes and pilots—one a victim of 'friendly fire'.

Although the Typhoon went on to a highly successful career as a low-level fighter-bomber, earning particular notoriety for the havoc it wrought on German armour and road transport during the Battle of Falaise in August 1944, it never really excelled as a fighter. Even with the bugs ironed out of its engine the Typhoon never overcame its tendency to fly erratically at high speeds, a problem that was eventually traced to compressibility—local airflow exceeding the speed of sound. As early as 1940 Camm had been working on a solution in the form of a laminar-flow wing of elliptical configuration, similar to that of the Spitfire. The new wing was installed on the Typhoon II, but its thinner cross section—with a root thickness five inches less than that of the original Typhoon—necessitated the transfer of fuel tanks from the wings to the fuselage, which consequently had to be lengthened. A dorsal tail fin was added, along with so many other changes that the final result was given a new name entirely. As first test-flown on 2 September 1942 the prototype Hawker Tempest Mk V was powered by the same 2,180 hp Napier Sabre II engine as the Typhoon but sustained a higher speed of 430 mph at 20,300 feet. Other variants with other engines were under development, but the RAF's demand for a fighter with the Tempest V's performance to match *Luftwaffe* counterparts such as the Me 109G led to the decision to put the proven version into production without further delay. First flown on 21 June 1943, the production Tempest Mk V reached a speed of 434 mph at 22,800 feet and climbed to 20,000 feet in 6 minutes 36 seconds. Its armament consisted of four short-barrelled 20mm Hispano V cannon as well as eight underwing rockets or 2,000 pounds of bombs.

The first Tempests were earmarked to replace the Typhoons of No 486 (New Zealand) Squadron in January 1944 but as that unit was engaged in attacks on German flying-bomb sites being established along the French coast it had no time to train in the new fighters. Instead the first machines went to No 3 Squadron at Manston in February, while No 486 got its first Tempest in March. Both units, along with Typhoon-equipped No 56 Squadron, made up No 150 Wing under Wing Commander Roland Prosper Beamont.

A veteran fighter and test pilot, 'Bea' Beamont still believed in leading by example—as shown by his scoring the Hawker Tempest's first aerial victory. On 8 June Beamont, flying Tempest V JN751 bearing his personal initials 'R-B', was leading some of his Wing on a sweep north of Rouen when they encountered Me 109Gs and he shot down the first of them. Moments later Flight Lieutenant A. R. Moore and Pilot Officer G. A. Whitman of No 3 Squadron accounted for two more Messerschmitts.

Soon after this fair start, however, the Tempest squadrons were withdrawn from cross-Channel operations to defend Britain against a new threat. On 13 June the first of thousands of pulse-jet-powered, guided glider bombs—officially given the deceptive designation of FZG-76 (*Flakzielgerät*, or anti-aircraft target device) but more widely referred to as *Vergeltungswaffe* (Vengeance Weapon) or V-1s by the Germans and as 'buzz bombs,' 'doodlebugs' or 'divers' by the British—hurtled skywards from ten launching ramps in France, to fall with often devastating effect on London and other cities.

When it came to intercepting these prototypical cruise missiles, the Tempest proved to be a textbook case of the right plane entering service at the right time. It was fast enough to overtake a V-1 and its guns could blow one up at sufficient distance to avoid the sometimes fatal damage that the exploding robot bomb could otherwise inflict on its pursuer. Because of its controllability at high speed, however, the Tempest's pilots also had the option of coming up alongside the V-1 and gradually raising a wing-tip under one of the robot bomb's, letting the resulting air pressure lift the robot's wing until its gyrocompass guidance system was upset and the 'diver' would fall out of control and crash in an unpopulated area.

One RAF response to the V-1 menace was to form a fighter flight within its Fighter Interception Unit, consisting of Tempest Vs and Merlin-engine Mustang IIIs, to patrol the southern approaches against the robot weapons. Among the flight's personnel was Flight Lieutenant Joseph Berry, who earlier had flown

Bristol Beaufighter Mk VIFs over the Mediterranean, downing a Ju 88 on 9 September 1943. Now flying a Tempest, he opened his V-1 account with two 'divers' on 28 June, followed by one the next day and three on the night of 30 June. Berry scored regularly throughout the month, including a record seven V-1s on the night of 23 July. His sourest moment occurred on 27 July when he pursued a V-1 over West Malling airfield before finally hitting the 'buzz bomb' and suffering damage to his Tempest in the explosion—and then learning to his chagrin that he would have to share credit for the victory with a Mosquito that had also been involved in the chase, in spite of testimony from his FIU colleagues that the Mosquito had fired at 1,000 yards and 'missed hopelessly'. Of the 86½ 'divers' destroyed by the FIU, Berry accounted for 52½ before being placed in command of No 501 Squadron on 16 August 1944. He had added seven more to his tally by the end of September, making him the highest-scoring of the 'diver aces'. Beamont also excelled at hunting 'doodlebugs', adding a total of 32 of them to the six enemy planes and shared credit in two others on his final wartime record.

Once the V-1 threat was under control the Tempests returned to the offensive, serving with Nos 2, 33, 56, 80, 222, 274 and 486 Squadrons. Operating from bases in the Netherlands and Belgium, Tempests of the Second Tactical Air Force added twenty manned jets, in the form of Me 262s, to their laurels before hostilities ceased. Although the Tempest never attained the fame of the Spitfire (but then, what British fighter did?), it was nevertheless the fastest and most powerfully armed single-engine fighter to see RAF service during World War II, and it went on to a worthy postwar career as well.

In June 1942, while the Hawker Typhoon was flying its first missions over the Channel, another cannon-armed fighter was having an even less auspicious debut over China. Armed with a 20mm cannon and two 12.7mm machine guns, the Japanese Army Air Force's first Kawasaki Ki-45 twin-engine fighters were about to test their mettle against more nimble single-seat fighters, flown by some of the deadliest pilots in Asia at that time—the 'Flying Tigers' of the American Volunteer Group. Built to a requirement issued to Mitsubishi, Nakajima and Kawasaki by the *Koku Hombu* in March 1937, the Ki-45 was one of several twin-engine, multi-seat, strategic fighters that came into vogue in the mid-1930s, other examples including the Bell YFM-1 Airacuda, the Messerschmitt Bf 110, the PZL P.38 *Wilk*, the Fokker G.I and the Potez 63. The idea of a modern long-range, general-purpose fighter had obvious appeal to the Japanese Army, but its requirements were so broad and poorly defined that Nakajima designer Hideo Itokawa withdrew from the project, while Mitsubishi declined even to tender a proposal. Kawasaki, on the other hand, were eager to try their hand at a modern aeroplane design, and in spite of the firm's inexperience its chief project engineer, Isamu Imashi, came up with the Ki-38, a semi-monocoque cantilever monoplane with semi-retractable landing gear and powered by two Kawasaki Ha.9-II-Ko 12-cylinder, water-cooled engines. Just as the Ki-38 mock-up was nearing completion, however, the *Koku Hombu* ordered further work to be stopped pending the resolution of differences between the Army and the Air Technical Research Institute in regard to speed, endurance and manoeuvrability requirements. A compromise was reached two months later and Kawasaki were ordered to revise their design to use 820 hp Nakajima Ha.20-Otsu nine-cylinder radial engines, with an armament of one 20mm Ho.3 cannon and two 7.7mm Type 89 machine guns.

By then Takeo Doi had succeeded Imashi as Chief Project Engineer and work proceeded on the revised and redesignated Ki-45, the design for which was completed in October 1938 and of which the first of three prototypes rolled out of Kawasaki's Gifu plant in January 1939. Problems immediately surfaced with the unreliable engine, combined with excessive drag which several redesigned engine cowlings seemed unable to remedy. The hand-operated chain-and-sprocket retraction system for the landing gear also was unpopular, though it was eventually supplemented with an electrical system. The Ki-45's maximum speed of 298 mph fell short of the 335 mph requirement and mock combats showed the aircraft to be unable to compete with Kawasaki's old Ki-10 biplane fighter let alone the Nakajima Ki-27. The plane's flexibly mounted rear 7.7mm machine gun was judged to be virtually useless at high speeds, and in general the Ki.45 was pronounced 'incapable of performing the missions considered necessary for a two-seat fighter'.

Further testing was curtailed while the *Koku Hombu* reviewed the feasibility of the entire strategic fighter concept. Then Kawasaki was ordered to try again—by adapting its airframe to the Nakajima Ha.25, a 14-cylinder, twin-row radial that produced 1,050 hp while possessing a slightly smaller diameter than the Ha.20. After being redesigned to handle greater stress, having its centre of gravity altered and being given deeper nacelles to accommodate both the engines and a fully retractable, electrically operated undercarriage, the fourth pre-series Ki-45 underwent its first test in July 1940. During the first flight the plane was barely controllable and suffered damage in a forced landing, but after repairs and further modifications it showed much improvement, including a speed of 323 mph. Doi and his design team continued to refine their design until it bore only a basic conceptual resemblance to the first prototype, completing the Ki-45-Kai in May 1941. The new fighter's overall lines were straighter and less curvaceous than the original's, but during flight testing in September–October 1941 it showed viceless flying characteristics which contrasted radically with those of the earlier prototype.

The Kawasaki design team's persistence was finally rewarded with a production contract in November 1941. The first batch of aircraft were to be powered by Ha.25 engines, later to be supplanted by more reliable 1,080 hp Mitsubishi Ha.102 14-cylinder radials. In its first production form the Ki-45-Kai-Ko, dubbed *Toryu* (Dragon Slayer) by the Army, retained the 20mm Ho.3 cannon firing through a ventral fuselage tunnel offset to starboard but the nose armament was increased with twin 12.7mm Ho.103 Type 1 machine guns while the rear observer was furnished with a 7.92mm Type 98 machine gun (based on the German MG 15). In addition to its heavier punch, the Ki-45 was one of the first Japanese fighters to have pilot armour and fuel tank protection. Although it was still criticized for its inability to manoeuvre as well as Japan's single-seat fighters—a virtually impossible task for any plane of its configuration—the Ki-45 was nevertheless one of the most agile twin-engine aircraft of World War II.

Given the many setbacks in the course of its development, there is a certain consistency in the Ki-45's baptism of fire. The first five production planes were sent to Canton, China, and attached to the 21st *Hikotai*, a composite unit of bombers and fighters also known as Nagano Force. The flight was led by Sergeant Jiro Ieiri and the new fighters' first mission was to supplement Nagano Force's Ki-27s in escorting Kawasaki Ki-48 medium bombers in a series of bombing attacks on Liuzhou, Kweilin and other airfields in East China between May and June 1942. For four weeks the raids went unchallenged and Ieiri decided to put his *Toryu*s to use in the ground attack role, loading the forward guns with explosive shells and mounting 110-pound bombs under the wings.

The tedium of the *Toryu* crews' routine was about to change, however. In the evening of 11 June eleven Curtiss P-40Cs and new P-40Es of the 1st Squadron of Colonel Claire L. Chennault's American Volunteer Group arrived at the hitherto unoccupied airfield at Kweilin, which the Japanese had bombed earlier that day. In anticipation of another visit, Chennault called reveille at 3.00 the next morning and the appearance of a Japanese reconnaissance plane at 5.00 gave his men all the warning they needed. By 5.58, when five Ki-48s of the Nanking-based 90th *Sentai*, eight Ki-27s of the 54th *Sentai* and the five Ki-45s of Nagano Force arrived over Kweilin, all three flights of the Flying Tigers were up and circling, at altitudes of 15,000, 18,000 and 21,000 feet, ready to pounce on their would-be assailants.

After dropping their bombs from an altitude of 16,600 feet the Ki-48s turned for home, but in the process their formation strayed from those of the escorts, at which point George T. Burgard, leading the uppermost flight of Flying Tigers, put his P-40C into a dive and attacked the bombers. He scored some hits on one of them before being attacked by one of the Ki-27s and was soon engaged with three of the fighters. Allen Wright's P-40C was hit by one of the Ki-48 gunners but he went on to attack three of what he thought were 'light bombers' until driven away from them by another Ki-27. Burgard spotted Wright's plane going down with smoke streaming from its engine and descended 2,000 feet to drive the Ki-27 off his tail. He then escorted Wright to the airfield, where the damaged P-40 bellied in and flipped over, spraining Wright's back.

Climbing to re-join the fight, Burgard was partnered by Lieutenant Romney Masters, a US Army Air Forces pilot who had recently joined the AVG in anticipation of its imminent transition from the Chinese Air Force to the USAAF. The two pilots encountered a Ki-27 and a twin-engine aeroplane, the former of which Burgard took on while Masters engaged the other. Burgard's quarry eluded him so he had a go at the twin-engine machine. 'The bomber was light, fast and exceptionally manoeuvrable,' Burgard reported afterwards. 'He dove sharply for the ground and made a sharp turn.'

At that moment the Ki-27 returned and put a hole in Burgard's left aileron, then dived away with Burgard in pursuit, firing long bursts until he saw it skid and fall off on a wing. 'I pulled up,' he wrote, 'and saw he had run into the side of a sharp peak and blew up.'

Burgard could not see Masters and his 0.50-calibre machine guns had stopped, but he still wanted to deal with the twin-engine 'light bomber', which he saw 'hedge-hopping through the sharp hills'. After half a dozen unsuccessful attempts to get on the evasive machine's tail, Burgard caught it in a valley, 'but he turned almost 90 degrees and began making 360-degree vertical turns around a sharp cone . . . we were never more than 150 feet from the ground'. During one pass, however, Burgard's machine guns started working again and he managed to set the enemy plane's left engine on fire. 'I throttled back,' he wrote, 'and continued to shoot until he dragged his wing on a small knob and mushed in.' Unknown to the AVG pilots at the time, Wright had been attacking three of the new Ki-45s when the Ki-27 jumped him, while Burgard had accounted for their leader. Sergeant Ieiri was killed but his gunner, Corporal Kei Honda, survived to be taken prisoner.

Camille J. Rosbert, flying a new P-40E in the lowest AVG formation, attacked another 'bomber' only to see it loop up and over him and speed off in the opposite direction. Using his dive speed to regain altitude, he gave chase and fired a burst that tore off part of the enemy plane's wing, after which, he said, 'the Jap spun down toward the mountains below'. Robert H. Neale was attacking a Ki-48 when he found one of the new *Toryus* on his tail. 'Thought it was an Me 110,' he wrote. 'Had a hell of a time getting away.'

Charles R. Bond Jr attacked another Ki-45, but its gunner put a bullet through the coolant system of his P-40E. His hydraulic system and his guns also failed, as smoke curled from behind his instrument panel. He then noticed two Ki-27s on his tail, one of which followed his descending plane to 1,000 feet before turning and climbing away, probably convinced that he was done for. Bond's propeller stopped moments later and he glided in and made a crash landing in a rice paddy. Although he gashed his forehead on his gunsight, Bond was otherwise unhurt and with the aid of local farmers and a Catholic missionary, Herbert Elliott, he eventually made his way back to his squadron.

The Flying Tigers claimed a total of nine enemy aircraft in the fight, which were credited to George Burgard, Joe Rosbert, John J. Dean, William E. Bartling and John R. Rossi. Their celebrations that night were enhanced when Reverend Elliott telephoned to report that 'old hard-luck Bond' was all right and when the Chinese brought in Ieiri's gunner, Corporal Honda. A chicken farmer before joining the army, Honda had been a bomber gunner for two years before joining Nagano Force in February 1942. His reference to his aircraft as a 'Model 45' marked the first time that Chennault heard a JAAF plane referred to by its *kitai* number, and his description of its nose cannon, in which every second shell was an explosive round, was sobering news to the Americans, who had hitherto considered their superior firepower to be a consistent advantage. 'No more head on runs for me,' Neale remarked. After Burgard was introduced to him as the man who had brought him down, Honda posed for a photograph with his captors in front of one of their shark-mouthed fighters before being returned to the Chinese.

In Tokyo a newspaper reported that 'Nine American aircraft of the Curtiss Hawker P-40 type were downed by the Japanese Air Unit in a fierce combat' on 12 June, for the loss of only two Japanese planes. The JAAF aircrews in China knew better—that the actual casualties in the day's fighting were roughly the opposite. One Ki-48 had crashed near Kweilin—apparently shot down by Bartling—and two others were so badly damaged that they were written-off upon their return. Only one Ki-27 was lost (though Burgard, Bartling and Rossi were credited with one each), but two of the new *Toryu*s had been destroyed near Kweilin by Burgard and Rosbert while a third, also credited to Rosbert, had crashed on the way back and the fuselages of the remaining two Ki-45s showed wrinkles that suggested that they could not stand up to the stress of high-g manoeuvring. The Japanese had brought down two P-40s but both of their pilots, Wright and Bond, had survived. After analyzing the raid's results the JAAF summarily cancelled further operations against Kweilin.

The *Koku Hombu* subjected the Ki-45 to yet another reappraisal (whether or not it noted the irony of the heavily armed fighter's first victory being scored by a rear gunner's relatively puny weapon is unknown). Although the *Toryu* had not exactly disgraced itself in its first combat, its performance as an escort fighter had fallen short of expectations, much as that of the Me 110 had during the Battle of Britain. When the Ki-45-Kai-ko entered service in quantity over China in November 1942 it was with a *chutai* of the 16th *Sentai*, replacing that squadron's Mitsubishi Ki-30 light bombers. At about the same time the newly activated 21st *Sentai* in Hanoi, Indo-China, replaced its initial complement of Ki-27s with Nakajima Ki-43s and Ki-45s, and in April 1943 the 13th *Sentai* in New Guinea began to receive Ki-45s to supplement its Ki-43s. In all of those units, and the 5th *Sentai* which joined the 13th in New Guinea in July 1943, the Ki-45s served primarily in the fighter-bomber role, attacking ground targets and small Allied vessels.

Late in 1943 the Ki-45-Kai-Otsu was introduced, with the 20mm cannon moved to the nose in place of the twin 12.7mm machine guns and its position in the ventral tunnel taken up by a 37mm, hand-loaded, Type 98 cannon. In early 1944 an increase in nocturnal bombing raids by Consolidated B-24 Liberators led Ki-45 units in the South Pacific area to turn their planes into improvised night fighters by removing the fuel tank in the upper fuselage aft of the cockpit and installing twin, oblique-firing 12.7mm Ho.103 machine guns or 20mm Ho.5 cannon in its place, similar to the mounting used in the Navy's Nakajima J1N1-C-Kai *Gekko* and to the *Schräge Muzik* arrangement employed in night fighters by the *Luftwaffe*. Although the modified Ki-45s carried no radar, the 5th and 13th *Sentai*s claimed some successes over the East Indies, New Guinea and Rabaul, prompting Kawasaki to standardize the oblique 20mm Ho.5 mounting in a final production variant, the Ki-45-Kai-Hei, which also replaced the Type 98 cannon with a semi-automatic, recoil-operated Ho.203 cannon, which had a slightly lower muzzle velocity than the hand-loaded weapon but which could use a 25-shell magazine with rate of fire of 130 rounds per minute. One Ki-45-Kai-Hei was trial-fitted with an airborne interception radar but this was never standardized in production aircraft.

In April 1944 the first Ki-45-Kai-hei fighters emerged from Kawasaki's Akashi plant and were delivered to the 4th *Sentai* based at Kozuki and the newly formed 53rd *Sentai* at Matsudo. By then the *Toryu* had a new dragon to slay—the Boeing B-29 Superfortress. On the night of 15 June 1944, 68 B-29s of the Twentieth Air Force's 58th Very Heavy Bombardment Wing left their base at Chengtu, China, to bomb the Imperial Iron and Steel Works at Yawata in northern Honshu—the first Allied bombing raid against mainland Japan since the Doolittle Raid of 18 April 1942. Among the Japanese fighters that rose to challenge the bombers were eight Ki-45s of the 4th *Sentai*, which claimed seven of the B-29s. First Lieutenant Isamu Kashiide claimed two, plus one whose fate could not be positively determined, while Second Lieutenant Sadamitsu Kimura was credited with two destroyed and three damaged, for which he received a personal citation from the commanding general of the Western Military District and was awarded a ceremonial sword.

The Americans had indeed lost seven bombers, but their reports told a different story. One B-29 from the 468th Bomb Group crashed shortly after take-off with no casualties and a second, from the 444th Group, subsequently crashed near Kiangyu, killing its entire crew. Four planes aborted their mission early and nine others which failed to reach the objective struck at alternative targets of opportunity. The 47 bombers that reached Yawata were hampered by cloud cover and haze over the target, preventing the 221 tons of bombs they dropped from causing much damage. A B-29 of the 368th Group's 792nd Squadron was shot down and six other planes were damaged by anti-aircraft fire. The Americans reported sixteen attacks by Japanese fighters, only three of which were by twin-engine aircraft and none of which scored significant damage on them. Two 368th Group B-29s crashed into mountains during the return flight over China, with the loss of both crews and *Newsweek* correspondent Robert Schenkel, while another plane from the 444th was forced to land at Heihsiang, where Japanese fighters and bombers destroyed it on the field the following morning. A total of 55 men were killed in the Yawata mission, but none of those losses was directly attributed to enemy aircraft.

Unaware of the Americans' assessment, the *Koku Hombu* was satisfied that the *Toryu* had found its operational niche at long last. Even though the Ki-45 lacked the radar and high-altitude performance to deal consistently with the B-29s, its 37mm shells could cause terrific damage whenever they were able to strike home. In the months that followed, Ki-45 crews of the 4th and 53rd *Sentais*, joined by the 5th, which was recalled from New Guinea, distinguished themselves in defence of the Japanese homeland.

While some Western nations were still wrestling with the feasibility of mounting cannon on single-engine aircraft, Japan entered the Pacific War with two 20mm cannon—albeit low-velocity weapons—in the wings of its principal air superiority fighter, the Mitsubishi A6M2 Zero. That in itself was a significant increase in armament, though the fighter that carried it had made extraordinary concessions in structure and protection in order to compensate for its weight. Even while the A6M was under development, however, discussions took place between its chief designer, Dr Jiro Horikoshi, and the Bureau of Aeronautics for the Imperial Navy regarding a radical departure from the established Japanese formula—a powerful, heavily armed interceptor built with an emphasis on speed and climb rate rather than manoeuvrability. The need to complete the A6M held up further work on the project, but in September 1939 the Navy issued a specification for an interceptor capable of 373 mph at 19,685 feet, the ability to reach that altitude in 5.5 minutes and provision for two 7.7mm machine guns, two 20mm cannon and an armoured pilot's seat.

Given a choice of the 1,185 hp V-12 Aichi Ha-60 Atsuta—based on the Daimler-Benz DB 601A—and the 1,440 hp Mitsubishi Ha-32 Kasei Model 13 14-cylinder, twin-row, radial engine, Horikoshi opted for the latter as he, Yoshitoshi Sone and Kiro Takahashi began work on the new interceptor in early 1940. In order to compensate for the radial engine's size—it was considerably larger than the Zero's Nakajima Sakae 12—Horikoshi's team extended the shaft to its three-blade propeller and housed the engine in a long, tapered cowling with an engine-driven fan to suck in cooling air. The higher priorities afforded to Zero production and initial problems with engine cooling delayed the completion of the prototype J2M1 until February 1942, by which time the overworked and weary Dr Horikoshi had relinquished his post as Chief Designer to Takahashi.

After flying it for the first time on 20 March, test pilot Katsuzo Shima judged the plane's stability and controllability to be excellent, though the ailerons tended to stiffen up at speeds above 323 mph. He also reported the forward view to be unacceptable and that the undercarriage would not retract at speeds exceeding 100 mph. The 359 mph speed and 7.8 minute climb to 19,685 feet fell short of the requirement, but the Navy decided that these shortcomings could be rectified by using the more powerful 1,870 hp Mitsubishi MK4R-A Kasei 14 Model 23ko engine, then under development, and a Sumitomo four-blade propeller. A modified version of the aircraft was therefore earmarked for production on 13 October 1942 as the J2M2 *Raiden* (Thunderbolt) Model 11, armed with two 7.7mm machine guns in the fuselage and two high-velocity 20mm Type 99 Model 2 cannon in the wings.

The production order proved to be premature. During test flights the Kasei 23ko engine, which had provision for water-methanol injection, emitted excessive smoke and tended to vibrate at maximum power, often to a critical degree. The latter problem was eventually alleviated by fitting more rigid propeller blades and more resilient engine-mounting shock absorbers, but further problems delayed the development of the J2M2 and not all of them had been solved when the first production machines were finally accepted by the Navy in December 1943. The oscillation problems persisted and in January 1944 the first of several incidents occurred in which J2Ms disintegrated in mid-air for reasons that were never conclusively explained.

In October 1943 the J2M3 appeared, replacing the fuselage-mounted 7.7mm machine guns with a pair of wing-mounted 20mm Type 99 Model 1 cannon, which had both a lower muzzle velocity and a lower rate of fire than the Model 2 but which greatly increased the interceptor's overall firepower. That type was accepted over the J2M2 in February 1944, but in June the production tempo of the later model was also reduced as a result of the Navy's disenchantment with the J2M's teething troubles and its increasing interest in Kawanishi's N1K1-J *Shiden* interceptor. Although *Raiden* development continued, production of all J2M variants totalled no more than 476—too few for it to affect the outcome of the Pacific War, no matter how good it ultimately turned out to be.

The first J2M2s were flown to Toyohashi, south-east of Nagoya, and from there they were assigned to fighter *Hikotai* (Squadron) *602* of the 381st *Kokutai*, then based at Kendari on the island of Celebes, to assist in the defence of the Balikpapan oilfields. Ten *Raiden*s were on hand in February 1944, but the further problems they were experiencing at Toyohashi dampened hopes of their completely replacing the Zeros on the 381st *Kokutai*'s inventory. In mid-March six of the *Raiden*s were detached to Balikpapan via Davao and took a direct part in air defence operations thereafter.

Hikotai 602 still had nine *Raiden*s on hand—though only seven were in operational condition—on 5 September when 58 Consolidated B-24 Liberators of the Fifth Air Force's 380th Heavy Bombardment Group attacked its air base at Menado, Celebes, destroying or damaging seventeen aircraft on the ground. The squadron's Zeros and *Raiden*s rose to oppose them, and during the action the Japanese fighters resorted to dropping No 3 phosphorus bombs into the bomber formations. Warrant Officer Keizu Kamihara of *Hikotai 602* was credited with three of the B-24s (although two were subsequently rated only as 'probables') as well as two of their Lockheed P-38 escorts.

At 12.40 in the morning of 30 September, 24 Liberators of the Thirteenth Air Force's 5th Bomb Group and 24 from the 307th began taking off from Kornasoren, Noemfoor, to carry out the first of five strikes on Balikpapan. Requiring a 2,600-mile round trip, this was the longest daylight mission ever undertaken by B-24s in formation, and 46 more Liberators of the Fifth Air Force's 90th Bomb Group also participated, flying 1,243 miles to reach the target. The 5th Group was 250 miles from Balikpapan when it encountered two Japanese fighters, and soon the B-24s were running the gauntlet of anti-aircraft fire and 30 more fighters. By the time the Liberators reached their target—the Pandansari refinery—they were fending off attacks by Zeros, *Raiden*s and J1N1-S *Gekko* night fighters of the 381st *Kokutai* as well as Zeros of the 331st *Kokutai*'s *Hikotai 309*. Flak damaged fifteen of the 5th Group's bombers and fighters downed three of them, including that of the deputy group commander. The Japanese fighters also accounted for a B-24J of the 90th Group's 319th Squadron. In spite of intermittent cloud cover that frustrated the 307th and 90th Group bombardiers' efforts, the bomber crews reported 37 direct bomb hits on the refinery as well as nine enemy fighters shot down.

The two Thirteenth Air Force groups returned to Balikpapan on 3 October and 40 Japanese fighters engaged the 307th in a 70-minute running fight that cost the group seven of its twenty B-24s as they bombed Pandansari. The 307th's gunners made a typically exaggerated claim of having shot down nineteen enemy planes, but Lieutenant (jg) Keisaburo Uchiyama and Chief Petty Officer Kitami Kikuchi of *Hikotai 602* were killed that day, though the Americans' unfamiliarity with the J2M2 makes it impossible to ascertain whether they were flying Zeros or *Raidens* and, if the latter, whether their deaths were due to combat or aircraft failure. The nineteen Liberators of the 5th Group maintained a tighter formation than the 307th as they struck at the Edeleanu refinery, claiming three enemy planes for the loss of two bombers.

For the next strike on 10 October, V Fighter Command dispatched sixteen Republic P-47s of the 35th Fighter Group from its newly acquired advance air base on Morotai—American Thunderbolts unwittingly stalking Japanese Thunderbolts! Preceding the bombers to the target area, the P-47s jumped 25 Japanese fighters and claimed a dozen of them—including three 'Oscars' by Captain William H. Strand of the 40th Squadron—for the loss of one Thunderbolt.

Fourteen Lockheed P-38Js of the 49th Fighter Group's 9th Squadron also flew ahead of the bombers and encountered six dark green, radial-engine aircraft cruising between 3,000 and 7,000 feet which the Lightning pilots identified as 'Oscars' of the JAAF but which were more probably the still unknown J2M2s because one of the American element leaders, Major Richard I. Bong, also spotted a naval 'Irving' at 5,000 feet—one of the J1N1-Ss of *Hikotai 902*, the 381st *Kokutai*'s night fighter element.

With Captain Robert Baker following in close support, Bong did an abrupt wing-over, overtook the 'Irving', shot it down for his 29th victory and noticed at least one of its crewmen take to his parachute. The other P-38s engaged the 'Oscars', one of which was so agile that Lieutenant Warren Curton went into a momentary high-speed stall while trying to follow it in a turn. Swiftly recovering, Curton set another antagonist's engine ablaze while Bong sent a further aircraft down in a ball of fire. Major Wallace Jordan caught another 'Irving' at 12,000 feet and sent it into the sea in flames, probably killing *Hikotai 902*'s division officer, Lieutenant Sadao Ozaki. Jordan then got one of the 'Oscars' for his fifth victory before the others got into such an advantageous position that he and his wingman, Captain Willie Williams, beat a prudent retreat. Lieutenant Edward Howes sent a Zero crashing into the ocean and then reported seeing one of two 'Oscars' drop two aerial bombs at some departing B-24s, though they exploded too far aft of the bomber to cause serious damage. Chief Petty Officer Eizo Ota of *Hikotai 602* was among the Japanese pilots killed in the day's fighting, as was

Lieutenant Akira Tanaka, group leader of the 331st *Kokutai*'s *Hikotai 309*, and two of his pilots, CPO Tsumiro Tanaka and PO1C Akio Fukui.

While the American fighters were trying to clear the way for them, 21 B-24s of the 90th Group had to fight their way through still more Japanese fighters to bomb Pandansari and Edeleanu. The group's gunners claimed sixteen of their assailants for the loss of one Liberator, which exploded after being struck by a phosphorus bomb dropped by one of the Japanese fighters. The 22nd Bomb Group's eighteen B-24s hit Padansari next, one of its planes claiming six enemy fighters before damage from numerous 20mm hits compelled it to crash-land on Batoedaka island. A second Liberator exploded after being rammed by a Zero and a third was shot down. The 43rd Bomb Group went in next, losing none of its nineteen planes and claiming thirteen of the enemy's. The 5th's 24 Liberators reported only half-hearted opposition as they went after Balikpapan's paraffin plant, suggesting that the Japanese fighter groups were a spent force, and the 307's 25 B-24s enjoyed an equally easy run against the cracking plants.

The next raid, on 14 October, was also escorted, with the 35th Fighter Group's Thunderbolts preceding the bombers by fifteen minutes and again claiming to have taken a heavy toll of the defenders in advance—nineteen, including two 'Oscars' each by Captains Strand and Alvaro J. Hunter of the 40th Squadron over Balikpapan at 10.30 a.m. and two more by First Lieutenant James D. Mugavero of the 41st at Manggar at 10.42, for the loss of four P-47s. The 'Jugs' were followed by P-38s of the 49th Fighter Group, joined by Major Thomas J. McGuire, the commander and leading ace of the 431st Fighter Group, who was obsessed with overtaking Bong's score. Again the Lightning pilots reported a mixed bag of opposition—Zeros, 'Oscars' and 'Tojos', the last of which again suggest confused identification of the new J2M2s. In any case, Major Gerald R. Johnson and Lieutenant Edward Cooper, of the 9th Squadron, and McGuire each claimed one of the 'Tojos'.

Also present over Balikpapan were two P-38Js of the 8th Fighter Group, flown by the group's commander, Lieutenant-Colonel Earl Dunham, and by Captain Kenneth Ladd, commander of the 36th Squadron. As they approached the target they encountered four 'Oscars,' the leader of which Ladd attacked and sent down, the Japanese pilot being last seen climbing from his cockpit to bail out. Dunham saw Ladd score hits on another enemy fighter before they became separated in the mêlée. After the fight broke up Dunham climbed to 19,000 feet and radioed Ladd but got no response. When he returned to Morotai he heard reports of a P-38 with a smoking engine still being engaged by Japanese fighters, but nothing more was ever learned of Ladd's fate. He was the only Lightning pilot lost, while his colleagues claimed a total of sixteen enemy fighters. The Thirteenth Air Force dispatched 42 of its own Lightnings to Balikpapan, but only six of the 68th Fighter Squadron's planes reached the target, to claim a 'Tojo' and a 'Tony'.

While the Thunderbolts and Lightnings were eliminating the aerial opposition, 49 Liberators of the 90th Group dropped two 1,000-pound and one 500-pound bomb each on Edeleanu; they were followed by 40 Thirteenth Air Force machines. Only one of the 90th's Liberators was lost in the most effective attack on the refineries so far, which was commended as 'magnificent' by General Douglas MacArthur himself. The Thirteenth Air Force tried to follow up with one more strike on 18 October but foul weather prevented its planes from accomplishing much, though it also prevented the Japanese fighters from intercepting the bombers.

The Japanese claimed a total of 80 American planes during the Balikpapan raids. The Fifth and Thirteenth Air Forces had actually lost 22 B-24s—from which 60 crewmen were eventually recovered—as well as six P-47s and three P-38s. The total of 433 tons of bombs dropped by the Liberators on Balikpapan did not cripple the complex but they did reduce its petroleum output for a while. It cannot be positively ascertained how much of a contribution the 381st Kokutai's *Raiden*s made to the American casualties, but the fact that they were no longer on group strength suggests that all were either shot down or written off in the course of the five air battles.

In spite of the *Raiden*'s gallant but less than outstanding debut, Japan's position at that point was desperate enough to assure the interceptor a role in her defence. As early as March 1944 Lieutenant (jg) Sadaaki Akamatsu, newly transferred to the 302nd *Kokutai* at Atsugi, was training in a new J2M3 which he would fly on and off until August 1945. In the hands of an expert like the irascible, alcoholic but brilliant Akamatsu, 'Jack,' as the Allies called the *Raiden*, proved to be not only a formidable interceptor for bringing down a Boeing B-29 but a fighter capable of besting a Grumman F6F Hellcat—Akamatsu accounting for four and five 'probables' among the latter.

After capturing a 'Jack' outside Manila in February 1945 and restoring it to flyable condition, the Americans tested it against their best fighters as well as several other Japanese and German fighters and were impressed with its speed, outstanding climb rate, stability and take-off and landing qualities. Significantly, their principal criticism centred on the Achilles' heel that had prevented the J2Ms from becoming a significant threat from the very start—poor mechanical reliability. Nevertheless, such *Raiden*s as were available were distributed among the best-trained of the home defence air groups and fought with distinction right up until Japan's surrender.

Chapter 17

DUELLING IN THE DARK

Night Fighters, 1940–1944

Nocturnal operations, like most aspects of aerial warfare, originated during World War I. As early as 1915 reconnaissance aircraft were making stealthy flights over the lines under the cover of darkness, as were German Zeppelins when improved air defences made it too dangerous to bomb Britain's cities by day. By 1918 modified British fighters, such as the Sopwith Comic (a Camel with the cockpit moved back and twin Lewis machine guns installed above the wing so that their flash would not ruin the pilot's night vision) were playing a nocturnal game of cat-and-mouse with Gotha G.Vs and Zeppelin-Staaken *Riesenflugzeuge* (Giant Aeroplanes), while some German fighters did the same with intruding French Voisins. As with some other World War I innovations, little substantial progress was made in that form of aerial warfare at the time, but it did set a precedent for further development during the post-war years.

The real foundations for nocturnal warfare were laid on 26 February 1935 when Robert Alexander Watson-Watt and his assistant, A. F. Wilkins, successfully demonstrated a means of locating and pinpointing flying objects by reflecting radio waves of ultra-high frequency off its surface. The British development of radio detection and ranging—radar—led to the establishment of stations along the coast that would be a decisive factor in the Battle of Britain. Inevitably, the advancing state of the art also made it possible to build radar units small enough to install in aeroplanes themselves, giving them the ability to navigate and to detect other aircraft in the dark.

Within the first year of the Second World War British and German bombers were suffering such severe losses at the hands of each other's fighters that by the autumn of 1940 both sides were making the nocturnal bombing of cities a standard practice. It all began on the night of 19 March 1940 when thirty Armstrong Whitworth Whitley Mk Vs of Nos 10, 51, 77 and 102 Squadrons, followed by twenty Handley Page Hampdens of No 5 Group, attacked the German floatplane base at Hörnum on the Frisian island of Sylt. Only one plane failed to return the next morning, but later reconnaissance flights of the area determined that this, the first deliberate British bombing attack on German soil, had not been very effective.

By what amounted to an unwritten mutual agreement, British and German cities were bombarded with nothing more than propaganda leaflets in the first months of the war, but on the night of 11/12 May 1940 Monchengladbach became the first town to suffer a bombing raid, albeit a modest one by 37 aircraft. Strategic night bombing commenced in earnest on the night of 15/16 May when a total of 99 RAF bombers struck at sixteen industrial targets in the Ruhr while twelve others attacked communications points in Belgium. Again, little damage was done, but no planes were lost. However, at that point the Germans decided to take serious steps to deal with the situation. *Oberst* Josef Kammhuber, a former Junkers Ju 88A bomber pilot, was put in charge of organizing night air defences, including a network of radar installations and the first *Nachtjgdgeschwader*, *NJG I*, under the command of *Major* Wolfgang Falck.

Kammhuber proved to be an outstanding organizer and Falck's enthusiastic leadership also contributed to the rapid growth and sophistication of the *Luftwaffe*'s nocturnal fighter component. Its primary weapon was the Me 110, which was soon to be proved ineffective in its original role as a general-purpose fighter by day but would be an excellent night fighter since it was faster and could climb higher than any British bomber and at the same time could be adapted to carry an increasingly advanced array of airborne radar. Supplementing the Me 110s were the first of several bombers converted to night fighters—the Dornier Do 17Z-6 *Kaus* (Screech Owl) and Do 17Z-10 *Kaus II* and the Ju 88C. The Ju 88, in particular, would be a highly successful variant of an airframe of seemingly limitless versatility: although less manoeuvrable than the Me 110, it could carry just as potent an array of guns and electronics, and with a range of 1,800 miles and an endurance of five hours it could stay in the air three times as long as an Me 110.

Ironically, none of the above-mentioned aircraft were involved in the *Luftwaffe*'s first successful nocturnal interception. On the night of 8/9 July 1940 *Oberfeldwebel* Paul Forster of *IV Gruppe (Nacht)* of *Jagdgeschwader 2* was patrolling in an Me 109E when he saw a twin-engine bomber caught in the searchlights, attacked it and sent it crashing into the sea off Heligoland. Forster, whose victim was a Whitley Mk V of No 10 Squadron, later stated quite frankly that he had just chanced to be at the right place at the right time.

The first success for one of the *Nachtjäger* came soon afterwards. On the night of 20/21 July *Hauptmann* Werner Streib of *NJG 1* was flying an Me 110C over the Ruhr when he spotted another twin-engine aeroplane that he at first thought was another Me 110. As he approached it, however, he identified it as a British bomber, a conclusion that was confirmed when he closed to 250 yards abeam of the intruder and its tail gunner opened fire at him. Turning right to position himself behind and below the enemy plane, Streib sent a volley of cannon and machine-gun fire into the target and saw flames erupt from the starboard engine, followed by the sight of crewmen bailing out as their plane went down. Both Nos 58 and 78 Squadrons lost Whitleys that night, but none of their crews survived to testify as to which had been Streib's victim.

The first German bombs to fall on London were dropped by mistake on 24 August 1940 but they led to a reprisal raid on Berlin by the RAF the following night, which in turn led Adolf Hitler to order an all-out retaliation against Britain's cities. This shifting of aerial priorities at a time when the *Luftwaffe* was coming tantalizingly close to annihilating the RAF's fighter defences was one of the decisive German blunders of the Battle of Britain. It also led to such heavy bomber losses that after 30 September the Germans resorted exclusively to night bombing. As the Germans had done, the British adapted such fighters as they could to the night interception role, the most successful at first being the Boulton Paul Defiant turret fighter. Better planes were needed, and they would not be long in coming.

At the forefront of British night fighter development was Bristol. Its first such aeroplane was nothing more than a fighter version of the Blenheim Mk I bomber, with a ventral rack of 0.303-inch Browning machine guns installed in place of the bomb bay. Its first mission took the form of a daylight strafing raid when Blenheim IFs of Nos 25 and 601 Squadrons attacked the *Luftwaffe* seaplane base at Borkum on 28 November 1939. Its first use as a night fighter occurred on 21/22 July 1940 when Sergeants Arthur J. Hodgkinson and Bertram E. Dye of No 219 Squadron took off from Redhill and made contact with an unidentified enemy plane west of Church Fenton, which they claimed to have damaged before it slipped away. The team subsequently claimed to have damaged a Junkers Ju 88 near Flamborough Head on August 15.

Given the Blenheim's obsolescence as a high-speed bomber, let alone a fighter, the first confirmed success for the nocturnal Mk IF was remarkably impressive. On the night of 4/5 September 1940 Squadron Leader Michael J. Herrick, a New Zealander assigned to No 25 Squadron, caught and shot down a Heinkel He 111 over Braintree at 12.45 a.m. followed by a Dornier Do 17 over Rendlesham 25 minutes later. The Blenheim IFs had further successes thereafter but it was clear that their run of good fortune could not last.

Bristol was swift to provide a successor in the form of another, even more serendipitous improvisation—a long-range fighter derived from the Beaufort torpedo-bomber that was proposed in October 1938, just days after the first Beaufort flew. The Type 156, later christened Beaufighter, was to have four Hispano 20mm cannon in the fuselage, a foreshortened nose to compensate for larger propellers and the Blenheim's four-man crew reduced to a pilot and a rear observer/navigator. The first production Beaufighter, powered by two 1,400 hp Bristol Hercules III engines driving de Havilland non-feathering, bracket-type airscrews, was not quite as potent as Bristol hoped because the Hercules VI engines and Rotol constant-speed propellers the firm had wanted to use were not available, but it was deemed good enough to warrant a 300-plane contract on 3 July 1939. At that point the 1938 Munich Crisis had awakened Britain to the need to modernize its defences in all forms, and the slow pace at which Westland was developing its Whirlwind twin-engine fighter compelled the RAF to hedge its bets with Bristol's alternative. As it turned out, the Whirlwind ended up having a disappointing career whereas the versatile Beaufighter would serve the RAF exceptionally long and well.

Cleared for RAF service on 26 July 1940, the first four Beaufighters were allotted, one apiece, to Nos 25, 29, 219 and 604 Squadrons on 2 September. Six days later No 600 Squadron received its first machine. Although too late to participate in the Battle of Britain, the 'Beaus' soon got the chance to show their capabilities during the 'Winter Blitz' that the German bombers pursued against British cities after abandoning their all-out air offensive in October 1940.

After the first 50 Beaufighters had been built, the plane's armament was increased by adding six Browning 0.303-inch machine guns to the wings—two port and four starboard—making it the most heavily armed fighter of the war. More significant was the experimental installation of the AI (Airborne Interception) Mk IV radar in an early production Beaufighter Mk I at the Fighter Interception Unit at Ford, followed by the modification of further aircraft from September 1940 onwards.

The first operational sortie by a night-fighting 'Beau' was flown by No 29 Squadron on 17 September. Although the plane's speed and climb were disappointing, crews found the aircraft more manoeuvrable and generally more pleasant to fly at night than their old Blenheims. The early radar proved to have some early developmental problems, however, with ground echoes limiting its range, and the first Beaufighter night fighter pilots claimed to have had more success without the help of the radar than with it.

The first confirmed success for the Beaufighter was scored on the night of 25 October by a machine of No 219 Squadron piloted by Sergeant Hodgkinson. The first radar-assisted victory was achieved by No 604 Squadron on 19/20 November when Flight Lieutenant John Cunningham and his observer, Sergeant J. R. Phillipson, destroyed a Ju 88A-5 of *3. Staffel, Kampfgeschwader 54*, north of Bridge Norton. The team struck again on the night of 23/24 December, shooting down an He 111 belonging to *3. Staffel* of a radar-equipped pathfinder unit, *Kampfgruppe 100*, between Alderney and Cherbourg. It was not until January

1941, however, with the introduction of GCI (Ground Controlled Interception), allowing controllers to plot fighters and their targets simultaneously on a PPI (plan position indicator) and vector the Beaufighters to the vicinity of the enemy, that the night fighters really came into their own. Successes grew until the night of 19/20 May when the *Luftwaffe* mounted its last major raid on London and lost 24 aircraft to RAF night fighters compared with only two to anti-aircraft fire.

The best of the British night fighters evolved from the RAF's most versatile multi-role aircraft, the de Havilland D.H.98 Mosquito. Captain Geoffrey de Havilland's 'Wooden Wonder' was itself a 1938 derivative of his previous Comet racer and Albatross airliner, with the original purpose of building a high-speed bomber constructed of non-strategic material—wood—with a range of 1,500 miles and a bomb load of 1,000 pounds. At first the Air Ministry rejected de Havilland's proposal because he refused to arm his design, relying on speed alone for protection. On 29 December 1939, however, de Havilland was authorized to proceed, and in the course of building his prototype he had the foresight to allow for the accommodation of cameras for photo-reconnaissance duties and four 20mm cannon under the crew floor for a possible fighter variant. Less than eleven months after serious design work had begun on it, the first prototype was flown by Geoffrey de Havilland Jr on 25 November 1940. Not only was its manoeuvrability impressive for a twin-engine aeroplane but, with a speed of 382 mph for the PR Mk I variant, it was the fastest combat plane at that time, and would remain for so the next two and a half years. De Havilland had already been awarded a contract for 50 bombers on 1 March 1940, which was later altered to 20 bombers and 30 fighters. Full-scale production orders, involving manufacture in Britain and Canada, soon followed.

The Germans soon became interested in the new de Havilland, and a German spy, air-dropped near Salisbury Field on 13 May 1941, was caught the following day, just twenty-four hours before the prototype night fighter version, the NF Mk II, made its first flight. The Mosquito NF Mk II had strengthened wing spars to stand up to high-speed manoeuvring, an armament of four 20mm Hispano cannon and four 0.303-inch Browning guns and an AI Mk IV radar with an 'arrowhead' aerial in the nose. Its maximum speed was 370 mph.

The first squadron to be equipped with the night fighting Mosquito was No 157, formed at Debden under the command of Wing Commander Gordon Slade on 13 December 1941 and then moved to Castle Camps, where it received its first T III trainer on 26 January 1942. While the air crews worked up, British bombers had struck the historic city of Lübeck on the night of 28/29 March 1942 and Hitler responded by ordering a series of 'Baedeker' raids, specifically targeting historic or scenic cities such as Exeter and Bath. Amid this atmosphere of terror and increasing civilian casualties, three Mosquito NF Mk IIs of No

157 Squadron, equipped with AI Mk V radar, flew the first operational sorties on 27/28 April, joining nineteen Beaufighters and Spitfires in an attempt to intercept a Baedeker raid on Norwich and the dropping of mines by Ju 88As of *KG 30* off the Norwich coast. Although some radar contacts were made, the Mosquitos failed to accomplish anything, the eyesight of crews being plagued by cannon flash as well as burning from the exhausts and cowlings. De Havilland swiftly responded to the air crews' complaints by installing flash eliminators on the guns and shrouds over the exhausts.

Meanwhile the Baedeker raids continued, with York the target on the night of 28 April. On the following night No 151 Squadron flew its first Mosquito sortie, and a Mosquito of No 157 Squadron stalked a Dornier Do 217 until the Germans spotted it in the moonlight and evaded their pursuer. On 19 May one of No 157 Squadron's planes fell victim to engine failure and crashed at Castle Camps, killing both crewmen. There would be two other accidents in May, but the Mosquitos accomplished nothing until the night of 29/30 May when a plane of No 151 Squadron caught and shot up a Dornier Do 217E-4 during a German raid on Grimsby. The Mosquito was in turn damaged by return fire and its pilot had to fly 140 miles back to the squadron's base at Wittering on one engine. A second No 151 Squadron Mosquito, crewed by Pilot Officer John Wain and Flight Sergeant Thomas S. G. Grieve, damaged another Do 217E-4 from *KG 2*, while Squadron Leader G. Ashfield of No 157 Squadron claimed to have 'probably' downed a Do 217E-4 south of Dover.

Official success continued to elude the Mosquitos until the night 24/25 June when the Germans struck at Nuneaton. One of the aircraft sent up to intercept the raiders was a Mosquito piloted by Wing Commander Irving Stanley Smith, the New Zealand-born leader of No 151 Squadron who had previously scored four victories in Hawker Hurricanes and one while flying a Defiant. At 11.30 he detected an He 111, closed to 300 yards, opened fire and reported seeing it dive away with fuel trailing from its port tanks. His opponent, which was counted only as 'damaged,' was probably an He 111H-6 of *Erprobungs und Lehr Kommando 17* which did indeed limp back to its base in the Netherlands. However, the plane lost its radio operator, *Oberfeldwebel* Paul Wilhelm Krause, who panicked and bailed out when the Mosquito's gunfire set off the bomber's flares; his body was washed ashore at Pakefield on 5 July.

The night was still young for 'Black' Smith. Ten minutes after attacking the Heinkel he was vectored to a Do 217, opened fire at a range of 100 yards and sent the bomber into the sea, where it exploded. The Mosquito had drawn first blood at last, and *II./KG 40* recorded the loss of a Do 217E-4 and its crew. At 11.48 Smith made radar contact with another Do 217E-4, this time a plane from *I./KG 40* flown by *Leutnant* Karl von Manowarda. Closing to 200 yards, the New Zealander fired again and both of the bomber's wings exploded in flames. After closing to fire one more burst Smith saw his second confirmed victory of the night—and his eighth of the war—crash into The Wash.

The team of Wain and Grieve forced an He 111H-6 down in the North Sea on the following night, and when the Germans bombed Norwich on the night of 26/27 June it cost them a Do 217E-4 piloted by *Feldwebel* Hans Schrödel of *3./KG 2*, courtesy of another of No 151 Squadron's Mosquitos.

While the Mosquito NF Mk II was proving its worth in the defensive role, a new Mosquito unit, No 23 Squadron, based at Ford, began flying offensive missions against German air bases in France, using NF Mk IIs with their radar deleted so that it would not fall into enemy hands if one of the planes was brought down. The first of such missions was flown on the night of 5/6 July by Wing Commander Bertie Rex O'Bryen Hoare, who was already credited with one confirmed and one 'probable' victory in the Blenheim IF as well as two enemy planes shot down, four damaged and one probably destroyed on the ground while flying Douglas Havocs. On the following night 'Sammy' Hoare, who boasted a handle-bar moustache that measured 'six inches wing tip to wing tip,' destroyed a Do 217 sixteen miles east of Chartres for the first Moquito night intruder victory. He downed another enemy plane over Orléans on 30/31 July.

From that time on the Mosquito went on to serve as the RAF's premier night fighter throughout the war, with as much success as it enjoyed in the light bombing, pathfinder and reconnaissance roles. One of the plane's many note-worthy proponents was Norwegian ace of aces Svein Heglund, who scored the last three of his seventeen victories in Mosquito Mk 30s of No 85 Squadron and who described just how different the night-fighting environment was when compared to his previous experience as a Spitfire pilot:

> It was like another, fantastic world, with all sorts of lights, flares and fires punctuating the darkness. I saw V-1 jet missiles skimming along the ground, and V-2 rockets on their way to England—I sometimes tried to intercept them, only to see them go up at ever increasing speed into the stratosphere. The pathfinder aircraft dropped markers on bombing targets, in all sorts of colours. During bombing raids, huge fires would cause smoke and clouds to rise 20–30,000 feet into the air—then all would be quiet again. One saw signal rockets being fired to alert German night fighters, tracer bullets during air-to-air encounters—it was all amazing.

The RAF made far more offensive use of night fighters in the intruder role than did the *Luftwaffe*, primarily because of Hitler's preference for the populations of German cities being able to see their attackers going down in flames. By late 1942, however, the growing use of Mosquitos to precede British bombers to the target or to prowl around the peripheries to pick off German night fighters had become a serious menace to the *Luftwaffe's* air defences. The Germans responded with a new generation of specialized night fighters, including a 'wooden wonder' of their own, the Kurt Tank-designed Focke-Wulf Ta 154, which was even christened with the sobriquet *'Moskito'* by its builders. The first prototype flew on 7 July 1943 and 250 were ordered in November, but a series of crashes held up the type's operational debut: it was eventually ascertained that the glue used to bond its wooden components contained too much acid which weakened, rather than strengthened, the joints.

The closest thing to a 'Mosquito-swatter' that the Germans were able to produce in quantity had originally been conceived by Ernst Heinkel AG as a *Zerstörer*, with provision for use as a short- to medium-range bomber or a torpedo-bomber. The design had been rejected by the *Reichluftfahrtministerium*, but as British bombing attacks against German cities increased in late 1941 the RLM asked Heinkel to resurrect his design, this time as a night fighter. Work began at Rostock in January 1942 but just as the drawings were completed they were destroyed in a series of RAF strikes during March and April. Heinkel transferred their development office to Vienna-Schwechat and literally went back to the drawing board. The result of that interrupted effort, the first He 219 V1 *Uhu* (Owl) did not fly until 15 November 1942. Powered by two 1,750 hp Daimler-Benz DB603A engines, the prototype showed excellent flying qualities from the outset, and in April 1943 four of Heinkel's factories were building the first of 300 He 219A-0s that had been ordered.

By that time concern over the Mosquito had reached the highest levels of the Nazi government, causing an urgent demand for a *Moskito-Jäger* (Mosquito hunter). That in turn threatened the He 219's future, as Kurt Tank offered his economically attractive Ta 154 as the ideal solution while Erhard Milch, resolutely opposed to the idea of diluting German industrial efforts on the production of specialized aircraft, advocated a night fighter version of the Junkers Ju 188. Sensing that it would take some tangible proof to save his fighter from cancellation, Ernst Heinkel rushed several prototypes, armed with a battery of four 30mm MK 108 (in the He 219A-0/R1) or MK 103 cannon (in the He 219A-0/R2) housed in a ventral fuselage tray, as well as two MG 151 machine guns in the wing roots, to *1./NJG 1*'s base at Venlo in the Netherlands. There he urged *Major* Werner Streib, by then commander of the wing's *Gruppe Stab* (Group Staff), to put the new fighters to the test—in combat.

The opportunity soon arose. On the night of 11 June 1943 RAF Bomber Command launched a 'maximum effort' of 693 planes to Düsseldorf with Mosquito pathfinders marking the target. Aided by a well-established *Himmelbett* GCI system composed of a network of *Freya*, *Wurzburg* and *Giant Wurzburg* radar stations, Streib took off in the He 219 V9 attached to *Stab/NJG 1* and was guided to multiple targets by his *Bordfunker* (radio operator), *Unteroffizier* Fischer. Handling his untried aeroplane with consummate skill, Streib wrought havoc among the bombers, shooting down a remarkable total of five, of which two were positively identified as a Handley Page Halifax Mk IIs of No 78 Squadron and an Avro Lancaster Mk II of No 115 Squadron. *NJG 1*'s Me 110s took a grisly toll on the bombers as well.

As he returned to Venlo and entered his final landing approach, Streib tried to lower his flaps but the lever failed to lock and the flaps retracted again. At that critical moment the He 219 went out of control and the starboard engine seized. The plane came down hard on the runway, at which point the starboard engine broke away from the wing and sliced into the cockpit section, breaking the plane's back. Streib and Fischer, still strapped to their seats, skidded down the runway behind the still-intact nosewheel until they finally came to a stop about 150 feet ahead of their wrecked plane. To the amazement of both men, neither had been hurt in this spectacularly disastrous finale to a spectacularly successful combat debut.

Milch conceded that Streib had put on an impressive show but added that he was good enough a pilot to have done the same with any other night fighter. In spite of Streib's crash landing, however, *NJG 1* crews flew further combat missions in the remaining He 219s and claimed twenty more victories over the next ten days. RLM officials continued to baulk at accepting the He 219, expressing misgivings about its tricycle landing gear and the close proximity of its propellers to the cockpit, although Ernst Heinkel addressed the latter complaint by installing the first ejection seat system in the plane. Production and development of the *Uhu* proceeded in the face of almost constant opposition. Virtually all of the 268 He 219s built were committed to the defence of the Reich, along with all twenty pre-production aircraft, and they proved to be outstanding whenever they got the chance to fight. The vast majority of Germany's night fighter force, however, consisted of improved versions of established designs converted to the role, mainly the Me 110G and Ju 88G. Prodigious feats were performed in them, Streib bringing his personal tally up to 68 before being killed on 21 January 1944. Germany would also produce the highest-scoring night fighter pilot in history, Heinz-Wolfgang Schnaufer, who scored his 121 victories in Me 110s. Other types were pressed into nocturnal service, such as the Do 217N and the most effective *Moskito-Jäger* of all, the Messerschmitt Me 262 jet. Belatedly committed to battle on 17 December 1944 with *10./NJG 11* under the command of *Oberleutnant* Kurt Welter, 25 Me 262A-1as and seven Me 262B-1a/U1 two-seaters equipped with *Neptun* radar managed to bring down a total of 48 Mosquitos by 7 May 1945. By then, however, there was no *Reich* left to defend.

Japan, like the other powers, adapted several of her aircraft to night fighting tasks as necessity dictated, but the career of her most successful night fighter represented a double change in role. When the Nakajima J1N *Gekko* (Moonlight) was originally designed for the Imperial Japanese Navy in 1938 it was to have been a twin-engine, long-range escort fighter like the Messerschmitt Me 110. Powered by twin 1,130 hp Nakajima NK1F Sakae 21 radial engines which gave it a speed of 329 mph at 19,685 feet and fitted with long, fabric-covered ailerons and slotted flaps, the J1N1 was exceptionally nimble—it was even able to hold its own in a dogfight with a Mitsubishi A6M2 Zero—but the Navy became fixated over the practicality of the two dorsal barbettes, each housing a 7.7mm machine gun, which were to be remotely controlled by the navigator. By 1941 the single-engine Zero had proved itself more than adequate for the fighter escort role, and by the time the *Gekko*'s protracted development reached fruition in July 1942 the Navy had decided to use a three-seat version, the J1N1-C, with its operational ceiling of 33,795 feet, as a high-altitude reconnaissance plane instead.

At least two J1N1-Cs were on strength with the 251st *Kokutai* at Rabaul in the spring of 1943 when the group's executive officer, Commander Yasuna Kozono, came up with an idea. At that time Boeing B-17s of the US Fifth Air Force were mounting night bombing attacks on Japanese bases throughout the Solomon Islands. The raids were more of a sleep-disrupting nuisance than a major threat, but Japanese morale was affected by the fact that nothing could be done to stop them. Kozono proposed to arm the *Gekko* with upward and downward-firing 20mm cannon mounted at an oblique angle behind the pilot so that the gun flashes would not affect his night vision. Navy General Headquarters dismissed his idea as absurd but Kozono went all the way to Japan to argue his case and eventually he persuaded them to modify two *Gekko*s in accordance with his concept. After being tested at Toyohashi the two J1N1-C-kais, as they were designated, arrived at Rabaul and were assigned to the 251st *Kokutai* on 10 May. The J1N1-C-kai had no radar so its crew had to depend on searchlights or the moon to help locate the target. The pilot and observer were given injections to aid their night vision just before a mission, but the substance that was administered has never been identified.

The night-fighting *Gekko*'s first test came when B-17s of the 64th Squadron, 43rd Bomb Group, left their base at Port Moresby, New Guinea, just after midnight on 21 May 1943 and headed for Rabaul. Japanese coastwatchers alerted Rabaul of the bombers' approach and both J1N1-C-kais commenced hunting. At 3.37 a.m. 23-year-old Chief Petty Officer Shigetoshi Kudo and his observer, Lieutenant (jg) Akira Sugawara, spotted a B-17E that was caught in a searchlight. Kudo slipped underneath the unsuspecting bomber and pumped shells into its underside. The plane crashed in St George's Channel, killing Major Paul Williams and all but one of his crew. The sole survivor, Master Sergeant Gordon Manuel, later reported: 'I heard one dull explosion, then a series of smaller ones. The ship wrenched to the left and shuddered . . .'

The night was still young and at 4.08 Kudo and Sugawara located another B-17 silhouetted in the thirteen-day-old moon, though they were unable to get into a good firing position before the aircraft escaped. Twenty minutes later they encountered another B-17E of the 64th Squadron and, after Kudo fired his single gun once more, that plane too descended in flames. He had expended 178 rounds in the course of the night's actions.

Kozono's theories had been proved in spectacular style, although the Americans at first attributed the loss of the two bombers to anti-aircraft fire or other operational causes. They should have had cause for concern after 5 June, however, when two Consolidated B-24s fell victim to another of the 251st *Kokutai*'s *Gekko*s, crewed by CPO Satoshi Ono and Lieutenant (jg) Kisaku Hamano. On 10 June Ono and Hamano claimed another two B-17s, of which one—again from the 64th Bomb Squadron—was subsequently confirmed.

The team of Kudo and Sugawara scored again on 11 and 13 June, the second victim being Lieutenant John Woodward's B-17E *Georgia Peach* of the 65th Squadron, 43rd Bomb Group, caught in the searchlights and dispatched at 3.14 a.m. to crash at Ulamona, New Britain. Of the two crewmen who got out, only one, bombardier Lieutenant Jack Wisener, survived his captivity; the navigator, Lieutenant Philip Bek, was killed by his captors.

Kudo was credited with another double victory on the night of the 15th and scored his seventh kill on 26 June when B-17E *Naughty But Nice* of the 65th Bomb Squadron was caught in the searchlights during an attack on Vunakanau airfield. Rabaul's anti-aircraft fire, though dangerous by day, had been notoriously inaccurate at night so the B-17's crew were little concerned until their plane was suddenly raked by 20mm fire from a J1N1-C-kai crewed by Kudo and Michitaro Ichikawa. Two engines caught fire and the Fortress went into a spin. Its navigator, First Lieutenant Jose L. Holguin, was wounded in the chin and left leg but he was trying to help a crewman strap on a parachute when he was sucked out of an open escape hatch. Battered by a tree as he parachuted down, 'Joe' Holguin suffered a broken back but he survived 27 days in the jungle until natives carried him to their village. He was subsequently turned over to the 6th *Kempei Tai* (Japan's notorious military police), but survived the war in their prisoner of war camp as well. The rest of *Naughty But Nice*'s crew were killed. Kudo and Sugawara finished out the month with a B-17 on the 30th.

In early July the *Gekko*s were moved up to Balale airfield in response to American attacks in the Buin area. The redoubtable team of Kudo and Sugawara were among them and on 7 July they scored their eighth and final night victory when they downed a Lockheed Hudson over Buin airfield. A month later the 'King of the Night,' as Kudo had come to be called, was awarded a ceremonial sword by Rear-Admiral Ninichi Kusaka, commander of Rabaul's 11th Air Fleet, for his distinguished service. Although badly injured in a crash in May 1945, Kudo survived the war with a total of nine victories but he died in 1960 of complications resulting from his wartime injury. Satoru Ono would also survive the war with the commissioned rank of Lieutenant Junior Grade and a total of eight enemy planes to his credit.

Kudo's success persuaded the Japanese to give the *Gekko* a new lease of life exactly as the Germans had with their Me 110—by giving full priority to the production of a night fighter version, with a smoother cabin outline and radar in the nose, as the J1N1-S. Now truly worthy of its 'moonlight' sobriquet—though the Allies knew it by the code-name 'Irving'—the J1N1-S represented the majority of the 477 *Gekko*s produced and was fairly successful until mid-1944, when the Boeing B-29 Superfortress outperformed it in speed and altitude.

A latecomer in dealing with the threat of night attack, the United States got its first convincing 'wake-up call' during the Guadalcanal campaign when Japanese aircraft attacked the US Marines at Henderson Field at night with everything from sleep-depriving nuisance raids by Mitsubishi F1M2s (nicknamed 'Washing Machine Charlies' by the Marines because of the sound of their engines) to more serious attacks by Mitsubishi G4M1 'Betty' medium bombers. The most spectacular Japanese success of the campaign occurred near Rennell Island on the night of 30 January 1943 when flare-equipped G4M1s, soon to be dubbed 'Tojo the Lamp-Lighter' by their opponents, illuminated the heavy cruiser *Chicago*, which was then torpedoed by the bombers and finished off by more G4M1s the following day.

As with the other warring powers, the United States Army Air Forces responded by converting a variety of day fighter and bomber types to the night fighter role, most notably the Douglas A-20 Havoc (which in its radar-equipped night fighter guise was known as the P-70) and the Lockheed P-38M Lightning. In November 1943 the US Navy enjoyed some success by using a radar-equipped Grumman TBF-1C Avenger to vector two F6F-3 Hellcats to their targets, but it would do better in the following year by installing a radar in one of the Hellcat's own wings, as the Grumman F6F-5N.

Even while such improvisations tided over the American air bases and carriers, a new, more specialized aeroplane was in the works—in fact, the only night fighter of World War II designed from the outset as such to achieve production status. In 1944 the USAAF was ready to unleash the Northrop P-61A Black Widow.

During the autumn of 1940 US Army observers in Britain had taken note of the nocturnal missions already being carried out by the RAF and the *Luftwaffe*. As a result, on 21 October 1940 the Army Air Corps Material Command presented John K. Northrop with a requirement for a specialized night fighter. Two weeks later, on 5 November, he and his assistant, Walter J. Cerny, were presenting their proposal at Wright Field, Ohio. After undergoing some revisions the design was approved for development on 30 January 1941, and on 26 May 1942 Vance Breese took the XP-61 prototype up for its first test flight.

Jack Northrop's creation was an all-metal, twin-boom, twin-tail monoplane, 66 feet 0¾ inches in wingspan and 49 feet 7 inches long. With an empty weight of 24,000 pounds and a maximum loaded weight of 32,400 pounds, it was three times heavier than a P-51 and almost twice as heavy as a P-47. As with other large American fighters, all that weight was compensated for by the engines—two 18-cylinder Pratt & Whitney R-2800-65 twin-row, air-cooled radials generating more than 2,000 hp each. Double-slotted flaps reached along almost the full span of the wings, which also featured small ailerons and lateral-control spoilers, an overall arrangement that was years ahead of its time and endowed the big plane with astonishing agility. With a range of 1,000 miles it could cover a wide area, and with a maximum speed of 366 mph at 20,000 feet it could fly as fast as many single-engine fighters.

The first of thirteen pre-production YP-61s flew on 6 August 1943 and provided much critical data that would go into the P-61A, which entered service in March 1944. Early Widows had four 20mm cannon housed in a ventral fairing and a dorsal barbette with four 0.50-calibre machine guns, though buffeting problems encountered when elevating or rotating the latter resulted in the barbettes being removed after the first 37 P-61A-1s had left the Northrop assembly line in October 1943. Equally important to the plane's success was the new SCR-720 AI radar housed in the nose of the fuselage nacelle.

In March 1944 personnel of the 422nd Night Fighter Squadron (NFS) arrived at Scorton, England, and began training in their new P-61A-5s and A-10s, to be joined in June by the 425th NFS. At about the same time Widows arrived in the Pacific to replace P-70s in the 6th NFS on 1 May and those of the 419th NFS two days later.

As much as the European P-61 crews were dying to match wits with the *Luftwaffe*'s best, it would be in the Central Pacific that the Black Widow would bite first. Like most P-61 pilots, Second Lieutenant Dale F. Haberman had undergone his initial training in the new type with the 481sth Night Fighter Operational Training Group at Orlando Field, Florida, before being assigned in March 1944 to the 6th NFS, Seventh Air Force, at John Rogers Airport,

Oahu, in the Hawaiian Islands. From there Haberman and eight other pilots and their ROs (Radar Operators) were detached from the squadron and sent to Isley Field on the newly taken island of Saipan, arriving on 21 June.

Flying with Flight Officer Raymond P. Mooney as his RO in a plane christened *Moonhappy*, Haberman claimed a 'probable' about a week before scoring his—and the Black Widow's—first confirmed victory. On 30 June Haberman and Mooney took off to investigate an unidentified plane, which they located about 50 miles east of Saipan. Haberman recalled:

> We were vectored on the bogey at 7,000 feet, with Mooney insisting that we had two targets in formation on our scope. We chased them from 7,000 to 22,000 over a 25-minute time period, never quite reaching their altitude. I discovered later that I had forgotten the radio, leading in on 'Transmit', so the whole intercept was broadcast over the entire Saipan area.
>
> I finally got a visual on the two bogeys. A 'Betty' with a Zero on her right wing were turning toward the island and at a much higher altitude than we were. I pulled the 'Widow' up on her tail and nailed the 'Betty' with a five-second burst. The 'Betty' burst into flame behind the left engine. The flame trailed for some time, then the aircraft exploded and was seen crashing into the ground.

Haberman then performed a high-speed stalling turn and went into a power dive with the Zero in pursuit. Although the P-61 reached 475 mph the Japanese fighter closed in on its tail. Glancing back, Mooney yelled to Haberman: 'Twist port to starboard! Let's get the hell out of here! The wingman is right there!' Haberman saw tracers flash by his plane and wondered if his wings would come off, but the Black Widow held together and he managed to lose the Zero in a cloud.

Pulling out at 1,500 feet, Haberman returned to Saipan only to be fired on by his own troops, who were not familiar with the new aeroplane. After having to dodge his own flak at tree-top level Haberman finally brought *Moonhappy* down safely on Isley Field. He would later add two more to his score and his colleagues did yeoman service in protecting the vital Boeing B-29 air bases of Saipan, Guam and Tinian from further nocturnal attacks by the Japanese.

Back in England the P-61 aircrews became livid with rage to learn that they were being barred from operations because their aircraft had been declared inferior to the Mosquito. The 422nd NFS demanded a fly-off, and when the RAF granted its request First Lieutenant Donald J. Doyle went up to defend the Widow's honour against an equally determined RAF champion on 7 July. The result was that the P-61 outran, outclimbed and out-turned the Mosquito at 5,000, 10,000 and 20,000 feet. Besides that convincing show, the appearance of growing numbers of V-1 pulse-jet powered guided bombs over Britain since mid-June led to the lifting of the ban on P-61 operations. The Widow crews' first job would be to join the RAF fighters in 'Anti-Diver' missions against Hitler's latest 'vengeance weapon'.

On the night of 14/15 July Second Lieutenant Herman E. Ernst, with Flight Officer Edward H. Kopsel as his RO, was cruising over the Channel at an altitude of 7,500 feet when the two men spotted a V-1 at 2,000 feet. Ernst dived after the 'diver', which he noted was racing along towards England at 340 mph. He recalled:

> All of a sudden there was a loud boom and a tremendous amount of noise in the cockpit. Kopsel was screaming into the intercom, but I could not understand a word. My first thought was that a German nightfighter had gotten behind us and shot us down . . . and on our very first mission!

Ernst's plane was still responding to the controls, so he brought it back to his base at Ford, to discover that the plexiglass tail cone had disintegrated due to the air pressure. A flat piece of plexiglass was installed in its place and the following night Ernst and Kopsel went up again. Again they encountered a V-1, and again Ernst dived after it. 'This time we closed the gap and fired several 20mm rounds,' he reported. 'They found their mark all over the propulsion unit and the bomb lost power, nosed over and went into the sea.'

The 422nd NFS had scored the first victory for the P-61 in Europe—over a pilotless flying robot. The Black Widows would have ample opportunity to strike against *Luftwaffe* aircraft in the months to come, however. In spite of—or perhaps because of—its late arrival in the night fighting arena, the Black Widow's career was as distinguished as it was brief. Sixteen squadrons operated P-61s on all fronts in which the USAAF operated and at least three pilots—one in the Pacific, two in Europe—would 'make ace' in Black Widows. Herman Ernst would be one of them, adding three Ju 87s, a Ju 188 and an Me 110 to his score by May 1945.

Chapter 18

Odds and Ends

Improvisations and Developmental Dead-Ends, 1940–1945

War induces combatants to seek advantages by any means possible. With regard to World War II aircraft, the quest for an 'edge' encompassed numerous aspects, such as size, bomb capacity, speed, rate of climb, altitude, manoeuvrability and potency of armament. Even though the fundamental configurations of aircraft had been established by the end of World War I, the pursuit of an advantage in the air brought a spate of new variations into the sky. For every successful innovation, such as the radar-equipped all-weather fighter, there were interesting failures, such as the turret fighter and the lightweight interceptor. And for every evolved or carefully conceived design there was a wartime improvisation that occasionally worked—though not always as originally intended.

The British should have known better than to develop the turret fighter. The two-seat fighter from which it evolved, the Bristol F.2B of 1917, had achieved its phenomenal success by being flown as a single-seater with a sting in the tail rather than relying primarily on the rear gunner's weapon. The F.2B's successor in 1931, the Hawker Demon, differed little from it in armament but the problems encountered by the gunner in handling a 0.303-inch gun in the open cockpit of an aeroplane flying at nearly twice the Bristol's speed led the Air Ministry to seek a more advanced weapons system.

One solution to the problem was offered by Boulton Paul Aircraft Ltd, which had been subcontracted to build Demons for the RAF and which had also obtained the rights to produce an electro-hydraulically operated turret invented by French engineer J. B. A. de Boysson, capable of traversing 360 degrees and incorporating either a 20mm cannon or four 0.303-inch machine guns. After seeing the turret demonstrated in the nose of a Boulton Paul Overstrand bomber, the Air Ministry issued a specification for a fighter armed with four machine guns in the de Boysson turret and capable of flying as fast as the Hawker Hurricane fighter. Since Hurricanes were expected to protect the turret fighter from enemy fighters while it attacked enemy bombers from the side or below, the specification limited armament to the turret. Such a mea-

263

sure saved weight but in essence it made the pilot nothing more than a chauf-feur for his gunner—hardly a role that went over well with aggressive fighter pilots.

Designed by J. D. North, the Boulton Paul Defiant was a commendably clean and compact aeroplane powered by the same 1,030 hp Rolls-Royce Merlin III engine as that used in the Hurricane and the Spitfire. A retractable fairing helped to smooth the airflow behind the rear turret when it was not in use, and in spite of the drag that the turret still imposed on it—as well as a gross weight of 8,600 pounds compared to the Hurricane's 6,218—the Defiant managed a maximum speed of 302 mph at 16,500 feet compared to the Hurricane's 316. It took the Defiant 11.4 minutes to climb to that altitude, however, whereas the Hurricane could reach it in only 6½ minutes. First flown on 11 August 1937, the Defiant was approved for production, but because Boulton Paul were then relocating from Norwich to a new plant at Wolverhampton the first operational Defiants were not deployed with No 264 Squadron until December 1939. When the Germans invaded the Low Countries on 10 May 1940 the unit moved from its training base at Martlesham Heath to Duxford; from there 'A' Flight flew to Horsham St Faith and 'B' Flight returned to Martlesham where it would oper-ate alongside the Spitfires of No 66 Squadron.

The Defiants did their intended job fairly well in their first combat. On 12 May Flight Lieutenant Nicholas G. Cooke led 'A' Flight on a patrol off the Dutch coast accompanied by six Spitfires of No 66 Squadron. They soon encountered enemy aircraft and the Defiants drew first blood five miles south of The Hague as a Junkers Ju 88A fell victim to No 264's commander, Squadron Leader Philip A. Hunter, and his gunner, Sergeant F. H. King, while a second was claimed by the team of Squadron Leader Michael H. Young and Leading Aircraftsman S. B. Johnson. Cooke added a third victory to the squadron's opening tally when he caught an He 111 six miles south of The Hague and his gunner, Corporal Albert Lippett, shot it down.

On the following morning six Defiants of 'B' Flight, accompanied by six Spitfires of No 66 Squadron's 'A' Flight, were flying another sweep over the Dutch coast when they spotted Junkers Ju 87Bs dive-bombing a railway line and attacked. Between them the British claimed ten of the Stukas before themselves coming under attack by Messerschmitt Me 109Es of *5. Staffel, Jagdgeschwader 26*. Flight Lieutenant Kenneth McLeod Gillies, a Spitfire pilot who had shot down a Stuka east of Rotterdam, damaged an Me 109 before No 66 Squadron disengaged. One Spitfire fell victim to *Leutnant* Hans Krug but its pilot managed to force-land his damaged plane in Belgium.

The fight had a much grimmer outcome for No 264 Squadron. In their first encounter with enemy fighters the six Defiant crews found themselves unable to evade the Me 109Es and five were shot down in short order, although only one German, *Feldwebel* Erwin Stolz, initially identified his adversary as a Defiant; the other victors, *Leutnant* Eckardt Roch (who claimed three), *Leutnant* Krug, *Unteroffizier* Hans Wemhöhner and *Feldwebel* Wilhelm Meyer, all claimed Spitfires before subsequently learning the true identity of their adversaries. The sole Defiant crew that returned claimed that five German fighters went down in the course of the massacre and they were duly credited to the squadron.

In actuality the Defiants had managed to shoot down only one of their assailants, who—contrary to popular misconception—already knew what he was up against and fell victim to overconfidence rather than from mistaking the turret fighter for a single-seater. As *Leutnant* Karl Borris himself recorded it in his diary:

> Enemy contact with a mixed British formation . . . bank toward a Defiant, I can clearly see the four machine guns in its turret firing; however, I do not think they can track me in a dogfight. I approach closer, and open fire at about seventy metres' range. At this moment, something hits my aircraft, hard. I immediately pull up into the clouds and examine the damage. The left side of my instrument panel is shot through; a round had penetrated the Revi [reflex gunsight] and a fuel line has obviously been hit—the cockpit is swimming in gasoline. The engine coughs and quits, starved of fuel. I push a wing over and drop from the clouds. Unbuckle, canopy off, out!

Borris parachuted on to a dyke wall near the mouth of the Rhine and made his way back to *5./JG 26* four days later. He would survive the war with 43 victories.

For the next ten days No 264 Squadron refrained from operations but on 23 May its Defiants joined in the RAF's desperate effort to provide air cover for the evacuation of Allied troops from Dunkirk. By the end of the month the squadron had claimed 48 victories—27 on 29 May alone—but lost nine planes, including that of Cooke and Lippett, killed on the 31st. Occasionally, the Defiant's superficial resemblance to the Hurricane did mislead German fighters into attacking them from the rear, with sometimes fatal results for the latter. Soon the Germans learned to distinguish between the Defiant and its single-seat stablemates, however, with results that spoke for themselves. A second Defiant unit, No 141 Squadron, had a disastrous combat debut on 28 June when nine of its planes tangled with Me 109Es and lost seven while claiming only four victories. On 19 July nine more Defiants of No 141 Squadron encountered Me 109Es of *JG 51* and again lost seven planes, while one of the two surviving crews, Flight Lieutenant Hugh N. Tamblin and Sergeant S. W. H. Powell, claimed one of the enemy in return. In August the Defiant units' air bases were moved farther north, but the RAF's need for anything that could fly and fight at that time kept them engaged—and suffering mounting losses. By late 1940 the Defiant Mk Is were being relegated to the night fighting role and a radar-equipped version, the Defiant Mk II, had been introduced. As such they did well, being in fact the most successful night fighters of 1941 until sufficient numbers of Bristol Beaufighters and de Havailland Mosquitos became available for them to be phased out of first-line service.

Another concept that persisted throughout World War II was that of the lightweight interceptor, inspired by the matter of mass production amid the exigencies of war. The lightweight fighters' exact roles varied as much as did their builders' approaches to achieving them, but they all sought to wring the highest possible performance from the smallest, lightest possible airframe, built using the greatest amount of easily available materials (usually wood) in lieu of strategic materials (such as aluminium). Another thing that most of them held in common was failure. Of the many lightweight interceptors created just before or during the war only three attained production status, and only one could truly be called successful.

During the mid-1930s the *Service Technique de l'Aéronautique* of the French *Armée de l'Air* laid down a specification for a lightweight interceptor that was influenced by the monoplanes which were then attracting much publicity in speed competitions. The chosen design, the Caudron C.710, was designed by Marcel Riffard and based on his sleek C.460 which between 1933 and 1936 had been outperforming larger, more powerful aircraft in international competitions. Like the racing plane, Riffard's C.710 fighter was of wooden, stressed-skin construction and was characterized by a long, slim fuselage. Its powerplant was a 500 hp Renault 12R 01 12-cylinder, inverted-vee, air-cooled engine. The first prototype had fixed, spatted landing gear and oval-shaped vertical tail surfaces when it first flew on 18 July 1937 and later carried two wing-mounted, drum-fed 20mm Hispano-Suiza HS-9 cannon. The second prototype, C.710-02, featured more angular vertical tail surfaces and the C.713 introduced retractable landing gear. A third version, the C.714, first flew on 6 July 1938 and differed from the C.713 primarily in its armament, the cannon being replaced by four 7.5mm MAC M39 machine guns housed in two underwing trays.

After some final modifications the C.714, also known as the *Cyclone*, was ordered into production on 5 November. The definitive C.714 featured an improved 12R 03 engine, which had a carburettor that allowed negative-g manoeuvres. It had a maximum speed of 286 mph at 16,450 feet and climbed to 13,125 feet in 9 minutes 40 seconds.

The original production order was for twenty C.714s with an option for a further 180, but once the fighter entered service the *Armée de l'Air* judged it to be unsuitable for combat. Six were sent to Finland but arrived too late to take part in the Winter War and, desperate though the Finns were for any combat aircraft, were never used in battle. The other *Cyclone*s were assigned to two train-ing squadrons at Lyon-Bron made up of expatriot Polish pilots. By 2 June a total of 39 C.714s had been delivered to the Poles, who flew them operationally as *Groupe de Chasse I/145*, also known as the *1ère Groupe Polonaise de Varsovie*, under the joint command of Major Józef Kepinski and his French advisor *Commandant* Lionel A. de Marmier, a six-victory World War I ace.

For all the *Cyclone*'s racy looks the Poles soon became disenchanted with their new mount. It required a long take-off and landing run; the landing gear release often jammed; the variable-pitch propeller mechanism was prone to failure; and the rate of climb was slow, as was the aileron response. Worst of all was the 12R 03 engine, which had trouble starting, was plagued by a weak crankshaft, had a tendency to overheat and suffered from fuel and oil leaks. *Sous-Lieutenant* Witold Dobrzynski was killed in a crash on 19 May and three other Caudrons were written off in landing accidents on 25 May. After inspecting *GC.I/145* on 25 May, Air Minister Guy le Chambre considered grounding the interceptors. Kepinski chose to keep them in spite of their faults, however. His men wanted to fight, and with the German offensive in the West under way they had little choice but to make do with the fighters they had until their intended replace-ments, Bloch M.B.152s, became available.

On 2 June *GC.I/145*'s *Cyclone*s flew from Villacoublay to the former RAF air-field at La Maison Blanche at Dreux. Combat was joined on 3 June when *Lieu-tenant* Tadeusz Czerwinski and *Sous-Lieutenant* Aleksy Zukowski dived on three He 111s and shot down two, though neither of their claims was confirmed. The unit carried out further patrols but its next fight did not occur until 8 June when a flight led by *Capitaine* Antoni Wczelik engaged at least fifteen Messer-schmitt Me 110Cs over Rouen. One Caudron was damaged but the French confirmed the destruction of two Me 110s by Czerwinski, one each by Wzelik and Zukowski and one shared between *Sous-Lieutenant* Jerzy Godlewski and *Caporal* Piotr Zaniewski. Kepinski and *Sous-Lieutenant* Czeslaw Glówczynski, who was already credited with 3½ enemy planes during the German invasion of Poland, scored 'probable' victories over another two Me 110s.

Perhaps inevitably, *GC.I/145*'s luck took a turn for the worse the next day when seventeen *Cyclone*s encountered 25 Dornier Do 17s escorted by twenty Me 109Es. Malfunctioning radios prevented the C.714 pilots from making a co-ordinated attack, and while Wczelik's flight hurled itself at the bomber forma-tion other Poles found themselves engaged in individual duels with the German fighters. 'Czesiek' Glówczynski got on a Messerschmitt's tail and hung on until he shot the aircraft down. Another Me 109 got on Glówczynski's tail and put a burst into his fuselage before *Sous-Lieutenant* Jerzy Czerniak, who had promised to guard his friend's rear, fired into the German fighter's cockpit and saw the aircraft crash in a farmyard south of Andelys. Glówczynski got a 'probable' credit for a second Me 109 and, after landing for hasty repairs, flew a further sortie that afternoon and probably downed another Do 17 (he would add one more German to his score on 30 December 1941 as a Spitfire pilot in the RAF). *Sergent* Mieczyslaw Parafinski was credited with another Me 109 in the 9 June mêlée, while Wczelik, *Lieutenant* Julian Kowalski and *Sergent* Antoni Markiewicz shared in the destruction of another of the bombers. *Lieutenant* Jan Obuchowski, *Sous-Lieutenant* Lech Lachowski-Czechowicz and *Caporal* Edward Uchto were killed, however, and Kowalski was wounded in the arm although he managed to land his damaged plane at Bernay. In addition the riddled Caudrons of Major Kepinski and *Sous-Lieutenants* Godlewski and Bronislaw Skibinski crash-landed in the Normandy countryside, Czerniak crash-landed his shot-up plane at Dreux and most of the other C.714s returned in variously damaged states.

Twelve of the group's thirteen remaining C.714s were operational as they attacked fifteen Do 17s and twelve Me 109s over Étampes on 10 June. The Poles' radios failed again as de Marmier led them in a head-on attack against the bombers. One Dornier fell to Czerniak and Zukowski downed a second, while *Capitaine* Piotr Laguna accounted for an Me 109 over Henonville following a long pursuit. Kepinski was wounded by Me 109s but in spite of a considerable loss of blood he managed to make a wheels-up landing in a field. *Capitaine* Juliusz Frey, *Lieutenant* Waclaw Wilczewski and *Lieutenant* Zdislaw Zadrozinski were also compelled to force-land their shot-up planes.

Kepinski's executive officer, *Capitaine* Laguna, took command of what remained of *GC.I/145* but there was little left to take charge of. On 11 June French technicians removed the instruments from eleven of the group's defective Caudrons and then burned the aircraft. The remaining twelve *Cyclones* were withdrawn to Sermaize, whence eight of *GC.I/145*'s pilots were assigned to *GC.I/1* and eight to *GC.I/8*, both of which were equipped with M.B.152s. The Poles continued to fly missions until 18 June, when they learned of France's capitulation. Released from French service, they departed by ship from La Rochelle on the 20th to carry on their fight in Britain. Using hit-and-run tactics to make the most of their faulty fighters, the aggressive Poles of *GC.I/145* had managed to shoot down twelve German aircraft and probably downed two others in the course of the Caudron C.714's brief fighting career.

The United States produced two lightweight fighters during World War II. One, the Bell XP-77, was not accepted for production. The other, the Curtiss-Wright CW-21, was—but not by the Americans. In the 1920s the Curtiss Wright Company established an independent division in St Louis, Missouri, under Vice-President of Engineering George Page. One of its early products was an all-metal, two-seat monoplane, the CW-19L, small quantities of which were sold to China and Cuba in 1937 as the A-19R military trainer. Although criticized for vicious stalling characteristics and a tendency to ground-loop, the CW-19 had an outstanding rate of climb—1,890 feet per minute and 23,000 feet in fifteen minutes with an 820 hp Wright engine. That capability inspired Page to design a lightweight interceptor. His specialized concept, which completely ignored dogfighting or tactical capabilities, ran counter to what the US Army Air Corps was looking for in a fighter but he proceeded with the CW-21's development with an eye on foreign customers.

Begun in 1938 under chief engineer Willis Wells, the CW-21 used a lot of CW-19 components but was trimmed down and strengthened. The landing gear retracted into two clamshell-shaped fairings under the wing. Its engine was a Wright Cyclone R-1820-G5 radial with a take-off rating of 1,000 hp. The original intended armament of four 0.30-calibre machine guns firing from inside the engine cowling was changed to two 0.50-calibre guns, effective beyond the range of a bomber's 0.30-calibre defences.

Using an Alclad semi-monocoque fuselage devoid of armour or fuel tank protection, the CW-21 weighed only 3,050 pounds empty and climbed at the phenomenal rate of 4,800 feet per minute, leading Curtiss-Wright to tout it as the 'mile-a-minute interceptor'. Its first flight was on 22 September 1938 with Ned Warren at the controls.

The first logical customer was China, where Curtiss-Wright was a shareholder in the Central Aircraft Manufacturing Company (CAMCO) at Nanking. On 24 January 1939 the first CW-21 prototype arrived by ship in Rangoon, Burma, then made its way up the Irrawaddy river by barge and finally by truck to Loiwing, where CAMCO had moved its facilities following the fall of Nanking to the Japanese in December 1938. Painted with blue and white Chinese tail stripes and test-flown by Curtiss Wright test pilot Robert Fausel in March, the plane proved to be surprisingly nimble as well as a fast climber: in a comparative dogfight with a Polikarpov I-152 Fausel managed to get on the biplane fighter's tail by means of a steep climb, followed by a wing-over. The Chinese were impressed but had reservations about the plane's $70,000 price tag and were concerned that it might be too 'hot' for the average Chinese pilot to handle. They also requested that two 0.30-calibre machine guns be added to the existing armament, along with provision for belly tanks and the replacement of the wrap-around Pyrolin plastic windshield, which yellowed on exposure to weather, with a three-piece armoured glass assembly, although that would reduce speed by an estimated four per cent.

While contract negotiations dragged on Fausel flew a patrol with a Chinese I-152 squadron on 29 March. When Japanese bombers attacked Chunking on 2 April Fausel took off just as the first bombs exploded and two minutes later he attacked a formation of Italian-built Fiat B.R.20s at 10,000 feet. On his third burst Fausel's machine guns jammed in the 'on' position until they ran out of ammunition but he saw one of the bombers smoking and later learned that it had belly-landed in Chinese territory, where its crew were taken prisoner.

Turned over to the Chinese at Kwang Yong Pa, the demonstrator aircraft is believed to have crashed in June 1939, but three more CW-21s, with increased armament and auxiliary fuel tanks as requested by the Chinese though retaining the original windshield, were soon produced at St Louis to serve as models for the assembly of 27 more by CAMCO. Shipped to Burma in May 1940, the CW-21s were to be flown from there to Kunming by pilots of the newly formed American Volunteer Group—Kenneth T. Merritt, Lacy F. Mangleburg and Erik E. Shilling—on 23 December 1941. Soon after taking off from Lashio, however, all three planes developed engine trouble, probably because of dirty fuel, and crash-landed on a mountain slope. Shilling and Merritt survived but Mangleburg was killed. In China two assembled CW-21s were almost ready for flight-testing when CAMCO, learning that advancing Japanese forces were only 60 miles away, burned them on 1 May 1942 and evacuated their equipment to India. By then the CW-21 was demonstrably obsolete and the type never saw use over Asia.

Meanwhile Curtiss-Wright had produced another trainer, the CW-23, which used landing gear that retracted inwards and flush under the wing rather than into underwing fairings. First flown in April 1939, the CW-23 failed to find any customers but its undercarriage was easily adapted to the CW-21, along with hydraulic wing flaps in place of the original chain-driven ones. Weight was increased and the climb rate reduced by 300 feet per minute, but the reduced drag produced by the new undercarriage increased the CW-21B's level speed by 18 mph.

During a sales visit to the Netherlands in January 1940 E. C. 'Red' Walton managed to interest the Dutch in ordering 36 CW-21Bs, although that order was later reduced to 24. The German conquest of the Netherlands on 14 May 1940, followed by the re-establishment of the exiled Dutch government in Britain, led to the CW-21Bs being shipped to the Dutch East Indies. By February 1941 twenty CW-21Bs had been assembled and were assigned to the 2nd *Jachtafdeling* (Fighter Squadron) of *Vliegtuig Groep* (Aircraft Group) *IV*, or *2-VlG-IV*, at Andir air base near Bandoeng, Java. Operational losses had lowered their number to seventeen by the time the Japanese invaded the East Indies in January 1942.

The CW-21B's first chance in combat occurred on 3 February when twelve of the fighters were scrambled from Perak airfield and spread out in three flights to intercept Japanese bombers heading for Soerabaja Naval Base. They did not find any bombers but they did encounter some of their escort—27 Mitsubishi

A6M2 Zeros of the 3rd *Kokutai*. In the dogfight that ensued the outnumbered Dutch learned that their CW-21Bs were no better protected than the Zeros but that the Japanese fighters were faster, more manoeuvrable and, with two 20mm cannon in the wings, better armed. In one flight Ensign J. Hogenes and Sergeant R. C. Halberstadt died in flames, but Second Lieutenant Kingma thought he shot two Zeros down before his own plane was set on fire. Kingma bailed out and survived, although he was badly burned. Sergeant H. M. Haye also shot down a Zero before force-landing his bullet-riddled CW-21B at Ngoro airfield.

Elsewhere First Lieutenant W. A. Bedet was wounded but managed to force-land at Perak and Ensign D. Dekker and Sergeants O. B. Roumimper and J. Brouwer also force-landed their damaged planes. The commander of *2-VlG-IV*, First Lieutenant R .A. D. Anemaet, found no enemy planes but as he returned to Perak he discovered that the field had already been attacked as his CW-21B crashed into a bomb crater. Ensign A. W. Hamming and Sergeant N. Dejalle landed safely but Sergeant F. van Balen was killed by Zeros as he made his landing approach.

The three Zero claims by Kingma and Haye may have been accurate since the 3rd *Kokutai* did lose three pilots—PO2C Hatsuma Yayama, PO3C Shoichi Shoji and PO3C Masaru Morita—in the 3 February raid. The Dutch had been decimated, however, losing eight CW-21Bs in 30 minutes.

The CW-21Bs fared no better in subsequent run-ins with such formidable adversaries as the Tainan *Kokutai* and later the Nakajima Ki-43-equipped 59th and 64th *Sentais*. After the Dutch surrendered on 9 March the Japanese recovered and flight-tested a number of intact Allied aircraft, including one CW-21B which was found in Singapore after the war.

In addition to France and the United States, Britain, Italy, Germany and the Soviet Union also tested a variety of lightweight fighters. Ironically the only country to succeed—the Soviet Union—had not given the lightweight concept serious consideration until 1941 when the *Voyenno-Vozdushny Sili* began pursuing two different directions of development with the Yakovlev Yak-1, a new fighter that held great promise but was handicapped by an unsatisfactory power-to-weight ratio. The *tyazhely* (heavy) variants took advantage of the new, boosted Klimov M-105PF engine, leading to the Yak-7A and the famous Yak-9. The other, *legky* (light) option involved taking radical steps to compensate for the existing engine with the smallest, simplest, cleanest airframe possible. Unlike Western designs, the *legky* fighter was intended to achieve local air superiority over the battlefield rather than be confined to point defence. In contrast to the similarly lightened Mitsubishi Zero, however, the Soviet fighter did not have to satisfy a long-range requirement, since it would be operating just over the lines during the sweeping land battles that could—and would—be fought on Russia's western steppes.

When the Germans invaded the Soviet Union on 22 June 1941 the *legky* project had to be shelved while production was concentrated on the existing Yak-1. Work on the 'lightened Yak' resumed in the late summer of 1942, resulting in the Yak-1M (*Modifikatsirovanny*, or 'Modified'), which incorporated aerodynamic refinements such as a shallower oil cooler intake and, most significantly, a cut-down rear fuselage with a three-piece canopy, affording the pilot a much-improved rearward view.

Even while that derivative was under way, one of Yakovlev's design team leaders, K. V. Sinelshchikov, was working on a more extensive redesign. His airframe looked like a that of a Yak-1M but the wingspan was decreased from 32 feet 9½ inches to 30 feet 2⅕ inches and the aspect ratio was also reduced. The canopy was shallower and had a one-piece, frameless windshield. The ventral radiator was moved farther aft, a retractable tailwheel was installed and the radio mast was discarded. The oil cooler was initially extended under the nose, but was later relocated in the left wing root.

Structurally, the Yak-3 was identical to the Yak-1M, with a two-spar, wooden wing skinned with highly polished plywood and a 27 foot 10¼ inch long fuselage consisting of a chrome-molybdenum steel tube frame covered by duralumin engine panels forward and plywood or fabric aft. All control surfaces were metal framed and fabric covered. Empty weight was 4,641 pounds and the normal maximum take-off weight was 5,862 pounds, making the Yak-3 the lightest non-Japanese fighter to see combat during World War II.

The Yak-1M was test-flown in late 1942 and its performance exceeded expectations, including a speed of 422 mph at 12,140 feet. At the same time the first prototype of Sinelshchikov's Yak-3 was well under way. Meanwhile Vladimir Klimov had developed a new, more efficient and more powerful four-valve version of his triple-valve M105, the M-107A, but since that engine was then being tested for use in the new Yak-9U an M-105PF-2 engine, with an output of 1,244 hp on take-off, was installed in the Yak-3. Armament consisted of a 20mm ShVAK cannon firing through the propeller shaft along with two nose-mounted 12.7mm Berezin UB machine guns.

During one of the Yak-3's first test-flights early in 1943 the left wing broke away during a snap roll. The pilot, S. N. Anokhin, bailed out at low altitude and parachuted into a marsh, which cushioned his landing enough to save his life. Despite the destruction of the first prototype a strengthened Yak-3 was factory-tested successfully in April and passed its official V-VS trials in October 1943. Maximum speed was 407 mph at 10,170 feet and with an initial climb rate of 3,800 feet per minute it could reach 16,405 feet in 4.1 minutes.

The first production Yak-3 left the factory on 1 March 1944 and the type entered front-line service with the 91st IAP in June 1944. Still-crude manufacturing standards reduced the plane's speed by as much as 12.4 mph and added half a minute to its climb to 16,400 feet in comparison with the prototype, but pilots still found the Yak-3's performance impressive. The 91st IAP was commanded by Lieutenant-Colonel A. R. Kovalev and almost half of its personnel were new replacements who were seeing combat for the first time. In a way that was fortunate for them, since they would be approaching the Yak-3 with an open mind and would be less prone to judge its flying characteristics against those of its predecessors. Its high wing loading took some getting used to at low speeds; its stalling speed was high; it had a tendency to drop a wing during a slow landing approach; and it had a tendency to ground-loop in the hands of an inexperienced pilot. During a high-speed, low-level dogfight, however, the Yak-3 was in its element and was clearly superior to both the Me 109G and the Fw 190A. It could do a 360-degree turn in only 18.5 seconds and could perform tight rolls and snap rolls with remarkable accuracy and smoothness.

The aircraft commenced operations over the Lwow area of Poland and its debut stood in marked contrast to those of its forebears, even the best of which could claim only qualified successes in their first encounters with the *Luftwaffe*. On 16 June 1944 eighteen Yak-3s of the 91st IAP charged headlong into 24 equally game German fighters and in the twisting aerial battle royal that ensued the Soviet pilots claimed no fewer than fifteen victories for the loss of one plane destroyed and one damaged. Although it is likely that the regiment's enthusiastic neophytes made exaggerated or duplicated claims, the virtual cessation of *Luftwaffe* activity over the Front on the following day suggests that the Germans found the new Soviet fighter to be an unpleasant surprise.

From that time on the Yak-3s were usually sent over the Front to strike at enemy airfields or engage enemy fighters about ten minutes ahead of the Ilyushin Il-2 or Petlyakov Pe-2 ground attack planes, at altitudes that seldom exceeded 11,500 feet. In the course of their next 431 missions the pilots of the 91st IAP accounted for twenty more German fighters and three Ju 87s, while two Yak-3s were lost in aerial combat and three others were damaged by anti-aircraft fire but returned to base.

Such early successes gave the Yak-3s instant popularity as more arrived at the Front. When offered their choice of the latest fighters, the French volunteers of the Normandie-Niemen Regiment unanimously requested Yak-3s, which started to reach them in mid-July 1944. During a ten-day rampage in October the regiment's four *escadrilles* claimed 119 victories out of their wartime total of 273. By late summer 1944 *Luftwaffe* units were receiving directives to 'avoid combat below 5,000 metres with Yakovlev fighters lacking an oil cooler under the nose'.

Early in 1944 the Yakovlev team unveiled an all-metal version of their light-weight wonder, the Yak-3U (*Usilenny*, or 'Strengthened'). Powered by the 1,650 hp M-107A engine, the Yak-3U had a speed of 447 mph at 18,045 feet and the ability to climb to 16,405 feet in 3.9 minutes—the highest performance of any piston-engine Yak. Armament consisted of two fuselage-mounted 20mm B-20 cannon. Nicknamed *Ubiytsa* (Killer) by its pilots, the Yak-3U was rushed into production in the autumn of 1944 but did not reach operational units before Germany surrendered. By the time the Yak-3U was phased out of production in early 1946 a total of 4,848 Yak-3s of all models had been built. If the Yak-3 was exceptionally successful for a lightweight fighter, it was also an exception that proved the rule, for, unlike its more original—and less successful—contemporaries, it was really a conventional fighter reduced in size and stripped to the bare essentials.

The Curtiss-Wright CW-21 was not the only fighter to be developed from a trainer. The crippling of the US Pacific Fleet at Pearl Harbor on 7 December 1941 and the equally disastrous losses of the British battleship *Prince of Wales* and battlecruiser *Repulse* in the Gulf of Thailand three days later resulted in Australia feeling largely isolated and left to her own devices. The only major aircraft factory in Australia at that time was the Commonwealth Aircraft Corporation (CAC) Ltd, at Fisherman's Bend, outside Melbourne, Victoria, then engaged in licence-production of the Bristol Beaufort torpedo-bomber and a version of the North American NA-33 single-engine, two-seat trainer called the CA-3 Wirraway ('Challenge' in the language of Australia's aborigines). With neither the time nor the resources to build a new fighter from scratch, CAC's design team, headed by Fred Davis, proposed a single-seat fighter based on the Wirraway's airframe and received the go-ahead for the project on 21 December 1941. Such importance was placed on the CA-12 Boomerang, as the new fighter was known, that the designers worked 70-hour weeks to complete it. The prototype flew for the first time on 29 May 1942, just five months after work on it had begun—a remarkable achievement for a company that had never built an original aeroplane before.

The Boomerang used as many Wirraway components as possible. The forward fuselage was strengthened to accept the largest engine then available in Australia—the 14-cylinder 1,200 hp Pratt & Whitney R-1830-S3C4G Twin Wasp that CAC was manufacturing under licence for its Beauforts. The outer wing panels were reduced to a span of 36 feet 3 inches and the fuselage was shortened to 25 feet 6 inches. A 1.25-inch armoured-glass windshield was installed, along with armour plate behind the pilot's seat. The rear fuselage and tail were also carried over from the Wirraway. The four 0.303-calibre Browning machine guns and two 20mm Hispano-Suiza cannon installed in the CA-12's wings were identical to the armament carried by the Spitfire Mk V. Hispano cannon were not being produced in Australia at that time but a single example of the weapon was located and, using it as a pattern, Harland Engineering Ltd established a production line to manufacture them. In addition to the guns a 500-pound bomb could be carried under the CA-12's fuselage. There was also provision for light bomb racks under the wings.

Considering its improvised origins, the Boomerang performed remarkably well, with a maximum speed of 296 mph and an initial climb rate of 2,940 feet per minute. The Australian fighter's normal 930-mile range of could be extended to 1,600 miles with the addition of a 70-gallon drop tank. Tested against the Curtiss P-40E Kittyhawk and the Bell P-39 Airacobra, the CA-12 outclimbed the P-40E and could outmanoeuvre both of its American counterparts, although they both possessed an edge in diving and level speed. One later example, designated the CA-14, was tested with a supercharger in an attempt to improve the plane's poor high-altitude performance but by the time it was built the crisis that had brought the Boomerang into being had passed.

Some minor teething troubles were experienced with the first CA-12s but by April 1943 the first Boomerang unit, No 84 Squadron RAAF, was operational over New Guinea and an improved version of the aircraft, the CA-13, was in production at Fisherman's Bend.

On 16 May two CA-12s from No 84 Squadron were performing a standing patrol over Torres Strait between Australia's Cape York Peninsula and Merauke, New Guinea, when they encountered three Mitsubishi G4M1 bombers. This, the first and only interception by Boomerangs, was not destined to be decisive— electrical failure caused one fighter's guns to jam while the other managed to loose off only one short burst of fire at the Japanese bombers before they disappeared into a cloud.

Swift though its genesis had been, at the time the Boomerang commenced operations it was no longer needed to defend Australia. By mid-1943 the RAAF had acquired enough British and American fighters to handle the threat of Japanese air attack. The Boomerang did, however, find another niche as a close-support aircraft. Jinking about over the mountainous rain forests of New Guinea, Bougainville, the Solomon Islands and Borneo, Boomerang pilots—known as 'Boomer Boys' to the troops they supported ('Boomer' being a reference to a male of the largest species of kangaroo)—became adept at ferreting out and eliminating enemy strongpoints. The Boomerang was the only indigenously designed Australian aircraft to see service during World War II and a total of 250 had been built by the time production was terminated in January 1945—105 CA-12s, 95 CA-13s, 49 CA-19 photo-reconnaissance planes and the single prototype CA-14—and they equipped five operational RAAF squadrons.

Australia's Japanese adversaries came up with a unique improvisation of their own when they went over to the defensive. The floatplane fighter, originally developed and employed with some success in World War I, declined in importance during World War II. Most such aircraft were land fighters modified to operate from island bases where airfields were unavailable, at the sacrifice of performance due to the weight and drag of the floats that replaced their retractable undercarriage. Such aircraft seemed to make sense to the Japanese, who after World War I had acquired a far-flung collection of island mandates in the Pacific. Two of their floatplane fighters, the two-seat Mitsubishi F1M2 biplane and the single-seat A6M2-N—the Nakajima-built floatplane version of the Zero—even enjoyed a modest degree of success in the Pacific War's first year. However, a more ambitious follow-up project by Kawanishi Kokoki K.K. ended up taking an unexpected turn: what began as a purpose-built floatplane fighter to supersede the A6M2-N evolved into a land fighter.

Begun by an engineering team led by Elizaburo Adachi, Toshibura Baba, Hiroyuki Inoue and Shizuo Kikuhara, the new Kawanishi floatplane was to feature a laminar-flow wing installed at mid-fuselage, a central float and stabilizing floats under each wing tip. The Kawanishi team used a 1,463 hp Mitsubishi Kasei 14 14-cylinder radial engine—partly because it was easier to maintain under primitive conditions than a water-cooled inline engine but mainly because it was readily available—and tried to compensate for its drag by using two contra-rotating propellers and a large spinner. In that form the N1K1 prototype first flew on 6 May 1942.

As early as December 1941 Kawanishi's experimental shop had been investigating the possibilities of building a land-based version of the new floatplane. The Japanese Navy rejected their proposal at that time but Kawanishi went ahead with the project as a parallel private venture. In addition to using an 1,820 hp Nakajima Homare 11 18-cylinder radial driving a four-blade propeller in place of the Kasei, Kawanishi's Model X-1 experimental land-based fighter required extra-long landing gear to compensate for its mid-wing configuration, a problem that the designers tried to remedy with a mechanism that would extend the undercarriage leg upon landing and contract it during retraction.

Troubles with the Kasei 14's contra-rotating installation resulted in the substitution of the more conventional Kasei 13 with a single three-blade airscrew in later prototype N1K1s as well as in the final production version of the N1K1 *Kyofu* (Mighty Wind), the first of which was delivered in July 1943. Service trials held up the new fighter's introduction until December, by which time the Navy's priorities had changed from offensive floatplane operations to land-based defence.

With a top speed of 304 mph at 18,700 feet the *Kyofu* was judged capable of intercepting a bomber if it could avoid the escort, so the first N1K1s were sent to defend the oil refineries at Balikpapan, Borneo, while the rest were kept at home, serving in the Otsu *Kokutai* from Lake Biwa on the island of Honshu. In January 1944 the Singapore-based 934th *Kokutai* received nine N1K1s and then set out via Java to Ambon Island, from which base it flew its first interception mission on 16 January. On that occasion the *Kyofus* engaged six Consolidated B-24s, one of which was claimed by Warrant Officer Kiyomi Katsuki, an exceptional floatplane pilot who had scored his first two victories in F1M2s (the second, a Boeing B-17E of the 72nd Bomb Squadron, being destroyed on 4 October 1942 by ramming, after which Katsuki and his observer bailed out of their plane) and at least three in A6M2-Ns before striking the first blow for the *Kyofu*. The 924th *Kokutai* engaged another twenty B-24s two days later, claiming one bomber destroyed and another probably shot down for the loss of one plane and pilot.

The Mighty Wind did not persist for long, however. On 1 March 1944 the 924th *Kokutai* was disbanded and its personnel returned to Soerabaya. By then its pilots had claimed 29 enemy aircraft and seven 'probables'—including five victories and shares in twelve others by Hidenori Matsunaga—for the loss of five pilots killed. Only 97 N1K1s were completed before production of the Mighty Wind petered out. The *Kyofu* had performed about as well as could have been expected of a floatplane fighter, but the concept on which it had been based was no longer relevant.

Fortuitous it was, then, that Kawanishi had persevered in ironing out the problems with its land fighter, installing an improved 1,990 hp Homare 21 engine, increasing the armament to two cowl-mounted 7.7mm machine guns, two wing-mounted 20mm Type 99 Model 2 cannon in the wings and two more cannon in underwing gondolas and making provision under the fuselage for a 400-litre auxiliary fuel tank. The company's efforts were finally rewarded when the Navy accepted the land interceptor for production as the N1K1-J *Shiden* (Violet Lightning) in December 1943.

Gearing up for production was slow, but by October 1944 Kawanishi's Naruo and Himeji plants had built 662 *Shidens* and they completed another 106 in that month. The first operational N1K1-Js went to the 341st or *'Shishi'* (Lion) *Kokutai*, commanded by Captain Motoharu Okamura. The group was divided into three *hikotais* or squadrons—the 401st commanded by Lieutenant Ayao Shirane, the 402nd led by Lieutenant Iyozo Fujita and the 701st under Lieutenant Kunio Iwashita. All three leaders were experienced pilots, Shirane having scored his first of nine victories in the first Zero action on 13 September 1940 and Fujita having flown Zeros at Pearl Harbor, Midway (where he was credited with three personal and seven joint victories on 4 June 1942), Guadalcanal and Rabaul. Between 31 August and mid-September *Hikotai 402* was dispatched to Takao (now Kaohsiung) on Formosa, where its 42 planes were to intercept

American aircraft en route to and from China. Opportunities for combat were few, which was just as well because the new *Shidens* were still proving to be mechanically unreliable.

The N1K1-J got its first real taste of combat on 12 October when the US Third Fleet struck at Formosa. The 401st and 701st *Hikotais* were moved to southern Kyushu and attached to the 2nd Air Fleet to assist in the island's defence while the 402nd, at that time led by Lieutenant Masaaki Asakawa, joined in from its base at Kaohsiung. Fielding 31 *Shidens* and one Zero, the 402nd alone claimed ten victories that day but lost fourteen planes and two pilots, Lieutenants (jg) Shigemi Wakabayashi and Katsumi Yamaguchi. Another of the 341st *Kokutai*'s pilots, CPO Tadashi Sakai, was killed in action the following day.

It remains difficult to determine which Americans first met the N1K1-Js in battle that day, though cases where 'Zekes', 'Oscars' and 'Tojos' were encountered at the same time (a suspicious mixing of Navy and Army types) may suggest that *Shidens* were engaged by Grumman F6F-5s of VF-15 from the carrier *Essex*, VF-18 from *Intrepid* and VF-20 from *Enterprise*. The Americans claimed a total of 500 Japanese planes destroyed in the air or on the ground between 12 and 16 October for the loss of 71 carrier planes. Japanese records claimed 112 American aircraft in that time while admitting to the destruction of 312 of their own.

On 17 October US Army troops landed at Leyte in the Philippines and 23 *Shidens* of the 341st *Kokutai* were dispatched south to reinforce the 201st *Kokutai*, based at Clark Field, Luzon. Battle was joined on the 24th as eighteen *Shidens* of *Hikotai 402* met a similar number of Hellcats, the Japanese claiming seven F6Fs but losing ten N1K1-Js and two of their pilots, Warrant Officer Minoru Shibamura and CPO Rokusaburo Shinohara. Undercarriage failures, oil leaks and strafing attacks by American fighters took their toll and by the end of the day only four N1K1-Js remained airworthy at Clark Field. Another was lost in action the following day along with its pilot, Lieutenant (jg) Misoru Sometani of *Hikotai 401*, and on 29 October CPO Kyoji Handa was killed over Manila.

At that point *Hikotai 701*, with Shirane commanding on behalf of the ailing Iwashita, was dispatched to Mabalacat airfield on Cebu island. Attrition on the ground continued, punctuated by occasional losses in the air, such as Ensign Munesaburo Takahashi, a veteran of service with the 13th and 12th *Kokutais* as well as aboard the carriers *Soryu* and *Hiyo*, who was killed over Tacloban on 18 November. A crippling blow to flagging morale in the 341st *Kokutai* occurred on 24 November when Shirane, then officially credited with nine victories, was killed along with CPO Sadao Koike during a fight between *Hikotai 701* and Lockheed P-38s of the 433rd Squadron, 475th Fighter Group, near Ponson island off the west coast of Leyte. Iwashita, recovered from his illness, reassumed command of *Hikotai 701* and led twelve *Shidens* during attacks on an American convoy off Mindoro, during which Lieutenant Sumio Arikawa and CPO Toshiharu Kagami of *Hikotai 701* were killed on 14 December and Lieutenant Seiya Nakajima, division leader of *Hikotai 402*, perished the following day. By the end of December eight N1K1-Js remained operational and some of the 341st's pilots were being selected to carry out *kamikaze* attacks on American shipping.

Thirteen new *Shidens* arrived from Japan on 3 January 1945 but on the following day they were caught on the airfield by two Republic P-47s which in moments set eight of them on fire and killed four pilots and five maintenance crewmen. When an American invasion force entered Lingayen Gulf on 7 January Iwashita led the 341st's four remaining *Shidens* on missions from Tuguegarao in northern Luzon until the last of them were destroyed a few days later. Most of the group's personnel were subsequently killed in ground fighting for Luzon, although a few, led by Fujita, managed to fight their way through a gantlet of Filipino guerrilla units back to Tuguegarao, whence they were evacuated by air to Japan.

Generally the 'George', as the Allies came to call the N1K1-J, had not made an impressive name for itself in its first actions. Its engine and undercarriage extending mechanism were both chronically prone to failure, and Fujita summed the new fighter's overall performance up in two words: 'No good.' Nevertheless Kawanishi were committed to production and eventually built 1,007 machines, including the N1K1-Ja, on which two of the wing cannon were transferred from underwing gondolas to the wings themselves.

Even while gearing up to produce the Shiden, Kawanishi's engineers were taking steps to address its shortcomings by repositioning the wings at the lower fuselage and enclosing the engine in a cleaner cowling. The resulting aeroplane, which first flew on 21 December 1943, also had a longer fuselage, redesigned tail surfaces and a shorter, simpler, sturdier undercarriage. The N1K2-J *Shiden-kai* (Violet Lightning, Modified) had a maximum speed of 369 mph at 13,375 feet—23 mph slower than the Army's Nakajima Ki-84 *Hayate* but 6 mph faster than the *Shiden* and 4 mph faster than the Mitsubishi J2M3 *Raiden*. It was also superior in manoeuvrability, visibility, range and overall performance to both Navy types. In spite of the Homare 21 engine's persistent problems the N1K2-J was lauded by its pilots and accepted by the Japanese Navy as its principal interceptor, though only 428 would be built between December 1943 and August 1945.

As had been the case with the original *Shiden*, the Japanese could not afford to spend much time equipping and training its units for action in the *Shiden-kai*. The 343rd *Kokutai*, a group that had been annihilated in Yap, Guam and

Saipan in July 1944, was reconstituted on 25 December under the command of Captain Minoru Genda. At the end of January 1945 its three 48-plane fighter *hikotais*, *301*, *701* and *407*, commenced training in N1K1-Js at Matsuyama, Oita and Izumi air bases respectively. In addition the 4th *Hikotai*, with 24 Naka-jima C6N1 *Saiun* (Iridescent Cloud) reconnaissance planes, was attached to the group to provide advance intelligence on enemy activity. N1K2-Js finally began arriving in mid-February, by which time the type was having its baptism of fire with another unit.

On 16 February carriers of US Task Force 58, conducting a pre-emptive strike in support of the invasion of Iwo Jima, attacked air bases in the Tokyo area—the first appearance of American aircraft over the Japanese capital since the Doolittle Raid of 18 April 1942. Among the Zeros and other fighters that rose to challenge them were a handful of *Shiden-kai* and J2M *Raiden* interceptors attached to the evaluation section of the Yokosuka *Kokutai*, Japan's oldest naval air group, which since 1916 had been responsible for testing new aircraft types and training new pilots. At the controls of an N1K2-J was Ensign Kaneyoshi Muto, a 28-year-old veteran of exceptionally short stature who nevertheless was described by his comrade and fellow ace Saburo Sakai as 'the toughest fighter pilot in the Imperial Navy'. Joining other aircraft from the Yokosuka *Kokutai*'s fighter element, Muto took part in a fierce engagement with F6F-5s of VF-82 from the carrier *Bennington* over Atsugi, during which four Hellcats were shot down.

After two days of mammoth air battles the American departed, claiming the destruction of 332 Japanese planes in the air and another 177 on the ground, for the loss of 52 F6Fs and sixteen F4Us to all causes, some 49 being destroyed in combat. The Japanese Navy in turn claimed that its airmen had downed at least 98 American planes while admitting to the loss of 78 fighters, with fourteen of its pilots killed. The defenders, who included some of the best pilots Japan had left, had done a creditable job, but amid the deteriorating wartime situation it was not good enough for the Japanese press, which seized on Muto's successful first fight in the *Shiden-kai* and beefed it up for public consumption. In consequence Japanese propaganda described Muto as taking on twelve Hellcats single-handed, dispatching each of his four victims with a single burst in a display of martial skills that the press compared with those of seventeenth-century *samurai* and master swordsman Miyamoto Musashi. In so doing they had inflated Muto's actual exploit to the realm of myth—a myth that still persists more than 50 years later.

By mid-March 1945 there were enough *Shiden-kais* for the three *hikotais* of the 343rd *Kokutai* to operate formations of sixteen each. Then, on 19 March, Task Force 58 returned, this time striking at the Kure naval base. Ready or not, the 343rd *Kokutai* would have to fight.

Their morale buoyed by a long series of successes in the past year, the Americans were confident that they were facing a spent force when F6F-5s of VBF-17 from the carrier *Hornet* ran into elements of the 407th and 701st *Hikotais*. A vicious mêlée ensued, during which Lieutenant (jg) Byron A. Eberts claimed two 'Georges', Ensign Robert A. Clark downed another 'George' and Lieutenant Edwin S. Conant claimed two 'Franks'. These aircraft, along with a 'Zeke' claimed by Eberts, were more likely to have been *Shiden-kai*s, matching the six actually lost by the 343rd *Kokutai* in that fight. VBF-17 in turn lost six planes: the Hellcat had met its match.

Hitotai 301, commanded by Lieutenant Naoshi Kanno, was even more active that morning, starting with a wild engagement with Marine F4U-1Ds of VMF-123, also operating from *Bennington*, north of Kure. After disengaging off the western coast of Shikoku island and reassembling his squadron, Kanno sought out more trouble. He found it—or rather it found him—in the form of two F4U-1Ds of *Intrepid*'s VBF-10 flown by Lieutenant Robert Hill and Ensign Roy Erickson which jumped the Japanese fighters from behind and sent their leader down in flames. Kanno bailed out and a Corsair passed by close enough for Erickson to notice the astonished look that was still on Kanno's face. Suffering burns to his hands and face, Kanno parachuted into a field near Matusyama Castle and was menacingly approached by an elderly farmer armed with a pitchfork who thought Kanno to be American until he heard the curses levelled at him in Japanese. Kanno then appropriated a bicycle and pedalled back to his base.

With Kanno out of the picture, CPO Shoichi Sugita, a veteran of fighting over the Solomons, took charge of a flight and quickly accounted for three Hellcats. Another member of *Hikotai 301*, 21-year-old CPO Katsue Kato, was involved in several fights that resulted in the destruction of nine Hellcats, all of which were subsequently credited to him alone by the Japanese press. Even in such desperate times Kato's superiors would not officially confirm such a fantastic score, although they did cite him by name in the Naval All Units Proclamation afterwards.

By morning's end the 343rd *Kokutai* had claimed 53 Hellcats and Corsairs as well as four Curtiss SB2C Helldivers for the loss of thirteen pilots. Any impact the *Shiden-kai* may have had on its American opponents was somewhat overshadowed by the dive-bombing and near-loss of the carrier *Franklin* that day, but, as far as the Japanese were concerned, the N1K2-J was an unqualified success. Superb fighter though it was, however, it had appeared too late to stave off their ultimate defeat. One by one even its greatest exponents were overwhelmed and killed—Sugita, by Lieutenant-Commander Robert Weatherup, an F6F-5 pilot of VF-46 from *Independence* on 15 April; Kato on 16 April, by Hellcats of

Hornet's VF-17; and Kanno following an engagement with B-24s on 1 August. Nevertheless the final variant of what began as a floatplane fighter was one of the war's outstanding land-based fighters—and, given its genesis, one of the most unusual.

When one thinks of unique aircraft, however, there can be little argument that the Messerschmitt Me 163 is the all-time champion, being the only tailless fighter to serve during World War II and the only rocket-powered manned aircraft ever to see combat under the stratosphere. Its roots lay both in Dr Alexander Lippisch's tailless glider experiments during the 1920s and in Hellmuth Walter's development of a rocket engine suitable for aircraft in 1936. In March 1938 the two elements were combined in a conception by the *Deutsches Forschungs-institut für Segelflug* (German Sailplane Research Institute), the DFS 194. Development of the design was transferred to Messerschmitt in January 1939 and after the poor showing made by another rocket-powered design, the Heinkel He 176, its Walter R I-203 engine was installed in the tailless, swept-wing airframe of the DFS 194 and flown with encouraging results—a speed of 342 mph, a fast rate of climb and, most notably, pleasant handling characteristics. In the spring of 1941 gliding trials began with the Me 163 V1, the only snag encountered being the aircraft's tendency to keep gliding even when the pilot was trying to bring it down for a landing. Using the rocket propellant between July and September 1941, test pilot Heinrich Dittmar pushed the speed envelope ever higher until he reached a maximum of 623.85 mph on 2 October—a world record. In December Lippisch and his design team began work on an operational fighter version.

Although none of the other Western powers had come anywhere near the Germans' level of rocket aircraft development, the latter were not quite alone in such endeavours. Scientists in the Soviet Union had also been experimenting with liquid rocket propellants in the 1930s, and in the spring of 1941 the Viktor Bolkhovitinov design bureau had begun work on an aeroplane to use the D-1-A rocket motor, fuelled by kerosene with concentrated nitric acid as the oxidizer. An airframe was designed by Aleksandr Bereznyak and Alexei Isaev and, given the high fuel consumption of the powerplant, it was intended as a short-range point interceptor—essentially the same role that would later be envisaged for the Me 163. Combining a bullet-shaped fuselage with conventional straight wings and tail surfaces, all constructed of plywood and fabric, the Bereznyak-Isaev BI fighter made its first powered flight on 15 May 1942. Captain Grigori Bakhchivandzhi reported that everything went smoothly and that 'the aircraft performed stable decelerations, gliding and handling like any ordinary aircraft'.

Armed with two nose-mounted 20mm cannon, a handful of BI-1 rocket interceptors were built and assigned to a squadron, making it the first rocket-powered fighter to see military service. On 27 March 1943, however, Bakhchivandzhi put the third prototype through a test flight, accelerated to a speed of 497 mph at 6,500 feet and suddenly went into a dive from which he was unable to recover. Testing of the BI continued in the hands of Konstantin Gruzdev and Boris Kudrin, but the death of Bakhchivandzhi—who was posthumously awarded the Gold Star of a Hero of the Soviet Union—left V-VS personnel uneasy about the 'devil's broomstick', as they came to call the BI, and about the rocket fighter concept in general. The BI was never used operationally and the Soviet Union, the first nation to develop a rocket fighter, also became the first to abandon it.

Even while the Bereznyak-Isaev fighter was being readied for its first test flight, the Me 163 V3 was being completed in May 1942, fitted with Walter's HWK R.II engine which used *T-Stoff* (hydrogen peroxide and water) as a fuel and calcium permanganate as a catalyst. The latter tended to clog the jets, however, so Walter devised another motor, the HWK 509, which employed *C-Stoff* (hydrazine hydrate and methyl alcohol) as the catalyst. Using the latter power-plant, the Me 163 V3 made its first powered flight at Peenemünde in August.

As the Allied bombing campaign against Germany increased, the new aeroplane was ordered into production at Messerschmitt's Regensburg plant and at the end of June 1944 the first Me 163B-1 *Komet* fighters were ready to commence operations with *1. Staffel, JG 400*. The first interceptor mission by the new plane, however, had already been flown a month earlier.

In May 1942 a test unit, *Erprobungskommando 16*, had been established at Bad Zwischenahn under the command of *Oberleutnant* Wolfgang Späte, a prewar glider pilot and crack fighter ace who already had 72 victories to his credit when he was recalled from the Eastern Front. After two years of test-flying and training pilots on the new plane, the newly promoted *Major* Späte was notified by his superiors that, since the actual combat unit was still undergoing training, he would demonstrate the new interceptor's capabilities on 13 May 1944. When he entered the hangar that morning he was astonished to find the only combat-ready machine, an Me 163B V41, overpainted entirely in tomato red. His own mechanics had finished it in Manfred von Richthofen's colours in the hope that it would bring him luck in the revolutionary machine. Späte did not appreciate the gesture, declaring that at least the Baron had scored some victories in his plane before having it painted red—and, on a more practical level, the extra paint added 40 pounds to an aeroplane whose rocket motor gave limited endurance as was. At least the unit's morale was in the right place, though, and when ground radar detected enemy fighters in the sky Späte took off, hoping that its garish finish or its long exhaust trail would not attract every other enemy plane in the area.

Once he reached his operating altitude Späte levelled off and spotted two Republic P-47 Thunderbolts ahead of him and two other Thunderbolts above. Switching on his Revi 16 gunsight and cocking his 20mm MG 151 cannon, Späte began a tight weaving manoeuvre to let the higher P-47s get ahead of him, during which he inadvertently released the control column, causing his engine to flame out. He then had to go into a shallow glide for two minutes, helpless until he could restart the motor. Once he did, however, he found that none of the American pilots was aware of his presence. Two of the P-47s were three miles distant, so Späte slid the throttle forward to 100 per cent power, bringing his airspeed past 550 mph, and soon had one of the silver fighters in his sight. He was about to open fire when the Me 163's left wing abruptly snapped down and the aeroplane went into a dive, vibrating dangerously and creating negative gs that caused the motor to flame out again. Späte eased back the throttle and regained control, as the shaking slowly ended.

Chastened and frustrated, Späte brought his *Komet* down safely at Bad Zwischenahn, having still gone completely unnoticed by his quarry. He had been undone by an encounter with the compressibility threshold known as the sound barrier, a sometimes fatal phenomenon that occurred more often with diving aircraft rather than with one engaged in roughly level flight as his had been. Späte, transferred out of *EK 16* after May, would never get another chance to claim an enemy plane while flying the Me 163 but he would later have the privilege of claiming five victories in the jet-powered Me 262, as *Gruppenkommandeur* of *III./JG 7*.

On 31 May a photo-reconnaissance Spitfire of the RAF, flying at altitudes of 37,000 to 41,000 feet, provided the Allies with the first report of an aeroplane that rose quickly, leaving three white trails behind it, and which seemed to be 'nearly all wing', possibly with a marked sweep-back. At about that same time the Germans had discovered why the Me 163 tended to cut out as it levelled off at the summit of its rapid climb—the fuels would slop around in their tanks, which in turn activated a safety device that would automatically cut the motor off, since any change in the ratio of its two unstable fuels might cause an explosion. The installation of additional baffle plates to the fuel tanks partially, but never completely, solved that problem.

Another flaw lay in the motor's running time, which the Walter firm had claimed would be twelve minutes but which in practice barely lasted four before all the fuel was consumed. For example, *I./JG 400*'s first combat mission, in which *Unteroffizier* Konrad Schiebeler tried to intercept a Lockheed F-5 reconnaissance plane on 7 July, ended in frustration when his fuel ran out. While Walter laboured on to increase the fighter's endurance the Me 163B-1 was physically confined to the point-interception role, using its rocket motor to shoot it above an incoming Allied bomber stream then gliding through the formation firing its two wing-mounted 30mm MK 108 cannon or its supplemental under-wing armament of R4M rockets, its pilot hoping to have conserved enough of a fuel reserve for an accelerated getaway if enemy escort fighters should inter-vene. By late July the newly expanded *I. Gruppe* of *JG 400* was assigned to defend the oil refinery at Merseberg-Leuna, in spite of the protests of its commander, *Hauptmann* Rudolf Opitz, that its base at Brandis, east of Leipzig and 40 kilome-tres from the target area, made it more difficult to carry out the mission.

On 29 July the Eighth Air Force dispatched 569 Boeing B-17s to bomb the Merseberg-Leuna petroleum complex. As the bombers passed over Brandis seven Me 163s, including those flown by *Leutnante* Hans Bott and Hartmut Ryll and by *Feldwebels* Siegfried Schubert and Hans Glogner, shot up to engage them. At 9.45 a.m. crewmen of the 96th, 388th and 452nd Bomb Groups began call-ing out the positions of strange aerial projectiles approaching them. Schubert, whose early mastery of the Me 163 had earned him delegated leadership of the formation, bought his flight above the bombers then dived through them. The Germans misjudged their closing speed, however, and found themselves with no time to select a target.

Colonel Avelin P. Tacon Jr was leading eight North American P-51s of the 359th fighter Group at 25,000 feet when he reported:

> One of my pilots called in two contrails at 6 o'clock high and five miles back at 32,000 feet. I identified them immediately as jet-propelled aircraft. Their contrails could not be mistaken and looked very dense and white, somewhat like an elongated cumulus cloud some three-quarters of a mile in length.

His flight turned 180 degrees and went to engage five of the Germans, three of which were gliding down with their motors cut off. The two whose rockets were on moved towards the bombers but at 3,000 yards' distance turned towards the oncoming Mustangs instead. 'In this turn they banked about 80 degrees but their course changed only about 20 degrees,' Tacon reported. 'Their turn radius was very large but their rate of roll appeared excellent. Their speed I estimated was 500 to 600 mph.' The *Komets* passed 1,000 feet under the Ameri-cans, but when the Americans went after them one shot up towards the sun, its rockets bursting intermittently 'as though it was blowing smoke rings', as one of Tacon's pilots described it. The other glided down and by the time Tacon turned his attention to that German 'he was five miles away at 10,000 feet'.

Six Me 163s rose to intercept a force of 647 bombers attacking Merseberg on 29 July but again failed to draw blood. One B-17 of the 100th Bomb Group was returning from the mission at 11,000 feet when an Me 163 came up behind it near Wesermünde at 11.45 a.m. Captain Arthur F. Jeffrey and three other

Lockheed P-38 pilots of the 434th Squadron, 479th Fighter Group, had been watching over the straggler and now he and his wingman, Second Lieutenant Richard G. Simpson, dived to attack the rocket, which began to climb and weave before breaking off to the left. Cutting inside its turn, Jeffrey got in a deflection shot from 300 yards, observed hits and then tried to follow the rocket in a vertical dive until his P-38 reached a speed of 500 mph and he was compelled to pull out at 1,500 feet, blacking out in the process. An examination of Jeffrey's camera film led to his being awarded credit for destroying the enemy plane, but German records indicated no Me 163 losses that day.

The remaining two P-38s of Jeffrey's flight had stayed 16,000 feet above and behind the bomber when a second Me 163 appeared at 11.48 and dived out of the sun at the B-17. It made a 70-degree firing pass but failed to score hits, then dived into a cloud deck before the startled P-38s could even begin pursuing it.

In spite of days of interception attempts, the Me 163s did nothing to prevent the substantial crippling of Merseberg's fuel-producing facilities. On 2 August Lieutenant Gerald M. Adams of the 14th Squadron, 7th Photo Reconnaissance Group, was flying a Lockheed F-5 to assess the damage when he found himself being pursued at 33,000 feet by an extraordinarily fast aeroplane which swiftly closed the range to 1,000 yards and started firing at him. Adams recalled:

> This was a very startling revelation to find something that much faster than the P-38, so I pointed the nose straight down toward a low cloud deck at about 8,000 feet and fortunately made it, but the old P-38 was bucking like a bronc all the way. The Me 163 followed me all the way down making firing passes, but was never able to maneuver into a good tail chase position, fortunately. The cloud deck extended far enough to lose the Me 163, or his fuel was short.

The Eighth Air Force struck at Merseburg again on 5 August and air crews of both the 94th and 352nd Bomb Groups reported seeing ten of the rockets. The 486th Group spotted eight and the 490th reported 'bat-type wing' fighters leaving smoke trails at 28,000 feet. Sergeant Charles M. Nevaskil, radio operator in *The Royal Flush*, a B-17 of the 100th Bomb Group, reported seeing three Me 163s

> . . . about 35,000 feet high and about 9 o'clock to our course. They flew in the direction of our formation, then turned left to attack three P-51s, which were flying approximately 3,000 feet above and to the left of our formation. The 'Jets' dived on to the P-51s, which were about 8 o'clock to our formation at the time. The Me 163s were in trail as they swooped down on the P-51s. The attacks were pressed to almost point-blank range, then the enemy aircraft zoom-dived into the clear blue sky above. I saw each of the three P-51s catch fire and dive earthward.

The 352nd Fighter Group did lose two Mustangs and the 20th Group lost another during the 5 August mission but, curiously, none of them had been flying together at the times they were shot down. On the same day Mustangs of the 361st Fighter Group tried to engage three Me 163s of *2. Staffel, JG 400*, operating from Venlo, but were unable to catch them even in level flight.

Thus far the Me 163 had been making its enemies uneasy but for all the *Sturm und Drang* it had done little material damage. Then, on 16 August, 1,096 B-17s and B-24s set out to bomb Zeitz, Rositz, Leuna, Boehlen, Halle, Dresden and Koethen. Only five Me 163s were operational, but all five were launched and at 10.45 a.m. began making rear-end attacks on B-17s of the 91st and 305th Bomb Groups. *Feldwebel* Herbert Straznicky made a determined attack on Second Lieutenant D. L. Waltz's B-17 of the 305th Group, closing to 50 yards before peeling off. Equally determined, however, was the bomber's tail gunner, Sergeant H. J. Kaysen, who began firing at 1,000 yards and kept firing bursts until he saw the rocket go down, emitting smoke from 23,000 feet. Wounded in the left arm and thigh, Straznicky bailed out and parachuted safely near Brandis.

Near Waltz's plane, First Lieutenant W. E. Jenks's B-17 became the target of another gliding Me 163. Both the upper turret gunner, Tech. Sergeant H. K. Tubbs, and the navigator, Second Lieutenant W. G. McGregor, fired back at the *Komet* between 800 and 200 yards' distance then saw it pass under their bomber and dive away. A third *Komet*, flown by *Leutnant* Ryll, attacked Second Lieutenant C. J. Laverdiere's B-17, pressing his attack so aggressively that the tail gunner bailed out. Closing to point-blank range, Ryll struck both inboard engines, the flaps and tail and killed a waist gunner. He then turned and resumed his attack from 2 o'clock low, blasting the B-17's ball turret and its gunner out of the plane. The Germans subsequently credited the Fortress to Ryll but in fact Laverdiere managed to bring his severely mauled plane back to base.

Shooting away from the 305th's formation, Ryll went after fresh prey in the form of *The Outhouse Mouse*, a B-17G of the 91st Bomb Group piloted by First Lieutenant W. Reese Mullins and limping along with two superchargers out after a previous attack by Fw 190s of *IV./JG 3*. During that earlier attack 20mm shells had struck the tail gunner, Staff Sergeant M. D. Barker, in the right leg and severed the ammunition train to his right gun, while in the top turret Tech. Sergeant Carl A. Dickson was hit in the face with shell splinters. Firing back with his one working weapon, Barker saw an Fw 190 go down on fire but 'Moon' Mullins had been compelled to drop out of formation, jettison his bombs to lighten the plane and head for home. *The Outhouse Mouse* was therefore not in the best of shape when Ryll came at it, but the B-17's plight had not gone unnoticed by friendlier eyes either.

Lieutenant-Colonel John B. Murphy of the 359th Fighter Group and his wingman, First Lieutenant Cyril W. Jones Jr, were surveying three boxes of

B-17s when he looked over his shoulder and saw Ryll's contrail. Murphy knew about the new German fighter and doubted that he could intercept it until he noticed *The Outhouse Mouse* two miles to his right at 25,000 feet. Expecting the ailing 'Fort' to attract enemy attention, he led Jones in a dive towards it. Even at a speed well past 400 mph, however, he and Jones were unable to reach the B-17 before Ryll did.

The Outhouse Mouse's radioman, Tech. Sergeant James R. Knaub, had dragged Barker to the waist gunner's position to treat his leg wound and the bomber's crew were preparing for the homeward flight when Staff Sergeant Robert D. Loomis, who had taken Barker's place at the tail gun, remarked in his Montana drawl: 'One of them things they been tellin' us about is messing' around back here.' 'If he starts to come at us, let me know,' replied Mullins over the radio. Second later, Loomis calmly announced, 'Here he comes', and Mullins and his co-pilot, Second Lieutenant Forrest B. Drewry, manhandled their B-17 into a three-second dive with alternating rudder action. Loomis assured the crew that 'he's shootin' at us and I'm shootin' at him', but the B-17's desperate evasive manoeuvres prevented Ryll from doing any further serious damage before he broke sharply to the right.

For more than half a minute the Me 163 flew alongside *The Outhouse Mouse*, then, to its crew's surprise and relief, it dived away. The reason became clearer to them when two P-51s flashed by. Closing to 1,000 feet, Murphy opened fire just as the *Komet* was pulling out of its dive, observing hits on the tail and left side of its fuselage before overshooting it and being forced to pull up violently to the left. Jones, trailing Murphy by 1,000 feet, came at the Me 163 from below and slightly to the left but as he opened fire he saw the German go into a split-S, rolling inverted and then diving. Going down after the rocket, Jones scored some hits on its canopy before his Mustang struck the enemy plane's backwash and he blacked out. He recovered at 14,000 feet, by which time Murphy had re-joined the chase, staying with the turning, descending *Komet* to an altitude of 8,000 feet. Firing a continuous burst as he closed to 100 feet, he saw multiple hits along the fuselage and pieces fly off until the entire left side of the fighter, from the cockpit back, blew away. As he passed through the smoke Murphy noticed 'a strange chemical fume' seeping into his cockpit. At that point he saw another Me 163 about two miles off but, because he was running low on fuel, he and Jones decided to set course for England and home. Aboard *The Outhouse Mouse* the ventral ball turret gunner, Staff Sergeant Kenneth L. Blackburn, saw Murphy's victim spiral into the ground, followed by an explosion and a tall column of smoke. The Germans subsequently determined that Ryll, the first combat casualty in a rocket fighter, had suffered fatal head and chest wounds before crashing just west of Brandis at 10.52.

At 11 a.m. two other Mustang pilots of the 359th Group, Captain C. W. Hipscher and Lieutenant James Shoffit, saw a rocket fighter ten to twelve miles away swiftly ascending to 32,000 feet to attack a formation of B-17s. Shoffit went after it and as he approached he got into a head-on gun duel with the Me 163. Neither plane scored hits but the *Komet* turned away from the bombers and Shoffit continued to engage it until the German applied full power and left the Mustang behind as if it were standing still.

Another of the 305th Group's 'Forts' came under attack at 11.02. The ball turret gunner, Sergeant J. D. Adriano, saw an Me 163 approach from 9 o'clock low, fired at 800 yards as it passed under his formation, and saw it dive into a cloud, smoking.

At Brandis the pilots of *I./JG 400* assessed the results of fifteen intense minutes with mixed feelings. The frustration of the past month had finally been broken by Hartmut Ryll's B-17 kill (understandably, nobody was aware that his adversary would actually survive the punishment he had inflicted on it) but the cost had been Ryll himself, cut down while trying to score a second success. The fighting on 16 August 1944 would not be typical. The Germans built 364 Me 163s before production ceased in February 1945 but their pilots were credited with no more than sixteen aerial victories—a number far exceeded by their losses. The vast majority of Me 163 fatalities were not in combat but in the act of taking off or landing, when a sharp bump could be enough to make the plane's unstable fuel explode. All of the Allied powers acquired Me 163s to evaluate after the war, but while it was unquestionably a spectacular weapon the *Komet* would remain the only rocket-powered fighter ever to be used in combat.

One other German fighter design that saw brief service involved a mismatch of concepts. As the war turned irretrievably against the Third Reich, *Reichsmarshall* Hermann Göring proposed a *'Volksjäger'* or 'People's Fighter'—a cheap, simple jet made of non-strategic materials and capable of being flown even by hastily trained Hitler Youth. *Projekt Salamander*, issued on 8 September 1944, was not beyond the technical capabilities of Germany's advanced aircraft industry at that time but the requirement that the design be drafted in twelve days and the prototype be flying within 90 days placed it in the realm of fantasy. *Generalmajor* Adolf Galland, chief of the *Jagdwaffe*, opposed the whole idea and only the Ernst Heinkel Flugzeugwerke made a serious effort to fulfil it. Working round the clock, the Heinkel designers managed to come up with a basic layout in four days. Of mixed construction, the Heinkel He 162 V1 had a fuselage of light steel with a wooden nose cone, a single-piece wooden wing with metal down-angled tips and twin vertical stabilizers at the ends of a V-shaped tailplane. A BMW 003E axial-flow turbojet engine, producing a maximum of 2,028 pounds of thrust, was mounted above the fuselage, aft of the cockpit.

First flown on 6 December 1944—incredibly, within the required time frame—the He 162 V1 displayed a good turn of speed but marked instability along its longitudinal axis. During a subsequent flight on 10 December it reached a speed of 560 mph at 20,000 feet—faster than an Me 262—but during a final high-speed run at low altitude the He 162 suddenly rolled hard to the right and crashed in a fireball, killing its pilot.

By that time Göring had already committed Heinkel to the production of his pet project, so its engineers did their best to make it more stable, increasing the wing area and the span of its tailplane. Because the twin 30mm MK 108 cannon intended for it placed excessive stress on its light airframe, two fuselage-mounted 20mm MG 151s had to be installed instead. The final version, the He 162A-2, was rushed into production, but a two-seat variant was never built and training consisted of veteran pilots getting a cockpit briefing at *Erprobungs-kommando 162* at Rechlin-Roggenthin and then going up to take its measure solo. In February 1945 the He 162 *Spatz* (Sparrow) entered service in *JG 1*, com-manded by *Oberstleutnant* Herbert Ihlefeld.

By mid-March *JG 1* had 25 combat-ready He 162s but the loss of nine expe-rienced pilots killed and five injured in accidents, against only one to enemy action, gave a clue as to how the '*Volksjäger*' would have fared in the hands of a neophyte *Hitlerjugend*. Operations against low-flying Allied fighter-bombers formally began on 21 April 1945. Three days later *Hauptmann* Paul Heinrich Dähme, a *Gruppenkommandeur* and a *Ritterkreuz* recipient with 99 victories previ-ously scored over the Eastern Front, lost control of his He 162 and crashed near Warnemünde.

On 1 May *JG 1* was based at Leck in Schleswig-Holstein, from which base *Leutnant* Rudolf Schmitt of *1./JG 1* was flying his fifth mission when he caught a low-flying Hawker Typhoon and sent it crashing to earth on 4 May. That would have been a thrilling first success for a remarkable if hair-raising aeroplane—had it not been disputed by a local *Flak* unit, which got the credit instead. Any further hopes for the *Volksjäger* ended twenty-four hours later as British troops occupied Leck.

Because of Göring's crash programme numerous He 162s were available for the Allies to evaluate—and later to preserve in their museums. While the Me 262 pointed to the future, however, the He 162 endures merely as a monument to desperation, a far-fetched deviation along the road to jet-plane development and an aeronautical curiosity.

Chapter 19

DAWN OF A NEW ERA

Messerschmitt Me 262 and Gloster Meteor, 1944

In the early morning hours of 27 August 1939 Ernst Udet, chief of the *Technisches Amt* of the *Reischsluftfahrtministerium* (RLM), was awakened by a telephone call from the Heinkel works' airfield at Rostock-Marienehe. 'Good morning,' said Ernst Heinkel, 'I just wanted to inform you that *Flugkapitän* Warnitz has just successfully flown the world's first jet plane, the Heinkel He 178, and landed safely.' Udet paused a moment to gather his drowsy thoughts, then congratulated Heinkel and asked that he be allowed to get back to sleep.

At the moment—and for some time thereafter—neither Udet nor the *Luftwaffe* were quite aware of the significance of what had occurred. In fact Udet's rude awakening had been amidst the dawn of a new era in aviation, for the Heinkel He 178 that Erich Warsitz had test-flown was indeed the first turbojet-powered aeroplane to take to the air. And just a few days later Adolf Hitler's invasion of Poland would plunge Germany into a war that would compel the *Luftwaffe* to accelerate the development of Heinkel's experimental He 178 into a practical weapon.

Heinkel had also built an aeroplane powered by a liquid-fuel rocket, the He 176, which Warsitz had successfully test-flown at the Peenemünde experimental rocket station in June 1939. It was the jet, however, that proved to have the greater potential, and Heinkel proceeded with the development of a twin-jet fighter, the He 280, which made its first powered flight on 20 March 1941. By then, however, Heinkel was not alone: his rivals at the Messerschmitt plant at Augsburg were working on a jet fighter of their own, and in Britain Frank Whittle had long been working on a jet engine and an airframe on which to demonstrate it—the Gloster E.28/39, which finally got into the air on 15 May 1941.

Jet development proceeded apace over the next two years, with Heinkel and Messerschmitt vying for a production order until 27 March 1943 when the German chief of aircraft procurement, *General-Luftzugmeister* Erhard Milch, informed Heinkel that his He 280 had been passed over in favour of Messerschmitt's Me 262. Although the He 280 was faster, had a higher rate of climb and a higher service ceiling, its twin vertical tail surfaces were suspect and its range was only two-thirds that of the Me 262's.

First proposed to the RLM in the summer of 1938 as a research aircraft to use the new BMW P 3032 gas turbine engine, Messerschmitt's *Projekt* P.1065 was developed into an airframe by a design team led by Dr Woldemar Voigt. Intended as an interceptor from the outset—even though the *Luftwaffe* requirement had not specified that role for it—the original Me 262 had a tailwheel, which was soon replaced by a tricycle landing gear arrangement. The wings had a slight sweepback, which was incorporated with the centre of gravity, rather than aerodynamic qualities, as the causal factor. The airframe, powered by a single 690 hp Junkers Jumo 210 piston engine, was taken up for its first test flight from Messerschmitt's airfield at Augsburg by *Flugkapitän* Paul Wendel on 18 April 1941.

Although Hitler is popularly blamed for holding up the Me 262's development with his much-publicized fixation on using it as a high-speed fighter-bomber, the real delaying factor was the engine. The Bayerische Motoren Werke had claimed that its P 3302 engine could be made to produce 600 kilograms (about 1,300 pounds) of thrust by the end of 1939, but when one of the engines was bench-tested at the end of 1940 it produced only 260 kilograms (570 pounds). Meanwhile Heinkel had developed his own engine, capable of producing 500 kilograms of thrust, to power his He 178 on its historic first flight. The first of BMW's P 3302 engines—redesignated BMW 003s—did not arrive at Augsburg until November 1941 and, shortly after Wendel took the Me 262 up for its first jet-powered flight on 25 March 1942, both of them failed, requiring him to return using the piston engine.

By then the Junkers Jumo 004 turbojet had been developed and tested, producing 1,000 kilograms (2,200 pounds) of thrust. Two of them were installed in the wings of the third prototype and on 18 July 1942 Wendel took off from Leipheim in the Me 262 V3 for a successful twenty-minute flight. Even after plane and engine went into full production, however, the Jumo 004 would be an Achilles' heel for the Me 262. Chromium and nickel, essential for the steel alloys necessary to operate at a jet engine's high temperatures, were in short supply and substitute metals, such as ordinary steel with a spray coating of aluminium, were prone to burn and adversely affected engine life. At the end of the war the average engine life of an Me 262 was only 25 hours, with a time between overhauls of ten hours.

So secret was the new plane's development that *General der Jagdflieger* Adolf Galland knew nothing of it until he finally got his chance to fly the fourth prototype on 22 May 1943. He was instantly impressed, declaring that flying the jet felt 'as if an angel were pushing', and recommended that Me 109 production be halted so that Messerschmitt could concentrate on the all-out manufacture of the new jet fighter. His influence did speed things up: 72 hours later Milch ordered the Me 262 into series production. The first 100 Me 262s to be built would be issued to special test units, or *Erprobungskommandos*, that would give the fighter its first operational exposure to the enemy and simultaneously identify and iron out any shortcomings as they arose.

In mid-1943 the German air defences had been holding their own against British and American bombers. At the same time, however, the failed British raid on Dieppe in August 1942, followed by the successful Allied invasions of North Africa in November 1942, of Sicily in July 1943 and of Italy in September, had alerted Hitler to the danger of an Allied invasion of France. Concluding that the best way to repel such an invasion would be a series of lightning air strikes on the beach-head, he became adamant about developing a high-speed 'Blitz bomber'. Such was the situation on 2 November 1943 when Hermann Göring, while visiting the Augsburg plant, first asked Willy Messerschmitt if the Me 262 could be adapted to the bombing role. '*Herr Reichsmarschall*, from the very outset we have provided for the fitting of two bomb pylons so it can carry bombs—either one 500 kg or two 250 kg,' Messerschmitt replied. He went on to state his confidence that the payload could be doubled and that such a modification could be completed in a couple of weeks.

On 26 November the Me 262 was demonstrated to Hitler at Insterburg and he, too, broached the question. Again, Messerschmitt answered affirmatively, and the *Führer* blissfully assumed that his wish would be carried out. Unknown to him, however, Messerschmitt proceeded with the Me 262 as an anti-bomber interceptor, with a quartet of four 30mm Mk 108 low-velocity cannon in the nose.

The *Luftwaffe* accepted its first sixteen pre-production Me 262A-0 fighters, which had been lying at Lechfeld waiting for engines, between 18 and 29 April 1944 and at the end of that month *Erprobungskommando 262* was formed at Lechfeld, Bavaria, under *Hauptmann* Werner Thierfelder. Even while they gained experience in the new type, the special test unit's pilots were writing an operating manual for the Me 262A-1a fighter.

On 23 May Hitler summoned Göring, Milch, Galland and other senior *Luftwaffe* officers, as well as Albert Speer and officials from his armament ministry, to Berchtesgaden to discuss fighter production. The *Führer* listened somewhat lackadaisically to Milch's statistics, but when he mentioned progress on the Me 262 fighter programme Hitler interrupted him: 'I thought the 262 was coming as a high-speed bomber? How many of the 262s already manufactured can carry bombs?'

'None, *Mein Führer*,' Milch replied. 'The Me 262 is being manufactured exclusively as a fighter aircraft.' There was an awkward silence, then Milch added that extensive design changes would be necessary to convert the jet into a bomber, and even then it would not be able to carry more than 500 kilograms.

'Never mind!' Hitler exclaimed, 'I wanted only one 250-kilo bomb.' Losing his composure, he demanded precise weight statistics on the fighter's armour, guns and ammunition. 'Who pays the slightest attention to the orders I give?' he railed. 'I gave an unqualified order, and left nobody in any doubt that the aircraft was to be equipped as a fighter-*bomber*.'

Hitler's confidence in Milch was irreparably shattered by the meeting in Berchtesgaden, and Milch would be progressively stripped of his authority in the weeks that followed. Göring was made personally responsible for the implementation of the Blitz bomber programme.

On 27 May a furious Hitler ordered that the Me 262 not be regarded as a fighter but that it enter service exclusively as a fighter-bomber. He relented somewhat a few days later, allowing testing of the fighter to continue, but with the proviso that the first operational units must be equipped with the bomber. Messerschmitt responded by mounting two pylons, each capable of carrying a 550-pound SC 250 bomb, under the nose of the tenth prototype and fitting an extra fuel tank with a capacity of 600 litres (132 Imperial gallons) in the rear fuselage. To compensate for the weight two of the MK 108 nose cannon and most of the armour plating from the cockpit were removed. While the Me 262A-2a *Sturmvogel* (Storm Bird) was hastened into production, a unit of *Kampfgeschwader 51*, commanded by *Major* Wolfgang Schenck, was detached and sent to Lechfeld to train on the new Blitz bomber. After about a month of conversion training the first nine Me 262A-2as of *Erprobungskommando Schenck* were transferred to Châteaudun, France, on 20 July. By then Allied forces had already landed in Normandy on 6 June and the taking of St Lô on July 18 had ended weeks of stalemate in the hedgerow country of the Cotentin pensinsula. Hitler, however, still did not realize that his original hope of using Blitz bombers to drive the Allies from their beach-head was long gone. He was still convinced that Normandy was a feint and that the main Allied landing was yet to come at Calais, for which event the *Sturmvogel* would surely be ready.

Meanwhile *Erprogungskommando 262* opened its account on 26 July when *Leutnant* Alfred Schreiber, flying Me 262A-1a No 130017, call-letter 'White 4', caught and shot down a de Havilland Mosquito engaged on a solitary high-altitude photo-reconnaissance mission over the Alps. A former Me 110 pilot of *Zerstörergeschwader 26*, 'Bubi' Schreiber repeated the performance on 2 August, downing a Supermarine Spitfire that was also engaged on a PR mission. He shot down a Lockheed F-5, the photo-reconnaissance version of the P-38 Lightning, on 28 October, and on the following day he shot down a second F-5 and then accounted for a Spitfire by the unorthodox means of ramming it—or colliding with it—after which he bailed out. Schreiber's impressive run of luck in the Me 262 ended on 26 November as the new ace was taking off with a comrade on an intercept mission and his engine suffered a flame-out. Schreiber tried to land but ran into a trench and was crushed to death when his plane turned over on top of him.

On 20 September Hitler, conceding the reality of Germany's situation, finally shifted the priority of Me 262 production to the fighter version. By then Me 262As were making their presence felt among the American bomber streams and, to a considerably lesser degree, among the Allied ground forces. They were, however, 'too little and too late' to affect the course of the air war over Europe. The presence of the long-ranging North American P-51D Mustang and the steady Allied advance across the Continent brought Me 262 air bases within range of an increasing number of Allied fighters. If the jets were too fast to catch in the air (though some were shot down by a handful of lucky pilots), they could be—and often were—ambushed as they took off or landed.

While the Me 262 pilots were putting up a gallant but futile fight against overwhelming numerical odds, another jet fighter was entering service on the Allied side—the Gloster Meteor. Since the early 1930s, while Ernst Heinkel worked on his jet engine, Frank Whittle had been engaged in a double struggle—with the problems of perfecting a gas turbine driving a series of enclosed impellers and with trying to interest the RAF in his project. In 1939 Whittle joined creative forces with George Carter, chief designer for the Gloster Aircraft Company, and at about the same time the Air Ministry finally took an interest in the jet concept, issuing a contract to Gloster for an experimental airframe which could be adapted for operational use with minimum modification.

The result of Whittle's and Carter's efforts, the single-engine Gloster E.28/39, finally flew at RAF Cranwell on 15 May 1941. Although the maiden flight lasted little more than a quarter of an hour, test pilot P. E. G. Sayer emerged from the cockpit praising the plane, convinced that the jet was indeed the way of the future. The RAF was convinced of it too, for it had already issued Specification F.9/40 calling for 500 twin-engine fighters using Whittle's engine.

Eight developmental aircraft were built, the fifth of which, DG206, made the F.9/40's first flight from RAF Cranwell on 5 March 1942. Whittle's WSB engines were still being built at the Rover plant in Coventry, so de Havilland H1 Halford engines were substituted for the first flight. Although the plane exhibited a few problems, including a tendency to yaw violently as its speed approached 230 mph, the Air Ministry found it promising enough to continue development. Trials were switched to Newmarket Heath, then to Barford St John and finally Moreton Valence, once a hardened runway was completed at the last field. Policemen closed the roads whenever the Meteor, as the new jet was then being called, flew. Test flights were usually conducted when there was low cloud cover, to reduce the odds of unauthorized eyes seeing the top-secret fighter.

Meteor DG205/G, fitted at last with the Whittle-developed W2B engine, made its first flight on 17 June 1943. Development continued at a rather slow pace until the first production Meteor F.1, EE210/G, flew from Moreton Valence on 12 January 1944. The production aircraft used Rolls-Royce-built W1B Welland I engines, but apart from a modified canopy and the installation of four 20mm Hispano cannon in the nose it differed little from the prototype. Rated at 1,600 hp, the Welland I was a reliable and tractable powerplant but because of the Meteor's size, rather than its modest weight, the plane was only able to reach a speed of about 390 mph at sea level and a maximum of 415 mph at higher altitudes, with a service ceiling of 40,000 feet. Given that less than exhilarating performance, some RAF people suggested that it was fit only to serve as a trainer. By then, however, the Air Ministry was aware of the Me 262 and of its imminent introduction to service and consequently judged it psychologically important that the RAF have a jet of its own in front-line squadrons.

Another psychological factor arose that would serve as the ultimate call to arms for the Meteor. On 12 June 1944 the first V-1 was launched against London in reprisal for the Allied landings in Normandy six days earlier. To the RAF it seemed almost a matter of destiny that its first jet should be among the aircraft mobilized to defend England against these swift, small, jet-propelled flying robots.

The unsuspecting first recipient of the Meteor was No 616 Squadron, Auxiliary Air Force, which in June 1944 was flying Spitfire Mk VIIs from Culmhead, Somerset, on escort missions for bombers striking at German tactical targets in France. Rumours had been rife since the spring that the squadron was to be re-equipped, but most pilots believed that the replacements would be Spitfire Mk XIVs, two of which arrived at Culmhead in June. Shortly afterwards Squadron Leader Andrew McDowall and five other pilots were summoned to Farnborough to acquaint themselves with the new aircraft, but when they returned they announced that No 616 Squadron's replacements would be jets—and unanimously added that once they had become accustomed to their tricycle landing gear they were delightful machines to fly.

The first two Meteor Is, EE213 and EE214, began flying with No 616 Squadron on 12 July 1944. Five more Meteors arrived on the 14th, and by the 25th squadron strength had reached a dozen, completely replacing its Spitfire VIIs. On 21 July two of the Meteors, escorted by the squadron's Spitfires, flew to Manston airfield in Kent, followed two days later by five more of the jets. From there newly promoted Wing Commander McDowall, Wing Commander

Wilson, Squadron Leader Leslie William Watts, Flying Officers McKenzie, Clark and Dean and Warrant Officer Wilkes commenced operations against the V-1s.

On 27 July 1944 Watts, Dean and McKenzie flew their first 'diver patrols', as the RAF code-named its efforts to stop the flying bombs. Dean and McKenzie failed to intercept any bombs but Watts caught up with a V-1 over Ashford. With the 'diver' in his gun sight, Watts pressed the trigger button on the control column but nothing happened. His guns had jammed and the V-1 escaped and went on to hit its target. After that setback it was decided that patrols against the vengeance weapons should be carried out by pairs of aircraft, since the odds of both Meteors' guns jamming were unlikely. In order to increase their time in the air the squadron moved its Meteors to a dispersal aerodrome near Ashford, reducing the distance they had to fly to reach the V-1s' expected routes.

Finally, on the evening of 4 August, Dean was only minutes from take-off at Ashford when he spotted a V-1 ahead of and below him, moving toward Tunbridge Wells. Going into a shallow dive, Dean increased his speed to 385 mph then got in a brief burst of his guns before they jammed. Dean brought the Meteor alongside the V-1 as close as he felt safe, slid his wing under that of the V-1 and slowly pushed his control column to the left. As Dean's plane banked, the force of air lifted the robot's wing, unbalancing the autopilot in the bomb until it abruptly flicked over on its back and dived into the ground, exploding harmlessly in the open countryside. Contrary to popular belief, the wing tip of the Meteor did not actually touch the V-1 during these 'tip and run' tactics since there was too much chance of damaging the fighter or even losing valuable pilots and aircraft. Air pressure sufficed to do the job.

Within minutes of Dean's success Flying Officer J. L. Rogers closed on another 'diver' over Tunbridge and opened fire with his four 20mm cannon. This time the weapons did not jam and the V-1 went down in open countryside near Tenterden.

After that No 616 Squadron relayed two-plane patrols throughout the day, each flight lasting about 30 minutes. By 10 August Dean had added two more 'divers' to his score. On 16 and 17 August the Meteors accounted for five more of the robot bombs. A total of thirteen V-1s were destroyed in one way or another by 616's 'Meatboxes'—modest in number but providing a great boost to public morale.

Aside from its guns the Meteor gave no trouble, and its two engines needed less servicing than the single engine of a Spitfire. Indeed, the only thing bad that happened to No 616 Squadron was when one of its Meteors was almost shot down in error by a Spitfire and had to land under control of the elevator trimmers.

For the remainder of 1944 No 616 Squadron's Meteors operated from Debden, where they were used to acquaint RAF and USAAF units with the characteristics of jets and to help them develop tactics to counter the Me 262As that were starting to take their toll of bomber formations. After being subjected to hit-and-run strikes by the Meteors, the American P-51 and P-47 pilots concluded that the only way to protect the bombers was to increase their numbers 5,000 feet above them, allowing the fighters time to build up speed to intercept the German jets. Such tactics required split-second timing at high speeds, but they paid off as several Americans added Me 262s to their scores while on escort duty.

On 18 December No 616 Squadron received its first two Meteor F Mk IIIs, EE231 and EE232, which were powered by Rolls-Royce Derwent engines in revised nacelles. In addition to improved performance, the F.III had a larger fuel capacity which gave it an hour's longer endurance, an enlarged, more stream-lined windscreen and a rear-sliding, bulged bubble canopy in place of the F.I's side-hinged canopy. Three more Meteor IIIs were on strength by January 1945 when the unit moved to Colerne, Wiltshire. There the squadron exchanged the last of its Mk Is for the newer type and on 20 January one of the flights was dispatched across the Channel to Melsbroek, near Brussels, to join No 84 Group of the 2nd Tactical Air Force. For some weeks the Meteors flew patrols over local Allied airfields, primarily to acquaint them with the new jet's silhouette. The rest of the squadron arrived on 31 March and in early April it resumed offensive operations from Gilze-Rizen in the Netherlands as part of No 122 Wing.

As was the case with the German jet fighter units, No 616 Squadron's person-nel now included some skilled veterans, including Wing Commander Warren Edward Shrader, from Wellington, New Zealand, who had previously flown Hawker Tempests with No 486 Squadron and had eleven victories, plus two shared, to his credit. Wing Commander McDowell, from Kirkenner, Scotland, had an identical victory tally, but he had achieved his in Spitfires with No 602 Squadron. Much to the disappointment of the pilots, however, no contact was made with the *Luftwaffe* in the course of their short patrols and in consequence they were employed in the armed reconnaissance and ground-attack roles.

On 13 April No 616 Squadron moved to Nijmegen and on the 14th Flight Lieutenant Cooper became the first 'Meatbox' pilot to fire his guns in anger over the Continent when he spotted a large German truck near Ijmuiden and in a single firing pass sent it careening off the road, to burst into flames seconds later. On the 24th McDowell, flying Meteor Mk I 'YQ-A', led four others on a strike against an enemy airfield at Nordholz, Germany. Diving out of the sun from 8,000 feet, he destroyed a Ju 88 on the ground and shot up a vehicle. Flying Officer Wilson set two petrol bowsers on fire and used up the rest of his shells on other airfield installations. Flying Officer Moon roamed the perimeter of the field, strafing a dozen railway trucks and destroying a Flak post. Flying Officer Clegg attacked a large vehicle full of German troops who, thinking the twin-engine jet to be one of their own, waved and cheered until Clegg opened fire.

Up to that time No 616 Squadron had taken no casualties, but that unblemished record came to a tragic end on 29 April when Squadron Leader Watts, who had been with the unit since August 1943, collided with Flight Sergeant Cartmell in a cloudbank. The two planes exploded and both pilots were killed.

On 2 May Wing Commander 'Smokey' Shrader replaced McDowell as commander of No 616 Squadron. On the same day one of the 'Meatbox' pilots encountered a Fieseler Fi 156 *Storch* but the nimble liaison plane was able to outmanoeuvre the fighter and landed—after which the Meteor strafed it to destruction. On 3 May Shrader, flying Meteor 'YQ-F', led the squadron in an attack on Schonberg air base near Kiel during which six aircraft were destroyed on the ground, Shrader personally accounting for an Me 109, an He 111 and a Ju 87. On another occasion four Meteors encountered some Fw 190s but their hopes of adding some air-to-air victories to the squadron tally were again frustrated when some Spitfires and Hawker Tempests mistook the British jets for Me 262s and prepared to attack, compelling the Meteors to abandon their attempt against the Germans. On the following day No 616 Squadron's pilots destroyed one locomotive and damaged another, knocked out ten vehicles and two half-tracks and strafed a number of installations. At 5 p.m. the unit was ordered to suspend offensive operations. Four days later, Germany surrendered.

It is probably fortunate for the Meteor pilots that they never had to do battle with the Me 262s—all other things being equal, neither their aircraft nor their own level of expertise would have matched the performance of the German fighter, nor of the crack *Experten* who were flying it in the final weeks of the war. Nevertheless the 'Meatbox' proved to have considerable development potential, and on 7 November 1945 a Meteor F Mk 3 reached a record speed of 606 mph. Progressively improved marks were to follow, serving in the fighter, reconnaissance and night fighter roles until September 1961, by which time a total of 3,875 Meteors had been built.

It had been a remarkable thirty years. At the start of 1915, the fighter plane did not exist and airmen were trying to figure out how to fire a machine gun around the propeller. By the end of 1945 there would no longer be a propeller in the way, as fighters took to the sky using means of propulsion that few would have envisaged three decades earlier. A new, frightening, exciting era of aerial combat had begun.

BIBLIOGRAPHY

Ashley, Glenn, *Meteor in Action*, Squadron/Signal Publications, Carrollton, 1995

Bailey, Frank W., and Chamberlain, Paul, 'L'Escadrille de Chasse Spa. 57', *Cross & Cockade Journal*, Vol. 26, No 1

Barker, Ralph, *The RAF At War*, Time-Life Books, Alexandria, 1981

Barnett, Corelli, *Engage the Enemy More Closely: The Royal Navy in the Second World War*, W. W. Norton & Co., London, 1991

'Beaufighter—Innovative Improvisation by Bristol', *Air Enthusiast International*, Vol. 6, No 1, January 1974

Beedle, J., *43 Squadron, Royal Flying Corps, Royal Air Force*, Beaumont Aviation Literature, London, 1966

Birdsall, Steve, *Log of the Liberators*, Doubleday & Co, Garden City, 1973

Bond Jr, Charles R., and Anderson, Terry H., *A Flying Tiger's Diary*, Texas A&M University Press, College Park, 1984

Bishop, Edward, *Hurricane*, Airlife Publishing, London, 1986

Böhme, Erwin, (ed. J. Werner), *Briefe eines Deutschen Kampffliegers an ein junges Mädchen*, Leipzig, 1930

Botquin, Gaston, 'Un Bon Chasseur pour la "Drole de Guerre"', *Le Fanatique de l'Aviation*, No 103, June 1978

Bowman, Martin, *Mosquito Fighter/Fighter-Bomber Units of World War II*, Osprey Publishing, London, 1998

Brown, Capt Eric, 'The Fortuitous Fulmar', *Air Enthusiast*, Vol. 13, No 2, August 1977

Bruce, J. M., 'Bristol's Fighter Manqué', *Air Enthusiast*, 32, December 1986–April 1987

———, *Hanriot HD.1* (Windsock Datafile 8), Albatros Productions, Berkhamsted, 1988

———, *Morane-Saulnier Types N, I, V* (Windsock Datafile 58), Albatros Productions, Berkhamsted, 1996

———, *RAF SE5* (Windsock Datafile 30), Albatros Productions, Berkhamsted, 1991

———, 'Sopwith's Pedigree Pup', *Air Enthusiast Quarterly*, 4

———, *Spad 13.C1* (Windsock Datafile 32), Albatros Productions, Berkhamsted, 1992

———, *Spad 7.C1* (Windsock Datafile 12), Albatros Productions Berkhamsted, 1988

———, *The De Havilland D.H.2*, Profile Publications, Leatherhead, 1966

———, *The De Havilland D.H.5*, Profile Publications, Leatherhead, 1967

———, *War Planes of the First World War: Fighters*, Vols I, II and V, Doubleday & Co, Garden City, 1965–68

Caldwell, Donald L., *JG 26: Top Guns of the Luftwaffe*, Orion Books, New York, 1991
———, *JG 26 War Diary. Vol. One: 1939-1942*, Grub Street, London, 1996
Campbell, Jerry L., *Messerschmitt Bf 110 Zerstörer in Action*, Squadron/Signal Publications, Carrollton, 1977
Cattaneo, Gianni, *Fiat CR.42*, Profile Publications, Leatherhead, 1965
Christienne, Charles, and Lissarague, Pierre, (trans. Kianka, Francis), *A History of French Military Aviation*, Smithsonian Institution Press, Washington, 1986
Cieslak, Krzysztof; Gawrych, Wojciech; and Glass, Andrzej, *Samoloty Mysliwskie wresnia 1939*, Aerohobby, Warsaw, 1987
Cloe, John Haile, *The Aleutian Warriors: A History of the 11th Air Force and Fleet Air Wing 4*, Pt I, Pictorial Histories Publishing Co, Missoula, 1991
Cooksley, Peter, *Bristol Fighter in Action*, Squadron/Signal Publications, Carrollton, 1993
Cooper, Ann, 'A Black Widow strikes at night to down a Japanese Betty bomber over the Pacific during World War II', *Aviation History*, March 1997
Cornelius, Wanda, and Short, Thayne, *Ding Hao: America's Air War in China, 1937–1945*, Pelican Publishing Co, Gretna, 1980
Courteville, Pierre, 'Viewed from the Cockpit: The Bloch M.B.152', *Air International*, Vol. 14, No 4, April 1978
Cynk, Jerzy B., *The Polish Air Force at War: The Official History, Vol. 1, 1939–1943*, Schiffer Publishing, Atglen, 1998
Duiven, Richard, 'Das Königliches Jagdgeschwader Nr II', *Over the Front*, Vol. 9, No 3, Fall 1994
Durkota, Alan; Darcey, Thomas; and Kulikov, Victor, *The Imperial Russian Air Service*, Flying Machines Press, Mountain View, 1995
'End of an Era . . . Polikarpov's Chaika', *Air Enthusiast*, Vol. 1, No 1, June 1971
Ethell, Jeffrey L., *Komet: The Messerschmitt 163*, Sky Books Press New York, 1978
Ethell, Jeffrey L., and Price, Alfred, *The German Jets in Combat*, Jane's Publishing Co, London, 1980
Ewing, Steve, and Lundstrom, John B., *Fateful Rendezvous: The Life of Butch O'Hare*, Naval Institute Press, Annapolis, 1997
Ferguson, S. W. and Paskalis, William K., *Protect and Avenge: The 49th Fighter Group in World War II*, Schiffer Publishing, Atglen, 1996
'Firefly: A Masterpiece for the Matelots', *Air Enthusiast*, Vol. 2, No 3, March 1972
Ford, Daniel, *Flying Tigers*, Smithsonian Institution Press, Washington, 1991
Francillon, René J., *American Fighters of World War II*, Vol. 1, Doubleday & Co, Garden City, 1969
———, *Kawanishi Kyofu, Shiden and Shiden Kai Variants*, Profile Publications, Windsor, 1970
Franks, Norman L. R.; Guest, Russell; and Alegi, Gregory, *Above the War Fronts*, Grub Street, London, 1997
Franks, Norman; Bailey, Frank W; and Guest, Russell, *Above the Lines*, Grub Street, London, 1993
Freeman, Roger A., *The Mighty Eighth*, Jane's Publishing, New York, 1970
Gordon, Yefim, and Khazanov, Dmitri, *Soviet Combat Aircraft of the Second World War. Vol. One: Single-Engined Fighters*, Midland Counties Publications, Earl Shilton, 1998

Goworek, Tomasz, 'The US Army Air Service's first air-to-air victim may have arranged his own capture', *Military History*, October 1994

Gray, Peter L., *The Fokker D.VII*, Profile Publications, Leatherhead

Green, William, *Fighters of World War II*, Vol. 1, Doubleday and Co, Garden City, 1968

———, *Warplanes of the Second World War: Fighters*, Vol. 1, Doubleday and Co, Garden City, 1965

Grosz, P. M., *Fokker D.VIII* (Windsock Datafile 25), Albatros Productions, Berkhamsted, 1991

———, *SSW D.III–D.IV* (Windsock Datafile 29), Albatros Productions, Berkhamsted, 1991

Grosz, Peter M, and Ferko, Ed, 'Biplanes for the Fliegertruppe', *Air Enthusiast*, 14, December 1980–March 1981

Grosz, Peter M.; Haddow, George; and Schiemer, Peter, *Austro-Hungarian Army Aircraft of World War One*, Flying Machines Press, Mountain View, 1993

Gunston, Bill, 'Birth of the Jet Fighter', *Royal Air Force Yearbook*, 1984.

Guttman, Jon, 'Plumage: Spa 156: L'Escadrille des Deux Martinets', *Over the Front*, Vol. 9, No 1, Spring 1994.

———, 'The first cannon-armed fighter owed its modest success to outstanding pilots', *Aviation Heritage*, September 1991

———, *Nieuport 28* (Windsock Datafile 36), Albatros Productions, Berkhamsted, 1992

Guttman, Robert, 'Arming a fighter plane with nothing more than a four-gun turret proved unique—but not brilliantly successful', *Aviation History*, September 1996

———, 'A speedy fighter of 1916 was rejected out of hand because it had only one wing in a biplane era', *Aviation History*, November 1996

———, 'The Triplane Fighter Craze of 1917', *Aviation History*, March 1995

Hall Jr, Grover C., *1000 Destroyed: The Life and times of the 4th Fighter Group*, Aero Publishers, Fallbrook, 1978

Hata, Ikuhiko, and Izawa, Yasuho, (trans. Gorham, Don Cyril), *Japanese Naval Aces and Fighter Units in World War II*, Naval Institute Press, Annapolis, 1989

Haugland, Vern, *The Eagles' War*, Tab Books, Blue Ridge Summit, 1992

Holmes, Tony, *Hurricane Aces 1939–40*, Osprey Publishing, London, 1998

Hooton, Edward R., 'Air War Over China', *Air Enthusiast*, 34, September–December 1987

Howson, Gerald, *Aircraft of the Spanish Civil War 1936–1939*, Smithsonian Institution Press, Washington, 1990.

Hylands, Dennis, *Georges Guynemer*, Albatros Productions, Berkhamsted, 1987

Imrie, Alex, *The Fokker Triplane*, Arms & Armour Press, London, 1992

Jackson, Robert, 'Flight of the Meteor', *The Elite: The Bombers*, National Historical Society, Harrisburg, 1989

———, *Spitfire: The Combat History*, Motorbooks International, Osceola, 1995

Jones, Wg Cdr Ira, *Tiger Squadron*, White Lion Publishers, London, 1954

Keskinen, Kalevi; Stenman, Kari; and Niska, Klaus, *Finnish Fighter Aces*, Tietoteos, Espoo, 1978

Kilduff, Peter, *Richthofen: Beyond the Legend of the Red Baron*, Arms & Armour Press, London, 1993

————, *That's My Bloody Plane*, The Pequot Press, Chester, 1975

————, *The Red Baron Combat Wing: Jagdgeschwader Richthofen in Battle*, Arms & Armour Press, London, 1997

Krybus, Josef, *The Avia B.534*, Profile Publications, Leatherhead, 1968

Kuipers, Lieutenant J. P., 'Un spectacle fascinant', *Icare*, winter 1976/77

Leyvastre, Pierre, 'Gallic Guardian', *Air Enthusiast*, Vol. 5, Nos 3 and 4, September and October 1973

Lighthall, W. S., 'The Royal Air Force in the Palestine Campaign, 1917–1918', *Cross & Cockade (USA) Journal*, Vol. 11, No 2, Summer 1970

Martinez, Luis García, 'Los Katiuskas', *Air Enthusiast*, 32, December 1986–April 1987

Mendenhall, Charles A., *Wildcats & Hellcats: Gallant Grummans in World War II*, Motorbooks International, Osceola, 1984

'Messerschmitt over Spain', *Air Enthusiast*, 8, October 1978–April 1979

Morgan, Hugh, and Weal, John, *German Jet Aces of World War 2*, Osprey Publishing, London, 1998

Morison, Samuel Eliot, *History of US Naval Operations in World War II. Vol. III. The Rising Sun in the Pacific, 1931–April 1942*, Little, Brown & Co, Boston, 1988

Morton, Fred, '5 jours de folles batailles', *Icare*, winter 1976/77

Moyes, Philip J. R., *The de Havilland Mosquito Mks I–IV*, Profile Publications, Leatherhead, 1965

Mullins, Jon D., *An Escort of P-38s: The First Fighter Group in World War II*, Phalanx Publishing Co, St Paul, 1995

'Nakajima Demonology . . . The Story of the Shoki," *Air International*, Vol. 3, No 1, July 1972

Nohara, Shigeru, *A6M Zero in Action*, Squadron/Signal Publications, Carrollton, 1983

'Of Chaika and Chato', *Air Enthusiast*, 11, October 1979–April 1980

Ostric, Sime I., and Janic, Cedomir J., *IK Fighters (Yugoslavia: 1930–40s)*, Profile Publications, Windsor, 1972

'Pacific Peregrine . . . The Nakajima Ki-43 Hayabusa', *Air International*, Vol. 18, No 1, January 1980

Poiencot, Kelly P., 'The Father of Aerial Combat', *Aviation History*, July 1996

Price, Alfred, *Spitfire at War*, Ian Allan, London, 1974

————, *The Spitfire Story*, Jane's Publishing Co, London, 1982

'Raiden: The Asiatic Thunderbolt', *Air Enthusiast*, Vol. 1, No 2, July 1971

Revell, Alex, *High in the Empty Blue: The History of 56 Squadron, RFC RAF 1916–1919*, Flying Machines Press, Mountain View 1995

Ries, Karl, and Ring, Hans, *The Legion Condor*, Schiffer Publishing, West Chester, 1992

Rimell, R. L., and Grosz, P. M., *Pfalz DIII* (Windsock Datafile 7), Albatros Productions, Berkhamsted, 1988

Robertson, Seona, and Wilson, Les, *Scotland's War*, Mainstream Publishing Co, Edinburgh, 1995

Roscoe, Theodore, *United States Submarine Operations in World War II*, US Naval Institute, Annapolis, 1958

Rust, Kenn C., *Twentieth Air Force Story*, Historical Aviation Album, Temple City, 1979

Rust, Kenn C., and Bell, Dana, *Thirteenth Air Force Story*, Historical Aviation Album, Terre Haute, 1981

Sakai, Saburo, with Caidin, Martin, and Saito, Fred, *Samurai!*, Bantam Books, New York, 1978

Sakaida, Henry, *Imperial Japanese Navy Aces of World War 2, 1937–45*, Osprey Publishing, London, 1998

———, *Japanese Army Air Force Aces, 1937–45*, Osprey Publishing, London, 1997

———, *The Siege of Rabaul*, Phalanx Publishing Co, St. Paul, 1996

Scutts, Jerry, *German Night Fighter Aces of World War 2*, Osprey Publishing, London, 1998

———, *Mustang Aces of the Ninth and Fifteenth Air Forces and the RAF*, Osprey Publishing, London, 1995.

Seidl, Hans D., *Stalin's Eagles*, Schiffer Publishing, Atglen, 1998

Shores, Christopher, *Dust Clouds in the Middle East*, Grub Street, London, 1996

———, *Spanish Civil War Air Forces*, Osprey Publishing, London, 1977

Shores, Christopher, and Cull, Brian, with Izawa, Yasuho, *Bloody Shambles: The First Comprehensive Account of Air Operations over South-East Asia, December 1941–May 1942*, Grub Street, London, 1993

Shores, Christopher, and Cull, Brian, with Maliza, Nicola, *Air War for Yugoslavia, Greece and Crete 1940–41*, Grub Street, London, 1987

Shores, Christopher, and Cull, Brian, with Malizia, Nicola, *Malta: The Hurricane Years, 1940–41*, Grub Street, London, 1987

Shores, Christopher; Franks, Norman; and Guest, Russell, *Above the Trenches*, Grub Street, London, 1990

Shores, Christopher, and Williams, Clive, *Aces High*, Grub Street, London, 1994

Skelton, Marvin L., 'Major H. D. Harvey-Kelly, Commanding Officer, No. 19 Squadron', *Cross & Cockade (USA) Journal*, Vol. 16, No 4, Winter 1975

'Slayer of Dragons', *Air Enthusiast*, Vol. 5, Nos 5 and 6, November and December 1973

'Soviet Flies in Spanish Skies', *Air Enthusiast*, 1, December 1975

Stapfer, Hans-Heiri, *LaGG Fighters in Action*, Squadron/Signal Publications, Carrollton, 1996

Stenman, Kari, '38 to 1: The Brewster 239 in Finnish Service', *Air Enthusiast*, 46, June-August 1997

Styling, Mark, *Corsair Aces of World War 2*, Osprey Publishing, London, 1996

Sullivan, Jim, *F4U Corsair in Action*, Squadron/Signal Publications, Carrollton, 1994

Terlinden, Lt-Col Michael C., '18 Days of Hell', *Air Classics*

'The Agile Asian . . . Japan's Type 97 Fighter', *Air Enthusiast*, 6, March–June 1978

'The Era of the Gull', *Air Enthusiast*, No 28, 1985

'The Zero Precursor . . . Mitsubishi's A5M', *Air Enthusiast*, 19, August–November 1982

Thompson, Warren, *P-61 Black Widow Units of World War 2*, Osprey Publishing, Wellingborough, 1998

Weal, John, *Focke-Wulf Fw 190 Aces of the Western Front*, Osprey Publishing, London, 1996

'Whirlwind—First of the Four-Cannon Fighters', *Air Enthusiast*, Vol. 4, No 7, July 1973

Wixey, Ken, 'Corpulent Feline: Grumman's F4F Wildcat', *Air Enthusiast*, 70, July–August 1997

INDEX

INDEX

319